The BIG BOOK *of*
LOW-SODIUM
RECIPES

The BIG BOOK of
LOW-SODIUM
RECIPES

More Than 500 Flavorful, Heart-Healthy Recipes, from Sweet Stuff Guacamole Dip to Lime-Marinated Grilled Steak

Linda Larsen

Aadamsmedia

Avon, Massachusetts

Published by
Adams Media, a division of F+W Media, Inc.
57 Littlefield Street, Avon, MA 02322. U.S.A.
www.adamsmedia.com

Contains material adapted from *The Everything® Low-Salt Cookbook* by Pamela Rice Hahn, copyright © 2004 by F+W Media, Inc., ISBN 10: 1-59337-044-X, ISBN 13: 978-1-59337-044-2.

ISBN 10: 1-4405-9165-2
ISBN 13: 978-1-4405-9165-5
eISBN 10: 1-4405-9166-0
eISBN 13: 978-1-4405-9166-2

Printed in the United States of America.

10   9   8   7   6   5   4   3   2   1

Library of Congress Cataloging-in-Publication Data
Larsen, Linda.
  The big book of low-sodium recipes / Linda Larsen.
      pages cm
  ISBN 978-1-4405-9165-5 (pb) -- ISBN 1-4405-9165-2 (pb) -- ISBN 978-1-4405-9166-2 (ebook) -- ISBN 1-4405-9166-0 (ebook)
1. Salt-free diet--Recipes. I. Title.
  RM237.8.L36 2015
  641.5'6323--dc23

                         2015020862

Always follow safety and commonsense cooking protocol while using kitchen utensils, operating ovens and stoves, and handling uncooked food. If children are assisting in the preparation of any recipe, they should always be supervised by an adult.

Many of the designations used by manufacturers and sellers to distinguish their products are claimed as trademarks. Where those designations appear in this book and F+W Media, Inc. was aware of a trademark claim, the designations have been printed with initial capital letters.

Cover design by Erin Alexander.
Cover images © StockFood/Adam, Frank.

This book is available at quantity discounts for bulk purchases.
For information, please call 1-800-289-0963.

CONTENTS

3 Salads and Salad Dressings ...81

4 Condiments 109

5 Stocks, Soups, and Stews

6 Snacks and Appetizers

7 Pasta Dishes

8 Poultry Main Dishes 229

11 Fish and Seafood Main Dishes 325

12 Vegetarian Main Dishes ...355

13 Vegetables and Side Dishes.......................**385**

14 Desserts 415

Appendix A:
Spice Blends 447

INTRODUCTION

IN TODAY'S BUSY WORLD IT CAN BE TEMPTING to grab a meal from a fast-food chain or open up a box of prepared food, but these processed foods are loaded with unnecessary fat, calories, and salt. This high concentration of sodium can wreak havoc on your body's systems, raising your blood pressure and cholesterol and endangering your heart health. Fortunately, with *The Big Book of Low-Sodium Recipes* you can lower your salt intake and still enjoy what you eat!

Throughout this book you'll find more than 500 recipes with fewer than 140mg of sodium per serving that are so flavorful you won't need to reach for the salt shaker. With recipes ranging from Blueberry-Stuffed French Toast for breakfast to Pineapple Curry Chicken for dinner to Peanut Butter S'mores Bars for dessert, you'll find that cooking without the salt can be easy, fun, and out-of-this-world delicious.

Whether you are looking into a low-sodium diet out of curiosity or a dietary need, this book will make your life on a low-sodium diet easy and pleasurable. Inside you'll find recipes to make your own breads, like Peach Pecan Bread and Flaky Crescent Rolls. You can explore simple salads like Lemon Chicken Avocado Salad, or easy meat dishes like Slow Cooker Pot Roast with Creamer Potatoes, Maple-Orange–Glazed Pork Tenderloin, and Spicy Salmon Tostadas. You can also delve into vegetarian meals, pasta dishes galore, and mouthwatering desserts. You'll never get bored with the versatile and flavorful dishes in this book. *The Big Book of Low-Sodium Recipes* will help you eat the same foods you've always enjoyed (and even add some new favorites) without the negative effects of sodium. Enjoy!

CHAPTER 1

BREAKFAST AND BRUNCH

KEDGEREE

Kedgeree is an English breakfast that is unusual and delicious. Serve this tasty dish with some fresh fruit, coffee, and orange juice for a great start to any day.

SERVES 4

1 cup basmati rice

2 teaspoons curry powder

½ teaspoon turmeric

2 cups chicken stock

2 (6-ounce) salmon fillets

4 large eggs

¼ cup light cream

⅛ teaspoon white pepper

2 tablespoons unsalted butter

2 tablespoons lemon juice

¼ cup chopped flat-leaf parsley

1. In medium saucepan, combine rice, curry powder, and turmeric. Add chicken stock and bring to a simmer over high heat. Reduce heat to low, cover, and cook for 15–20 minutes or until rice is tender and liquid is absorbed. Remove from heat.

2. Place salmon on a broiler pan. Broil 6" from heat for 8–9 minutes until salmon is just cooked through and flakes when tested with a fork. Set aside.

3. In small bowl, beat eggs with cream and pepper.

4. Melt butter in a medium skillet over medium heat. Add the eggs to the saucepan and cook them, stirring, until curds form. When eggs are just cooked, but still soft and shiny, remove from heat.

5. Fluff the rice with a fork. Stir in the salmon, eggs, lemon juice, and parsley. Serve immediately.

PER SERVING: Calories: 491 | Total Fat: 22g | Saturated Fat: 8g | Cholesterol: 290mg | Protein: 30g | Sodium: 132mg | Potassium: 625mg | Fiber: 1g | Carbohydrates: 41g | Sugar: 1g

BAKED SAVORY OATMEAL

Most breakfast recipes using oatmeal are sweet. But this whole grain can be made into a savory dish that is a great twist on the classic baked oatmeal. Mushrooms, onions, and garlic pair well with this grain in this easy recipe. Serve with orange juice and coffee, perhaps with some fresh fruit on the side.

SERVES 4

2 tablespoons unsalted butter, plus more for greasing

1 medium red onion, chopped

1 clove garlic, minced

1 cup sliced mushrooms

1¼ cups rolled oats (not instant or quick cooking)

1¼ cups whole milk

1 large egg, beaten

½ teaspoon dried thyme leaves

2 tablespoons grated Parmesan cheese

1. Preheat oven to 375°F. Grease a 9" square pan with unsalted butter and set aside.

2. In medium skillet, melt butter over medium heat. Add onion, garlic, and mushrooms and cook until tender, stirring occasionally, about 4–5 minutes. Remove from heat and place in medium bowl.

3. Add oats, milk, egg, and thyme to mixture in bowl and mix well. Spoon into prepared pan. Sprinkle with cheese.

4. Bake for 30–40 minutes or until top is light golden brown and the mixture is set. Cut into squares to serve with maple syrup, if desired.

PER SERVING: Calories: 253 | Total Fat: 11g | Saturated Fat: 6g | Cholesterol: 78mg | Protein: 9g | Sodium: 96mg | Potassium: 381mg | Fiber: 3g | Carbohydrates: 27g | Sugar: 8g

DUTCH BABY

A Dutch baby is a large pancake that's baked in the oven instead of cooked on the stovetop. It's a great way to serve pancakes for several people, since you don't have to stand at the stove turning them. The pancake will puff up in the oven, then fall, creating a natural crater to fill with fresh fruit and whipped cream, if you're feeling decadent.

SERVES 4

2 tablespoons sugar

3 large eggs, at room temperature

1½ teaspoons vanilla

½ cup whole milk

2 tablespoons lemon juice

½ cup plus 2 tablespoons flour

1 tablespoon cornstarch

⅛ teaspoon cinnamon

¼ cup unsalted butter

2 tablespoons powdered sugar

1 cup fresh raspberries

½ cup chopped strawberries

1 tablespoon chopped fresh mint

⅓ cup maple syrup

1. Preheat oven to 425°F. Place a 10" ovenproof skillet in the oven to heat.

2. In large bowl, combine sugar with eggs and vanilla and beat until light and fluffy. Beat in milk and lemon juice.

3. In small bowl, combine flour, cornstarch, and cinnamon and mix well. Beat into egg mixture until smooth.

4. Carefully, using a pot holder, remove the hot skillet from the oven and let sit for 2 minutes. Add butter to skillet and swirl to coat the bottom and sides.

5. Pour the batter into the skillet; it will start sizzling. Immediately place into the oven. Bake for 16–20 minutes or until puffed and light golden.

6. Remove the skillet from the oven; the pancake will sink. Sprinkle with powdered sugar, then fill with the berries and mint and serve with maple syrup.

PER SERVING: Calories: 392 | Total Fat: 16g | Saturated Fat: 9g | Cholesterol: 192mg | Protein: 8g | Sodium: 70mg | Potassium: 266mg | Fiber: 3g | Carbohydrates: 52g | Sugar: 30g

HARD-COOKED EGGS

Hard-cooked eggs are not hard-boiled eggs! Eggs should never be boiled; that just makes them tough and makes a green ring around the yolk. That green ring is formed when hydrogen sulfide from the egg white reacts with iron in the yolk. Don't overcook the eggs and it won't happen!

SERVES 8

8 large eggs

1. Place the eggs in a large saucepan and add cold water to cover. Bring to a boil over high heat.

2. When the water comes to a rolling boil, cover the pan, remove it from heat, and let stand for 15 minutes.

3. Then place the pan with the eggs in the sink. Run cold water into the pan until the eggs are cold.

4. Crack the eggs under the water and let sit for 5 minutes; then peel.

5. Or put one egg into a glass and add a little water. Cover the top with your hand and shake well over the sink. The shell should slip right off.

6. Cover the eggs and store in the fridge up to 4 days.

PER SERVING: Calories: 77 | Total Fat: 5g | Saturated Fat: 1g | Cholesterol: 212mg | Protein: 6g | Sodium: 62mg | Potassium: 63mg | Fiber: 0g | Carbohydrates: 0g | Sugar: 0g

BAKED CRANBERRY ORANGE OATMEAL WITH ORANGE SAUCE

This simple recipe has a lot of flavor and is attractive, too. Serve it for Christmas morning breakfast with some warmed maple syrup, your own homemade sausages, orange juice, fresh fruit, and coffee.

SERVES 8

2½ cups rolled oats

½ cup chopped pecans

½ cup brown sugar

½ teaspoon cinnamon

⅛ teaspoon cardamom

1 teaspoon grated orange rind

⅔ cup dried cranberries

1 cup whole milk

1 cup light cream

1⅓ cups orange juice, divided

2 large eggs

¼ cup unsalted butter, melted, divided

1 tablespoon cornstarch

¼ cup granulated sugar

1 tablespoon unsalted butter

1. Preheat oven to 375°F. Grease a 13" × 9" pan with unsalted butter and set aside.

2. In large bowl, combine oats, pecans, brown sugar, cinnamon, cardamom, orange rind, and cranberries, and mix well.

3. In medium bowl, combine milk, cream, ⅓ cup orange juice, eggs, and half of the melted butter and beat well.

4. Stir the milk mixture into the oats. Spread into prepared pan and drizzle with remaining melted butter.

5. Bake for 35–45 minutes or until top is golden and the mixture is set.

6. Meanwhile, combine 1 cup orange juice, cornstarch, granulated sugar, and 1 tablespoon unsalted butter in a small saucepan and bring to a boil. Reduce heat to low and simmer for 3–4 minutes until thickened.

7. Slice the baked oatmeal into squares and serve drizzled with the orange sauce.

PER SERVING: Calories: 430 | Total Fat: 21g | Saturated Fat: 9g | Cholesterol: 94mg | Protein: 7g | Sodium: 48mg | Potassium: 324mg | Fiber: 4g | Carbohydrates: 53g | Sugar: 31g

WILD RICE WAFFLES

Waffles are a wonderful treat for breakfast. Add some wild rice to the batter for a great look, slightly crunchy texture, and nutty taste. If you have leftover wild rice, refrigerate or freeze it to use later in this recipe. Otherwise, cook the rice before you start to make the batter.

SERVES 4

⅔ cup wild rice

1⅓ cups water

1⅓ cups flour

1 tablespoon cornstarch

½ teaspoon baking powder

½ teaspoon cinnamon, if desired

3 large eggs

2 tablespoons sugar

¾ cup milk

2 tablespoons orange juice

¼ cup unsalted butter, melted

1. In small saucepan, combine wild rice and water. Bring to a boil over high heat, then reduce heat to low, cover, and simmer for 35–45 minutes or until rice is just tender. Drain, if necessary, and spread on a plate to cool.

2. When rice is cool, combine flour, cornstarch, and baking powder (and cinnamon, if using) in a medium bowl and mix.

3. In a large bowl, beat eggs with sugar until light and lemon colored. Beat in milk, orange juice, and melted butter. Fold in flour mixture. Fold in wild rice.

4. Preheat your waffle iron. Make waffles according to manufacturer's instructions. Serve immediately with maple syrup and fresh berries.

PER SERVING: Calories: 460 | Total Fat: 16g | Saturated Fat: 9g | Cholesterol: 192mg | Protein: 14g | Sodium: 77mg | Potassium: 356mg | Fiber: 3g | Carbohydrates: 63g | Sugar: 10g

BLUEBERRY-STUFFED FRENCH TOAST

This casserole serves a crowd and should be made the night before. This recipe is much easier than making French toast one or two or three at a time, even with a big skillet. The filling is made of blueberries and slightly sweetened mascarpone cheese. Serve for a holiday or a special birthday breakfast.

SERVES 6

¾ cup mascarpone cheese

3 tablespoons powdered sugar

½ teaspoon grated lemon zest

12 slices French Bread (Chapter 2), sliced 1" thick on a diagonal

1 cup fresh blueberries

1 cup milk

3 large eggs, beaten

2 tablespoons unsalted butter, melted

1½ teaspoons vanilla

1. In medium bowl, combine mascarpone cheese, powdered sugar, and lemon zest and mix well.

2. Place bread on work surface. Spread half of the slices with the cheese mixture and top with the blueberries, dividing evenly. Place remaining slices of bread on top and press together slightly to make sandwiches.

3. Arrange the bread sandwiches in a 13" × 9" glass baking dish.

4. In small bowl, combine milk, eggs, melted butter, and vanilla and beat until smooth. Pour into baking dish over bread.

5. Cover and refrigerate overnight.

6. In the morning, preheat the oven to 350°F. Uncover the baking dish and bake for 30–40 minutes or until tops of bread are golden brown. Serve immediately with maple syrup and more fresh blueberries.

PER SERVING: Calories: 398 | Total Fat: 20g | Saturated Fat: 20g | Cholesterol: 153mg | Protein: 11g | Sodium: 116mg | Potassium: 176mg | Fiber: 2g | Carbohydrates: 41g | Sugar: 8g

SAUSAGE AND VEGGIE SCRAMBLED EGGS

Eggs scrambled with sausage and vegetables make a hearty and delicious breakfast. If you ordered this recipe in a restaurant it would be loaded with sodium from the sausage and the cheese. Make it yourself for a better, tastier version that is much healthier.

SERVES 6

1 cup Maple Turkey Sausage (see recipe in this chapter)

2 tablespoons unsalted butter

1 medium onion, chopped

½ cup sliced mushrooms

1 medium red bell pepper, chopped

6 large eggs, beaten

¼ cup sour cream

2 tablespoons milk

½ teaspoon dried thyme leaves

⅛ teaspoon white pepper

⅓ cup shredded mozzarella cheese

1. In a large skillet over medium heat, cook the sausage, stirring to break up meat, until browned and cooked through. Remove sausage from skillet. Drain fat from skillet, but do not wipe pan.

2. Return skillet to heat and add butter. Add onion, mushrooms, and bell pepper and cook until vegetables are tender, about 4–5 minutes.

3. Meanwhile, in medium bowl beat eggs, sour cream, milk, thyme, and white pepper until smooth. Pour into skillet over vegetables.

4. Cook, stirring occasionally, and lifting the egg mixture to let uncooked egg flow underneath, until the eggs are just set but still moist.

5. Stir in sausage and add cheese. Cover and let stand off heat 4 minutes, then serve.

PER SERVING: Calories: 215 | Total Fat: 15g | Saturated Fat: 7g | Cholesterol: 248mg | Protein: 16g | Sodium: 140mg | Potassium: 166mg | Fiber: 0g | Carbohydrates: 4g | Sugar: 3g

GLAZED LEMON MUFFINS

This recipe is delicate and light, but full of flavor. Almond flour and ground coconut add a sweet and nutty taste to these muffins, and the lemon glaze on top adds the perfect finishing touch. To grind coconut, just put some in a blender or food processor, cover, and blend or process until fine crumbs form.

YIELDS 12 MUFFINS

1½ cups flour

⅓ cup almond flour

3 tablespoons ground coconut

1 teaspoon baking powder

½ teaspoon baking soda

1 cup granulated sugar

½ cup milk

⅓ cup sour cream

4 tablespoons lemon juice, divided

1 teaspoon grated lemon zest, divided

1 teaspoon vanilla

¼ cup unsalted butter, melted

1 large egg

1½ cups powdered sugar

1. Preheat oven to 375°F. Line a 12-cup muffin tin with paper liners and set aside, or spray each cup with nonstick baking spray containing flour.

2. In large bowl, combine flour, almond flour, ground coconut, baking powder, baking soda, and granulated sugar and whisk to combine.

3. In small bowl, combine milk, sour cream, 2 tablespoons lemon juice, ½ teaspoon lemon zest, vanilla, melted butter, and egg and beat until smooth.

4. Stir milk mixture into dry ingredients and stir just until combined.

5. Spoon batter into prepared muffin tin. Bake for 17–22 minutes or until the muffins are very light golden brown and spring back when lightly touched with your finger.

6. While muffins are baking, combine powdered sugar, 2 tablespoons lemon juice, and ½ teaspoon zest in small bowl. When the muffins are done baking (and still in the pan), drizzle some of this glaze over each muffin, using about half of the glaze.

7. Remove muffins from muffin tin and let cool on wire rack. When cool, drizzle with remaining glaze.

PER SERVING: Calories: 257 | Total Fat: 8g | Saturated Fat: 4g | Cholesterol: 28mg | Protein: 3g | Sodium: 72mg | Potassium: 105mg | Fiber: 1g | Carbohydrates: 43g | Sugar: 30g

FARRO PORRIDGE WITH NUTS

Farro is a whole grain that has a wonderful nutty flavor with a chewy texture. It is fabulous for breakfast when cooked as a hot cereal. Combine it with some dried fruit and crunchy toasted nuts for a healthy and nutritious breakfast. Choose unpearled farro for more texture, or if you like a creamy hot cereal, look for pearled farro.

SERVES 4

1 cup farro, rinsed

¾ cup water

¾ cup almond milk

⅓ cup orange juice

¼ cup brown sugar

1 teaspoon vanilla

⅓ cup chopped walnuts, toasted

⅓ cup chopped cashews, toasted

1. Combine the farro, water, almond milk, orange juice, and brown sugar in a medium saucepan over medium heat. Bring to a boil, stirring occasionally.

2. Reduce heat to low and cook, stirring occasionally, until the mixture is creamy and the farro is tender but still chewy, about 25 minutes. Stir in vanilla and nuts and serve immediately.

PER SERVING: Calories: 402 | Total Fat: 14g | Saturated Fat: 1g | Cholesterol: 0mg | Protein: 11g | Sodium: 32mg | Potassium: 186mg | Fiber: 8g | Carbohydrates: 57g | Sugar: 16g

ALMOND-BUTTER CRANBERRY OATMEAL BARS

Almond butter is made of ground almonds just as peanut butter is made of ground peanuts. It's nutty and creamy and rich. You can find no-salt versions of it in most regular grocery stores. Combined with oatmeal and cranberries, it makes an elegant breakfast bar.

SERVES 36

⅓ cup no-salt-added almond butter

⅔ cup unsalted butter, melted

½ cup granulated sugar

½ cup brown sugar

¼ cup honey

2 teaspoons vanilla

3 cups rolled oats

⅔ cup dried cranberries

½ cup slivered almonds

1. Preheat oven to 375°F. Spray a 13" × 9" pan with nonstick baking spray containing flour and set aside.

2. In large bowl, combine almond butter, butter, granulated sugar, brown sugar, and honey and mix well.

3. Beat in vanilla, then stir in oats, cranberries, and almonds. Press into prepared pan.

4. Bake for 15–20 minutes or until the edges are golden brown and mixture is set. Let cool completely, then cut into bars.

PER SERVING: Calories: 114 | Total Fat: 6g | Saturated Fat: 2g | Cholesterol: 8mg | Protein: 1g | Sodium: 2mg | Potassium: 61mg | Fiber: 1g | Carbohydrates: 14g | Sugar: 9g

RAISIN APPLE STRATA

A strata is a mixture of cubed bread and a custard made of milk and eggs, baked until crisp and crunchy on top but tender within. This casserole will feed a crowd, so it's perfect for holiday breakfasts and brunches. It must be made ahead and refrigerated overnight. All you have to do in the morning is bake it and eat!

SERVES 12

3 Granny Smith apples, peeled, cored, and chopped

2 tablespoons brown sugar

1 tablespoon granulated sugar

2 tablespoons orange juice

1 teaspoon cinnamon

¼ teaspoon nutmeg

16 slices Raisin Bread (Chapter 2), cubed

⅓ cup maple syrup

½ cup chopped toasted pecans

½ cup raisins

8 large eggs, beaten

1¾ cups whole milk

2 teaspoons vanilla

1. Preheat oven to 350°F. Spray a 9" × 13" glass baking dish with nonstick cooking spray.

2. Combine chopped apples, brown sugar, granulated sugar, orange juice, cinnamon, and nutmeg in baking dish and toss to coat.

3. Top apples with raisin bread, maple syrup, pecans, and raisins and toss to mix. Spread evenly in baking dish.

4. In large bowl, combine eggs, milk, and vanilla. Pour evenly over bread mixture. Cover and refrigerate overnight.

5. In the morning, uncover the strata. Bake for 55–65 minutes or until the strata is set, with golden brown edges and light golden top. Cut into squares to serve.

PER SERVING: Calories: 104 | Total Fat: 4g | Saturated Fat: 1g | Cholesterol: 38mg | Protein: 2g | Sodium: 23mg | Potassium: 88mg | Fiber: 1g | Carbohydrates: 15g | Sugar: 7g

APPLE TURNOVERS

Turnovers are flaky pastries filled with fruit. They are crunchy, creamy, sweet, and tart and the perfect treat for a special breakfast. Most recipes call for canned apple pie filling, but making your own filling is easy and fun.

SERVES 9

3 Granny Smith or Braeburn apples, peeled, cored, and chopped

2 tablespoons unsalted butter

⅔ cup brown sugar

1 teaspoon cinnamon

¼ teaspoon nutmeg

1 tablespoon flour

1 tablespoon orange juice

2 teaspoons vanilla, divided

⅓ cup dried cherries, chopped

⅓ cup chopped toasted pecans

1 (17-ounce) package frozen puff pastry, thawed

1¼ cups powdered sugar

1–2 tablespoons cherry juice

1. In medium saucepan over medium heat, combine chopped apples, butter, brown sugar, cinnamon, and nutmeg. Cook, stirring, until apples are tender, about 5 minutes.

2. In small bowl, combine flour and orange juice and mix well. Stir into apple mixture and cook, stirring, for another 1–2 minutes or until mixture has thickened.

3. Remove apple mixture from heat, stir in 1 teaspoon vanilla, dried cherries, and pecans, and set aside to cool for 45 minutes.

4. When apple mixture has cooled for 45 minutes, preheat oven to 400°F.

5. Unfold the puff pastry sheets and place on lightly floured board. Cut each sheet into 4 squares, making 8 squares total.

6. Divide the apple mixture among the squares. Fold the puff pastry over the apples to make triangles. Press edges with a fork to seal.

7. Place turnovers on a parchment paper–lined baking sheet. Bake for 20–30 minutes or until turnovers are puffed and light golden brown. Cool on wire rack.

8. To make the glaze: combine powdered sugar, cherry juice, and 1 teaspoon vanilla in a medium bowl until a thick glaze forms. Drizzle this over the cooled turnovers and let stand until set.

PER SERVING: Calories: 541 | Total Fat: 30g | Saturated Fat: 7g | Cholesterol: 6mg | Protein: 5g | Sodium: 139mg | Potassium: 162mg | Fiber: 3g | Carbohydrates: 64g | Sugar: 37g

STREUSEL FRENCH TOAST

French toast is always a delicious breakfast recipe, but adding streusel takes it to the next level. Use one of the bread recipes from Chapter 2 to make sure the sodium content stays nice and low.

SERVES 8

8 (1") slices French Bread or other bread (Chapter 2), cut on the diagonal

3 large eggs

1 cup whole milk

¼ cup plus 3 tablespoons granulated sugar, divided

½ cup plus 2 tablespoons unsalted butter, melted, divided

1½ teaspoons cinnamon, divided

⅛ teaspoon cardamom

1 teaspoon vanilla

½ cup brown sugar

½ cup flour

½ cup rolled oats

½ cup chopped pecans

1. Place the bread slices in a greased 9" × 13" glass baking dish.

2. In medium bowl, combine eggs, milk, ¼ cup granulated sugar, 2 tablespoons melted butter, ½ teaspoon cinnamon, cardamom, and vanilla and mix well. Pour over the French bread, saturating each piece. Cover with foil and refrigerate overnight.

3. In small bowl, combine brown sugar, flour, oats, pecans, 3 tablespoons granulated sugar, and 1 teaspoon cinnamon and mix. Add ½ cup melted butter and mix until crumbly. Cover with foil and refrigerate overnight.

4. In the morning, preheat oven to 375°F. Uncover the pan with the bread. Sprinkle each piece of bread with some of the oat-streusel mixture.

5. Bake for 30–40 minutes or until the bread is golden brown. Serve immediately with maple syrup.

PER SERVING: Calories: 475 | Total Fat: 28g | Saturated Fat: 11g | Cholesterol: 119mg | Protein: 8g | Sodium: 68mg | Potassium: 204mg | Fiber: 3g | Carbohydrates: 48g | Sugar: 22g

OVEN OMELET

Making a good omelet takes years of practice. But you can make a wonderful version in the oven with no experience necessary! You can vary the vegetables in this recipe to suit your tastes and what looks good in the market or your garden.

SERVES 6

2 tablespoons unsalted butter, divided

⅓ cup chopped mushrooms

¼ cup chopped yellow summer squash

2 tablespoons chopped green onions

6 large eggs

½ cup milk

½ teaspoon dried thyme leaves

⅛ teaspoon pepper

½ cup shredded whole milk mozzarella cheese

1. Preheat oven to 375°F. Grease a 9" glass pie plate with 1 teaspoon unsalted butter and set aside.

2. In small skillet over medium heat, melt remaining butter. Add mushrooms, squash, and green onions; cook and stir for 4–5 minutes or until vegetables are tender. Arrange in prepared pie plate.

3. In medium bowl, combine eggs, milk, thyme, and pepper and beat well. Pour over vegetables in pie plate. Sprinkle with cheese.

4. Bake for 20–30 minutes or until set. Cut into wedges to serve.

PER SERVING: Calories: 146 | Total Fat: 11g | Saturated Fat: 5g | Cholesterol: 231mg | Protein: 9g | Sodium: 138mg | Potassium: 138mg | Fiber: 0g | Carbohydrates: 2g | Sugar: 1g

CHICKEN SALAD ON WILD RICE WAFFLES

In the South, it's customary to serve fried chicken on waffles. While this combination is delicious, it's also difficult to eat, and full of fat and sodium. Now you can switch it up and serve a delicious and tender chicken salad on some waffles made with wild rice.

SERVES 4

4 Wild Rice Waffles (see recipe in this chapter), toasted

4 cups Chicken Wild Rice Salad (Chapter 3)

While waffles are still hot, top each with a cup of the chicken salad. Serve immediately.

PER SERVING: Calories: 584 | Total Fat: 25g | Saturated Fat: 4g | Cholesterol: 71mg | Protein: 35g | Sodium: 95mg | Potassium: 664mg | Fiber: 4g | Carbohydrates: 56g | Sugar: 14g

VEGGIE FRITTATA

A frittata is different from an omelet or scrambled eggs because it's first cooked on the stovetop, then finished under the broiler. The texture is firmer than an omelet. You can serve a frittata straight from the broiler or let it cool and serve it lukewarm. This type of recipe is a great way to use up leftover veggies.

SERVES 4

1 cup grape tomatoes, chopped

1 tablespoon sliced fresh basil leaves

1 tablespoon minced green onion

2 tablespoons olive oil

½ cup diced red onion

½ cup chopped red bell pepper

½ cup chopped peeled zucchini

½ cup chopped mushrooms

6 large eggs

⅓ cup whole milk

½ teaspoon dried basil leaves

⅛ teaspoon white pepper

2 tablespoons grated Parmesan cheese

1. Use an ovenproof 8" skillet, or cover the wooden handle of a skillet with foil to protect it.

2. In small bowl, combine grape tomatoes, fresh basil, and green onion and set aside.

3. In the skillet, heat olive oil over medium heat. Add red onion, bell pepper, zucchini, and mushrooms and cook until lightly browned, about 6–7 minutes.

4. Meanwhile, in medium bowl combine eggs, milk, dried basil, and white pepper, and beat well. Pour into skillet over vegetables.

5. Cook over medium heat for 5–10 minutes, lifting egg mixture occasionally to let uncooked egg flow underneath and shaking pan, until the bottom is golden brown.

6. Meanwhile, preheat broiler to high. Sprinkle frittata with cheese and place under broiler. Broil for 10–12 minutes, moving skillet around under the broiler, until frittata is set and top is light golden brown.

7. Cut frittata into wedges and serve with the grape-tomato mixture for a topping.

PER SERVING: Calories: 223 | Total Fat: 16g | Saturated Fat: 4g | Cholesterol: 320mg | Protein: 12g | Sodium: 137mg | Potassium: 397mg | Fiber: 1g | Carbohydrates: 8g | Sugar: 6g

PEAR PECAN MUFFINS

Canned pears are low in sodium and delicious when puréed and stirred into batter for breads and muffins. Buy pears in light syrup; otherwise they will be too sweet. Drain the pears and reserve the liquid; it's delicious in waffle and pancake batters, as well as in other quick bread recipes.

YIELDS 18 MUFFINS

½ cup unsalted butter, softened

¼ cup safflower or peanut oil

¾ cup granulated sugar

½ cup brown sugar

2 large eggs

2 egg whites

1 (15-ounce) can pear halves, drained, reserving liquid

⅓ cup lemon juice

2 teaspoons vanilla

3 cups flour

1 teaspoon baking powder

½ teaspoon baking soda

1 cup chopped toasted pecans

1 cup powdered sugar

1. Preheat oven to 350°F. Line 18 muffin cups with paper liners and set aside, or grease with unsalted butter.

2. In large bowl, combine butter, oil, sugar, and brown sugar and beat until fluffy. Add eggs and egg whites and beat well.

3. Mash the drained pear halves and add to the batter along with lemon juice and vanilla, and mix well.

4. Stir in flour, baking powder, and baking soda and mix just until combined. Stir in pecans.

5. Fill prepared muffin cups ⅔–¾ full. Bake for 17–22 minutes or until the muffins are light golden brown and spring back when lightly touched. Remove from tins and place on wire racks.

6. In small bowl, combine powdered sugar and 2 tablespoons reserved pear liquid and mix well. Glaze the warm muffins with this mixture, then let cool completely.

PER SERVING: Calories: 335 | Total Fat: 18g | Saturated Fat: 4g | Cholesterol: 37mg | Protein: 4g | Sodium: 52mg | Potassium: 149mg | Fiber: 2g | Carbohydrates: 40g | Sugar: 22g

MAPLE TURKEY SAUSAGE

This delicious homemade sausage is scented with sage and has a nice maple-y kick! These sausages are subtly sweet and absolutely delicious.

SERVES 4

1 pound lean ground turkey

1 tablespoon maple syrup

¼ teaspoon freshly ground black pepper

⅛ teaspoon mustard powder

⅛ teaspoon ground cloves

⅛ teaspoon ground sage

Pinch ground cinnamon

Pinch ground allspice

Pinch ground mace

Optional: ¼ teaspoon natural maple flavoring

1. Mix together all the ingredients in a bowl. Cover and refrigerate overnight.

2. Shape the mixture into 4 flat patties. Cook over medium heat in a medium nonstick skillet or grill pan for 3 minutes on each side or until a food thermometer registers 165°F.

PER SERVING: Calories: 167 | Total Fat: 7g | Saturated Fat: 0g | Cholesterol: 65mg | Protein: 22g | Sodium: 81mg | Potassium: 14mg | Fiber: 0g | Carbohydrates: 3g | Sugar: 3g

BANANA WALNUT BREAKFAST COOKIES

Cookies for breakfast are a fun way to get some nutrition into your kids before they head out the door. These cookies are healthier than a doughnut or sweet roll. Store them airtight at room temperature for up to 5 days.

YIELDS 24 COOKIES

⅓ cup unsalted butter, softened

⅓ cup unsalted peanut butter

2 medium bananas, mashed

1 large egg

½ cup brown sugar

2 tablespoons honey

2 teaspoons vanilla

1 cup all-purpose flour

¼ cup whole-wheat flour

½ teaspoon baking powder

1½ cups rolled oats

1 cup dried cherries

½ cup chopped walnuts

1. Preheat oven to 350°F.

2. In large bowl, combine butter and peanut butter and mix well. Add mashed banana and egg and stir until combined.

3. Beat in brown sugar, honey, and vanilla and mix well. Add flour, whole-wheat flour, baking powder, and oats and mix until combined. Stir in cherries and walnuts.

4. Drop dough by tablespoons onto a cookie sheet. Bake for 11–16 minutes or until the cookies are light golden brown and set. Remove to wire rack to cool completely before storing.

PER SERVING: Calories: 141 | Total Fat: 6g | Saturated Fat: 2g | Cholesterol: 15mg | Protein: 3g | Sodium: 5mg | Potassium: 123mg | Fiber: 1g | Carbohydrates: 18g | Sugar: 8g

SAUSAGE AND EGG BAKE

Traditionally this recipe would usually be very high in sodium, but this version uses your own homemade sausage. Serve it with a fresh fruit salad, coffee, cinnamon rolls or muffins, and orange juice.

SERVES 10

1 recipe Peppery Turkey Sausage (see recipe in this chapter)

1 medium onion, chopped

1 cup sliced mushrooms

1 medium red bell pepper, chopped

2 cloves garlic, minced

14 large eggs

½ cup light cream

3 tablespoons Mustard (Chapter 4)

¼ teaspoon pepper

1. Preheat oven to 350°F. Spray a 9" × 13" glass baking dish with nonstick cooking spray and set aside.

2. In large skillet, cook sausage, stirring to break up meat, until meat is thoroughly cooked, about 7–8 minutes. Remove sausage from pan and place in baking dish; drain skillet, but do not wipe out.

3. Add onion, mushrooms, bell pepper, and garlic to skillet; cook and stir for 7–9 minutes or until mushrooms give up their liquid and the liquid evaporates. Place in baking dish on top of sausage.

4. In large bowl, beat eggs with cream, mustard, and pepper until combined. Pour into baking dish on top of sausage and vegetables.

5. Bake for 25–35 minutes or until the eggs are puffy and top just begins to brown. Cut into squares to serve.

PER SERVING: Calories: 202 | Total Fat: 12g | Saturated Fat: 3g | Cholesterol: 331mg | Protein: 18g | Sodium: 137mg | Potassium: 180mg | Fiber: 0g | Carbohydrates: 3g | Sugar: 1g

APPLE POTATO PANCAKES

Life on a low-sodium diet can be inconvenient. Save yourself some time and hassle by doubling pancake recipes like this one on the weekends. Place leftovers between small sheets of waxed paper, store in plastic bags, and freeze. A frozen pancake will defrost in minutes.

SERVES 4

½ cup potato flakes

1½ cups boiling water

4 large eggs

2 teaspoons granulated sugar

½ teaspoon ground cinnamon

1 cup peeled and grated Granny Smith apple

¼ cup chopped pecans

Optional: Plain nonfat yogurt, sour cream, or applesauce

1. To prepare the potatoes, add potato flakes to a large bowl. Gradually pour the boiling water over the potato flakes, whisking continuously to mix and whip.

2. In small bowl, beat together the eggs, sugar, and cinnamon. Beat into the potatoes. Fold in the grated apple and chopped pecans.

3. Heat a nonstick skillet or griddle treated with nonstick spray over medium heat. (If using an electric griddle, preheat to 350°F–380°F.) Cook the pancakes on both sides until golden brown. Serve hot—plain or topped with plain nonfat yogurt, sour cream, or applesauce.

PER SERVING: Calories: 176 | Total Fat: 10g | Saturated Fat: 2g | Cholesterol: 211mg | Protein: 7g | Sodium: 78mg | Potassium: 209mg | Fiber: 1g | Carbohydrates: 13g | Sugar: 5g

PEPPERY TURKEY SAUSAGE

Perfect for those avoiding pork or just looking for another lean breakfast meat.

SERVES 8

1 pound lean ground turkey

¼ teaspoon garlic powder

¼ teaspoon onion powder

¼ teaspoon dried sage

½ teaspoon freshly ground black pepper

⅛ teaspoon ground cloves

Pinch ground allspice

1. In a mixing bowl, combine all the ingredients until well mixed. Form into 8 equal-sized patties.

2. Pan-fry on a nonstick grill pan or prepare in a covered indoor grill (such as a George Foreman–style indoor grill). The sausage is done when the juices run clear and a food thermometer registers 165°F. You can also cook the sausage as you would any ground meat, stirring to break up the meat.

PER SERVING: Calories: 76 | Total Fat: 3g | Saturated Fat: 0g | Cholesterol: 32mg | Protein: 11g | Sodium: 40mg | Potassium: 4mg | Fiber: 0g | Carbohydrates: 0g | Sugar: 0g

FRUIT SMOOTHIE

Thick, creamy, and absolutely delicious, this smoothie is a great alternative to those high-fat frozen treats sold in stores.

SERVES 2

½ cup frozen strawberries, unsweetened

1 tablespoon apple juice concentrate

3 tablespoons water

½ medium banana, sliced

8 ounces peach nonfat yogurt

Put all the ingredients in a blender or food processor and process until thick and smooth. Serve immediately.

PER SERVING: Calories: 158 | Total Fat: 0g | Saturated Fat: 0g | Cholesterol: 2mg | Protein: 5g | Sodium: 68mg | Potassium: 411mg | Fiber: 1g | Carbohydrates: 34g | Sugar: 29g

TOFU SMOOTHIE

A protein-packed power breakfast! Feel free to change this up by substituting another type of fruit for the peach slices.

SERVES 2

1 cup frozen unsweetened peach slices

1 large banana, sliced

½ cup soft silken tofu

2 teaspoons honey

4 teaspoons toasted wheat germ

Chilled water, as needed

Put all the ingredients in a food processor or blender and process until smooth. Add a little chilled water, if necessary. Serve immediately.

PER SERVING: Calories: 166 | Total Fat: 0g | Saturated Fat: 0g | Cholesterol: 0mg | Protein: 6g | Sodium: 10mg | Potassium: 485mg | Fiber: 4g | Carbohydrates: 32g | Sugar: 20g

STRAWBERRY EGG-WHITE PANCAKES

Weekends are made for hot, fluffy pancakes! This recipe is great with any type of flour or any other type of fruit jam.

SERVES 4

½ cup oats

8 egg whites

1 tablespoon lemon juice

2 tablespoons strawberry jam

⅛ cup unbleached all-purpose flour

1. Process the oats in a blender or food processor until ground.

2. Whisk the egg whites in a medium metal or glass bowl until soft peaks form.

3. Mix the lemon juice and jam together in a small bowl (this will thin the jam and make it easier to fold into the egg whites).

4. One at a time, fold the thinned jam, ground oatmeal, and flour into the egg whites.

5. Preheat a nonstick pan or griddle treated with cooking spray over medium heat. Pour ¼ of the mixture into the pan and cook for about 4 minutes or until the top of the pancake bubbles and begins to get dry. Flip the pancake; cook until the inside of the cake is cooked. Repeat until the remaining 3 pancakes are done.

PER SERVING: Calories: 111 | Total Fat: 0g | Saturated Fat: 0g | Cholesterol: 0mg | Protein: 9g | Sodium: 113mg | Potassium: 160mg | Fiber: 1g | Carbohydrates: 17g | Sugar: 5g

BUCKWHEAT PANCAKES

The amount of milk can vary in this recipe depending on the consistency you like for your pancakes.

SERVES 4

½ cup whole-wheat flour

½ cup unbleached all-purpose flour

½ cup buckwheat flour

½ teaspoon baking powder

1 large egg, separated

3 tablespoons apple juice concentrate

1 tablespoon lemon juice

1¼–1½ cups skim milk

1. Sift the flours and baking powder together in a large bowl.

2. Combine the egg yolk, apple juice concentrate, lemon juice, and 1 cup of the skim milk in a small bowl. Add the milk mixture to the dry ingredients and mix well, but do not overmix. Add the remaining milk if necessary to reach your desired consistency.

3. In small bowl, beat the egg white until stiff peaks form. Fold into the batter until just combined.

4. Cook the pancakes, using ¼ cup measure for each one, in a nonstick skillet or on a griddle treated with nonstick spray over medium heat until the top of the pancake bubbles and the edges begin to look dry. Flip pancakes using a spatula; cook for 1–2 minutes until browned. Repeat with remaining batter.

PER SERVING: Calories: 222 | Total Fat: 2g | Saturated Fat: 0g | Cholesterol: 54mg | Protein: 9g | Sodium: 117mg | Potassium: 541mg | Fiber: 3g | Carbohydrates: 42g | Sugar: 8g

SPICED APPLE EGG CLOUDS ON TOAST

This combination of tastes seems tailor-made for fall. The warmth of the eggs, the tang of the apple, the sweet spiciness of the ginger and cinnamon—it's a perfect breakfast for those crisp mornings!

SERVES 2

4 egg whites

1 teaspoon powdered sugar, sifted

2 teaspoons unsalted butter

1 large apple, peeled, cored, and thinly sliced

2 teaspoons lemon juice

1 teaspoon brown sugar

¼ teaspoon cinnamon

Pinch ground cloves

Pinch ground ginger

Pinch ground allspice

2 cups water

2 slices low-salt bread

Optional: Freshly ground nutmeg

1. In a medium metal or glass bowl, beat the egg whites until they thicken. Add the powdered sugar, and continue to beat until stiff peaks form.

2. Heat a small sauté pan over medium heat; add the butter. Toss the apple slices in the lemon juice and add them to the pan. Sprinkle the brown sugar, cinnamon, cloves, ginger, and allspice over the apples; sauté, stirring occasionally, until the apples are tender and glazed, about 5–6 minutes.

3. While the apples cook, bring the water to a simmer in a large, deep nonstick sauté pan over medium-low heat. Drop the egg whites by the tablespoonful into the simmering water. Simmer for 3 minutes, then turn the egg white "clouds" over, and simmer for an additional 3 minutes. Remove egg white clouds from pan with a large strainer one at a time, and briefly drain on paper towels to remove excess water.

4. Toast the bread and divide the apples over the slices, then top with the "clouds." Sprinkle with nutmeg, if desired. Serve immediately.

PER SERVING: Calories: 190 | Total Fat: 4g | Saturated Fat: 2g | Cholesterol: 10mg | Protein: 9g | Sodium: 116mg | Potassium: 242mg | Fiber: 2g | Carbohydrates: 28g | Sugar: 13g

OVERNIGHT FRUIT AND OATMEAL

A simple, hot, and filling breakfast is especially great in fall and winter. This oatmeal is as sweet and delicious as those instant packets, but without the high sodium content.

SERVES 4

1 cup steel-cut oats

14 dried apricot halves, chopped

1 dried fig, chopped

2 tablespoons golden raisins

4 cups water

½ cup whole milk

¼ teaspoon cinnamon

⅛ teaspoon grated orange zest

Pinch ground cloves

Pinch ground ginger

Pinch ground allspice

Combine all the ingredients in a slow cooker with a ceramic interior; set to low heat. Cover and cook overnight (for 8–9 hours). Stir and serve.

PER SERVING: Calories: 122 | Total Fat: 1g | Saturated Fat: 0g | Cholesterol: 0mg | Protein: 3g | Sodium: 2mg | Potassium: 262mg | Fiber: 3g | Carbohydrates: 26g | Sugar: 10g

LEMON CREPES

Serve theses crepes by placing fresh fruit or a little jelly in a line in the center of the crepe. Roll the crepe and place seam-side down on the plate. Dust with a little powdered sugar for a more attractive presentation.

SERVES 10

2 large eggs

¾ cup unbleached all-purpose flour

1 tablespoon lemon juice

⅛ teaspoon lemon extract

1 cup skim milk

1 tablespoon nonfat dry milk

⅛ teaspoon baking powder

Pinch baking soda

1. Combine all the ingredients in a blender or food processor and process until the mixture is the consistency of cream.

2. Treat an 8" nonstick skillet with nonstick spray and heat over medium heat. Pour about 2 tablespoons of the crepe batter into the hot pan, tilting in a circular motion until the batter spreads evenly over the pan. Cook the crepe until the outer edges just begin to brown and loosen. Flip the crepe over to the other side and cook for about 30 seconds. Using a thin spatula, slide the crepe from the pan onto a warm plate or baking sheet set in a warm oven. Continue until all the crepes are done.

3. Garnish and serve as desired.

PER SERVING: Calories: 59 | Total Fat: 1g | Saturated Fat: 0g | Cholesterol: 42mg | Protein: 3g | Sodium: 44mg | Potassium: 82mg | Fiber: 0g | Carbohydrates: 8g | Sugar: 1g

CHAPTER 2

BREADS

CORNBREAD

There is a debate over whether sugar belongs in cornbread. If you aren't adding salt, sugar really accents the corn flavor and brings out its sweetness. Using cornmeal and puréed corn makes this recipe very delicious. Use it to make turkey or pork stuffing, or serve it hot out of the oven with some unsalted butter and honey.

SERVES 9

1 cup frozen corn kernels, thawed and drained

¼ cup apple juice

½ cup whole milk

1 tablespoon lemon juice

2 tablespoons honey

5 tablespoons unsalted butter, melted

2 large eggs, beaten

1⅔ cups yellow cornmeal

⅔ cup flour

1 teaspoon baking powder

½ teaspoon baking soda

¼ cup granulated sugar

1. Preheat oven to 400°F. Spray a 9" square baking pan with nonstick baking spray containing flour; set aside.

2. In food processor or blender, combine corn kernels and apple juice. Purée until smooth. Pour into large bowl.

3. Add milk, lemon juice, honey, melted butter, and eggs to corn mixture and stir until combined.

4. Add cornmeal, flour, baking powder, baking soda, and sugar and mix just until combined. Spoon into prepared pan.

5. Bake for 25–30 minutes or until cornbread is light golden brown, bread pulls away from sides of pan, and a toothpick inserted in the center comes out clean. Let cool for 10 minutes, then serve.

PER SERVING: Calories: 276 | Total Fat: 8g | Saturated Fat: 4g | Cholesterol: 64mg | Protein: 5g | Sodium: 94mg | Potassium: 202mg | Fiber: 1g | Carbohydrates: 45g | Sugar: 11g

WILD RICE BREAD

Wild rice is delicious in bread, which is especially good toasted and spread with unsalted butter for breakfast. Because there is no salt in this bread, the amount of yeast must be reduced so the bread doesn't rise too much and then collapse in the oven.

YIELDS 1 LOAF; 16 SERVINGS

⅓ cup wild rice, rinsed and drained

1 cup water

1 cup bread flour

½ cup whole-wheat pastry flour

1½ teaspoons active dry yeast

Pinch salt

1 cup whole milk

1 teaspoon lemon juice

1 teaspoon sugar

2 tablespoons unsalted butter

1½ cups all-purpose flour

1. In small pan, combine rice and water; bring to a simmer over medium heat. Reduce heat to low, partially cover the pan, and simmer until the rice is tender, about 30–40 minutes. Drain if necessary and set aside.

2. In large bowl, combine bread flour, whole-wheat pastry flour, yeast, and salt; mix until combined.

3. In small saucepan, combine milk, lemon juice, sugar, and butter and heat until the butter melts. Let cool to 120°F. Add to the bread-flour mixture along with the wild rice and beat well.

4. Add enough of the all-purpose flour to form a firm dough. Knead on a lightly floured surface for 5–7 minutes or until dough is springy.

5. Grease a 9" × 5" loaf pan with unsalted butter. Roll the dough out into a 12" × 4" rectangle. Roll up tightly, starting from short end, sealing seams. Place seam-side down in the loaf pan.

6. Cover dough with a cloth and let rise until doubled, about 35–40 minutes. Preheat oven to 375°F. Remove the cloth and bake bread for 35–45 minutes or until the bread is golden brown and has pulled away from the pan sides. Remove immediately from pan and let cool on wire rack.

PER SERVING: Calories: 122 | Total Fat: 2g | Saturated Fat: 1g | Cholesterol: 5mg | Protein: 3g | Sodium: 7mg | Potassium: 65mg | Fiber: 1g | Carbohydrates: 21g | Sugar: 1g

SOURDOUGH BREAD

If you want to make "real" sourdough bread, you have to begin with a starter. That can be finicky and difficult to keep alive. Let's shortcut the process and add acidic ingredients to a bread recipe to add tang and strengthen the gluten bonds that make bread chewy. This recipe is easy enough for beginners!

YIELDS 1 LOAF; 16 SERVINGS

1½ cups bread flour

2 teaspoons sugar

1¾ teaspoons active dry yeast

½ cup whole milk, divided

⅓ cup plain yogurt

⅓ cup buttermilk

2 teaspoons lemon juice

1 tablespoon unsalted butter

1 large egg

1¼–2 cups all-purpose flour

1 tablespoon yellow cornmeal

1. In large bowl, combine bread flour, sugar, and yeast.

2. In small saucepan, combine all but 1 tablespoon milk, yogurt, buttermilk, lemon juice, and butter. Heat over low heat until the butter melts. Cool to 120°F.

3. Add milk mixture to the bread-flour mixture along with the egg and beat well. Gradually stir in enough all-purpose flour to make a firm dough.

4. Knead the dough on a floured surface for 3–5 minutes until smooth.

5. Grease a 9" × 5" loaf pan with unsalted butter and dust with cornmeal. Roll out the dough to a 12" × 4" rectangle. Roll up, starting with short side, and seal edges. Place seam-side down in pan; brush with 1 tablespoon milk.

6. Cover with cloth and let rise for 35–45 minutes or until almost doubled. Preheat oven to 375°F. Place a pan of water on the bottom rack. Remove the cloth and put the pan with the dough on the top rack. Bake for 30–40 minutes or until golden brown. Remove from pan and cool on wire rack.

PER SERVING: Calories: 107 | Total Fat: 1g | Saturated Fat: 0g | Cholesterol: 16mg | Protein: 3g | Sodium: 14mg | Potassium: 65mg | Fiber: 0g | Carbohydrates: 18g | Sugar: 1g

HONEY SESAME BATTER BREAD

Batter breads are much easier to make than kneaded breads. Less flour is used, so the "dough" is loose and soft. You beat it well instead of kneading it. The grain is more open and the texture is a bit rougher, which makes this bread perfect for toasting for breakfast. Spread with unsalted butter and some whipped honey.

YIELDS 1 LOAF; 12 SERVINGS

2½–3 cups all-purpose flour, divided

½ cup whole-wheat pastry flour

1½ teaspoons active dry yeast

Pinch salt

3 tablespoons honey

2 tablespoons butter

1 cup whole milk

½ cup buttermilk

3 tablespoons sesame seeds, toasted, divided

1 tablespoon light cream

1. In large bowl, combine 1½ cups all-purpose flour, the whole-wheat pastry flour, yeast, and salt; mix well.

2. In medium saucepan, combine honey, butter, milk, and buttermilk. Heat until the mixture is warm; butter does not need to melt.

3. Add the honey mixture to the flour mixture and beat by hand for 2 minutes. Gradually add enough of the remaining all-purpose flour to make a stiff batter. Stir in 2 tablespoons of the sesame seeds.

4. Grease a 9" × 5" loaf pan with unsalted butter. Spoon batter into prepared pan and smooth top.

5. Cover bread with a cloth and let rise until the batter comes to the top of the pan, about 30 minutes. Preheat oven to 375°F.

6. Brush top of bread gently with the light cream and sprinkle with remaining 1 tablespoon sesame seeds. Bake bread for 30–40 minutes or until golden brown and firm. Remove from pan and cool on wire rack.

PER SERVING: Calories: 176 | Total Fat: 4g | Saturated Fat: 2g | Cholesterol: 8mg | Protein: 4g | Sodium: 34mg | Potassium: 97mg | Fiber: 1g | Carbohydrates: 29g | Sugar: 5g

PEACH PECAN BREAD

Flavored quick breads are a great introduction to bread making. Making these breads is like making a cake, except you bake the batter in a loaf pan. The texture is fine, with a dense crumb and lots of flavor. They're great for breakfast on the run; you can also toast them or use them in sandwiches.

YIELDS 2 LOAVES; 20 SERVINGS

½ cup unsalted butter, softened

¼ cup safflower or peanut oil

¾ cup granulated sugar

½ cup light brown sugar

3 large eggs

1 (16-ounce) can peach halves in light syrup, drained

7 tablespoons lemon juice, divided

2 cups all-purpose flour

1 cup whole-wheat pastry flour

1 teaspoon baking powder

½ teaspoon baking soda

½ teaspoon cinnamon

1 cup chopped pecans

½ cup powdered sugar

1. Preheat oven to 350°F. Grease two 9" × 5" loaf pans and set aside.

2. In large bowl, combine butter, oil, granulated sugar, and brown sugar and beat well. Add eggs, one at a time, beating until fluffy.

3. Place drained peaches in a blender or food processor with 5 tablespoons of the lemon juice; blend or process until smooth.

4. In medium bowl, combine all-purpose flour, whole-wheat pastry flour, baking powder, baking soda, and cinnamon, and mix well.

5. Add flour mixture alternately with peach mixture to butter mixture, stirring just until combined. Stir in chopped pecans.

6. Spoon batter into prepared pans. Bake for 40–50 minutes or until the bread is light golden brown and begins to pull away from the sides of the pan.

7. Let cool in pan 5 minutes, then remove to wire rack.

8. In small bowl, combine remaining lemon juice and powdered sugar; drizzle over loaves. Let cool completely.

PER SERVING: Calories: 254 | Total Fat: 13g | Saturated Fat: 3g | Cholesterol: 43mg | Protein: 3g | Sodium: 45mg | Potassium: 99mg | Fiber: 1g | Carbohydrates: 32g | Sugar: 17g

CIABATTA ROLLS

Ciabatta rolls are crusty and light, with large air holes. The dough is wetter than typical roll dough; this helps more gluten form and the yeast grow faster, which creates the unique structure of this Italian treat. Use a stand mixer, if you have one, for the easiest way to make these rolls. Ciabatta rolls are fabulous for sandwiches.

YIELDS 12 ROLLS

1⅔ cups warm water, divided

1 teaspoon active dry yeast, divided

⅔ cup bread flour

Pinch salt

3 cups all-purpose flour, divided

½ teaspoon lemon juice

1 tablespoon solid shortening

2 tablespoons yellow cornmeal

1. In large bowl, combine ⅓ cup warm water, ½ teaspoon yeast, and bread flour. Mix well and let stand at room temperature for 2 hours.

2. Add remaining 1⅓ cups water, remaining ½ teaspoon yeast, salt, and 1 cup of the all-purpose flour; beat for 1 minute.

3. Add the remaining all-purpose flour ½ cup at a time, beating well after each addition, until the dough is very thick but still wet. Beat in lemon juice, then beat the dough for another 3 minutes.

4. Dust work surface with flour. Add the dough, dust top with more flour, and pat into a rectangle. Cut into 12 pieces; shape into rough rectangles.

5. Grease a large cookie sheet with solid shortening and dust with cornmeal. Place rolls on the sheet using floured fingers.

6. Cover the rolls and let rise for 1 hour or until almost doubled. Preheat oven to 425°F.

7. Bake rolls for 18–20 minutes or until golden brown. Remove from sheet and let cool on wire rack. Store in airtight container for 2 days at room temperature, or freeze up to 3 months.

PER SERVING: Calories: 157 | Total Fat: 1g | Saturated Fat: 0g | Cholesterol: 0mg | Protein: 4g | Sodium: 16mg | Potassium: 50mg | Fiber: 1g | Carbohydrates: 30g | Sugar: 0g

PITA BREAD

Premade pita breads usually have about 130mg of sodium for a small round. Make it yourself for a delicious bread with almost no sodium.

YIELDS 12 PITA BREADS

1 teaspoon active dry yeast

1½ cups water

½ teaspoon honey

3 tablespoons olive oil

2 cups bread flour

1 cup whole-wheat flour

Pinch salt

¾ cup all-purpose flour

1. In large bowl, combine yeast, water, and honey and mix well. Let stand for 20 minutes until the mixture starts to foam.

2. Add oil and bread flour; beat well. Add the whole-wheat flour and salt and mix well. Add enough of the all-purpose flour to make a firm dough.

3. Knead dough on floured surface until smooth and elastic, adding more all-purpose flour as needed. Cover bowl and let rise for 30 minutes.

4. Punch down dough and divide into 12 pieces. Roll out each piece to a 6" circle, and cover with a cloth.

5. Preheat oven to 475°F. Bake 4 pita breads at a time on an ungreased cookie sheet for 4–6 minutes or until the breads are puffed and light golden brown.

6. Transfer pitas to wire rack and let cool for 10 minutes, then cover with kitchen towels. Repeat with remaining breads. Store in airtight containers at room temperature up to 2 days; freeze for longer storage.

PER SERVING: Calories: 176 | Total Fat: 3g | Saturated Fat: 0g | Cholesterol: 0mg | Protein: 4g | Sodium: 16mg | Potassium: 37mg | Fiber: 2g | Carbohydrates: 30g | Sugar: 0g

FLAKY CRESCENT ROLLS

Use these rolls in place of "crescent dough" called for in many recipes; this recipe will replace three (8-ounce) tubes. Just roll out the dough into a large rectangle and cut into 4" × 6" rectangles, or roll dough into rounds and use as directed in the recipe. Freeze any leftover dough.

YIELDS 36 ROLLS

2 cups bread flour

2¼ cups all-purpose flour, divided

⅓ cup sugar

Pinch salt

1½ teaspoons active dry yeast

½ cup unsalted butter

1¼ cups whole milk

3 large eggs

5 tablespoons unsalted butter, softened

1. In large bowl, combine bread flour, 1 cup all-purpose flour, sugar, salt, and yeast and mix well. Cut in ½ cup butter until particles are fine.

2. In medium saucepan, heat milk to 120°F.

3. Add milk to flour mixture along with eggs; beat well. Gradually add enough remaining all-purpose flour to make a soft dough. Cover dough with cloth and let stand for 20 minutes.

4. Divide dough into three parts. Roll out each part to a 12" circle. Spread each circle with 1 tablespoon softened unsalted butter, then cut each circle into 12 wedges. Roll up each wedge, starting with the wide side. Place on baking sheet and curve ends to form a crescent shape. When all rolls are formed, brush crescents with remaining softened butter.

5. Cover and let rise for 35–45 minutes until almost doubled. Preheat oven to 400°F. Bake rolls for 12–17 minutes or until light golden brown. Cool on wire racks, then store in airtight container at room temperature.

PER SERVING: Calories: 110 | Total Fat: 5g | Saturated Fat: 2g | Cholesterol: 29mg | Protein: 2g | Sodium: 15mg | Potassium: 38mg | Fiber: 0g | Carbohydrates: 13g | Sugar: 2g

FOCACCIA

Focaccia is a flatbread; you can use it for a pizza crust, or top it with salsa or chopped tomatoes and basil for an appetizer.

YIELDS 1 LOAF; 8 SERVINGS

1¼ cups water

¼ cup whole milk

1½ teaspoons active dry yeast

2 cups bread flour

Pinch salt

2½ cups all-purpose flour

½ cup extra-virgin olive oil, divided

1 tablespoon minced fresh rosemary

1 tablespoon minced fresh oregano leaves

¼ teaspoon freshly cracked black pepper

1. In a large bowl, combine water, milk, and yeast. Stir and let stand until bubbly, about 20 minutes.

2. Add bread flour and salt and beat well. Gradually add enough all-purpose flour to make a soft and wet dough.

3. Brush a 15" × 10" jellyroll pan with 2 tablespoons of the olive oil. Put the dough into the pan and stretch and press so the dough fills the pan. Then, using your fingertips, make dimples in the dough's surface.

4. Drizzle the dough with the remaining olive oil and sprinkle with the rosemary, oregano, and pepper. Let rise in a warm place for about 45 minutes.

5. Preheat oven to 400°F. Bake the focaccia until golden brown, about 30–35 minutes. Remove to a wire rack to cool.

PER SERVING: Calories: 410 | Total Fat: 15g | Saturated Fat: 2g | Cholesterol: 3mg | Protein: 9g | Sodium: 37mg | Potassium: 137mg | Fiber: 2g | Carbohydrates: 56g | Sugar: 1g

HAMBURGER BUNS

Most people just buy packages of hamburger buns without thinking of the sodium content. But an average package of this product bought at any grocery store or bakery can contain 206mg of sodium per bun! Make your own for better flavor and much less sodium.

YIELDS 8 HAMBURGER BUNS

½ cup bread flour

½ cup whole-wheat flour

2½ cups all-purpose flour, divided

1½ teaspoons active dry yeast

Pinch salt

½ cup plus 1 tablespoon whole milk, divided

½ cup water

¼ cup oil

3 tablespoons honey

1 large egg

2 tablespoons sesame or poppy seeds

1. In large bowl, combine bread flour, whole-wheat flour, 1 cup of the all-purpose flour, yeast, and salt, and mix well.

2. In a medium saucepan, combine ½ cup milk, water, oil, and honey and heat to 120°F. Add to the flour mixture along with the egg and beat well.

3. Gradually beat in enough of the remaining all-purpose flour to make a soft dough. Turn out onto floured surface and knead until smooth.

4. Divide dough into eight pieces. Form each into a round about 4" wide and place on a greased baking sheet. Brush each bun with some of the remaining 1 tablespoon milk and sprinkle with sesame or poppy seeds. Cover and let rise for about 40–50 minutes or until almost doubled.

5. Preheat oven to 400°F. Bake the buns for 10–15 minutes or until golden brown. Remove from baking sheet and let cool on wire rack.

PER SERVING: Calories: 313 | Total Fat: 9g | Saturated Fat: 1g | Cholesterol: 27mg | Protein: 7g | Sodium: 40mg | Potassium: 117mg | Fiber: 2g | Carbohydrates: 49g | Sugar: 7g

DINNER ROLLS

The dinner roll is another hidden-sodium bomb. Most rolls are made with lots of salt to control the yeast development. We'll make our rolls richer so they don't need salt. Butter and eggs also help control yeast development. These rolls freeze well; just cool them completely, package them in hard-sided freezer containers, and freeze up to 3 months.

YIELDS 24 ROLLS

4½ cups all-purpose flour, divided

1 package active dry yeast

Pinch salt

½ cup light cream

¼ cup milk

¼ cup water

¾ cup unsalted butter, divided

3 tablespoons sugar

2 large eggs

1. In a large bowl, combine 2 cups flour, yeast, and salt; mix well.

2. In a medium saucepan, combine cream, milk, water, ½ cup butter, and sugar and heat to 120°F. The butter doesn't need to melt.

3. Add the warm cream mixture to the flour mixture and beat well. Beat in the eggs.

4. Gradually add enough of the remaining flour to make a soft dough. Turn out onto floured surface and knead for 5 minutes.

5. Divide dough into quarters, and divide each quarter into sixths to make 24 balls. Cover half of the balls with a towel so they don't dry out. Spray two 12-cup muffin tins with nonstick baking spray containing flour. Melt the remaining ¼ cup butter.

6. Divide each of the balls into three pieces; place the three pieces in a muffin cup side by side to make cloverleaf rolls. Repeat with remaining dough. Brush all of the little buns with the remaining ¼ cup butter.

7. Cover with a towel and let rise for 50–60 minutes or until the rolls are almost doubled. Preheat oven to 350°F.

8. Bake rolls for 12–17 minutes or until they are light golden brown. Remove from pans and cool on wire racks.

PER SERVING: Calories: 159 | Total Fat: 7g | Saturated Fat: 4g | Cholesterol: 36mg | Protein: 3g | Sodium: 17mg | Potassium: 48mg | Fiber: 0g | Carbohydrates: 19g | Sugar: 1g

RAISIN BREAD

This raisin bread makes the world's best toast. Spread it with unsalted butter and some whipped honey for a wonderful treat. Instead of rolling up the cinnamon-raisin mixture in the bread, you simply knead it a bit. This avoids the large air pockets that can form around the cinnamon spiral. The bread also freezes well.

YIELDS 1 LOAF; 12 SERVINGS

1 cup bread flour

1¼ teaspoons active dry yeast

Pinch salt

1⅔ cups all-purpose flour, divided

¾ cup whole milk

2 tablespoons water

3 tablespoons granulated sugar

5 tablespoons unsalted butter, divided

1 large egg

¼ cup brown sugar

2 teaspoons ground cinnamon

½ cup raisins

1. In large bowl, combine bread flour, yeast, salt, and ½ cup of the all-purpose flour and mix well.

2. In medium saucepan, combine milk, water, granulated sugar, and 3 tablespoons butter and heat to 120°F. Pour into flour mixture and beat well. Beat in egg.

3. Gradually add enough of the remaining all-purpose flour to make a firm dough. Knead on floured surface for 3 minutes.

4. In small bowl, combine remaining butter, brown sugar, and cinnamon and mix well. Stir in raisins. Knead this mixture into the dough until the dough is marbled.

5. Roll out dough on floured surface to 10" × 4" rectangle. Roll up, starting with the short side, and place in a greased 9" × 5" loaf pan.

6. Cover with a towel and let rise until almost doubled, about 50 minutes. Preheat oven to 350°F.

7. Bake bread for 35–45 minutes or until bread is golden brown. Remove from pan and cool on wire rack.

PER SERVING: Calories: 213 | Total Fat: 5g | Saturated Fat: 3g | Cholesterol: 31mg | Protein: 4g | Sodium: 39mg | Potassium: 128mg | Fiber: 1g | Carbohydrates: 36g | Sugar: 12g

FLAKY BISCUITS

With practice, you should be able to whip these up in just a few minutes to serve with chili, soup, or a chicken dinner. While you can cut these biscuits into rounds for a classic shape, you'll get more biscuits if you simply pat the dough into a square and cut into smaller squares. It's easier too!

YIELDS 12 BISCUITS

1¾ cups plus 2 tablespoons all-purpose flour

2 tablespoons cornstarch

2 teaspoons baking powder

¼ teaspoon baking soda

3 tablespoons solid shortening

¼ cup unsalted butter

⅓ cup whole milk

⅓ cup buttermilk

1 tablespoon water

1. Preheat oven to 425°F.

2. In large bowl, combine 1¾ cups plus 2 tablespoons flour, cornstarch, baking powder, and baking soda.

3. Using two knives or a pastry blender, cut in the solid shortening and butter until particles are the size of small peas.

4. Add whole milk, buttermilk, and water and mix just until a dough forms.

5. Sprinkle more flour on a work surface. Pat dough out to an 8" × 6" rectangle. Cut into 12 squares and place on a baking sheet.

6. Bake for 12–17 minutes or until the biscuits are light golden brown. Serve warm.

PER SERVING: Calories: 145 | Total Fat: 7g | Saturated Fat: 3g | Cholesterol: 11mg | Protein: 2g | Sodium: 37mg | Potassium: 125mg | Fiber: 0g | Carbohydrates: 17g | Sugar: 0g

BASIC WHITE BREAD

As with many bread recipes, humidity and other factors can affect how much flour is needed, so more or less may be needed. If it takes more, continue to add flour 1 tablespoon at a time in Step 2 until you get the described results.

YIELDS 1 LOAF; 12 SERVINGS

1 teaspoon active dry yeast

1 teaspoon granulated sugar

1⅓ cups lukewarm water (about 105°F)

2 tablespoons extra-virgin olive oil

¼ teaspoon fine sea salt

4 cups unbleached bread flour

1. To make the dough: In the bowl of a heavy-duty electric mixer fitted with a dough-hook attachment, combine the yeast, sugar, and water. Mix on lowest speed to blend. Let stand until the yeast bubbles, about 5 minutes.

2. Add the oil and salt; mix on lowest speed to blend. Add 3 cups of the flour and resume mixing at the lowest speed, adding the remaining flour a little at a time until the flour has been absorbed and the dough forms a ball and pulls away from the side of the mixer. Increase mixer to the speed recommended by the manufacturer for kneading dough; mix until the dough is soft and has a satiny sheen, about 4–5 minutes. Or you can knead the dough by hand for 5 minutes.

3. Transfer the dough to a bowl that has a capacity of 3 times the size of the ball of dough; cover tightly with plastic wrap and place in the refrigerator. Let the dough rise in the refrigerator until doubled in bulk, 8–12 hours. The dough can be kept for 2–3 days in the refrigerator. Simply punch down the dough as it doubles.

4. To bake the bread: Treat a 9" × 5" bread pan with olive oil or nonstick cooking spray. Remove the dough from the refrigerator and punch down. Work the dough by folding it over itself a few times, pinching the resulting "seam" together. Arrange in the pan, seam-side down. Brush a little oil over the top of the dough. Cover with a cotton towel and set in a warm place, and let the dough rise until doubled in size. Preheat oven to 350°F.

5. Cut 1 or 2 slits in the top of the dough. Bake for 30–40 minutes, or until the loaf has a hollow sound when "thumped." Let cool in the pan for a few minutes, then remove from the pan and cool on a wire rack.

PER SERVING: Calories: 168 | Total Fat: 0g | Saturated Fat: 0g | Cholesterol: 0mg | Protein: 4g | Sodium: 47mg | Potassium: 50mg | Fiber: 0g | Carbohydrates: 32g | Sugar: 0g

SAVORY BEER BREAD

If you are short on time, you can make this dough all the way through Step 4 and then you can cover the bowl with plastic wrap and let the dough rise overnight in the refrigerator. If you do, allow the dough to come to room temperature before you proceed with Step 5 the next day.

YIELDS 1 LOAF; 12 SERVINGS

¾ cup warm beer

2 teaspoons active dry yeast

1 tablespoon granulated sugar

2¼ cups unbleached all-purpose flour

½ cup oat bran or rye flour

¼ teaspoon salt

¼ cup walnut or other cold-pressed oil, plus extra for greasing bowl

½ cup minced sweet onion

6 tablespoons coarsely chopped walnuts

1 small egg

1 teaspoon water

1. In a microwave-safe cup, heat the beer to lukewarm (105°F–115°F), about 20–30 seconds in the microwave on high. Add the yeast and sugar; let stand for 10 minutes or until the yeast begins to bubble.

2. Combine the flour, oat bran, and salt in a large bowl. Make a well in the center. Pour the yeast mixture and ¼ cup walnut oil into the well; stir until blended. The dough should form a ball and easily pull away from the bowl. If not, add flour 1 tablespoon at a time.

3. Turn the dough out onto a floured surface. Sprinkle flour over the top of the dough and pat some onto your hands. Knead the dough by pressing it against the floured surface with the heels of your hands, then fold it back onto itself. Knead until the dough is glossy, smooth, and elastic, about 10 minutes.

4. Grease a large bowl with walnut or other cold-pressed oil. Place the kneaded dough in the bowl and turn to coat with oil. Cover with a damp cotton towel and let rise in a warm place until doubled in size, about 1 hour. (Alternatively, you can place in the refrigerator overnight.)

5. Punch down the dough; add the onion and walnuts, and knead into the dough until evenly distributed throughout.

6. Preheat oven to 375°F.

7. Turn the dough out onto a floured surface. Divide the dough into thirds. Using your hands, roll each of the pieces into a 12"-long rope. Braid 3 ropes together to form a loaf. Tuck the ends under and place on an 18" × 12" baking sheet. Cover with a cotton towel and let rise until doubled in bulk, about 45 minutes to 1 hour.

8. In a small bowl, beat together the egg and water. Brush the top of the loaf with the egg wash.

9. Bake for 45–50 minutes or until crusty and brown. (The bread should sound hollow when you thump it with your fingers.) Cool on the pan for 10 minutes. Turn out onto a wire rack to cool completely. Slice with a serrated bread knife.

PER SERVING: Calories: 160 | Total Fat: 4g | Saturated Fat: 0g | Cholesterol: 14mg | Protein: 2g | Sodium: 54mg | Potassium: 72mg | Fiber: 0g | Carbohydrates: 22g | Sugar: 0g

OLD-STYLE WHOLE-WHEAT BREAD

Bread recipes need some sugar or sweetener, such as honey, to "feed" the yeast. This helps the yeast work, which in turn helps the bread rise.

YIELDS 2 LOAVES; 24 SERVINGS

1¼ teaspoons active dry yeast

1 cup warm water

1½ cups unbleached all-purpose or bread flour

1 tablespoon granulated sugar

¼ cup hot water

¼ teaspoon salt

⅛ teaspoon mustard powder

⅛ teaspoon grated lemon zest

¼ cup brown sugar

1½ tablespoons solid shortening

1½ cups whole-wheat flour

1. Add the yeast to the warm water. Stir in the all-purpose flour and granulated sugar. Beat the mixture until smooth, either by hand or with a mixer. Set the mixture in a warm place to "proof" until it becomes foamy and bubbly (up to 1 hour).

2. Combine the hot water, salt, mustard powder, lemon zest, brown sugar, and shortening; stir. Allow to cool until lukewarm. (Stirring until the brown sugar dissolves should be sufficient to cool the water; test to be sure, because adding liquid that's too warm can "kill" the yeast. The water should not be warmer than 120°F.) Add to the bubbly flour mixture (the "sponge"). Stir in the whole-wheat flour and beat until smooth, but *do not knead*.

3. Divide the dough into 2 loaf pans treated with nonstick spray; cover and set in a warm place until doubled in size.

4. Preheat oven to 350°F and bake for 50 minutes.

PER SERVING: Calories: 85 | Total Fat: 1g | Saturated Fat: 0g | Cholesterol: 0mg | Protein: 1g | Sodium: 29mg | Potassium: 18mg | Fiber: 1g | Carbohydrates: 16g | Sugar: 3g

FRENCH BREAD

To keep homemade bread fresh and ready for use, slice cooled bread, put the slices together and wrap them in aluminum foil, then place the foil-wrapped slices in a plastic bag. You can freeze the package. The slices will easily break apart and thaw rapidly.

YIELDS 2 LOAVES; 24 SERVINGS

2½ teaspoons active dry yeast

2½ cups warm water

2 cups unbleached bread flour

2 cups unbleached all-purpose flour

¼ teaspoon salt

Optional: Cornmeal

1. Add the yeast to the water; stir to dissolve. Set aside for 5–10 minutes, until the yeast is bubbling to the top. Add the flours and salt to a mixing bowl. If using an electric mixer, use the dough hook and mix on low to combine. Pour in the yeast-water mixture. Mix on low until combined; the dough should form a ball and pull away from the sides of the bowl.

2. Add more water or flour, if necessary. If your mixer can handle this much dough, knead at medium-high speed for 5 minutes or until the dough is glossy and elastic. (You should be able to pull the dough gently without it sticking to your fingers.) Otherwise, knead by hand for about 15 minutes by pressing it against a lightly floured surface with the heels of your hands, then folding it back onto itself.

3. Form the dough into a round and cover with a bowl turned upside down over the top. Let rise for 2 hours. Punch down, cover, and let rise for another 1½ hours. Punch down again and divide the dough in half. Roll each half into an elongated loaf. Place on a heavy baking pan treated with nonstick spray or dusted with cornmeal. Use a sharp knife to cut several vents into the top of each loaf. Cover with a damp cotton towel and let rise until doubled.

4. As the loaves rise, place 1 shelf so that it's in the lower third of the oven and the top shelf so it's in the upper third. Preheat oven to 450°F. Place a pan of hot water on the bottom shelf; also have a mister filled with water at the ready.

5. Remove the cotton towel covering the loaves and place the baking sheet with risen bread loaves in the oven. Quickly mist water across the tops of the loaves. (This creates an immediate rush of steam and helps form a good crust.) Bake for 25 minutes or until the loaves are nicely browned and have a hollow sound when "thumped" on the bottom crust.

PER SERVING (1 slice): Calories: 78 | Total Fat: 0g | Saturated Fat: 0g | Cholesterol: 0mg | Protein: 2g | Sodium: 24mg | Potassium: 30mg | Fiber: 0g | Carbohydrates: 16g | Sugar: 0g

PIZZA CRUST

The cornmeal in this dough adds crispness, texture, and flavor. Make several of these crusts, prebake them, and freeze. When you want homemade pizza, take them out of the freezer, top with desired sauce and toppings, and bake until the crust is golden brown.

YIELDS 1 CRUST; 4 SERVINGS

1 cup bread flour

⅓ cup white cornmeal

¾ teaspoon active dry yeast

Pinch salt

1 tablespoon olive oil

⅔ cup warm water

½ cup all-purpose flour

1. In large bowl, combine bread flour, cornmeal, yeast, and salt, and mix well. Add oil and warm water and beat well. Add enough all-purpose flour until a firm dough forms.

2. Flour work surface and knead the dough for 1 minute. Then put the dough into a bowl coated with olive oil; turn so it's greased all over. Cover and let rise for 1 hour.

3. Grease a large cookie sheet with solid shortening. Roll out the dough directly on the cookie sheet until it's about ¼" thick. Let stand for 10 minutes.

4. Preheat oven to 425°F. Bake the crust for 8–9 minutes or until it's set and very light golden brown. Top as desired and bake for another 10–15 minutes or until crust is deep golden brown.

PER SERVING: Calories: 260 | Total Fat: 4g | Saturated Fat: 0g | Cholesterol: 0mg | Protein: 6g | Sodium: 48mg | Potassium: 85mg | Fiber: 1g | Carbohydrates: 47g | Sugar: 0g

BREAD MACHINE WHITE BREAD

Simple and yet oh so delicious. This recipe creates a soft bread with a nice brown crust. It's perfect for sandwiches and can be used to make homemade bread crumbs.

YIELDS 1 LOAF; 12 SERVINGS

1¼ cups skim milk

1 tablespoon light olive, canola, or other cold-pressed vegetable oil

½ teaspoon salt

2 tablespoons nonfat milk powder

4 cups unbleached all-purpose or bread flour

1 tablespoon granulated sugar

2½ teaspoons active dry yeast

Add the ingredients to your bread machine in the order recommended by the manufacturer (which is usually in the order given here), being careful that the yeast doesn't come in contact with the salt. Bake on light-crust setting.

PER SERVING: Calories: 176 | Total Fat: 0g | Saturated Fat: 0g | Cholesterol: 0mg | Protein: 4g | Sodium: 114mg | Potassium: 122mg | Fiber: 0g | Carbohydrates: 34g | Sugar: 2g

BREAD MACHINE HONEY WHOLE-WHEAT BREAD

Be sure to check the manufacturer's instructions for your bread machine; some aren't designed to handle whole grains.

YIELDS 1 LOAF; 12 SERVINGS

1¼ cups skim milk

1 tablespoon light olive, canola, or other cold-pressed vegetable oil

1 large egg, beaten

¼ cup oat bran

2 tablespoons nonfat buttermilk powder

½ teaspoon salt

3 cups unbleached all-purpose or bread flour

¾ cup whole-wheat flour

1 tablespoon honey

2½ teaspoons active dry yeast

Check the manufacturer's manual for whole-grain bread settings; otherwise, use the light-crust setting. Add the ingredients to your bread machine in the order recommended by the manufacturer (which is usually the order given here), being careful that the yeast doesn't come in contact with the salt. Bake at the wheat-bread setting, light crust.

PER SERVING: Calories: 178 | Total Fat: 2g | Saturated Fat: 0g | Cholesterol: 18mg | Protein: 6g | Sodium: 120mg | Potassium: 130mg | Fiber: 2g | Carbohydrates: 32g | Sugar: 2g

BUTTERY BATTER BISCUITS

Most commercial breads not only contain lots of preservatives; they also usually use shortening, which contains hydrogenated oil, a less healthy fat choice. You can substitute olive or other cold-pressed vegetable oil, such as expeller-pressed canola, for the butter in any bread recipe.

YIELDS 24 BISCUITS

3 cups unbleached all-purpose flour

¼ teaspoon salt

1½ teaspoons baking soda

1 tablespoon cream of tartar

1 teaspoon baking powder

½ cup unsalted butter

1⅓ cups 1% milk

1. Preheat oven to 400°F. For quick mixing, use a food processor. Add all of the ingredients and then pulse until just blended. Be careful not to overprocess this dough; if you do, the rolls won't be as light.

2. To mix by hand, sift together the dry ingredients, then cut in the butter using a pastry blender or fork until the mixture resembles coarse crumbs. Add the milk and stir until the mixture pulls away from the sides of the bowl.

3. Use 1 heaping tablespoon for each biscuit, dropping the dough onto baking sheets treated with nonstick spray. (You can also use pan liners, such as parchment or nonstick aluminum foil.) Bake until golden brown, about 20–30 minutes.

PER SERVING: Calories: 95 | Total Fat: 4g | Saturated Fat: 2g | Cholesterol: 10mg | Protein: 2g | Sodium: 108mg | Potassium: 58mg | Fiber: 0g | Carbohydrates: 12g | Sugar: 0g

BREAD MACHINE 7-GRAIN BREAD

Seven-grain cereal is usually a mix of wheat, rye, triticale, oats, oat bran, barley, brown rice, and flaxseed. You can substitute it in place of or for part of the oats in traditional recipes, such as cookies, breads, muffins, or pancakes. You can also cook it up like a hot breakfast cereal and serve it with dried fruit or nuts.

YIELDS 1 LOAF; 12 SERVINGS

1¼ cups skim milk

2 tablespoons nonfat milk powder

1 tablespoon extra-virgin olive oil

¾ cup dry 7-grain cereal

½ cup oat bran

¼ teaspoon sea salt

⅛ teaspoon grated lemon zest

Pinch mustard powder

2¼ cups unbleached all-purpose or bread flour

½ cup whole-wheat flour

1 tablespoon honey

2½ teaspoons active dry yeast

Add the ingredients to your bread machine in the order recommended by the manufacturer (which is usually the order given here), being careful that the yeast doesn't come in contact with the salt. Bake at the whole-wheat bread setting.

PER SERVING: Calories: 150 | Total Fat: 0g | Saturated Fat: 0g | Cholesterol: 0mg | Protein: 4g | Sodium: 74mg | Potassium: 132mg | Fiber: 2g | Carbohydrates: 28g | Sugar: 2g

BREAD MACHINE REDUCED-SODIUM CHEESY CORNBREAD

This cornbread strikes an ideal balance between sweet and savory. When choosing your Parmesan cheese, check its nutrition facts carefully; some brands have unwanted fat and sodium. BelGioioso Freshly Grated Parmesan is one of the lowest in both fat and sodium.

YIELDS 1 LOAF; 12 SERVINGS

1¼ cups water

¼ cup dried nonfat milk powder

1 tablespoon honey

2 tablespoons plus 2 teaspoons canola oil

2½ teaspoons active dry yeast

2½ cups bread flour

1 cup yellow cornmeal

¼ teaspoon mustard powder

¼ teaspoon sea salt

⅛ teaspoon grated lemon zest

½ cup grated Cheddar cheese

1 tablespoon grated Parmesan cheese

1. Bring the water to just below the boiling point by heating it in a saucepan over medium-high heat; remove from heat. Immediately whisk in the milk powder, honey, and oil; let cool to room temperature.

2. Add the remaining ingredients *except* the Cheddar and Parmesan cheeses in the order suggested by your bread machine manual, and process on the basic bread cycle according to the manufacturer's directions. Bake at the white-bread setting, light crust.

3. At the beeper (or the end of the first kneading), add the cheeses.

PER SERVING: Calories: 200 | Total Fat: 2g | Saturated Fat: 0g | Cholesterol: 4mg | Protein: 6g | Sodium: 70mg | Potassium: 118mg | Fiber: 0g | Carbohydrates: 34g | Sugar: 2g

BREAD MACHINE COTTAGE CHEESE BREAD

This recipe creates a hearty white bread that's great for sandwiches. You can use full-fat cottage cheese in this bread if you wish, but the nonfat version comes out delicious with nothing lacking in the taste department.

YIELDS 1 LOAF; 12 SERVINGS

¼ cup water

1 cup nonfat cottage cheese

2 tablespoons unsalted butter

1 large egg

1 tablespoon granulated sugar

¼ teaspoon baking soda

¼ teaspoon salt

⅛ teaspoon grated lemon zest

2¾ cups bread flour

¼ cup oat bran

2½ teaspoons active dry yeast

1. Add the ingredients to your bread machine in the order recommended by the manufacturer (which is usually the order given here), being careful that the yeast doesn't come in contact with the salt.

2. Check the bread machine at the "beep" to make sure the dough is pulling away from the sides of the pan and forming a ball. Add water or flour, if needed. (You do not want the dough to be overly dry.)

3. Bake on the white bread setting, light crust.

PER SERVING: Calories: 156 | Total Fat: 2g | Saturated Fat: 0g | Cholesterol: 22mg | Protein: 6g | Sodium: 120mg | Potassium: 80mg | Fiber: 0g | Carbohydrates: 26g | Sugar: 0g

BREAD MACHINE NEW YORK RYE

This bread is wonderful fresh out of the machine, warm with some unsalted butter on it. Or you can refrigerate it and then slice it for sandwiches.

YIELDS 1 LOAF; 12 SERVINGS

1⅛ cups water

2 tablespoons honey

¼ teaspoon salt

⅛ teaspoon mustard powder

⅛ teaspoon grated lemon zest

4 teaspoons olive or canola oil

1 large egg, beaten

¼ cup dried nonfat milk powder

1 tablespoon caraway seeds

2½ cups bread flour

1¼ cups rye flour

¼ cup whole-wheat flour

¼ cup oat bran

2½ teaspoons active dry yeast

1. Add the ingredients in the order suggested by your bread machine manual and process on the basic bread cycle according to the manufacturer's directions.

2. Bake on the white-bread setting, light crust.

PER SERVING: Calories: 196 | Total Fat: 2g | Saturated Fat: 0g | Cholesterol: 16mg | Protein: 6g | Sodium: 68mg | Potassium: 138mg | Fiber: 2g | Carbohydrates: 36g | Sugar: 4g

LEMON PEAR SCONES

You can underbake some of these scones and then, once they've cooled, wrap them in nonstick foil and freeze them until needed. When needed, pop the foil-wrapped scones into a preheated 350°F oven for 15–20 minutes.

SERVES 12

1 cup rolled oats or oat bran, or ½ cup of each

1 cup unbleached all-purpose flour

⅓ cup plus 2 tablespoons granulated sugar

1½ teaspoons low-salt baking powder

½ teaspoon baking soda

1 teaspoon dried ground ginger

¼ teaspoon cinnamon

¼ teaspoon nutmeg

Pinch salt

2 teaspoons grated lemon zest

3 tablespoons unsalted butter, cut into small pieces

⅔ cup plain nonfat yogurt

1 large egg, lightly beaten

1 teaspoon vanilla extract

1 teaspoon lemon extract

½ cup peeled and grated pear

1. Preheat oven to 400°F. Treat a baking sheet or jellyroll pan with nonstick cooking spray.

2. In large bowl, combine the rolled oats or oat bran or a combination of the two, flour, ⅓ cup of the sugar, baking powder, baking soda, ginger, cinnamon, nutmeg, salt, and lemon zest; mix well. Cut in the butter until crumbly.

3. In separate bowl, mix together the yogurt, beaten egg, vanilla extract, and lemon extract. Add to the dry ingredients, using a fork to mix the wet ingredients in to moisten the dry. Fold in the grated pear.

4. Drop ¼ cupfuls of batter in semiflattened mounds on the treated baking sheet. Sprinkle with the remaining sugar. Bake for 16–18 minutes, until light golden brown. Serve warm.

PER SERVING: Calories: 135 | Total Fat: 3g | Saturated Fat: 2g | Cholesterol: 24mg | Protein: 3g | Sodium: 69mg | Potassium: 149mg | Fiber: 1g | Carbohydrates: 22g | Sugar: 9g

POTATO WATER SOURDOUGH OAT BRAN BREAD

The sourdough starter will need to be made anywhere from 6–24 hours before you plan to make the bread, depending on how sour you wish the flavor to be. Store it in the refrigerator in a container with a small hole in the lid; the hole allows the gasses to escape. Replenish the starter as needed with equal parts water and flour.

YIELDS 1 LOAF; 12 SERVINGS

Sourdough Starter

1 cup potato water (water drained off of unsalted boiled potatoes)

¾ cup unbleached all-purpose flour

1 teaspoon granulated sugar

1 teaspoon active dry yeast

¾ teaspoon sea salt

Bread

1 cup nonfat milk

2 tablespoons extra-virgin olive oil

¾ cup oat bran

3¼ cups unbleached all-purpose flour

¼ teaspoon salt

2 teaspoons granulated sugar

1 teaspoon active dry yeast

1. To make the sourdough starter: Combine the potato water, ¾ cup flour, 1 teaspoon granulated sugar, 1 teaspoon yeast, and ¾ teaspoon salt in a glass container (such as a mayonnaise jar) and cover the jar with cheesecloth.

2. Allow to sit at room temperature. The length of time you leave the dough starter at room temperature will depend on how sour you like your bread. If you prefer a milder flavor, only allow the starter to sit for 6 hours. You can leave the starter at room temperature for up to 2 days. Stir the mixture or jiggle the jar occasionally to keep it mixed.

3. To make the bread: Add the milk, then the starter, and then the remaining ingredients to your bread machine in the order recommended by the manufacturer (which is usually in the order given here), being careful that the yeast doesn't come in contact with the salt. Set the bread maker at the white bread setting, light crust.

4. Check the bread machine at the "beep" to make sure the dough is pulling away from the sides of the pan and forming a ball. Add water or flour, if needed. (You do not want the dough to be overly dry.)

PER SERVING: Calories: 168 | Total Fat: 2g | Saturated Fat: 0g | Cholesterol: 0mg | Protein: 4g | Sodium: 90mg | Potassium: 112mg | Fiber: 0g | Carbohydrates: 30g | Sugar: 2g

REDUCED-SODIUM HAWAIIAN-STYLE BREAD

You can substitute ⅛ cup frozen unsweetened pineapple juice concentrate and ⅜ cup water for the unsweetened pineapple juice in this recipe.

YIELDS 1 LOAF; 12 SERVINGS

1 large egg

½ cup unsweetened pineapple juice

¾ cup water

2 tablespoons canola oil

1 teaspoon vanilla extract

1 teaspoon grated orange zest

½ teaspoon grated lemon zest

½ teaspoon dried ground ginger

¼ teaspoon salt

1½ cups unbleached bread flour

2¼ cups unbleached all-purpose flour

¼ cup granulated sugar

2 tablespoons dried nonfat milk

2½ teaspoons active dry yeast

Unless the instructions for your bread machine differ, add the ingredients in the order listed here. Bake on the light-crust setting.

PER SERVING: Calories: 202 | Total Fat: 2g | Saturated Fat: 0g | Cholesterol: 16mg | Protein: 4g | Sodium: 62mg | Potassium: 100mg | Fiber: 0g | Carbohydrates: 36g | Sugar: 6g

AWESOME ORANGE BREAD

Wake up to a bright citrus bread that is perfect for your morning toast.

YIELDS 1 LOAF; 12 SERVINGS

1 large egg

¼ cup frozen orange juice concentrate

1 cup water

2 tablespoons canola oil

1 teaspoon vanilla extract

1 teaspoon grated orange zest

½ teaspoon grated lemon zest

¼ teaspoon dried ground ginger

Pinch cinnamon

Pinch cloves

Pinch nutmeg

¼ teaspoon salt

⅛ cup oat bran

1½ cups unbleached bread flour

2¼ cups unbleached all-purpose flour

⅛ cup granulated sugar

2 tablespoons dried nonfat milk

2½ teaspoons active dry yeast

Unless the instructions for your bread machine differ, add the ingredients in the order listed here. Use the light-crust setting.

PER SERVING: Calories: 206 | Total Fat: 2g | Saturated Fat: 0g | Cholesterol: 16mg | Protein: 6g | Sodium: 60mg | Potassium: 132mg | Fiber: 0g | Carbohydrates: 36g | Sugar: 4g

WILD MUSHROOM BREAD

The quality of your bread pan, the humidity, the type of oven you use and how well it maintains the temperature, and other factors can all affect how bread turns out. Putting a pizza stone on a lower oven shelf can help maintain oven temperature, even when you're not baking directly on the stone.

YIELDS 2 LOAVES; 24 SERVINGS

1 cup water

3 ounces dried wild mushrooms, ground to a fine powder

¼ teaspoon mustard powder

¼ teaspoon salt

2 teaspoons granulated sugar

2½ teaspoons active dry yeast

½ cup warm skim milk (100°F–115°F)

3½–4 cups unbleached all-purpose flour

¼ cup canola or other cold-pressed vegetable oil, plus extra as needed

Nonstick cooking spray

1. Boil the water. In a medium bowl, combine the mushroom powder, mustard powder, and salt. Pour the boiling water over the mixture; cover and set aside.

2. Add the sugar and yeast to the warm milk; stir well and allow the yeast to proof for 5 minutes.

3. In another bowl, add 3 cups of the flour. Add the yeast mixture, mushroom mixture, and the ¼ cup canola oil. Stir well, adding additional flour 1 tablespoon at a time until the dough forms a ball that easily pulls away from the sides of the bowl.

4. Turn the dough out onto a floured surface. Sprinkle flour over the top of the dough and pat some onto your hands. Knead the dough by pressing it against the floured surface with the heels of your hands, then folding it back onto itself. Knead until the dough is glossy, smooth, and elastic, about 10 minutes.

5. Coat a large bowl with cold-pressed vegetable oil. Place the kneaded dough in the bowl and turn it to coat with oil. Cover with a damp cotton towel and let rise in a warm place until doubled in size, or about 1 hour.

6. Coat your hands with about ¼ teaspoon of vegetable oil. Punch down the dough. Divide the dough into 2 equal parts and shape into round loaves. Place the rounds about 8" apart on a baking sheet treated with the nonstick spray. Use a sharp knife to make 2 or 3 slits in the top of the dough rounds. Cover with a cotton towel and place in a warm place until doubled in size, about 35–45 minutes.

7. Preheat oven to 375°F. Lightly spray the top of the loaves with the cooking spray. Bake for 35–45 minutes, until crusty and brown. (The bread should sound hollow when you thump it with your fingers.) Cool on the pan for 10 minutes. Turn out onto wire rack to cool completely. Slice with a serrated bread knife.

PER SERVING: Calories: 101 | Total Fat: 2g | Saturated Fat: 0g | Cholesterol: 0mg | Protein: 2g | Sodium: 27mg | Potassium: 90mg | Fiber: 0g | Carbohydrates: 17g | Sugar: 0g

CORN TORTILLAS

You can use a mixer with a dough hook or a food processor to mix corn tortilla dough. As with bread, the dough needs to be kneaded until it's no longer sticky. Since corn flour doesn't have the gluten that wheat flour has, there's no need to worry that you are kneading too long.

YIELDS 16 TORTILLAS

2 cups masa harina (corn flour)

¼ teaspoon salt

¼ teaspoon mustard powder

2 tablespoons lard or solid shortening

1¼ cups warm water

1. Add the masa harina, salt, and mustard powder to a large bowl; mix well. Add the lard and warm water. Use your fingers to work the mixture into a soft dough. Knead the dough until it is no longer sticky. Divide the dough into 16 balls; cover with a cotton towel and let rest for 20 minutes at room temperature.

2. To use a tortilla press, place a small square of waxed paper on the bottom part of the open press. Place a corn tortilla ball almost on the center of the waxed paper—a little more toward the hinge of the press than the handle. Place a second waxed paper square on top of the ball and press to flatten slightly. Close the press firmly until the tortilla measures about 6 inches in diameter. Alternately, roll the tortillas by hand: Flatten each ball between 2 pieces of waxed paper and roll out with a rolling pin; or place each ball on a lightly floured surface, dust the top of the ball with some corn flour, and roll out with a rolling pin. (Try to use as little flour as possible.)

3. Place the tortilla on a moderately hot griddle treated with nonstick spray. Within a few seconds, the edges of the tortilla will begin to dry out. At this point, turn the tortilla. Allow the second side to cook for a slightly longer period until it is slightly browned. Flip it back onto the first side and let it finish cooking. Allow about 2 minutes total cooking time per tortilla.

PER SERVING: Calories: 66 | Total Fat: 2g | Saturated Fat: 0g | Cholesterol: 0mg | Protein: 1g | Sodium: 36mg | Potassium: 42mg | Fiber: 0g | Carbohydrates: 10g | Sugar: 0g

RAISED BUTTERMILK BISCUITS

Keep in mind that even when you use a nonhydrogenated oil shortening such as in place of butter or lard, it's still a fat. Each tablespoon of that shortening has 110 calories (13 grams of fat, 6 grams of saturated fat). You can sometimes substitute plain nonfat yogurt or applesauce for some of or all of the fat called for in a recipe.

YIELDS 24 BISCUITS

¾ cup cultured lowfat buttermilk, warm

⅛ cup granulated sugar

2½ teaspoons active dry yeast

2½ cups unbleached all-purpose flour

¼ teaspoon salt

½ teaspoon low-salt baking powder

¼ cup unsalted butter

¼ cup solid shortening

1. Put the buttermilk and sugar in a food processor and process until mixed. Sprinkle the yeast over the buttermilk-sugar mixture and pulse once or twice to mix. Allow the mixture to sit at room temperature for about 5 minutes or until the yeast begins to work and the mixture is bubbling. Add the remaining ingredients to the food processor and pulse just until mixed, being careful not to overprocess the dough.

2. Preheat oven to 400°F.

3. Drop by heaping teaspoon per biscuit onto a baking sheet treated with nonstick spray. Set the tray in a warm place and allow the biscuits to rise for about 15 minutes. Bake for 12–15 minutes.

PER SERVING: Calories: 88 | Total Fat: 1g | Saturated Fat: 4g | Cholesterol: 5mg | Protein: 1g | Sodium: 32mg | Potassium: 43mg | Fiber: 0g | Carbohydrates: 11g | Sugar: 1g

FLOUR TORTILLAS

Tortillas can also be "baked" on an outdoor grill over indirect heat; as you would for grilling pizza crust, just make sure the grids are clean and well-seasoned so that the dough doesn't stick.

YIELDS 12 TORTILLAS

2 cups unbleached all-purpose flour

¼ teaspoon salt

1 teaspoon low-salt baking powder

1 tablespoon lard or solid shortening

¾ cup cold water

1. Thoroughly mix the dry ingredients in a bowl. Use a pastry blender or fork to cut in the lard and enough water to make a stiff dough. Divide into 12 balls.

2. Roll out on a lightly floured board, making them as thin as possible. Bring a griddle or nonstick pan treated with nonstick spray to temperature over medium heat. Cook the tortillas by placing them on griddle or in pan 1 at a time. Turn the tortillas when the top side begins to show some puffiness or blisters; turn and cook until the other side is lightly browned. (Total cooking time will be about 2 minutes per tortilla.)

PER SERVING: Calories: 84 | Total Fat: 1g | Saturated Fat: 0g | Cholesterol: 0mg | Protein: 2g | Sodium: 48mg | Potassium: 63mg | Fiber: 0g | Carbohydrates: 15g | Sugar: 0g

THIN FLOUR TORTILLAS

Flour (or corn) tortillas can be stored flat for several days in the refrigerator, or frozen. There is no need to defrost them before reheating.

YIELDS 24 TORTILLAS

2 cups unbleached all-purpose flour

1 teaspoon low-salt baking powder

1 tablespoon solid shortening

¼ teaspoon salt

¾ cup cold water

1. Thoroughly mix the flour and baking powder together in a medium bowl. Using your fingers, rub the shortening into the flour.

2. Dissolve the salt in the water and add it to the flour mixture. Use your fingers to knead the mixture into a dough, kneading for about 3 minutes. Cover the bowl with a cotton towel; let the dough rest for at least 2 hours. (Do not refrigerate.)

3. After the dough has rested, knead it again. Divide the dough into 24 balls, each about 1½" in diameter. Cover with a cotton towel until needed.

4. To prepare the tortillas, dust your hands with flour. Flatten 1 of the tortilla dough balls between your hands. Transfer to a lightly floured surface and use a rolling pin to roll it into a 7"-diameter round. As you roll the dough, turning it occasionally as you apply the rolling pin helps keep it round.

5. Bring a griddle or nonstick skillet to temperature over medium heat. Place the rolled tortilla on the griddle or in the skillet. (The cooking surface should be hot enough that there is a slight sizzling sound when the dough hits the surface.) Cook for about 20 seconds or until bubbles appear on the surface and the underside is speckled with dark brown. (If it puffs up, use a heat-safe spatula to press it down.) Turn the tortilla; cook it for a slightly shorter time on the other side.

PER SERVING: Calories: 41 | Total Fat: 0g | Saturated Fat: 0g | Cholesterol: 0mg | Protein: 1g | Sodium: 24mg | Potassium: 31mg | Fiber: 0g | Carbohydrates: 7g | Sugar: 0g

INDIAN SPICED FLATBREAD

Charnushka is also known as nigella sativa, black cumin, black caraway, black onion seed, or kalonji. It's an ingredient in many garam masala recipes, and it's often used in Jewish rye bread. You can buy it at the specialty spice shops.

YIELDS 8 FLATBREADS

⅔ cup warm skim milk

1 teaspoon granulated sugar

5 teaspoons active dry yeast

4 cups unbleached all-purpose flour

1 teaspoon baking powder

⅛ teaspoon mustard powder

⅛ teaspoon grated lemon zest

1 teaspoon fennel seed

2 teaspoons charnushka

1 teaspoon cumin seed

2 tablespoons canola oil

⅔ cup plain nonfat yogurt

1 large egg, beaten

Olive oil spray

2 teaspoons poppy seeds

1. In a microwave-safe measuring cup, heat the milk until warm (15–20 seconds on high). Stir in the sugar and yeast. Set aside for 5 minutes for the yeast to proof.

2. Add the flour, baking powder, mustard powder, lemon zest, fennel seed, charnushka, and cumin seed to mixing bowl. Place a cover over the bowl and mix on low with the dough hook long enough to combine the ingredients.

3. Add the milk-yeast mixture, oil, yogurt, and egg. Mix on low until the dough begins to form a ball and pull away from the sides of the bowl, then knead until the mixture becomes elastic. Cover and let the mixture rise until doubled.

4. Place a heavy baking sheet in the oven; preheat oven to 475°F.

5. Turn out the dough onto a lightly floured surface. Punch down, then knead the dough for about 1 minute. Divide into 8 equal pieces; cover with a damp cotton towel and let rest for 15 minutes.

6. Roll each naan (flatbread) out to a teardrop (rather than round) shape, leaving the dough about 10 times the thickness of a tortilla or about half the height of a hamburger bun. (Keep the remaining dough covered with the towel while you roll out each naan.) Lightly spray the top of the naan with the olive oil spray and sprinkle ⅓ teaspoon poppy seeds over the top. Transfer to the baking pan. Bake for 3 minutes, until puffed, then place under the broiler until the top is lightly browned. Repeat with the remaining 7 naan segments. (If you prefer, you can bake the flatbreads 2 at a time.) The bread is best served warm, immediately after baking; however, it can be baked and then broiled later immediately before serving.

7. If preparing on the grill, grill over indirect heat until puffy, then turn the bread and grill an additional 15–30 seconds. Transfer to a plate. Treat the side of the bread that is brownest with the spray oil, sprinkle with the poppy seeds, and return to the grill—poppy seed–side up—for another 15–30 seconds.

PER SERVING: Calories: 303 | Total Fat: 5g | Saturated Fat: 0g | Cholesterol: 27mg | Protein: 9g | Sodium: 39mg | Potassium: 291mg | Fiber: 2g | Carbohydrates: 52g | Sugar: 3g

AMERICANIZED INDIAN FLATBREAD

Create brown-and-serve flatbreads. Omit brushing the tops with egg yolk. Don't bake them completely, just prebake them for 3–4 minutes; let cool and then store in a plastic bag for 1–2 days. When ready to use, spray the tops with your choice of spray oil and sprinkle them with sesame seeds or another topping of your choice.

YIELDS 12 FLATBREADS

2 cups bleached flour

½ teaspoon low-salt baking powder

½ teaspoon salt

3 tablespoons skim milk

1 cup plain nonfat yogurt

1 teaspoon granulated sugar

1 teaspoon active dry yeast

3 tablespoons canola or other cold-pressed vegetable oil, plus extra as needed

1 large egg, lightly beaten

1 egg yolk

Optional: Garlic powder

4 teaspoons sesame seeds

1. Mix together the flour, baking powder, and salt in large bowl; make a well in the center.

2. Mix together the milk and yogurt; heat to lukewarm temperature in a medium saucepan on the stovetop or in the microwave. Stir the sugar, yeast, oil, and the whole large egg into the milk mixture; pour into the well in the flour. Stir from the center until mixed to a smooth dough. Turn out onto a floured surface; knead for about 15–20 minutes. (The dough should be elastic but not sticky; sprinkle with a little flour if the dough is sticky.) Place the dough in a covered bowl and let rise until doubled in size, about 3–4 hours at normal room temperature.

3. Punch down the dough and turn out onto a floured surface; divide into 12 pieces. Rub a little oil on your hands. Knead each dough piece lightly, then flatten it between your hands, pulling it into an oval to form a pear shape. Put the formed flatbreads onto baking sheets treated with nonstick spray, cover with damp cloth, and let rise for 15 minutes.

4. While the dough rises, preheat the oven to 450°F. Beat the egg yolk and brush it over the tops of the flatbreads. Sprinkle with garlic powder, if using, and the sesame seeds. Bake for 8–10 minutes, until golden brown.

PER SERVING: Calories: 137 | Total Fat: 4g | Saturated Fat: 0g | Cholesterol: 35mg | Protein: 3g | Sodium: 121mg | Potassium: 118mg | Fiber: 0g | Carbohydrates: 18g | Sugar: 2g

CHAPTER 3
SALADS AND SALAD DRESSINGS

HONEY MUSTARD SALAD DRESSING

Use your own honey mustard to make a salad dressing that is the perfect complement for greens or pasta salad, or to brush on chicken or fish before you grill it.

YIELDS 1 CUP; 16 SERVINGS

⅓ cup Honey Mustard (Chapter 4)

½ cup Mayonnaise (Chapter 4)

2 tablespoons lemon juice

1 tablespoon extra-virgin olive oil

Combine all ingredients in a medium bowl and whisk together until blended. Store in a tightly sealed jar in the refrigerator up to 5 days.

PER SERVING: Calories: 133 | Total Fat: 13g | Saturated Fat: 2g | Cholesterol: 17mg | Protein: 0g | Sodium: 1mg | Potassium: 17mg | Fiber: 0g | Carbohydrates: 2g | Sugar: 1g

CREAMY ONION SALAD DRESSING

Commercial salad dressings are very salty, so even a green salad with vegetables, usually considered a health food, can be hazardous to those who must watch their sodium intake. This recipe is excellent on mixed salad greens topped with grilled sliced chicken breast, red bell peppers, green onion, and sliced fresh mushrooms.

YIELDS 1 CUP; 16 SERVINGS

½ cup Slow Cooker Caramelized Onions (Chapter 4)

⅓ cup Mayonnaise (Chapter 4)

2 tablespoons sour cream

2 tablespoons milk

1 tablespoon lemon juice

Combine all ingredients in small bowl and mix until combined. Store covered in refrigerator up to 5 days.

PER SERVING: Calories: 45 | Total Fat: 4g | Saturated Fat: 0g | Cholesterol: 6mg | Protein: 0g | Sodium: 2mg | Potassium: 18mg | Fiber: 0g | Carbohydrates: 0g | Sugar: 0g

CREAMY GRAPE SALAD

Grapes can be found in several colors: green (or white), red, purple, and black. Their flavors are slightly different, so they are delicious combined in this easy salad. Serve this as a side dish to grilled chicken or steak, or as a flavor and temperature contrast to hot soup.

SERVES 6

½ cup sour cream

2 tablespoons honey

2 tablespoons milk

¼ teaspoon dried thyme leaves

3 cups green grapes

3 cups red grapes

½ cup chopped toasted walnuts

1. In medium bowl, combine sour cream, honey, milk, and thyme leaves and mix with wire whisk.

2. Stir in grapes gently to coat. Cover and refrigerate for 1–2 hours before serving. Top each serving with some walnuts.

PER SERVING: Calories: 179 | Total Fat: 5g | Saturated Fat: 2g | Cholesterol: 10mg | Protein: 2g | Sodium: 20mg | Potassium: 336mg | Fiber: 1g | Carbohydrates: 34g | Sugar: 30g

GREEN GODDESS DRESSING

Green Goddess salad dressing is green because it's packed with fresh herbs. It's usually made with anchovies, which are loaded with salt. Adding one green olive, which adds only 24mg of sodium to the whole recipe, supplies a bit of the briny flavor of anchovies.

YIELDS 1 CUP; 16 SERVINGS

1 clove garlic, minced

½ cup Mayonnaise (Chapter 4)

⅓ cup sour cream

2 tablespoons lemon juice

¼ cup chopped flat-leaf parsley

¼ cup chopped fresh basil leaves

2 tablespoons fresh thyme leaves

2 tablespoons chopped green onion

1 tablespoon chopped chives

1 large green olive, pitted

⅛ teaspoon black pepper

Combine all ingredients in a blender or food processor and blend or process until smooth. Store covered in the refrigerator up to 1 week.

PER SERVING: Calories: 66 | Total Fat: 7g | Saturated Fat: 1g | Cholesterol: 11mg | Protein: 0g | Sodium: 8mg | Potassium: 19mg | Fiber: 0g | Carbohydrates: 0g | Sugar: 0g

PASTA FAZOOL SALAD

Pasta fazool, technically known as pasta e fagioli, is a hot main dish recipe made with pasta, beans, and lots of veggies. Turn it into a salad for the hot summer months for a delightful change of pace. You can add some chopped grilled chicken, shrimp, or steak to this recipe if you'd like, but it's delicious on its own.

SERVES 6

3 cups penne pasta

⅓ cup extra-virgin olive oil

⅓ cup white wine vinegar

2 tablespoons Mustard (Chapter 4)

2 tablespoons lemon juice

2 tablespoons chopped fresh basil leaves

2 tablespoons minced fresh thyme leaves

⅛ teaspoon black pepper

1 teaspoon granulated sugar

1 (15-ounce) can no-salt-added cannellini beans, rinsed and drained

1 pint grape tomatoes, rinsed and cut in half

1 medium yellow bell pepper, chopped

3 stalks celery, chopped

¼ cup sliced green onion

⅓ cup shredded Parmesan cheese

1. Bring a large pot of water to a boil. Cook pasta according to package directions; when al dente, drain.

2. Meanwhile, in large bowl combine olive oil, vinegar, Mustard, and lemon juice and beat with a whisk until blended. Stir in basil, thyme, black pepper, and sugar.

3. Add hot pasta to the dressing and stir. Stir in remaining ingredients and mix gently. Cover and chill for 1–2 hours before serving.

PER SERVING: Calories: 492 | Total Fat: 15g | Saturated Fat: 2g | Cholesterol: 4mg | Protein: 18g | Sodium: 120mg | Potassium: 794mg | Fiber: 8g | Carbohydrates: 68g | Sugar: 4g

COBB SALAD

You can serve this salad the classic way by layering ingredients in rows next to each other on the plate, or you can toss everything together.

SERVES 4

⅓ cup Mayonnaise (Chapter 4)

2 tablespoons Mustard (Chapter 4)

3 tablespoons extra-virgin olive oil

2 tablespoons lemon juice

2 tablespoons minced chives

1 clove garlic, minced

⅛ teaspoon white pepper

2 cooked chicken breasts, chopped

2 hard-boiled eggs, sliced

2 cups chopped romaine lettuce

2 cups chopped butter lettuce

2 tomatoes, seeded and chopped

1 medium red bell pepper, chopped

1 medium avocado, chopped

1. In small bowl, combine mayonnaise, mustard, olive oil, and lemon juice and mix with wire whisk. Add chives, garlic, and white pepper and set aside.

2. Either arrange remaining ingredients in rows on a large serving plate or combine in a large bowl. Drizzle with the dressing and serve immediately.

PER SERVING: Calories: 543 | Total Fat: 40g | Saturated Fat: 6g | Cholesterol: 201mg | Protein: 34g | Sodium: 103mg | Potassium: 828mg | Fiber: 6g | Carbohydrates: 12g | Sugar: 4g

ZIPPY COLESLAW

Coleslaw is a wonderful side dish that is delicious served with grilled meats in the summer, or all year round. You can buy preshredded cabbage and even coleslaw mixes in the store if you'd like, but it's cheaper to shred or chop the cabbage yourself.

SERVES 8

½ cup Mayonnaise (Chapter 4)

3 tablespoons Mustard (Chapter 4)

3 tablespoons milk

2 tablespoons lemon juice

2 teaspoons honey

½ teaspoon celery seed

⅛ teaspoon white pepper

6 cups shredded cabbage

1 medium red bell pepper, slivered

1 medium yellow bell pepper, slivered

¼ cup sliced green onions

1 jalapeño pepper, minced

1. In large bowl, combine mayonnaise, mustard, milk, lemon juice, honey, celery seed, and white pepper and mix well.

2. Stir in remaining ingredients to coat. Cover and refrigerate for 1–2 hours to blend flavors before serving.

PER SERVING: Calories: 161 | Total Fat: 13g | Saturated Fat: 2g | Cholesterol: 18mg | Protein: 2g | Sodium: 14mg | Potassium: 216mg | Fiber: 2g | Carbohydrates: 8g | Sugar: 4g

CAESAR SALAD DRESSING

To reduce the sodium and add meaty flavor to this dressing, add well-browned mushrooms to the recipe. This step adds "umami," a Japanese term for "meaty" or "savory."

YIELDS 1 CUP; SERVING SIZE 2 TABLESPOONS

1 tablespoon unsalted butter

2 small cremini mushrooms, sliced

2 cloves garlic, minced

⅓ cup Mayonnaise (Chapter 4)

¼ cup plain yogurt

2 tablespoons lemon juice

2 tablespoons Mustard (Chapter 4)

2 tablespoons grated Parmesan cheese

⅛ teaspoon white pepper

1. In small skillet, melt butter over medium heat. Add mushrooms and cook, stirring frequently, until browned, about 9–12 minutes. Add garlic and cook for another 30 seconds; remove from heat and cool.

2. When mushroom mixture is cool, place in food processor or blender. Add mayonnaise, yogurt, lemon juice, mustard, cheese, and pepper; process or blend until smooth.

3. Cover and store in refrigerator up to 3 days.

PER SERVING: Calories: 104 | Total Fat: 10g | Saturated Fat: 2g | Cholesterol: 16mg | Protein: 1g | Sodium: 23mg | Potassium: 56mg | Fiber: 0g | Carbohydrates: 1g | Sugar: 0g

TUNA WALDORF SALAD

Waldorf salad was invented at the Waldorf Astoria Hotel in the late 1800s. It is traditionally made of chopped apples, grapes, and walnuts in a creamy dressing. This version uses golden raisins and dried cherries instead of grapes, and adds freshly grilled tuna to make this wonderful dish a main course.

SERVES 6

3 (4-ounce) tuna steaks

1 tablespoon olive oil

⅛ teaspoon pepper

⅓ cup plain yogurt

¼ cup Mayonnaise (Chapter 4)

2 tablespoons Honey Mustard (Chapter 4)

2 tablespoons lemon juice

½ teaspoon grated lemon zest

3 Granny Smith apples, chopped

3 stalks celery, chopped

1 cup coarsely chopped walnuts, toasted

⅓ cup golden raisins

⅓ cup dried cherries

6 cups torn butter lettuce

1. Prepare and preheat grill. Brush the tuna steaks with olive oil and sprinkle with pepper; grill 6" over medium coals for 4–5 minutes per side until desired doneness.

2. Meanwhile, in large bowl combine yogurt, mayonnaise, honey mustard, lemon juice, and lemon zest and mix well.

3. Stir apples, celery, walnuts, raisins, and cherries into the dressing.

4. When tuna is done, set aside, covered, for 5 minutes; meanwhile, assemble the salads.

5. Arrange lettuce on plates and top with apple mixture. Slice the tuna and place on top; serve immediately.

PER SERVING: Calories: 318 | Total Fat: 15g | Saturated Fat: 2g | Cholesterol: 39mg | Protein: 16g | Sodium: 58mg | Potassium: 691mg | Fiber: 4g | Carbohydrates: 30g | Sugar: 22g

CHICKEN SALAD IN GRILLED AVOCADOS

Not many people have tried grilled avocados. They are delicious, but only when cooked for about a minute or two. If avocados are heated too long, they develop a bitter flavor. Grilling just adds a bit of smokiness and some beautiful grill marks. A simple chicken salad is perfect served in these tender avocado halves.

SERVES 5

3 poached (6-ounce) chicken breasts, diced

¼ cup diced celery

2 tablespoons diced red onion

½ cup Mayonnaise (Chapter 4)

2 tablespoons lemon juice

1 jalapeño pepper, minced

4 large avocados

1 tablespoon olive oil

1. In medium bowl, combine diced chicken breasts, celery, and red onion. Add mayonnaise, lemon juice, and jalapeño and stir to coat.

2. Prepare and preheat grill. Cut avocados in half and twist to separate. With a knife, hit the pit sharply, then use the knife to remove the pit. Brush the avocados with olive oil.

3. Grill the avocados for 2 minutes or until grill marks appear. Be careful not to overcook.

4. Place avocados, grilled-side up, on serving plate. Top each with a spoonful of the chicken salad and serve immediately.

PER SERVING: Calories 802 | Total Fat: 62g | Saturated Fat: 10g | Cholesterol: 145mg | Protein: 46g | Sodium: 111mg | Potassium: 1,295mg | Fiber: 11g | Carbohydrates: 19g | Sugar: 1g

PEACH TOMATO RASPBERRY SALAD

Peaches, tomatoes, and raspberries are all delicious in late summer, the perfect time to make this beautiful salad. Serve with grilled steak, chicken, or fish for a special dinner.

SERVES 4

¼ cup extra-virgin olive oil

3 tablespoons peach nectar

1 tablespoon lime juice

1 teaspoon honey

Pinch black pepper

2 ripe medium peaches

2 ripe beefsteak tomatoes

1 cup raspberries

1 tablespoon minced fresh basil leaves

1. In small jar with a tight-fitting lid, combine olive oil, peach nectar, lime juice, honey, and black pepper and shake well. Set aside.

2. To peel peaches, bring a small pot of water to a boil. Drop in the peaches and let sit for 10 seconds. Remove peaches and plunge into ice water. The skins will slip right off. Remove the pits and slice.

3. Slice the tomatoes. Arrange the fruits on a serving platter and drizzle with the prepared dressing. Sprinkle with basil and serve immediately.

PER SERVING: Calories: 187 | Total Fat: 13g | Saturated Fat: 1g | Cholesterol: 0mg | Protein: 1g | Sodium: 4mg | Potassium: 345mg | Fiber: 3g | Carbohydrates: 16g | Sugar: 12g

CHICKEN CAESAR SALAD

This version of the classic salad adds veggies for color and flavor and adds grilled chicken to make it a main dish. Purchased croutons, unfortunately, are loaded with salt, so make your own. They are much more delicious than the commercial variety and are simple to create.

SERVES 5

3 slices French Bread (Chapter 2)

3 tablespoons olive oil, divided

4 (6-ounce) boneless, skinless chicken breasts

6 cups torn romaine lettuce leaves

1 medium yellow bell pepper, chopped

1 small zucchini, sliced

1 cup sliced mushrooms

¼ cup sliced green onions

½ cup Caesar Salad Dressing (see recipe in this chapter)

1. Cut the French Bread into 1" cubes. In large skillet, heat 2 tablespoons olive oil over medium heat. Sauté the bread, stirring frequently, until golden brown. Remove to paper towel to drain; let cool.

2. Prepare and preheat grill. Brush chicken with remaining 1 tablespoon olive oil and grill over medium coals for 5–6 minutes per side, turning once, until a meat thermometer registers 160°F. Remove from heat and cover with foil.

3. Combine lettuce, bell pepper, zucchini, mushrooms, and green onions in large bowl. Add croutons and toss.

4. Cut chicken into cubes and add to salad. Drizzle with dressing and toss to coat. Serve immediately.

PER SERVING: Calories: 413 | Total Fat: 17g | Saturated Fat: 3g | Cholesterol: 123mg | Protein: 47g | Sodium: 125mg | Potassium: 615mg | Fiber: 2g | Carbohydrates: 15g | Sugar: 1g

PAELLA SALAD

You can make a delicious salad version of Spanish paella using fresh seafood that is healthy and colorful. Saffron, the world's most expensive legal crop, is essential to the flavor and color of paella. Just a couple strands are used to give the rice and dressing a beautiful golden hue.

SERVES 6

¾ cup basmati rice

1½ cups chicken stock

2 strands saffron threads, divided

⅓ cup extra-virgin olive oil

2 tablespoons sour cream

2 tablespoons Grainy Mustard (Chapter 4)

3 tablespoons lemon juice

1 tablespoon minced fresh thyme leaves

1 tablespoon olive oil

1 pound Arctic char fillets

1 medium onion, chopped

3 cloves garlic, minced

1 Poached Chicken Breast (Chapter 8), cubed

1 medium yellow bell pepper, sliced

2 cups frozen baby peas, thawed

4 cups arugula

1. In medium saucepan, combine rice, chicken stock, and 1 strand of the saffron. Bring to a boil, reduce heat, and simmer for 15–20 minutes or until rice is tender. Set aside.

2. In large bowl, combine extra-virgin olive oil, sour cream, grainy mustard, lemon juice, remaining strand of saffron, and thyme and mix well. Set aside.

3. Heat 1 tablespoon olive oil in large skillet. Add the Arctic char fillets and cook, turning once, until fish flakes when tested with a fork. Remove fish from skillet.

4. Add onions and garlic to skillet; cook and stir until tender, about 5–6 minutes. Remove to bowl with the dressing and let cool.

5. Fluff rice with a fork and add to bowl. Break fish into pieces and add to bowl along with chicken, bell pepper, and peas. Stir gently to coat. Cover and chill for 1–2 hours to blend flavors before serving. Serve on arugula.

PER SERVING: Calories: 398 | Total Fat: 19g | Saturated Fat: 3g | Cholesterol: 71mg | Protein: 29g | Sodium: 112mg | Potassium: 568mg | Fiber: 4g | Carbohydrates: 38g | Sugar: 3g

DEVILED EGG SALAD

Deviled eggs are made by beating mayonnaise, mustard, and spices into egg yolks and piling the mixture into egg white halves. Let's turn this classic treat into a salad by creaming the yolks and adding lots of goodies, then chopping the whites and adding them to the yolk mixture with vegetables.

SERVES 4

6 large eggs

⅓ cup Mayonnaise (Chapter 4)

3 tablespoons Mustard (Chapter 4)

1 tablespoon lemon juice

½ teaspoon grated lemon zest

1 medium yellow bell pepper, chopped

2 stalks celery, chopped

¼ cup chopped green onion

1. Place eggs in a medium saucepan and cover with cold water. Place over high heat and bring to a boil. When the water is boiling hard, cover the pan and remove from heat. Let stand for 14 minutes. Then place the pan in the sink and run cold water over the eggs until they are cold. Crack the eggs under the water and let stand for 5 minutes. Peel eggs. Cut in half and remove yolks.

2. Place yolks in a medium bowl and mash with a fork. Gradually add mayonnaise, mixing well, until the mixture is smooth. Add mustard, lemon juice, and lemon zest and mix well.

3. Chop the egg whites and add to the yolk mixture along with bell pepper, celery, and green onion. Cover and refrigerate 1–2 hours before serving.

PER SERVING: Calories: 305 | Total Fat: 25g | Saturated Fat: 5g | Cholesterol: 340mg | Protein: 11g | Sodium: 121mg | Potassium: 334mg | Fiber: 1g | Carbohydrates: 7g | Sugar: 2g

LEMON CHICKEN AVOCADO SALAD

Chicken salad is a classic recipe, comforting and delicious. It's best made with poached chicken so the meat is tender and moist. This recipe can be dressed up many ways, but sometimes the simplest is best. Add avocado and lemon to chicken for a tasty salad everyone will love.

SERVES 4

¼ cup Mayonnaise (Chapter 4)

¼ cup sour cream

3 tablespoons lemon juice

2 teaspoons honey

1 teaspoon grated lemon zest

1 tablespoon minced fresh thyme leaves

1 tablespoon minced flat-leaf parsley

4 Poached Chicken Breasts (Chapter 8), cubed

2 medium avocados, peeled, seeded, and cubed

1. In medium bowl, combine mayonnaise, sour cream, lemon juice, honey, lemon zest, thyme, and parsley.

2. Stir in chicken and avocados and mix gently. Serve immediately on lettuce-lined plates.

PER SERVING: Calories: 597 | Total Fat: 36g | Saturated Fat: 7g | Cholesterol: 171mg | Protein: 57g | Sodium: 139mg | Potassium: 829mg | Fiber: 7g | Carbohydrates: 10g | Sugar: 1g

AVOCADO SALAD DRESSING

The fats in avocado are very healthy, since they are mainly monounsaturated. These fruits are also cholesterol and sodium free and contain a good amount of vitamin C and vitamin B$_6$. And they're delicious! The only problem with this dressing is that it doesn't last very long in the fridge, so make it and use it right away.

YIELDS 1 CUP; SERVING SIZE 2 TABLESPOONS

1 large ripe avocado, peeled and cubed

3 tablespoons buttermilk

2 tablespoons lemon or lime juice

¼ teaspoon grated lemon or lime zest

¼ cup extra-virgin olive oil

1 tablespoon chopped basil or flat-leaf parsley

1 teaspoon honey

Pinch white pepper

2 tablespoons water

In blender or food processor, combine avocado, buttermilk, lemon juice, and zest and blend. Slowly add olive oil while running the machine. Add basil, honey, and white pepper and blend. Add water until desired consistency is reached. Serve immediately.

PER SERVING: Calories: 105 | Total Fat: 10g | Saturated Fat: 1g | Cholesterol: 0mg | Protein: 0g | Sodium: 6mg | Potassium: 136mg | Fiber: 0g | Carbohydrates: 3g | Sugar: 1g

FRESH CORN SALAD

You can buy all kinds of contraptions to remove kernels from an ear of corn, but not much beats a sharp knife and a bundt pan. Just set the corn into the hole in the pan and slice downward. The kernels will fall right into the pan!

SERVES 4

4 ears corn, leaves and silk removed

1 tablespoon sugar

¼ cup extra-virgin olive oil

2 tablespoons lemon juice

1 tablespoon Honey Mustard (Chapter 4)

1 tablespoon minced fresh basil leaves

1 cup grape or cherry tomatoes, cut in half

1 medium orange bell pepper, chopped

1 tablespoon minced green onions

2 tablespoons grated Parmesan cheese

1. Bring a large pot of water to a boil. Add the shucked corn and sugar and bring to a simmer. Simmer for 1 minute, then cover the pot and remove from heat. Let stand for 5 minutes, then remove corn from pot and let cool for 10–15 minutes.

2. Meanwhile, in large bowl combine olive oil, lemon juice, honey mustard, and basil and mix well.

3. Cut the kernels off the ears of corn and add to the dressing. Add tomatoes, bell pepper, green onions, and Parmesan cheese and toss. Serve immediately or cover and chill up to 2 hours before serving.

PER SERVING: Calories: 239 | Total Fat: 15g | Saturated Fat: 2g | Cholesterol: 2mg | Protein: 4g | Sodium: 46mg | Potassium: 352mg | Fiber: 3g | Carbohydrates: 26g | Sugar: 8g

CRANBERRY GOAT CHEESE MESCLUN SALAD

Goat cheese is one of the few cheeses that is relatively low in sodium. Look for different flavors, but make sure to check the sodium content. Combine goat cheese with dried cranberries, sugared almonds, and mesclun in a simple and tasty salad that's a good accompaniment to any grilled or roasted meat.

SERVES 4

½ cup sliced almonds

1 tablespoon unsalted butter

2 tablespoons brown sugar

¼ cup extra-virgin olive oil

3 tablespoons lemon juice

1 tablespoon Honey Mustard (Chapter 4)

1 tablespoon honey

1 tablespoon finely chopped red onion

½ teaspoon dried thyme leaves

Pinch pepper

6 cups mesclun greens or mixed greens

⅔ cup dried cranberries

½ cup crumbled goat cheese

1. Preheat oven to 350°F.

2. Place almonds on a parchment paper–lined baking sheet. In small microwave-safe bowl, combine butter and brown sugar; microwave on high for 30 seconds; stir. Drizzle over almonds and toss to coat. Bake almonds for 7–9 minutes or until glazed, stirring once. Remove and cool.

3. In small jar with tight-fitting lid, combine olive oil, lemon juice, honey mustard, honey, red onion, thyme, and pepper. Close jar and shake to blend.

4. In serving bowl, toss together mesclun and dried cranberries. Add salad dressing and toss again. Sprinkle with almonds and goat cheese and serve.

PER SERVING: Calories: 316 | Total Fat: 23g | Saturated Fat: 6g | Cholesterol: 20mg | Protein: 7g | Sodium: 103mg | Potassium: 261mg | Fiber: 3g | Carbohydrates: 23g | Sugar: 17g

CHICKEN WILD RICE SALAD

Wild rice is more expensive, but its nutty taste and chewy texture are worth every penny. Combine with tender chicken and pecans in a sweet cherry dressing for a memorable meal.

SERVES 6

6 (10-ounce) bone-in, skin-on chicken breasts

1 tablespoon olive oil

⅛ teaspoon white pepper

1½ cups wild rice, rinsed

3 cups water

⅓ cup extra-virgin olive oil

3 tablespoons cherry juice

½ teaspoon grated orange zest

1 tablespoon Mustard (Chapter 4)

1 tablespoon honey

⅛ teaspoon black pepper

½ teaspoon dried marjoram leaves

½ cup dried cherries

½ cup coarsely chopped toasted pecans

6 cups mixed salad greens

1. Preheat oven to 375°F.

2. Drizzle the chicken with 1 tablespoon olive oil and sprinkle with white pepper; place in baking dish. Bake for 45–55 minutes or until temperature registers 160°F. Remove chicken from pan and cover; let stand 10 minutes, then refrigerate.

3. Meanwhile, place wild rice and water in a medium saucepan. Bring to a boil over high heat, then reduce heat to low, cover partially, and simmer for 35–45 minutes or until rice is tender; drain if necessary and set aside.

4. In serving bowl, combine ⅓ cup extra-virgin olive oil, cherry juice, orange zest, mustard, honey, black pepper, and marjoram and whisk to combine.

5. Remove skin from chicken and remove meat from bones. Cube chicken and add to dressing in bowl. Add wild rice, cherries, and pecans and toss to coat. Cover and chill for 1–2 hours to blend flavors before serving. Serve on greens.

PER SERVING: Calories: 462 | Total Fat: 22g | Saturated Fat: 3g | Cholesterol: 65mg | Protein: 31g | Sodium: 88mg | Potassium: 599mg | Fiber: 3g | Carbohydrates: 34g | Sugar: 13g

GRILLED CHOPPED SALAD

A chopped salad is just that—lots of greens and veggies chopped to about the same size. But grilling each ingredient before chopping it adds great smoky flavor and changes the texture a bit. This salad can easily be a meal on a hot summer night. Serve with a glass of white wine and some fresh fruit for dessert.

SERVES 4

1 head romaine lettuce

1 medium zucchini, cut in half lengthwise

2 large portobello mushrooms, stems removed

1 cup cherry tomatoes

1 medium avocado, cut in half

¼ cup extra-virgin olive oil

3 tablespoons lemon juice

2 tablespoons Grainy Mustard (Chapter 4)

1 tablespoon maple syrup

1 tablespoon chopped fresh tarragon leaves

⅛ teaspoon pepper

1. Prepare and preheat grill. Cut the lettuce in half lengthwise and rinse well; shake to dry.

2. Place the lettuce on the grill, cut-side down, and grill for 2–3 minutes until light brown in spots, turning once. Place the zucchini on the grill, cut-side down, and grill until grill marks appear, about 3–4 minutes. Grill the mushrooms on both sides, turning once, until tender, about 4–5 minutes. Put cherry tomatoes in a grill basket and grill for 1–2 minutes or until brown spots appear. Grill the avocado, cut-side down, for 1 minute.

3. Chop the lettuce and all of the vegetables into bite-sized pieces.

4. In serving bowl, combine olive oil, lemon juice, grainy mustard, maple syrup, tarragon, and pepper and mix well.

5. Add all of the chopped vegetables to the dressing and toss gently to coat. Serve immediately.

PER SERVING: Calories: 287 | Total Fat: 22g | Saturated Fat: 3g | Cholesterol: 0mg | Protein: 6g | Sodium: 23mg | Potassium: 1,082mg | Fiber: 8g | Carbohydrates: 20g | Sugar: 8g

GREEN ON GREEN SALAD

This salad is a symphony in greens! You can use any green vegetable you'd like; add some zucchini, or different types of lettuce, or broccoli or asparagus. Serve this salad with a meatloaf in the winter and with grilled steak in summer for a delicious and healthy meal.

SERVES 4

1 medium cucumber, peeled

2 medium avocados, peeled, skin removed

2 cups frozen baby peas, thawed

1 cup sliced celery

2 cups chopped butter lettuce

2 cups arugula

½ cup Avocado Salad Dressing (see recipe in this chapter)

1. Cut the cucumber in half and remove the seeds with a spoon. Slice into half-moons. Cube the avocados.

2. Combine cucumber, avocados, peas, and celery in a medium bowl.

3. Combine lettuce and arugula in serving bowl and top with the cucumber mixture. Drizzle with the dressing and serve immediately.

PER SERVING: Calories: 324 | Total Fat: 25g | Saturated Fat: 3g | Cholesterol: 0mg | Protein: 6g | Sodium: 46mg | Potassium: 1,045mg | Fiber: 12g | Carbohydrates: 22g | Sugar: 7g

WHEAT BERRY VEGGIE SALAD

You can find wheat berries at most large grocery stores, or in co-ops or health food stores. They keep for a long while if you decant them into glass jars and store them in a dark, cool place.

SERVES 4

1½ cups wheat berries, rinsed

4 cups water

1 medium red bell pepper, chopped

3 stalks celery, chopped

1 cup sliced mushrooms

½ cup shredded carrot

¼ cup chopped green onion

2 tablespoons lemon juice

½ cup French Dressing (see recipe in this chapter)

1. Combine wheat berries and water in large saucepan; bring to a boil over high heat. Reduce heat to low, partially cover, and simmer until tender, about 50–60 minutes. Drain wheat berries and set aside.

2. In large bowl, combine bell pepper, celery, mushrooms, carrot, and green onion, and stir to blend. Add wheat berries, lemon juice, and French dressing and mix gently.

3. Cover and refrigerate for a few hours to blend flavors.

PER SERVING: Calories: 367 | Total Fat: 12g | Saturated Fat: 1g | Cholesterol: 0mg | Protein: 10g | Sodium: 54mg | Potassium: 362mg | Fiber: 11g | Carbohydrates: 56g | Sugar: 6g

TOFU, OIL, AND VINEGAR SALAD DRESSING

Silken tofu has a softer consistency than regular tofu and therefore the two types are not interchangeable in a recipe. Silken tofu is often sold in aseptic boxes that do not require refrigeration.

YIELDS ¼ CUP; SERVING SIZE 1 TABLESPOON

1 tablespoon extra-virgin olive oil

2 tablespoons silken tofu

1 tablespoon vinegar

1 teaspoon ground mustard

Optional: Choice of herbs, spices, and freshly ground black pepper

Put all the ingredients in a small bowl and whisk to combine. Drizzle over your choice of prepared salad greens and vegetables.

PER SERVING: Calories: 35 | Total Fat: 3g | Saturated Fat: 0g | Cholesterol: 0mg | Protein: 0g | Sodium: 0mg | Potassium: 10mg | Fiber: 0g | Carbohydrates: 0g | Sugar: 0g

ZESTY CORN RELISH

If it's in season in your part of the world, fresh corn would also work wonderfully in this recipe and take the taste up that extra notch.

SERVES 4

4 banana or jalapeño peppers, stemmed, seeded, and chopped

⅓ cup frozen corn, thawed

⅓ cup chopped red onion

⅛ teaspoon Texas Seasoning (Appendix A)

2 teaspoons lime juice

¼ teaspoon freshly ground black pepper

Combine all the ingredients in a bowl and toss to mix. This can be served immediately, or it can be chilled and served the next day.

PER SERVING: Calories: 25 | Total Fat: 0g | Saturated Fat: 0g | Cholesterol: 0mg | Protein: 0g | Sodium: 2mg | Potassium: 94mg | Fiber: 0g | Carbohydrates: 5g | Sugar: 1g

ROASTED SHALLOT VINAIGRETTE

Fruit and herb vinegars are usually flavored cider or wine vinegars. When a vinaigrette is too tart because of a strong vinegar, instead of adding more oil, try mixing in some frozen fruit juice concentrate, 1 teaspoon at a time.

**YIELDS 1¼ CUPS; SERVING SIZE 1
  TABLESPOON**

2 teaspoons unsalted butter

¼ cup chopped shallots

¼ cup cider vinegar

1½ tablespoons lemon juice

1 teaspoon Dijon mustard

1 cup extra-virgin olive oil

½ teaspoon fennel seeds, crushed

⅛ teaspoon freshly ground black pepper

Optional: 1 teaspoon frozen apple juice
  concentrate

1. Melt the butter in a sauté pan over medium heat. Add the shallots and sauté them, stirring or tossing them constantly to prevent them from burning, until they are caramelized (turn golden brown). Remove from heat and cool the shallots in the refrigerator.

2. Add the vinegar, lemon juice, mustard, olive oil, fennel seeds, and pepper to a covered jar. Shake well until the mixture is emulsified. (Alternatively, add the ingredients to a blender or a food processor and process until mixed.) Add the shallots and shake again. Store in the refrigerator up to 2 days.

PER SERVING: Calories: 100 | Total Fat: 11g | Saturated Fat: 1g | Cholesterol: 1mg | Protein: 0g | Sodium: 0mg | Potassium: 8mg | Fiber: 0g | Carbohydrates: 0g | Sugar: 0g

VEGGIE-FRUIT SALAD

For a zestier dressing, you can add a chopped jalapeño pepper or 1 tablespoon of a low-sodium fruit salsa. A sweet-peppery option that only adds a trace of sodium to each serving is to stir in 1 teaspoon jalapeño pepper jelly.

SERVES 4

1 medium ripe avocado, peeled and pit removed

½ cup plain nonfat yogurt

1 tablespoon mayonnaise

2 teaspoons lemon juice, divided

¼ teaspoon finely grated lime or lemon zest

1 tablespoon finely chopped fresh cilantro

1 tablespoon finely chopped fresh parsley

¼ teaspoon ground mustard

1 clove garlic, minced

4 scallions, white and green parts finely chopped

1 cup chopped poached chicken breast, unsalted

⅛ teaspoon freshly ground black pepper

2 cups salad greens, torn into bite-sized pieces

2 cups cubed cantaloupe

2 cups seedless green grapes

2 cups cherry tomatoes

1 cup diced celery

1. In a medium bowl, mash the avocado with a fork. Add the yogurt, mayonnaise, 1 teaspoon of the lemon juice, the zest, cilantro, parsley, ground mustard, garlic, and scallions; mix well.

2. In a large bowl, toss the chicken breast with the remaining teaspoon of lemon juice and the freshly ground black pepper. Add the salad greens, cantaloupe, grapes, cherry tomatoes, and celery; toss well. Divide the salad between 4 plates.

3. Divide the dressing between the 4 salads. Garnish with additional finely chopped cilantro or parsley, or freshly ground pepper.

PER SERVING: Calories: 288 | Total Fat: 12g | Saturated Fat: 1g | Cholesterol: 27mg | Protein: 15g | Sodium: 114mg | Potassium: 1,159mg | Fiber: 7g | Carbohydrates: 33g | Sugar: 24g

ROASTED RED (OR OTHER) PEPPERS

The traditional method to roast a red pepper is to hold it over an open flame until it's charred. Of course, there are a variety of other methods as well.

YIELD VARIES DEPENDING ON USE

1 medium red bell pepper

- Place the pepper directly on an electric or gas burner on the stove and turn it occasionally, until the skin is blackened. This should take about 4–6 minutes.

- You can also put the pepper over direct heat on a preheated grill. Use tongs to turn the pepper occasionally. This takes about 5–10 minutes. Close the lid on the grill between turns.

- Another method is to put a pepper on a broiler rack about 2 inches from the heat, turning the pepper every 5 minutes. Total broiling time will be about 15–20 minutes, or until the skin is blistered and charred.

- You can place a pepper on a baking sheet treated with nonstick spray. Bake in a 400°F oven for 20–30 minutes. (Using this method won't get the skin of the pepper as dark as does open roasting.)

- The key to peeling the pepper is letting it sit in its steam in a closed container until it is cool. Seal the pepper in a brown paper bag, a plastic bag, or a bowl covered with plastic wrap. Once the pepper is cool, the skin will rub or peel off easily. Keep the pepper whole to peel it, then cut off the top and discard the seeds and rib membrane.

- Store roasted peppers in a plastic bag in the refrigerator for a few days—or in the freezer for several months. To preserve in the refrigerator for a week, cover the roasted pepper completely with extra-virgin olive oil and refrigerate in an airtight container. You can use the oil, too! It absorbs some of the pepper's flavor and is a delicious addition to salad dressings.

PER SERVING: Calories: 36 | Total Fat: 0g | Saturated Fat: 0g | Cholesterol: 0mg | Protein: 1g | Sodium: 4mg | Potassium: 251mg | Fiber: 2g | Carbohydrates: 7g | Sugar: 4g

WARM BROCCOLI AND POTATO SALAD

It's true that the flavor of freshly squeezed fruit juice is wonderful, but it's not always practical. An (almost) equally delicious alternative is to keep your freezer stocked with fruit juice concentrates and mix your own "fresh" fruit juice as needed.

SERVES 8

6 medium-size potatoes, peeled and cubed

2 cups broccoli florets

¼ cup fresh orange juice

3 tablespoons white wine vinegar or champagne vinegar

½ teaspoon dried basil

1 clove garlic, minced

Pinch dried red pepper flakes

1–2 teaspoons dried parsley

⅛ teaspoon mustard powder

¼ teaspoon Dijon mustard

3 tablespoons extra-virgin olive oil

2 large green onions, white and green parts thinly sliced

⅛ teaspoon freshly ground black or white pepper

1. Preheat oven to lowest temperature.

2. Place the potatoes in a saucepan and cover with cold water. Bring to a boil, cover, and cook for 10 minutes or until fork tender. Remove the potatoes with a slotted spoon. Save the water, keeping the pan on the heat. Transfer the potatoes to a baking sheet and place in the warm oven.

3. Add the broccoli to the reserved water and blanch for 1 minute. Remove the broccoli with a slotted spoon and add to the potatoes in the oven.

4. In a small saucepan over medium-high heat, combine the orange juice, vinegar, basil, garlic, and red pepper flakes; bring to a boil. Remove from heat and whisk in the parsley, mustard powder, Dijon mustard, and olive oil. Add the onion and stir to mix.

5. Remove the vegetables from the oven and transfer to a serving bowl. Toss with the dressing, making sure all the potatoes and broccoli florets are thoroughly coated. Top with freshly ground white or black pepper. Serve immediately.

PER SERVING: Calories: 124 | Total Fat: 5g | Saturated Fat: 0g | Cholesterol: 0mg | Protein: 2g | Sodium: 11mg | Potassium: 351mg | Fiber: 2g | Carbohydrates: 18g | Sugar: 1g

SPICED TUNA SALAD WITH TOASTED SESAME SEED VINAIGRETTE

Bold flavors combine beautifully in this healthy, salt-free salad. With low-fat protein, vitamins, and nutrients, this makes a delicious one-dish meal.

SERVES 2

1 teaspoon sesame seeds

¼ cup minced shallots

1 tablespoon white wine vinegar

1 tablespoon rice vinegar

1 teaspoon mustard powder

Optional: ¼–½ teaspoon Oriental (hot) mustard powder

¾ teaspoon granulated sugar

2 tablespoons sesame oil

¼ teaspoon toasted sesame oil

¼ teaspoon ground coriander

¼ teaspoon ground star anise

¼ teaspoon ground cinnamon

¼ teaspoon ground cloves

⅛ teaspoon ground ginger

1 (6-ounce) can low-sodium chunk white water-packed albacore tuna, drained

1 teaspoon canola (or sesame) oil

2 cups prepared salad greens, torn into bite-sized pieces

2 large green onions, white and green parts finely sliced

Optional: Candied ginger

1. Toast the sesame seeds in a small skillet over medium heat until light golden brown.

2. Combine shallots, vinegars, mustard powders, and sugar in a blender; purée for about 2 minutes. While the blender is running, slowly add both sesame oils. Add the sesame seeds and blend for 1 minute.

3. In small nonstick sauté pan over medium heat, warm the coriander, star anise, cinnamon, cloves, and ginger until fragrant. Transfer the heated spices to a bowl.

4. Drain the tuna and mix it with the canola oil. Add the tuna to the sauté pan, adding the heated spices to taste; sauté until coated with the spices and heated through.

5. Toss the salad greens and sliced green onions with the vinaigrette. Divide between 2 plates. Top each lettuce serving with equal amounts of the sautéed tuna. Garnish with finely shaved slices of candied ginger, if desired.

PER SERVING: Calories: 205 | Total Fat: 8g | Saturated Fat: 1g | Cholesterol: 25mg | Protein: 23g | Sodium: 48mg | Potassium: 433mg | Fiber: 2g | Carbohydrates: 8g | Sugar: 4g

THOUSAND ISLAND DRESSING

According to The Oxford Companion to American Food and Drink, *Thousand Island dressing gets its name from its presumed place of origin, the Thousand Islands between Canada and the United States in the St. Lawrence River.*

YIELDS 1 CUP; SERVING SIZE 1 TABLESPOON

½ cup plain nonfat yogurt

2 tablespoons mayonnaise

2 tablespoons low-salt ketchup

1 tablespoon sweet pickle relish

1 teaspoon lemon juice

1 teaspoon apple cider vinegar

1 tablespoon finely chopped celery

½ teaspoon granulated sugar or ¼ teaspoon honey

¼ teaspoon celery seed

¼ teaspoon onion powder

¼ teaspoon yellow or Dijon mustard

⅛ teaspoon mustard powder

⅛ teaspoon freshly ground black pepper

1 large hard-boiled egg, minced

Add all ingredients to a jar. Cover and shake well to combine. Refrigerate between uses. This dressing can be stored 3–4 days. To serve, shake well to emulsify.

PER SERVING: Calories: 25 | Total Fat: 1g | Saturated Fat: 0g | Cholesterol: 12mg | Protein: 0g | Sodium: 26mg | Potassium: 32mg | Fiber: 0g | Carbohydrates: 1g | Sugar: 1g

RUSSIAN DRESSING

You can also use this recipe to make a creamy Russian dressing. To make a single serving of the creamy version, mix together 1 tablespoon of this Russian Dressing, 1 teaspoon of mayonnaise, and 2 teaspoons of plain nonfat yogurt.

YIELDS 1 CUP, 2 TABLESPOONS; SERVING SIZE 1 TABLESPOON

½ cup grapeseed or canola oil

¼ cup red wine vinegar or balsamic vinegar (or a combination)

¼ cup water

½ teaspoon Dijon mustard

1 teaspoon garlic powder

1 teaspoon onion powder

¼ teaspoon mustard powder

¼ teaspoon freshly ground black pepper

¼ teaspoon granulated sugar

¼ teaspoon dried basil

¼–½ teaspoon salt-free chili powder

¼–½ teaspoon sweet paprika

2 tablespoons no-salt-added tomato paste

Pinch dried red pepper flakes

1 tablespoon finely chopped green bell pepper

Add all the ingredients to a jar. Cover and shake well to combine. Refrigerate between uses. To serve, shake well to emulsify.

PER SERVING: Calories: 57 | Total Fat: 6g | Saturated Fat: 0g | Cholesterol: 0mg | Protein: 0g | Sodium: 2mg | Potassium: 27mg | Fiber: 0g | Carbohydrates: 0g | Sugar: 0g

SAFFRON VINAIGRETTE

Saffron is one of the world's most costly spices by weight. The saffron threads must be painstakingly plucked from the flowers of the saffron crocus plant and then dried. It adds a sweet flavor and a bright yellowish-orange color to foods.

YIELDS 2 CUPS; SERVING SIZE 2 TABLESPOONS

1 cup dry white wine

1 cup rice wine vinegar or white wine vinegar

1 tablespoon chopped shallot

3 peppercorns, crushed

½ teaspoon dried thyme

¼ teaspoon saffron strands

½ cup extra-virgin olive oil

½ tablespoon honey

1. Add the wine, vinegar, shallot, peppercorns, thyme, and saffron to a saucepan over medium-low heat; slowly reduce by half to yield ½ cup of liquid. Strain the mixture through a fine-mesh sieve.

2. Whisk in the olive oil and honey. Use immediately to wilt lettuce, or chill until ready to serve.

PER SERVING: Calories: 75 | Total Fat: 6g | Saturated Fat: 0g | Cholesterol: 0mg | Protein: 0g | Sodium: 0mg | Potassium: 2mg | Fiber: 0g | Carbohydrates: 0g | Sugar: 0g

WALDORF SALAD

Waldorf salad was invented not by a chef but by a maître d' at New York's Waldorf Astoria Hotel. The original version contained only apples, celery, and mayonnaise.

SERVES 4

1 cup peeled and diced apples

1 tablespoon lemon juice

1 cup diced celery

4 medium carrots, peeled and finely shredded

½ cup chopped walnuts

¼ cup raisins

¼ cup mayonnaise

¼ cup plain nonfat yogurt

Optional: 4 lettuce leaves

1. In a medium bowl, toss the apples with the lemon juice. Add the celery, carrots, walnuts, raisins, mayonnaise, and yogurt; mix well.

2. To serve, place a lettuce leaf on each plate. Evenly divide the salad, scooping it on top of the lettuce leaves.

PER SERVING: Calories: 205 | Total Fat: 13g | Saturated Fat: 1g | Cholesterol: 8mg | Protein: 2g | Sodium: 90mg | Potassium: 465mg | Fiber: 3g | Carbohydrates: 20g | Sugar: 13g

TABOULEH SALAD

Bulgur wheat, the main ingredient in tabouleh, is a staple of Middle Eastern cuisine. It is richer in nutrients and vitamins than refined wheat, and is also low in fat, high in fiber, and rich in minerals. You can also use bulgur in soups, pilafs, baked goods, and stuffing.

SERVES 4

1 cup bulgur

2 cups boiling water

½ cup chopped fresh parsley

2 large tomato, peeled and finely chopped

1 large cucumber, peeled, seeded, and finely chopped

2 medium carrots, peeled and shredded

2 large stalks celery, diced

2 tablespoons lemon juice

Optional: 2 tablespoons extra-virgin olive oil

¼ teaspoon freshly ground black pepper

1/16–1/8 teaspoon mustard powder

1 clove garlic, minced

¼ teaspoon celery seeds

1. Add the bulgur to a large mixing bowl and pour the boiling water over it. Cover and set aside for 30 minutes.

2. Add the remaining ingredients to the bowl and stir to combine. Cover and chill for at least 2 hours. (This gives the salad time to soak in its own juices and brings out the flavor of all the ingredients.)

PER SERVING: Calories: 116 | Total Fat: 0g | Saturated Fat: 0g | Cholesterol: 0mg | Protein: 4g | Sodium: 63mg | Potassium: 518mg | Fiber: 6g | Carbohydrates: 2g | Sugar: 4g

ITALIAN DRESSING

Many people put their spice racks close to the stove for easy access when cooking. But the proximity to heat and humidity can compromise the taste and longevity of your spices and make for lackluster flavors in dressings like this one. Store your spices and herbs in a cool, dark cabinet away from heat and cooking.

YIELDS 1 CUP; SERVING SIZE 1 TABLESPOON

½ cup extra-virgin olive oil

4 cloves garlic, crushed

¼ cup red or white wine vinegar, balsamic vinegar, or lemon juice

¼ cup water

¼ teaspoon Dijon mustard

¼ teaspoon mustard powder

¼ teaspoon freshly ground black pepper

¼ teaspoon granulated sugar

½ teaspoon dried basil

¼ teaspoon dried oregano

⅛ teaspoon dried rosemary

⅛ teaspoon dried thyme

Pinch dried red pepper flakes

1. Add all the ingredients to a jar. Cover and shake well to combine. Refrigerate overnight to allow the flavors to intensify and combine. Use a slotted spoon to remove and discard the garlic. Refrigerate between uses.

2. To serve, allow 10 minutes for the dressing to come to room temperature and for the olive oil to become liquid again. Shake well to emulsify.

PER SERVING: Calories: 59 | Total Fat: 6g | Saturated Fat: 0g | Cholesterol: 0mg | Protein: 0g | Sodium: 0mg | Potassium: 5mg | Fiber: 0g | Carbohydrates: 0g | Sugar: 0g

FRENCH DRESSING

No need to purchase commercial salt-filled French dressing when it is so easy to make a low-sodium version at home. No artificial additives, preservatives, or sweeteners, and it's delicious!

**YIELDS 1 CUP AND 2 TABLESPOONS;
SERVING SIZE 1 TABLESPOON**

2 tablespoons minced shallots

1 clove garlic, crushed

½ cup extra-virgin olive oil

¼ cup red wine vinegar

¼ teaspoon Dijon mustard

¼ teaspoon mustard powder

¼ teaspoon freshly ground black pepper

2 teaspoons honey

½ teaspoon dried basil

¼ teaspoon dried tarragon

⅛ teaspoon dried rosemary

⅛ teaspoon dried thyme

2 tablespoons no-salt-added tomato paste

1. Add all ingredients to a jar. Cover and shake well to combine. Let rest at room temperature for 30 minutes to bring out the flavors. Use a slotted spoon to remove and discard the garlic. Refrigerate between uses.

2. To serve, allow 10 minutes for the dressing to come to room temperature and for the olive oil to become liquid again. Shake well to emulsify.

PER SERVING: Calories: 56 | Total Fat: 5g | Saturated Fat: 0g | Cholesterol: 0mg | Protein: 0g | Sodium: 2mg | Potassium: 25mg | Fiber: 0g | Carbohydrates: 1g | Sugar: 0g

CHAPTER 4

CONDIMENTS

SLOW COOKER CARAMELIZED ONIONS

Onions are a very pungent vegetable, and can overpower a dish. But when caramelized they take on some fabulous characteristics and become sweet, nutty, and as soft as butter. Caramelized onions are a wonderful way to add flavor to just about any recipe, or you can serve them as-is.

SERVES 6

5 large onions, sliced

2 tablespoons olive oil

1 teaspoon lemon juice

⅛ teaspoon white pepper

1. Combine all ingredients in a 4-quart slow cooker.

2. Cover and cook on low for 8–10 hours, stirring occasionally, until the onions are deep golden brown and very soft. If the mixture is liquid, set the lid ajar and cook on low for another hour or two until the liquid evaporates.

3. Cover and refrigerate up to 3 days, or freeze in ¼-cup portions for up to 6 months.

PER SERVING: Calories: 86 | Total Fat: 4g | Saturated Fat: 0g | Cholesterol: 0mg | Protein: 1g | Sodium: 3mg | Potassium: 178mg | Fiber: 1g | Carbohydrates: 10g | Sugar: 5g

LEMONY PESTO

Pesto is a condiment that is very versatile. You can add it to soups, use it as a sandwich spread, or mix it with sour cream for a vegetable dip. It's also delicious as a salad dressing; just add more olive oil to reach the right consistency. Lemon is almost always used in pesto, but this recipe uses a larger amount for more flavor.

YIELDS 1½ CUPS; 24 SERVINGS

1½ cups packed whole basil leaves

¼ cup flat-leaf parsley

⅓ cup baby spinach leaves

¼ cup pine nuts

⅓ cup lemon juice

2 teaspoons grated lemon zest

3 tablespoons grated Parmesan cheese

⅔ cup extra-virgin olive oil

1. Combine all ingredients except olive oil in a blender or food processor. Lock top on and blend or process until finely chopped.

2. With the machine running, slowly add the olive oil and blend or process until a sauce forms.

3. Place in a small bowl and place plastic wrap directly against the surface of the pesto to prevent browning. Store in the refrigerator for up to 3 days. You can also divide this mixture into 2-tablespoon portions and freeze for up to 6 months.

PER SERVING: Calories: 63 | Total Fat: 6g | Saturated Fat: 0g | Cholesterol: 0mg | Protein: 0g | Sodium: 10mg | Potassium: 29mg | Fiber: 0g | Carbohydrates: 0g | Sugar: 0g

KALE PESTO

Kale pesto is delicious tossed with hot pasta, can be used as a sandwich spread or an appetizer dip, and is wonderful as a topping on tomato soup.

YIELDS 1 CUP; 16 SERVINGS

2 cups chopped kale

1 cup whole basil leaves

2 tablespoons chopped flat-leaf parsley

¼ cup pine nuts

2 tablespoons lemon juice

⅛ teaspoon white pepper

½ cup extra-virgin olive oil

1. Combine all ingredients except olive oil in blender or food processor. Cover and blend or process until finely chopped.

2. Slowly pour in the oil while the machine is running, blending or processing until a smooth sauce forms. Cover and store in the refrigerator for up to 3 days.

PER SERVING: Calories: 78 | Total Fat: 8g | Saturated Fat: 1g | Cholesterol: 0g | Protein: 0g | Sodium: 4mg | Potassium: 62mg | Fiber: 0g | Carbohydrates: 1g | Sugar: 0g

MUSTARD

It's easy to make your own mustard, and you can flavor it any way you'd like. This recipe does have to be started several days in advance, since the mixture needs to sit at room temperature to mellow. You can also add some roasted garlic, caramelized onions, or herbs such as thyme or oregano to your homemade mustard.

YIELDS 1 CUP; 16 SERVINGS

½ cup yellow mustard seeds

½ cup apple cider vinegar or white wine vinegar

⅓ cup water

2 tablespoons mustard powder

1 tablespoon brown sugar

1 tablespoon lemon juice

½ teaspoon turmeric

1. Combine all ingredients in a blender or food processor; blend or process until smooth.

2. Transfer to a small bowl and cover loosely with plastic wrap. Let stand at room temperature for 1–3 days, stirring a few times a day, until the mustard tastes good to you. Cover and store in the refrigerator for up to 3 weeks.

PER SERVING: Calories: 35 | Total Fat: 1g | Saturated Fat: 0g | Cholesterol: 0mg | Protein: 1g | Sodium: 1mg | Potassium: 45mg | Fiber: 0g | Carbohydrates: 2g | Sugar: 1g

HONEY MUSTARD

Honey mellows mustard and adds a wonderful flowery depth of flavor to this condiment. Look for locally sourced honey for the freshest flavor and add to your homemade mustard to suit your own tastes. This is really good served with grilled fish or chicken.

YIELDS 1 CUP; 16 SERVINGS

¾ cup Mustard (see recipe in this chapter)

3 tablespoons honey

1 tablespoon lemon juice

Combine all ingredients in a small bowl and mix well. Cover and store in refrigerator up to 3 weeks.

PER SERVING (1 tablespoon): Calories: 39 | Total Fat: 1g | Saturated Fat: 0g | Cholesterol: 0mg | Protein: 1g | Sodium: 1mg | Potassium: 35mg | Fiber: 0g | Carbohydrates: 5g | Sugar: 4g

GRAINY MUSTARD

Grainy mustard is as easy to make as regular mustard; you just don't grind all of the seeds. Brown mustard seeds are spicier and more pungent than yellow mustard seeds. Use the combination you like and don't be afraid to experiment.

YIELDS 1 CUP; 16 SERVINGS

¼ cup yellow mustard seeds, divided

3 tablespoons brown mustard seeds

1 tablespoon dry mustard powder

2 tablespoons brown sugar

⅓ cup apple cider vinegar

⅓ cup water

1. Grind 1 tablespoon of the yellow mustard seeds with a mortar and pestle or blender. Combine with the remaining ingredients in a small bowl.

2. Cover loosely with plastic wrap and let stand at room temperature for 3 days, stirring four times a day. Taste the mustard. If it's still too strong for you, let stand for another day or two, stirring four times a day.

3. When the flavor is right, cover the mustard tightly and refrigerate for up to 3 weeks.

PER SERVING: Calories: 18 | Total Fat: 0g | Saturated Fat: 0g | Cholesterol: 0mg | Protein: 0g | Sodium: 0mg | Potassium: 23mg | Fiber: 0g | Carbohydrates: 1g | Sugar: 0g

TARTAR SAUCE

When making your own tartar sauce use cucumbers for the crunch and add lemon juice and jalapeños for a sparkling bite. If you use purchased mayonnaise for this recipe, make sure to check the sodium levels on the label. Using your own homemade mayonnaise guarantees that the sodium level will be low.

YIELDS 1 CUP; 16 SERVINGS

⅔ cup Mayonnaise (see recipe in this chapter)

¼ cup finely chopped, seeded, peeled cucumber

1 tablespoon lemon juice

1 tablespoon Mustard (see recipe in this chapter)

1 jalapeño pepper, minced

Combine all ingredients in small bowl and mix well. Cover and store in refrigerator for up to 4 days.

PER SERVING: Calories: 75 | Total Fat: 7g | Saturated Fat: 1g | Cholesterol: 10mg | Protein: 0g | Sodium: 0mg | Potassium: 10mg | Fiber: 0g | Carbohydrates: 0g | Sugar: 0g

MAYONNAISE

Mayonnaise is another popular condiment that is very high in sodium—usually about 90-100mg per tablespoon! To make at home, be sure to use pasteurized eggs. Pasteurized eggs have been heated briefly to a temperature high enough to kill bacteria but low enough so the eggs don't cook.

YIELDS 1½ CUPS; 24 SERVINGS

2 pasteurized egg yolks

1 tablespoon lemon juice

2 teaspoons apple cider vinegar

1 teaspoon Mustard (see recipe in this chapter)

1⅓ cups peanut, olive, or safflower oil

Pinch white pepper

1. Combine egg yolks, lemon juice, vinegar, and mustard in blender or food processor. Blend until light yellow in color.

2. Slowly add the oil through the food processor feed tube or the little hole in the top of the blender cover, while the machine is running. When all the oil is added, the mayonnaise should be a light color and be smooth and thick.

3. Add the pepper and decant to a jar with a lid. Cover tightly and store in the refrigerator for up to 10 days.

PER SERVING (1 tablespoon): Calories: 113 | Total Fat: 12g | Saturated Fat: 2g | Cholesterol: 17mg | Protein: 0g | Sodium: 0mg | Potassium: 3mg | Fiber: 0g | Carbohydrates: 0g | Sugar: 0g

JERK SEASONING

Jerk is a type of cooking that is native to Jamaica. You can use jerk seasoning in many ways; add it to mayonnaise for a sandwich spread; rub it into chicken, beef, pork, or fish, then grill or broil; or sprinkle it on vegetables before they are roasted.

YIELDS ¼ CUP; SERVING SIZE 1 TEASPOON

2 teaspoons cayenne pepper

1 teaspoon black pepper

2 teaspoons onion powder

2 teaspoons garlic powder

2 teaspoons sugar

1 teaspoon smoked paprika

1 teaspoon dried thyme leaves

½ teaspoon ground allspice

¼ teaspoon cardamom

¼ teaspoon nutmeg

Combine all ingredients in small bowl and mix well. Store in tightly covered jar at room temperature.

PER SERVING: Calories: 6 | Total Fat: 0g | Saturated Fat: 0g | Cholesterol: 0mg | Protein: 0g | Sodium: 0mg | Potassium: 22mg | Fiber: 0g | Carbohydrates: 1g | Sugar: 0g

HERBED SUGAR

Adding herbs to sugar is a wonderful way to add more flavor to sweet recipes without adding salt. You can use any dried herb in this recipe: lavender, thyme, basil, rosemary, mint, lemon verbena, rose geranium, or sage. Store these flavored sugars in an airtight container at room temperature.

YIELDS 1 CUP; SERVING SIZE 1 TEASPOON

2–3 tablespoons dried herbs

1 cup granulated sugar

1. Place the herbs in a small bowl and crush them with the back of a spoon. Add the sugar and mix well.

2. Decant into small covered jar with a tight lid and store at room temperature. Ready to use in about 5–7 days.

PER SERVING: Calories: 16 | Total Fat: 0g | Saturated Fat: 0g | Cholesterol: 0mg | Protein: 0g | Sodium: 4mg | Potassium: 0mg | Fiber: 0g | Carbohydrates: 4g | Sugar: 4g

MOSTARDA

Mostarda is a condiment from Italy that is made from mustard and different types of fruit. Serve it with broiled or grilled chicken or fish, or with pot roast. It is also delicious as a dip with unsalted tortilla chips.

YIELDS 2 CUPS; SERVING SIZE 2 TABLESPOONS

1 cup chopped dried apricots

½ cup chopped dried cranberries

2 dried figs, diced

1 medium pear, peeled and diced

1 Granny Smith apple, peeled and chopped

½ cup brown sugar

⅓ cup Mustard (see recipe in this chapter)

1 tablespoon mustard seeds

1½ cups water

2 tablespoons lemon juice

1. Combine all ingredients in a heavy large saucepan and bring to a boil over medium-high heat.

2. Reduce heat to low and cook, stirring frequently, until the dried fruits are slightly plump and the pear and apple are tender, about 30 minutes.

3. Let cool and decant into jars. Store, tightly covered, in the refrigerator for up to 2 weeks.

PER SERVING: Calories: 100 | Total Fat: 0g | Saturated Fat: 0g | Cholesterol: 0mg | Protein: 1g | Sodium: 4mg | Potassium: 182mg | Fiber: 2g | Carbohydrates: 23g | Sugar: 19g

CHIMICHURRI

You can use just about any fresh green herb you'd like in this easy recipe; just keep the red wine vinegar, garlic, and olive oil. Pour it over steak, mix it with some Mayonnaise (see recipe in this chapter) for dipping crudités, serve it with chicken or fish, or mix it with roasted vegetables.

YIELDS 1 CUP; SERVING SIZE 2 TABLESPOONS

⅔ cup whole flat-leaf parsley leaves

2 tablespoons minced fresh basil leaves

1 tablespoon minced fresh oregano leaves

½ cup olive oil

¼ cup red wine vinegar

3 tablespoons lemon juice

2 cloves garlic, minced

¼ teaspoon dried mustard

⅛ teaspoon white pepper

⅛ teaspoon cayenne pepper

⅛ teaspoon crushed red pepper flakes

Combine all ingredients in a blender or food processor and blend or process until smooth. Cover and refrigerate for up to 4 days.

PER SERVING: Calories: 124 | Total Fat: 13g | Saturated Fat: 1g | Cholesterol: 0mg | Protein: 0g | Sodium: 4mg | Potassium: 48mg | Fiber: 0g | Carbohydrates: 1g | Sugar: 0g

LEMON CURD

Lemon curd is a delicious cake filling, pie filling, and cookie filling, or you can spread it on toast, waffles, or pancakes for a special breakfast. Use a food thermometer with this recipe so you can make sure that the eggs are thoroughly cooked.

YIELDS 2 CUPS; 16 SERVINGS

⅔ cup freshly squeezed lemon juice

1 tablespoon grated lemon zest

¾ cup plus 1 tablespoon sugar

4 large eggs

⅓ cup unsalted butter, cut into small pieces

1. In large saucepan, combine lemon juice, zest, sugar, and eggs and stir together with a wire whisk until blended.

2. Start cooking over low heat, whisking frequently, until the mixture is thickened and smooth. As the custard cooks, whisk more frequently.

3. Test whether it's done by dipping a spoon into the curd; you should be able to draw your finger on the back of the spoon, through the curd, and leave a distinct path. The temperature of the curd should be 160°F; this should take about 7–8 minutes.

4. Remove from heat and whisk in the butter, a bit at a time, until smooth. Let cool for 30 minutes, whisking occasionally. Then cover with plastic wrap placed directly on the surface and chill until cold. Store in the refrigerator in a tightly covered container for up to 1 week.

PER SERVING: Calories: 92 | Total Fat: 4g | Saturated Fat: 2g | Cholesterol: 62mg | Protein: 1g | Sodium: 17mg | Potassium: 30mg | Fiber: 0g | Carbohydrates: 11g | Sugar: 10g

BBQ SAUCE

Making your own BBQ sauce is easy, and it freezes really well too. Be sure to purchase low-salt and no-salt-added tomato products for this recipe. Even the no-salt-added varieties may contain some sodium, so always read labels carefully.

YIELDS 8 CUPS; SERVING SIZE 2 TABLESPOONS

2 tablespoons olive oil

2 medium onions, chopped

6 cloves garlic, minced

1–2 jalapeño peppers, minced

1 (6-ounce) can no-salt-added tomato paste

2 (8-ounce) cans no-salt-added tomato sauce

1 (28-ounce) can no-salt-added crushed tomatoes, undrained

2 cups beef broth

½ cup brown sugar

½ cup apple cider vinegar

⅓ cup Mustard (see recipe in this chapter)

1 tablespoon chili powder

½ teaspoon ground cumin

2 teaspoons black pepper

1 teaspoon cayenne pepper

1 teaspoon celery seeds

2 tablespoons lemon juice

1. In large heavy pot, heat olive oil over medium heat. Add onions and cook, stirring, for 5 minutes. Add garlic and jalapeños; cook, stirring, for another 3–4 minutes until tender.

2. Stir in tomato paste, tomato sauce, crushed tomatoes, beef broth, brown sugar, vinegar, mustard, chili powder, cumin, black pepper, cayenne pepper, and celery seeds and bring to a simmer.

3. Reduce heat to low and simmer, partially covered, stirring occasionally, for 40–50 minutes until slightly thickened. Taste and add more pepper or celery seeds if you'd like.

4. Stir in lemon juice and let cool for 30 minutes. Use immediately or cover and store in the refrigerator for up to 3 weeks. Freeze for longer storage. To thaw, let stand in the refrigerator overnight, then stir and use in recipes.

PER SERVING: Calories: 16 | Total Fat: 0g | Saturated Fat: 0g | Cholesterol: 0mg | Protein: 0g | Sodium: 6mg | Potassium: 63mg | Fiber: 0g | Carbohydrates: 2g | Sugar: 1g

MANGO CHUTNEY

Commercially made chutneys are very high in sodium. Most have almost 200mg of sodium per tablespoon. But it's easy and fun to make your own! Freeze this chutney in ⅓-cup portions, then thaw by putting in the fridge overnight. After you've made this once, you can vary it by using your own favorite fruits and spices.

YIELDS 4 CUPS; SERVING SIZE 1 TABLESPOON

2 large mangoes

2 Granny Smith apples, peeled and chopped

1 medium yellow bell pepper, chopped

1 medium onion, chopped

2 cloves garlic, minced

2 tablespoons minced fresh ginger root

1 cup granulated sugar

½ cup orange juice

¼ cup honey

¼ cup lemon juice

3 tablespoons apple cider vinegar

¼ cup raisins

¼ cup golden raisins

1 tablespoon curry powder

½ teaspoon cinnamon

⅛ teaspoon cardamom

⅛ teaspoon crushed red pepper flakes

⅛ teaspoon white pepper

1. To prepare mango, cut off the skin. Then hold each mango upright and cut down to remove the flesh, working around the large pit in the center. Chop the flesh.

2. Combine mangoes, apples, yellow pepper, onion, garlic, and ginger root in a large saucepan and mix.

3. Add sugar, orange juice, honey, lemon juice, and vinegar, and bring to a boil over medium heat.

4. Reduce heat to low and add raisins, golden raisins, curry powder, cinnamon, cardamom, crushed red pepper flakes, and white pepper. Simmer for 20–25 minutes or until chutney is thickened.

5. Decant into small jars, cover tightly, and refrigerate for up to 5 days. For longer storage, freeze in ⅓-cup portions for up to 6 months.

PER SERVING: Calories: 28 | Total Fat: 0g | Saturated Fat: 0g | Cholesterol: 0mg | Protein: 0g | Sodium: 0mg | Potassium: 38mg | Fiber: 0g | Carbohydrates: 7g | Sugar: 6g

DUXELLES

Duxelles is an essential condiment for low-sodium cooking. Most high-sodium condiments, such as soy sauce and fish sauce, add a rich and meaty taste to recipes along with a salty taste. The best way to add a meaty taste without sodium is to cook mushrooms until they are very deep brown.

YIELDS 2 CUPS

2 tablespoons unsalted butter

1 tablespoon olive oil

1 pound cremini mushrooms, chopped

½ pound portobello mushrooms, chopped

1 medium onion, chopped

4 cloves garlic, minced

1 tablespoon red wine

2 tablespoons lemon juice

3 tablespoons heavy cream

1 teaspoon dried marjoram leaves

⅛ teaspoon pepper

1. In a medium skillet, heat butter and olive oil over medium heat. Add cremini mushrooms, portobello mushrooms, onion, and garlic. Reduce heat to low.

2. Cook, stirring frequently, until the mushrooms give up their liquid and the liquid evaporates, about 7–8 minutes. Continue cooking and stirring until the mushrooms are deep brown, about 20–30 minutes longer.

3. Add wine, lemon juice, cream, marjoram, and pepper, and simmer for 5 minutes longer.

4. Mixture can be refrigerated up to 1 week, or frozen in 2-tablespoon portions for up to 3 months.

PER SERVING (2 tablespoons): Calories: 43 | Total Fat: 3g | Saturated Fat: 1g | Cholesterol: 7mg | Protein: 1g | Sodium: 4mg | Potassium: 204mg | Fiber: 0g | Carbohydrates: 2g | Sugar: 0g

SWEET PICKLED CHIPOTLE RELISH (CHIPOTLES EN ESCABÈCHE)

If the southwestern flavor of chipotle peppers isn't to your taste, substitute chopped bell peppers, carrots, cabbages, cauliflower, or your choice of other fresh, no-salt-added canned or thawed frozen vegetables and create a sweet vegetable relish instead.

YIELDS 3 CUPS; SERVING SIZE 1 TABLESPOON

4 ounces (about 50) dried chipotle peppers

Boiling water

1 cup cider vinegar

½ cup packed brown sugar

½ teaspoon dried thyme

½ teaspoon dried marjoram

3 bay leaves

1 medium-size white onion, finely minced

1 head garlic, cloves peeled and minced

2 teaspoons salt

1¼ cups water

Optional: 1 teaspoon each of celery seeds and mustard seeds

1. Put the chipotle peppers in a bowl or jar and pour enough boiling water over them to cover them completely. Keep the peppers submerged and let stand for 10 minutes. Drain off all the water. If the peppers aren't soft, cover with more boiling water and let stand for an additional 10 minutes. Drain.

2. Remove the stems and discard. Add the peppers to the bowl of a food processor; process until chunky. Drain off most of the liquid, then transfer the peppers to a glass jar that is large enough to comfortably hold all the ingredients and has a noncorrosive lid.

3. In a noncorrosive saucepan, combine all the remaining ingredients. Bring to a gentle simmer and stir until the sugar is completely dissolved, about 5 minutes. Pour the hot liquid over the peppers and stir to mix. The peppers should be completely submerged; if there's not quite enough liquid to cover them, add equal parts cider vinegar and water.

4. Cover and refrigerate for a day or more before serving. This recipe keeps for several weeks in the refrigerator.

PER SERVING: Calories: 10 | Total Fat: 0g | Saturated Fat: 0g | Cholesterol: 0mg | Protein: 0g | Sodium: 94mg | Potassium: 15mg | Fiber: 0g | Carbohydrates: 2g | Sugar: 2g

ROASTED GARLIC

When garlic is roasted it becomes creamy, nutty, tender, and slightly sweet. This is a wonderful ingredient to have on hand when you are cooking without salt. It's delicious stirred into soups, sauces, or hamburgers, spread on chicken or fish, or served alongside a grilled steak.

YIELDS 4 HEADS; 16 SERVINGS

4 heads garlic

3 tablespoons olive oil

2 teaspoons lemon juice

⅛ teaspoon white pepper

1. Preheat oven to 400°F. Cut the top ½" off of the tops of the garlic heads. Remove excess papery skins.

2. Place each head on a square of aluminum foil. Drizzle each with some of the olive oil and the lemon juice and sprinkle with pepper. Loosely close the foil around the garlic.

3. Place the foil bundles on a baking sheet. Roast the garlic for 40–50 minutes or until the heads are very soft when squeezed.

4. Let cool, then gently squeeze the heads to remove the cloves. Discard the skins. Put the cloves in a hard-sided freezer container and freeze up to 2 months. You can also mash the garlic and freeze the paste in ice cube trays. To use, add directly to soups or sauces, or thaw overnight in the fridge.

PER SERVING: Calories: 47 | Total Fat: 2g | Saturated Fat: 0g | Cholesterol: 0mg | Protein: 1g | Sodium: 2mg | Potassium: 68mg | Fiber: 0g | Carbohydrates: 5g | Sugar: 0g

YOGURT-MAYO SANDWICH SPREAD

Add 1 teaspoon of your choice of vinegar and 1 teaspoon of sugar or honey to 2 tablespoons of Yogurt-Mayo Sandwich Spread to create a salad dressing–style mayonnaise. Doing so adds less than 1 calorie per serving and no sodium.

YIELDS ½ CUP; SERVING SIZE 1 TABLESPOON

¼ cup drained nonfat yogurt

¼ cup mayonnaise

1. Measure the yogurt into a paper coffee filter. Wrap the filter up and around the yogurt and twist to secure. Place the filter in a strainer set to drain over a cup or bowl. Refrigerate for at least 1 hour. (While this step isn't necessary, it does help make for a creamier, thicker spread.)

2. In a small bowl, combine the drained yogurt with the mayonnaise. Use as you would mayonnaise. Store in the refrigerator in a covered container until the expiration date on the yogurt.

PER SERVING: Calories: 51 | Total Fat: 5g | Saturated Fat: 0g | Cholesterol: 4mg | Protein: 0g | Sodium: 46mg | Potassium: 21mg | Fiber: 0g | Carbohydrates: 0g | Sugar: 0g

TOFU-MAYO SANDWICH SPREAD

This sandwich spread is best when made the night before to allow time for the flavors to meld.

YIELDS ½ CUP; SERVING SIZE 1 TABLESPOON

2 ounces firm silken tofu

¼ cup mayonnaise

In a small bowl, combine the silken tofu with the mayonnaise. Use as you would mayonnaise. Store in the refrigerator in a covered container until the expiration date on the tofu.

PER SERVING: Calories: 53 | Total Fat: 5g | Saturated Fat: 0g | Cholesterol: 2mg | Protein: 0g | Sodium: 39mg | Potassium: 9mg | Fiber: 0g | Carbohydrates: 0g | Sugar: 0g

EASY HOMEMADE KETCHUP

If you like ketchup with a kick, you have several ways you can spice up Easy Homemade Ketchup. You can add crushed red peppers, Mrs. Dash Extra Spicy Seasoning Blend, or salt-free chili powder along with, or instead of, the cinnamon and other seasonings.

YIELDS 2 CUPS; SERVING SIZE 1 TABLESPOON

1 (15-ounce) can no-salt-added tomato sauce

2 teaspoons water

½ teaspoon onion powder

½ cup granulated sugar

⅓ cup cider vinegar

¼ teaspoon sea salt

¼ teaspoon ground cinnamon

⅛ teaspoon ground cloves

Pinch ground allspice

Pinch nutmeg

Pinch freshly ground pepper

⅔ teaspoon sweet paprika

1. Add all the ingredients except the paprika to a nonstick saucepan. Simmer over low heat for 15–30 minutes, until the mixture reduces to desired consistency.

2. Remove from heat and stir in the paprika. Allow the mixture to cool, then put it in a covered container (such as a recycled ketchup bottle). Store in the refrigerator until needed.

PER SERVING: Calories: 18 | Total Fat: 0g | Saturated Fat: 0g | Cholesterol: 0mg | Protein: 0g | Sodium: 19mg | Potassium: 51mg | Fiber: 0g | Carbohydrates: 4g | Sugar: 3g

TOMATO BUTTER

If you prefer not to take the time to peel and seed the tomatoes before cooking them, you can coarsely chop them instead. Prepare the recipe as directed; however, once it's been seasoned, force the mixture through a fine-meshed sieve using the back of a spoon to remove the seeds and skins.

YIELDS 2½ CUPS; SERVING SIZE 2 TABLESPOONS

½ teaspoon saffron threads

¼ cup Mushroom Broth (Chapter 12)

4 cups peeled, seeded, and diced fresh tomatoes (about 8 large)

½ pound unsalted butter, at room temperature

2 tablespoons white wine vinegar

½ teaspoon salt

Pinch freshly ground black pepper

1. Combine the saffron and broth in a small bowl; let stand for 15 minutes.

2. Bring a large, deep nonstick sauté pan to temperature over medium heat. Add the tomatoes and broth to the pan; bring to a boil, then lower heat. Simmer the tomatoes, stirring frequently, for 40–45 minutes or until the mixture is very thick and reduced in volume to less than 1 cup.

3. Add the butter several tablespoons at a time, whisking after each addition until it has been incorporated into the tomatoes.

4. Add the vinegar, salt, and pepper. This recipe can be stored in the refrigerator for several days or frozen for 3 months.

PER SERVING: Calories: 88 | Total Fat: 9g | Saturated Fat: 5g | Cholesterol: 24mg | Protein: 0g | Sodium: 62mg | Potassium: 90mg | Fiber: 0g | Carbohydrates: 1g | Sugar: 0g

MULTIPURPOSE GARLIC SPREAD

Thin this Multipurpose Garlic Spread with a little water and white wine vinegar to make a Caesar-style salad dressing or seasoned mayonnaise substitute. You can also heat it with a little milk to make a meatless pasta sauce or to use as a seasoning for mashed potatoes.

YIELDS ⅔ CUP; SERVING SIZE 1½ TABLESPOONS

1 ounce Parmesan cheese, cubed

4 cloves roasted garlic

1 teaspoon Dijon mustard

1 teaspoon dry white wine

½ teaspoon reduced-sodium Worcestershire sauce

Pinch freshly ground black pepper

½ cup firm silken tofu

1 tablespoon extra-virgin olive oil

1. Put the cheese cubes into a blender container and chop them on the lowest speed until the cheese settles into the bottom; gradually increase the speed until the cheese is grated.

2. Add the garlic, mustard, wine, Worcestershire sauce, pepper, and tofu to the blender; blend until smooth.

3. While the blender is running, drizzle in the olive oil and continue to process until mixed with the other spread ingredients. Store, covered, in the refrigerator.

PER SERVING: Calories: 40 | Total Fat: 3g | Saturated Fat: 0g | Cholesterol: 2mg | Protein: 2g | Sodium: 66mg | Potassium: 30mg | Fiber: 0g | Carbohydrates: 0g | Sugar: 0g

ROASTED APPLE AND ONION RELISH

Apple cider vinegar is made from leftover apple pressings, or must, that is first boiled down to form a syrup and then allowed to age.

SERVES 8

1 small sweet onion, minced

1 tart cooking apple, peeled, cored, and chopped

1 cup unsweetened, no-salt-added applesauce

1 tablespoon apple cider vinegar

1 teaspoon frozen apple juice concentrate

1 tablespoon lemon juice

⅛ teaspoon dried thyme

⅛ teaspoon freshly ground black pepper

Pinch grated orange zest

1. Preheat oven to 400°F. Spray a cookie sheet with sides with olive oil spray.

2. Mix together the minced onion and chopped apple; add to the prepared cookie sheet and spread out in a single layer. Lightly spray with olive oil spray. Bake for 10 minutes. Stir the mixture. Bake for 5–10 minutes, until tender and lightly browned.

3. Bring a small nonstick saucepan to temperature over low heat. Add the roasted apple-onion mixture and all of the remaining ingredients; simmer for 15–20 minutes, stirring frequently, until the mixture is reduced by half and light to medium brown in color. Note: Increase the stirring frequency halfway through and until the end of the cooking time, as the relish can easily burn once it's reduced.

4. Cool mixture for 30 minutes, then cover and store in refrigerator.

PER SERVING: Calories: 35 | Total Fat: 0g | Saturated Fat: 0g | Cholesterol: 0mg | Protein: 0g | Sodium: 4mg | Potassium: 92mg | Fiber: 0g | Carbohydrates: 9g | Sugar: 6g

RÉMOULADE SAUCE

This sauce, similar to a tartar sauce, is perfect to accompany your seafood dishes, and it is great on other meats, too.

YIELDS 1 CUP, 2 TABLESPOONS; SERVING SIZE 1 TABLESPOON

½ cup mayonnaise

½ cup plain nonfat yogurt

1 tablespoon lemon juice

1 tablespoon dill pickle relish

1 teaspoon capers, rinsed and crushed

1 tablespoon freeze-dried shallots

1 teaspoon freeze-dried chives

½ teaspoon dried parsley

¼ teaspoon freshly ground white or black pepper

In a bowl, combine all the ingredients until well blended. Refrigerate until needed. This sauce can be safely stored in the refrigerator until the expiration date on the yogurt.

PER SERVING: Calories: 30 | Total Fat: 2g | Saturated Fat: 0g | Cholesterol: 1mg | Protein: 0g | Sodium: 63mg | Potassium: 23mg | Fiber: 0g | Carbohydrates: 2g | Sugar: 1g

CHIPOTLE RÉMOULADE

A rémoulade sauce with a hot kick! This sauce will spice up your fish and meat dishes.

YIELDS 2 CUPS; SERVING SIZE 1 TABLESPOON

1 cup Chipotle Peppers in Adobo Sauce (see recipe in this chapter)

2 teaspoons lime juice

¼ cup mayonnaise

½ cup plain nonfat yogurt

¼ cup minced fresh cilantro

⅛ teaspoon freshly ground black pepper

1. Put the Chipotle Peppers in Adobo Sauce and lime juice in a blender or food processor; process until smooth.

2. Transfer to a bowl and mix together with the remaining ingredients. Refrigerate until needed. You can safely store this recipe in the refrigerator until the expiration date on the yogurt.

PER SERVING: Calories: 17 | Total Fat: 1g | Saturated Fat: 0g | Cholesterol: 0mg | Protein: 0g | Sodium: 36mg | Potassium: 58mg | Fiber: 0g | Carbohydrates: 2g | Sugar: 0g

CHIPOTLE PEPPERS IN ADOBO SAUCE

It is very important to not burn the chipotle peppers when roasting them in Step 1. If you do, the resulting sauce will be bitter.

YIELDS 1 CUP; SERVING SIZE 2 TABLESPOONS

7 medium-size dried chipotle chilies

⅓ cup chopped white or yellow onion

5 tablespoons apple cider vinegar

2 cloves garlic, sliced

4 tablespoons low-sodium ketchup

¼ teaspoon salt

3 cups boiling water

1. Remove the stems and seeds from the chilies, and slit the chilies lengthwise. Roast in a heavy skillet over medium-high heat, turning them occasionally; heat until puffed and just beginning to get brown, about 10 seconds each. (Do not burn.)

2. Combine all ingredients in a nonreactive pan and pour the boiling water over them. Cover and cook over very low heat for 1–1½ hours, until the chilies are very soft and the liquid has been reduced to 1 cup. Freeze leftovers, or they can be kept for several weeks in the refrigerator in an airtight container.

PER SERVING: Calories: 32 | Total Fat: 0g | Saturated Fat: 0g | Cholesterol: 0mg | Protein: 1g | Sodium: 82mg | Potassium: 184mg | Fiber: 1g | Carbohydrates: 5g | Sugar: 1g

CHIPOTLE-POBLANO SAUCE

Though not necessary, you can peel the peppers if you'd like. After they have been browned and soaked for 15 minutes in Step 2, remove them from the water with a slotted spoon and peel them before adding them to blender or food processor in Step 4.

YIELDS ½ CUP, 2 TABLESPOONS; SERVING SIZE 1 TABLESPOON

6 chipotle peppers

1 poblano pepper

½ cup boiling water

½ teaspoon cumin seed

½ teaspoon dried Mexican oregano

1 tablespoon dried minced onion

1 teaspoon onion powder

2 teaspoons roasted garlic powder

1 tablespoon olive oil

Pinch salt

1. Remove the stems and seeds from the peppers, and slit the peppers lengthwise. Roast in a heavy skillet over medium-high heat, turning them occasionally; heat until puffed and just beginning to get brown, about 10 seconds each. (Do not burn the peppers or the resulting sauce will be bitter.) As they're done, put the peppers in a bowl.

2. Pour the boiling water over the peppers; let soak for 15 minutes.

3. Dry-roast the cumin and oregano in the skillet until fragrant, being careful that the oregano doesn't burn.

4. Add the remaining ingredients to the bowl of a food processor or blender container. Process until mixed but still chunky. Leftovers can be stored for several days in the refrigerator.

PER SERVING: Calories: 20 | Total Fat: 1g | Saturated Fat: 0g | Cholesterol: 0mg | Protein: 0g | Sodium: 15mg | Potassium: 44mg | Fiber: 0g | Carbohydrates: 1g | Sugar: 0g

SESAME SALT (GOMASHIO)

Traditional gomashio is 15 parts toasted sesame seeds to 1 part sea salt. The version here has a 9-to-1 ratio, which works well to season vegetables and potatoes.

YIELDS 10 TEASPOONS; SERVING SIZE ¼ TEASPOON

3 tablespoons sesame seeds

1 teaspoon sea salt

1. Toast the sesame seeds in a heavy skillet over medium heat until they're light brown and aromatic. (The seeds may start to "pop" at this point.) Stir frequently to prevent the seeds from burning. Set aside to cool.

2. Add the salt to the toasted sesame seeds and mix well. Grind with a mortar and pestle until the seeds crack open; the mixture will be a coarse grind. (Alternatively, you can grind it in a spice grinder or food processor and pulse the mixture a few times.) Regardless of the method, do not overprocess it. Like peanuts, sesame seeds have natural oils that will turn it into a paste if you process it too much, and you'll end up with nut butter.

PER SERVING: Calories: 3 | Total Fat: 0g | Saturated Fat: 0g | Cholesterol: 0mg | Protein: 0g | Sodium: 58mg | Potassium: 2mg | Fiber: 0g | Carbohydrates: 0g | Sugar: 0g

ZESTY HERBED DILLY BEANS

Try adding Zesty Herbed Dilly Beans on a hamburger instead of dill pickles for that traditional flavor at a fraction of the sodium content. Green beans are blanched before being frozen, so using a package of frozen beans saves you that step. Frozen green beans are crisper than no-salt-added canned green beans.

SERVES 16

1 (16-ounce) package frozen cut green beans, thawed and drained

¾ cup apple cider vinegar

¾ cup water

¼ teaspoon cayenne pepper or dried red pepper flakes

2 cloves garlic, minced

2 teaspoons dill seeds

1 teaspoon dried dill weed

½ teaspoon salt

1. Put the thawed green beans in a glass jar or other covered container large enough to hold the beans and vinegar mixture.

2. In a medium nonreactive saucepan over high heat, bring the vinegar and water to a boil. Stir in the cayenne pepper (or pepper flakes), garlic, dill seeds and weed, and salt. Pour the vinegar mixture over the green beans. Allow to cool to room temperature.

3. Cover and refrigerate for 24 hours before serving. Store leftovers in the refrigerator. Use within 1 week.

PER SERVING: Calories: 10 | Total Fat: 0g | Saturated Fat: 0g | Cholesterol: 0mg | Protein: 0g | Sodium: 73mg | Potassium: 55mg | Fiber: 0g | Carbohydrates: 0g | Sugar: 0g

POMEGRANATE PIZZAZZ SALSA

Substitute mango for the peaches and/or frozen orange juice concentrate for the pomegranate concentrate or molasses in this recipe. If you're making salsa for a huge crowd, you can go crazy and even throw in some cooked sweet corn and chopped red and green bell pepper, too.

SERVES 16

1 large banana, peeled and chopped

2 limes, zested and juiced

1 teaspoon pomegranate concentrate or molasses

1 clove garlic, minced

1 jalapeño, seeded and minced

2 teaspoons Citrus Pepper (Appendix A)

¼ teaspoon mustard powder or Dijon mustard

Pinch (or to taste) dried red pepper flakes

Optional: 1 tablespoon water

1 large red or sweet onion, chopped

2 medium avocados, pitted, peeled, and diced

¼ cup chopped fresh cilantro

2 large tomatoes, peeled, seeded, and chopped

2 large peaches, peeled, pitted, and chopped

Optional: Freshly ground black pepper

1. Add the banana, lime zest and juice, pomegranate concentrate or molasses, garlic, jalapeño, Citrus Pepper, mustard powder or Dijon, and red pepper flakes to a blender or food processor; process until smooth. If the resulting banana-lime mixture is thicker than you prefer, add the optional water at this time and pulse to combine.

2. Add the onion, avocados, cilantro, tomatoes, and peaches to a bowl; stir to mix.

3. Pour the banana-lime mixture over the ingredients in the bowl and toss gently. Add black pepper, if using. Serve immediately. (If preparing in advance, add the avocados at the last minute.) Store leftovers, covered, in the refrigerator.

PER SERVING: Calories: 70 | Total Fat: 3g | Saturated Fat: 0g | Cholesterol: 0mg | Protein: 1g | Sodium: 5mg | Potassium: 287mg | Fiber: 2g | Carbohydrates: 9g | Sugar: 4g

HOLLANDAISE-STYLE SAUCE

If you love the taste of hollandaise sauce but fear the dreaded separation that can occur when making it, try this easy recipe that gives you the flavor without the fear.

YIELDS ½ CUP; SERVING SIZE 1 TABLESPOON

½ cup Mayonnaise (see recipe in this chapter)

1 tablespoon fresh lemon juice

1–2 tablespoons Honey Mustard (see recipe in this chapter)

Pinch dried red pepper flakes, crushed

⅛ teaspoon freshly ground black pepper

Add all the ingredients to a small serving bowl and whisk to combine. Refrigerate leftovers; this sauce can be safely kept (covered) in the refrigerator for 3 days.

PER SERVING: Calories: 141 | Total Fat: 15g | Saturated Fat: 1g | Cholesterol: 27mg | Protein: 0g | Sodium: 5mg | Potassium: 7mg | Fiber: 0g | Carbohydrates: 0g | Sugar: 0g

TOASTED GROUND ALMONDS

Almonds are high in monounsaturated fats and vitamin E and may help reduce cholesterol and the risk of heart disease.

SERVES 24

½ cup ground raw almonds

1. Add the raw almonds to a nonstick skillet over low heat. Toast until golden, shaking the pan or stirring the mixture frequently so that the nuts toast evenly. When the nuts reach a light brown color, remove from the heat and pour into a bowl.

2. Allow to cool completely, then store in an airtight container kept in a cool, dry place.

PER SERVING: Calories: 16 | Total Fat: 1g | Saturated Fat: 0g | Cholesterol: 0mg | Protein: 0g | Sodium: 0mg | Potassium: 20mg | Fiber: 0g | Carbohydrates: 0g | Sugar: 0g

TEXAS ROASTED ALMONDS

If you need to stretch this recipe for a crowd, you can turn it into Texas Popcorn by misting some air-popped popcorn with olive oil spray and tossing it with these Texas Roasted Almonds.

SERVES 16

2 teaspoons unsalted butter

½ teaspoon reduced-sodium Worcestershire sauce

½ teaspoon Texas Seasoning (Appendix A)

1 cup slivered almonds

1. Preheat oven to 350°F.

2. In a microwave-safe bowl, mix together the butter, Worcestershire sauce, and Texas Seasoning; microwave on high for 30 seconds or until the butter is melted; stir well.

3. Spread the almonds on a shallow baking sheet treated with nonstick spray. Bake for 12–15 minutes or until light gold, stirring occasionally.

4. Pour the seasoned butter over the almonds and stir to mix. Return to the oven and bake for 5 minutes. Cool, then store in airtight containers in a cool place.

PER SERVING: Calories: 55 | Total Fat: 5g | Saturated Fat: 0g | Cholesterol: 1mg | Protein: 1g | Sodium: 1mg | Potassium: 65mg | Fiber: 1g | Carbohydrates: 1g | Sugar: 0g

BERRY GOOD SALSA

A truly stellar salsa made from fresh blackberries. Sweet, spicy, and savory flavors meld together to create this mouthwatering salsa.

SERVES 16

1 cup blackberries

½ cantaloupe, diced

1 jalapeño or banana pepper

1 small red or green bell pepper

1 medium-size red onion, diced

1 tablespoon lemon juice

⅛ teaspoon freshly ground black pepper

Pinch mustard powder

⅛ teaspoon dried lemon granules, crushed

½ teaspoon dried cilantro or parsley

½ teaspoon Texas Seasoning (Appendix A)

Place all the ingredients in a food processor and process until well mixed. Do not overprocess—the salsa should remain somewhat chunky. Store leftovers, covered, in the refrigerator.

PER SERVING: Calories: 15 | Total Fat: 0g | Saturated Fat: 0g | Cholesterol: 0mg | Protein: 0g | Sodium: 3mg | Potassium: 78mg | Fiber: 0g | Carbohydrates: 3g | Sugar: 2g

MINCEMEAT-STYLE CHUTNEY

This chutney is also good if made with curry powder instead of the cinnamon and Pumpkin Pie Spice. Or, for a zesty change of pace, you can substitute chili powder for the Pumpkin Pie Spice.

SERVES 48

1 cup diced sweet onion

1 cup peeled and diced Granny Smith apples

1 cup peeled and diced bananas

1 cup peeled and diced peaches

¼ cup raisins

¼ cup dried cranberries

¼ cup dry white wine

¼ cup apple cider vinegar

1 teaspoon brown sugar

½ teaspoon cinnamon

½ teaspoon Pumpkin Pie Spice (Appendix A)

⅛ teaspoon freshly ground black pepper

⅛ teaspoon grated lemon zest

In a large saucepan, combine all the ingredients and cook over low heat for about 1 hour, stirring occasionally. Let cool completely. This recipe can be kept in the refrigerator for 1 week or in the freezer for 3 months.

PER SERVING: Calories: 15 | Total Fat: 0g | Saturated Fat: 0g | Cholesterol: 0mg | Protein: 0g | Sodium: 0mg | Potassium: 43mg | Fiber: 0g | Carbohydrates: 3g | Sugar: 2g

PLUM SAUCE

This sauce beautifully complements chicken and is so easy to make.

YIELDS 1¼ CUPS; SERVING SIZE 1 TABLESPOON

1 cup plum jam

½ teaspoon grated lemon zest

1 tablespoon lemon juice

1 tablespoon rice wine vinegar or white wine vinegar

½ teaspoon ground dried ginger

½ teaspoon crushed anise seeds

¼ teaspoon dry mustard

¼ teaspoon ground cinnamon

⅛ teaspoon ground cloves

⅛ teaspoon hot sauce

Heat the plum jam in a small saucepan over medium heat until melted. Stir in the remaining ingredients. Bring the mixture to a boil, lower the heat, and simmer for 1 minute, stirring constantly. Cool for 30 minutes, then store, covered, in the refrigerator up to a week.

PER SERVING: Calories: 45 | Total Fat: 0g | Saturated Fat: 0g | Cholesterol: 0mg | Protein: 0g | Sodium: 5mg | Potassium: 14mg | Fiber: 0g | Carbohydrates: 11g | Sugar: 7g

PEACH SAUCE

This peach sauce is wonderful over pork or chicken or can be used over ice cream or cake. Talk about a versatile sauce!

YIELDS ½ CUP; SERVING SIZE 2 TABLESPOONS

2 teaspoons olive oil

1 tablespoon chopped shallots

1 teaspoon grated fresh ginger

⅛ teaspoon grated lemon zest

½ teaspoon Pumpkin Pie Spice (Appendix A)

Pinch mustard powder

⅓ cup dry white wine

1 small peach, peeled and diced

1 tablespoon frozen orange juice concentrate

1 teaspoon Bragg Liquid Aminos

½ teaspoon cornstarch

1. Heat the olive oil in a nonstick saucepan over medium heat; sauté the shallots and ginger until soft.

2. Add the lemon zest, Pumpkin Pie Spice, mustard powder, and wine; simmer until reduced by half.

3. Add the diced peach, orange juice concentrate, and liquid aminos and bring to a simmer, stirring occasionally.

4. In a separate container, mix the cornstarch with 1 tablespoon of the sauce; stir to create a slurry, mixing well to remove any lumps. Add the slurry to the sauce and simmer until the mixture thickens. Transfer the mixture to a blender or food processor container and process until smooth.

PER SERVING: Calories: 56 | Total Fat: 2g | Saturated Fat: 0g | Cholesterol: 0mg | Protein: 0g | Sodium: 0mg | Potassium: 97mg | Fiber: 0g | Carbohydrates: 5g | Sugar: 4g

MOCK SOUR CREAM

The type of vinegar used in the Mock Sour Cream recipe will affect the "tang" of the sour cream taste. Apple cider vinegar, for example, has a stronger taste; white wine and champagne vinegar tend to be milder.

YIELDS 6 TABLESPOONS; SERVING SIZE 1 TABLESPOON

2 tablespoons plain nonfat yogurt

¼ cup cottage cheese

½ teaspoon vinegar

Put all the ingredients in a blender or food processor; process until smooth.

PER SERVING: Calories: 10 | Total Fat: 0g | Saturated Fat: 0g | Cholesterol: 1mg | Protein: 1g | Sodium: 34mg | Potassium: 20mg | Fiber: 0g | Carbohydrates: 0g | Sugar: 0g

SPICED MIXED NUT BUTTER

Serve this Spiced Mixed Nut Butter with toast points, crackers, or celery sticks. Refrigerate any leftovers.

YIELDS ¼ CUP; SERVING SIZE ½ TABLESPOON

2 tablespoons sesame seeds

2 tablespoons ground almonds

2 tablespoons sunflower seeds

1½ teaspoons honey

¼ teaspoon cinnamon

⅛ teaspoon Pumpkin Pie Spice (Appendix A)

Pinch unsweetened cocoa powder

Pinch grated lemon zest

1. Bring a large, deep nonstick sauté pan to temperature over medium heat. Add the sesame seeds, ground almonds, and sunflower seeds; toast for 5–7 minutes or until lightly browned, stirring frequently to prevent burning. Immediately transfer the nuts to a bowl and let cool.

2. Combine the cooled, toasted nuts with the remaining ingredients in a blender or food processor; process until the desired consistency is reached, scraping down the sides of the bowl as necessary. (Note: A mini food processor works best for a recipe this size.)

PER SERVING: Calories: 50 | Total Fat: 4g | Saturated Fat: 0g | Cholesterol: 0mg | Protein: 1g | Sodium: 1mg | Potassium: 53mg | Fiber: 0g | Carbohydrates: 2g | Sugar: 1g

CURRY POWDER

A dry-toasted curry powder blend lets you eliminate some of the butter or oil called for in a recipe. Curry powder is usually sautéed in some fat to bring out the flavors. If you aren't watching your fat intake, leave the fat in the recipe; it does add more flavor and texture to the finished dish.

YIELDS ABOUT ¼ CUP

1 tablespoon coriander seeds

½ tablespoon cumin seeds

½ teaspoon fennel seeds

¼ teaspoon whole cloves or ⅛ teaspoon ground cloves

¼ teaspoon mustard seeds

½ tablespoon cardamom seeds

½ tablespoon whole black peppercorns

½ teaspoon dried red pepper flakes, or crushed red peppers

½ tablespoon turmeric

⅛ teaspoon ground ginger

⅛ teaspoon ground cinnamon

1. Toast the coriander, cumin, fennel, cloves, mustard seeds, cardamom seeds, peppercorns, and red pepper flakes in a small, dry skillet over medium-low heat. Stir the spices often to prevent them from burning. Toast for a couple of minutes, or until the spices smell fragrant.

2. Add the toasted spices to a clean coffee grinder and grind into a fine powder. Add the turmeric, ginger, and cinnamon, and pulse the grinder a few times to combine them with the other spices. Use the spice blend immediately if desired, or, if stored in a sealed glass jar, it can be kept in a cool, dry place for 1 month. To freeze, decant into a hard-sided freezer container and freeze up to 1 year.

PER SERVING (1 tablespoon): Calories: 4 | Total Fat: 0g | Saturated Fat: 0g | Cholesterol: 0mg | Protein: 0g | Sodium: 0mg | Potassium: 23mg | Fiber: 0g | Carbohydrates: 0g | Sugar: 0g

STOCKS, SOUPS, AND STEWS

BEEF STOCK

Beef stock is made of beef bones, stew meat, and lots of vegetables. The key to making a good beef stock is to thoroughly brown the meat before everything simmers together for hours in a big pot. Freeze the stock in 1-cup portions and you'll always have some on hand.

YIELDS 12 CUPS

4 pounds meaty beef bones

2 pounds beef stew meat, cut into chunks

2 tablespoons olive oil

5 medium carrots, cut into chunks

3 large onions, sliced

16 cups water, divided

3 large tomatoes, cut into chunks

1 head garlic, cut in half crosswise

2 bay leaves

3 sprigs fresh thyme

1 sprig fresh oregano

1 tablespoon black peppercorns

1. Preheat oven to 425°F. Place the bones and stew meat in a large roasting pan and drizzle with olive oil; toss to coat. Roast for 45 minutes.

2. Add carrots and onions; roast for another 30 minutes.

3. Remove bones, meat, carrots, and onions to very large stock pot. Drain the fat from the roasting pan; do not wipe out.

4. Add 2 cups water to the roasting pan and stir to remove pan drippings. Add to pot with bones and vegetables.

5. Add all remaining ingredients to pot and bring to a boil. Reduce heat to low, partially cover, and simmer for 4–6 hours, skimming off the foam from the surface as needed, until liquid is deep brown.

6. Strain stock through a colander into another pot; discard meat and vegetables. Cool the stock, then refrigerate until cold. Remove fat from surface of stock and discard. Freeze the stock in 1-cup portions for up to 6 months.

PER SERVING: Calories: 20 | Total Fat: 0g | Saturated Fat: 0g | Cholesterol: 0mg | Protein: 2g | Sodium: 140mg | Potassium: 80mg | Fiber: 0g | Carbohydrates: 2g | Sugar: 1g

CHICKEN STOCK

Chicken stock is essential to so many recipes, from risotto to soups and stews. Make your own for a very rich taste and much less money than expensive boxed stocks. Every time you roast a chicken or bake or grill bone-in chicken, save the carcass and bones in the freezer. When you have enough, make stock!

YIELDS 8 CUPS

5 pounds chicken carcasses and/or bones, including fat and skin

2 pounds chicken wings

2 medium onions, chopped

4 cloves garlic, cut in chunks

3 medium carrots, sliced

3 celery stalks, sliced

1 sprig fresh thyme

3 sprigs flat-leaf parsley

5 whole black peppercorns

11 cups cold water

1. In very large stock pot, combine all ingredients. Bring to a boil, reduce heat, and skim foam off surface and discard the foam.

2. Simmer the stock, skimming the surface occasionally and discarding foam, until the liquid is reduced and it looks like chicken stock, about 3 hours.

3. Strain stock through a strainer, discarding bones, chicken, and vegetables. Cool stock, refrigerate, and remove and discard the fat. Freeze in 1-cup portions for up to 6 months.

PER SERVING: Calories: 20 | Total Fat: 0g | Saturated Fat: 0g | Cholesterol: 0mg | Protein: 4g | Sodium: 130mg | Potassium: 70mg | Fiber: 0g | Carbohydrates: 1g | Sugar: 1g

FISH STOCK

Fish stock is not something you find often in the grocery store. It is essential in fish soups, although most people just use chicken stock or vegetable broth instead. But when you need it, this is the recipe to use. Ask the fishmonger or butcher for fish bones and fish heads; he may even give them to you without charge.

YIELDS 6 CUPS

2 pounds fish bones

1 medium onion, chopped

1 leek, rinsed and chopped

2 medium carrots, cut into chunks

1 teaspoon black peppercorns

3 cloves garlic, cut in half

1 sprig fresh thyme

8 cups water

1. Combine all ingredients in a large pot and bring to a boil.

2. Reduce heat to low. Partially cover pot and simmer for 40 minutes.

3. Strain stock through a cheesecloth-lined colander, discarding solids. Cool stock, then freeze in 1-cup containers for up to 3 months.

PER SERVING: Calories: 36 | Total Fat: 0g | Saturated Fat: 0g | Cholesterol: 0mg | Protein: 0g | Sodium: 34mg | Potassium: 210mg | Fiber: 0g | Carbohydrates: 1g | Sugar: 1g

MUSHROOM HUMMUS SOUP

Hummus adds a rich and nutty note to this simple mushroom soup. Fresh and dried mushrooms add to the flavor of this recipe, along with your own homemade vegetable broth. Serve with a green salad and some Roasted Garlic Crackers (Chapter 6) for a hearty and nourishing meal.

SERVES 6

2 ounces dried porcini mushrooms

1 cup warm water

1 tablespoon unsalted butter

1 tablespoon olive oil

1 medium onion, chopped

3 cloves garlic, minced

1 (8-ounce) package fresh cremini mushrooms, sliced

6 cups Vegetable Broth (see recipe in this chapter)

1 bay leaf

1 cup Hummus (Chapter 6)

1 tablespoon lemon juice

½ teaspoon grated lemon zest

1. In small bowl, combine dried mushrooms and water; let stand for 15 minutes. Drain mushrooms, reserving liquid. Remove stems from dried mushrooms if needed and discard. Slice mushroom caps.

2. In large soup pot, melt butter and olive oil over medium heat. Add onion, and garlic; cook and stir for 5 minutes.

3. Add sliced cremini mushrooms and cook for another 4 minutes.

4. Add dried mushrooms, reserved mushroom liquid, vegetable broth, and bay leaf, and bring to a simmer.

5. Reduce heat to low and simmer for 30 minutes or until mushrooms are tender. Remove bay leaf and discard.

6. Place hummus in medium bowl and add two ladles of the hot broth. Stir with a wire whisk to combine.

7. Whisk the hummus mixture into the soup. Add lemon juice and lemon zest and heat through. Serve immediately.

PER SERVING: Calories: 357 | Total Fat: 18g | Saturated Fat: 3g | Cholesterol: 5mg | Protein: 15g | Sodium: 93mg | Potassium: 830mg | Fiber: 7g | Carbohydrates: 37g | Sugar: 5g

VEGETABLE BROTH

Vegetable broth is essential in vegetarian recipes, and adds a mild and slightly sweet flavor to soups. You can make this recipe for almost no money at all if you save vegetable trimmings and scraps.

YIELDS 6 CUPS

1 tablespoon olive oil

2 medium onions, chopped, including skins

2 cloves garlic, cut in half

2 medium carrots, cut into chunks

2 stalks celery, cut into chunks

¼ cup celery leaves

1 bay leaf

1 sprig fresh parsley

6 whole peppercorns

8 cups water

1. Combine all ingredients in a large pot and bring to a boil.

2. Reduce heat to low. Partially cover pot and simmer for 50 minutes.

3. Strain stock through a cheesecloth-lined colander, discarding solids. Cool stock, then freeze in 1-cup containers for up to 3 months.

PER SERVING: Calories: 15 | Total Fat: 0g | Saturated Fat: 0g | Cholesterol: 0mg | Protein: 0g | Sodium: 17mg | Potassium: 0mg | Fiber: 0g | Carbohydrates: 3g | Sugar: 2g

PEACH GAZPACHO

Cutting down on the tomatoes and adding peaches instead adds a new twist to this classic summer recipe. This is an excellent appetizer served before a grilled dinner; just serve the soup in shot glasses or small mugs. It can also be the centerpiece of a gorgeous lunch on the porch.

SERVES 4

5 medium peaches

2 cups grape tomatoes, chopped

1 cup peach nectar

2 tablespoons sliced green onion

¼ cup lemon juice

½ teaspoon grated lemon zest

2 tablespoons honey

2 tablespoons chopped fresh mint

1. Bring a large pot of water to a boil. Add the peaches; simmer for about 20 seconds. Plunge the peaches into cold water and let stand 5 minutes. Remove the peach skins and discard. Remove pits and discard, and chop the peaches.

2. In blender or food processor, combine peaches, tomatoes, peach nectar, green onion, lemon juice, lemon zest, and honey. Blend or process until almost smooth.

3. Transfer to pitcher or serving bowl and add mint. Cover and chill for 2–3 hours before serving.

PER SERVING: Calories: 159 | Total Fat: 0g | Saturated Fat: 0g | Cholesterol: 0mg | Protein: 2g | Sodium: 10mg | Potassium: 636mg | Fiber: 4g | Carbohydrates: 40g | Sugar: 35g

BEEF AND POTATO CHOWDER

Potato chowder is a wonderfully comforting food. Unfortunately, the best way to make a flavorful potato chowder or soup is to use a lot of salt. This recipe uses duxelles instead, which is mushrooms cooked down until they are very deep brown; it adds a meaty depth of flavor to the soup along with caramelized onions.

SERVES 6

1½ pounds sirloin tip, cut into strips

2 tablespoons flour

2 tablespoons unsalted butter

1 tablespoon olive oil

1 onion, chopped

4 cloves garlic, sliced

½ cup Duxelles (Chapter 4)

4 cups Beef Stock (see recipe in this chapter)

4 Yukon gold potatoes, peeled and chopped

⅔ cup light cream

1 teaspoon dried marjoram leaves

¼ teaspoon pepper

1. Toss beef with flour. In large pot, melt butter over medium heat. Add beef; brown, stirring frequently, for 5 minutes. Remove beef from pot.

2. Add olive oil to pot; add onion and garlic. Cook, stirring frequently, until the vegetables are tender, about 6 minutes.

3. Add duxelles and beef stock to the pot; bring to a simmer, stirring with a wire whisk.

4. Add beef and potatoes to the pot; bring to a simmer. Reduce heat to medium-low and simmer for 10–15 minutes or until potatoes are tender.

5. Add cream, marjoram, and pepper to the chowder; simmer for 5–10 minutes. Serve immediately.

PER SERVING: Calories: 421 | Total Fat: 21g | Saturated Fat: 10g | Cholesterol: 88mg | Protein: 30g | Sodium: 124mg | Potassium: 902mg | Fiber: 1g | Carbohydrates: 26g | Sugar: 2g

BEEF AND PEPPER CHOWDER

This chowder is warm and comforting and rich with beef and bell peppers. We are using cubed sirloin steak for a wonderfully meaty taste and thick texture.

SERVES 6

1 pound sirloin steak, cut into 1" pieces

2 tablespoons flour

1 teaspoon dried marjoram leaves

½ teaspoon dried basil leaves

⅛ teaspoon pepper

2 tablespoons olive oil

1 medium onion, chopped

3 cloves garlic, minced

⅓ cup red wine

1 medium red bell pepper, chopped

1 medium yellow bell pepper, chopped

1 medium green bell pepper, chopped

1 (15-ounce) can no-salt-added diced tomatoes, undrained

3 cups Beef Stock (see recipe in this chapter)

1 tablespoon brown sugar

½ cup light cream

2 tablespoons grated Parmesan cheese

1. Toss the beef with flour, marjoram, basil, and pepper.

2. Heat olive oil in a large pot over medium heat and add the beef. Brown on all sides, stirring frequently.

3. Add onion and garlic to the pot; cook and stir for 4–5 minutes until vegetables are crisp-tender. Add red wine; stir to remove pan drippings.

4. Add all of the bell peppers, tomatoes, stock, and brown sugar to the pot. Bring to a simmer, then simmer for 20 minutes or until peppers are tender.

5. Stir in the cream and heat for a few minutes, then sprinkle with cheese and serve.

PER SERVING: Calories: 302 | Total Fat: 17g | Saturated Fat: 6g | Cholesterol: 63mg | Protein: 21g | Sodium: 119mg | Potassium: 663mg | Fiber: 1g | Carbohydrates: 13g | Sugar: 4g

SWEET-AND-SOUR MEATBALL STEW

Sweet-and-sour flavors are achieved by combining something like pineapple, honey, or sugar with vinegar or lemon juice. Most sweet-and-sour stews also use soy sauce for depth of flavor. This stew uses duxelles to give that umami flavor with very little sodium.

SERVES 6

½ recipe Savory Meatballs (Chapter 9)

2 tablespoons olive oil

1 tablespoon unsalted butter

1 medium onion, chopped

2 cloves garlic, minced

2 medium carrots, sliced

1 medium red bell pepper, chopped

3 tablespoons no-salt-added tomato paste

1 (14-ounce) can no-salt-added diced tomatoes, undrained

2 cups Beef Stock (see recipe in this chapter)

½ cup Duxelles (Chapter 4)

2 tablespoons honey

2 tablespoons brown sugar

¼ cup apple cider vinegar

½ teaspoon smoked paprika

¼ teaspoon pepper

1. Prepare Savory Meatballs, bake, and set aside.

2. In large pot, heat olive oil and butter over medium heat. Add onion, garlic, carrots, and bell pepper; cook and stir for 5 minutes.

3. Add tomato paste to pot; let the tomato paste brown in a few spots. Then add the tomatoes and beef stock, stirring to remove pan drippings.

4. Add the meatballs, duxelles, honey, brown sugar, vinegar, paprika, and pepper to the pot. Simmer for 15–20 minutes until vegetables are tender, then serve.

PER SERVING: Calories: 344 | Total Fat: 20g | Saturated Fat: 8g | Cholesterol: 82mg | Protein: 19g | Sodium: 113mg | Potassium: 908mg | Fiber: 2g | Carbohydrates: 21g | Sugar: 14g

GREEN CHICKEN CHILI

This chili is delicious served with some Cornbread (Chapter 2), hot out of the oven and spread with unsalted butter and honey.

SERVES 6

2 (6-ounce) boneless, skinless chicken breasts, cubed

2 tablespoons flour

1 tablespoon chili powder

½ teaspoon cumin

⅛ teaspoon white pepper

2 tablespoons olive oil

1 medium onion, chopped

3 cloves garlic, minced

2 jalapeño peppers, minced

1 cup chopped tomatillos

2 medium green bell peppers, chopped

1 (15-ounce) can no-salt-added cannellini beans, rinsed and drained

2½ cups Chicken Stock (see recipe in this chapter)

½ cup sour cream

¼ cup shredded Monterey jack cheese

1. Sprinkle chicken with flour, chili powder, cumin, and white pepper.

2. Heat oil in large pot over medium heat. Add chicken; cook for 3–4 minutes, stirring frequently.

3. Add onion, garlic, jalapeños, and tomatillos to pot with chicken; cook and stir for 5 minutes. Add green bell peppers.

4. Add beans and chicken stock and bring to a simmer. Reduce heat to low and simmer for 10–15 minutes or until vegetables are tender. Serve with sour cream and cheese.

PER SERVING: Calories: 299 | Total Fat: 11g | Saturated Fat: 4g | Cholesterol: 47mg | Protein: 24g | Sodium: 126mg | Potassium: 795mg | Fiber: 6g | Carbohydrates: 25g | Sugar: 2g

CABBAGE MUSHROOM SOUP

This homey soup is very inexpensive to make but is flavorful and filling. A good variety of mushrooms adds interest to this recipe. Serve with a seasonal fruit salad—apples and oranges in the winter; grapes and cantaloupe in the spring.

SERVES 4

2 tablespoons olive oil

1 cup chopped leek

1 medium onion, chopped

3 cloves garlic, minced

1 cup sliced button mushrooms

1 cup sliced cremini mushrooms

1 cup sliced shiitake mushrooms

3 cups chopped green cabbage

3 cups Beef Stock (see recipe in this chapter)

1 teaspoon dried thyme leaves

1 bay leaf

1 tablespoon lemon juice

½ teaspoon grated lemon zest

⅛ teaspoon pepper

1. In large pot, heat olive oil over medium heat. Add leek, onion, and garlic; cook and stir for 5 minutes.

2. Add all of the mushrooms; cook and stir until mushrooms give up their liquid and the liquid evaporates, about 9–10 minutes.

3. Add cabbage; cook and stir for 3 minutes.

4. Add stock, thyme, bay leaf, lemon juice, lemon zest, and pepper and stir. Bring to a simmer, reduce heat, and simmer for 20–25 minutes or until cabbage is tender. Remove bay leaf and discard, then serve.

PER SERVING: Calories: 140 | Total Fat: 8g | Saturated Fat: 1g | Cholesterol: 0mg | Protein: 6g | Sodium: 70mg | Potassium: 489mg | Fiber: 2g | Carbohydrates: 14g | Sugar: 4g

ROASTED GARLIC TOMATO SOUP

Tomato soup can be pretty ordinary, but it's also delicious when made with in-season tomatoes, roasted garlic, and lots of fresh basil. You could omit the butter and use vegetable broth instead, for a vegan version.

SERVES 4

1 head Roasted Garlic (Chapter 4)

1 tablespoon olive oil

1 tablespoon unsalted butter

1 cup chopped leek

1 shallot, minced

4 cups chopped fresh tomatoes

½ teaspoon dried basil leaves

2 cups Chicken Stock (see recipe in this chapter)

2 tablespoons lemon juice

½ teaspoon grated lemon zest

1 teaspoon sugar

⅛ teaspoon pepper

⅓ cup light cream

2 tablespoons minced fresh basil

1. Remove the garlic from the peel; discard the peel and mash garlic.

2. Heat olive oil and butter in a large pot. Add leek and shallot; cook and stir for 4 minutes. Add the mashed garlic and stir well.

3. Add tomatoes and dried basil; cook and stir for 4 minutes. Then add chicken stock, lemon juice, lemon zest, sugar, and pepper and bring to a simmer.

4. Reduce heat and simmer for 15–20 minutes or until tomatoes are soft. Purée soup using an immersion blender.

5. Stir in the light cream and fresh basil. Heat and serve.

PER SERVING: Calories: 188 | Total Fat: 12g | Saturated Fat: 5g | Cholesterol: 26mg | Protein: 5g | Sodium: 53mg | Potassium: 610mg | Fiber: 2g | Carbohydrates: 17g | Sugar: 6g

SPICY THAI SOUP

Cremini mushrooms are easier to find than straw and shiitake in most areas of the country. Those are used in this spicy soup packed with chicken and vegetables. Serve with a cold beer and some fresh fruit.

SERVES 4

2 tablespoons olive oil

8 boneless, skinless chicken thighs, cubed

1 medium onion, chopped

1 cup sliced cremini mushrooms

1 tablespoon minced fresh ginger root

4 cloves garlic, minced

1 serrano pepper, minced

1 stalk lemongrass

1 medium yellow bell pepper, chopped

2 teaspoons curry powder

⅛ teaspoon crushed red pepper flakes

⅛ teaspoon white pepper

2 cups Chicken Stock (see recipe in this chapter)

1 (14-ounce) can coconut milk

2 tablespoons lime juice

½ teaspoon grated lime zest

2 tablespoons minced fresh basil

1. Heat olive oil in large pot over medium heat. Add chicken; cook, stirring frequently, until chicken is lightly browned, about 4–5 minutes. Remove chicken from pot and set aside.

2. Add onion, mushrooms, ginger root, garlic, and serrano pepper to pot. Cook, stirring to remove pan drippings, until crisp-tender, about 4–5 minutes.

3. Bend the lemongrass stalk several times to slightly crush it. Add it with the yellow bell pepper to the pot; cook and stir for 2 minutes longer.

4. Return chicken to the pot along with the curry powder, red pepper flakes, white pepper, and chicken stock. Bring to a simmer; reduce heat to low. Simmer for 10–15 minutes or until vegetables are tender.

5. Remove and discard lemongrass. Add coconut milk, lime juice, and lime zest. Simmer for 1 minute, then stir in basil and serve immediately.

PER SERVING: Calories: 403 | Total Fat: 25g | Saturated Fat: 4g | Cholesterol: 98mg | Protein: 31g | Sodium: 140mg | Potassium: 563mg | Fiber: 1g | Carbohydrates: 9g | Sugar: 2g

VEGETABLE MEATBALL SOUP

This hearty soup is a classic. You can substitute your own favorite vegetables for the ones given in this recipe—try adding turnips instead of the carrots, or use yellow summer squash instead of the zucchini. And try kidney or black beans in place of the cannellini beans.

SERVES 4

½ recipe Savory Meatballs (Chapter 9)

2 tablespoons olive oil

1 leek, chopped

2 cloves garlic, minced

2 medium carrots, sliced

1 (8-ounce) package sliced mushrooms

1 medium zucchini, sliced

1 (15-ounce) can no-salt-added cannellini beans, rinsed and drained

2 cups Beef Stock (see recipe in this chapter)

1 cup water

1 teaspoon dried marjoram leaves

⅛ teaspoon pepper

1 tablespoon lemon juice

1. Prepare meatballs; bake and set aside.

2. In large pot, heat oil over medium heat. Add leek and garlic; cook and stir for 4–5 minutes or until crisp-tender.

3. Add carrots and mushrooms; cook and stir for 3 minutes longer.

4. Add zucchini, beans, beef stock, water, marjoram, and pepper along with the meatballs and bring to a simmer.

5. Reduce heat, partially cover, and simmer for 20–25 minutes or until vegetables are tender.

6. Add lemon juice and serve.

PER SERVING: Calories: 379 | Total Fat: 18g | Saturated Fat: 6g | Cholesterol: 76mg | Protein: 27g | Sodium: 109mg | Potassium: 1,184mg | Fiber: 6g | Carbohydrates: 28g | Sugar: 4g

FAJITA SOUP

Fajitas are made by marinating and grilling meats and vegetables, then slicing the meat and serving everything with lots of toppings on warmed tortillas. This soup uses the same ingredients, but in a different way. The meat and veggies cook in the slow cooker all day. The tortillas are cut into strips, then baked until crisp and used as a garnish.

SERVES 8

1½ pounds sirloin tip, cut into cubes

1 medium onion, chopped

3 cloves garlic, minced

1 jalapeño pepper, minced

1 medium red bell pepper, chopped

1 medium yellow bell pepper, chopped

1 tablespoon chili powder

1 teaspoon smoked paprika

½ teaspoon ground cumin

½ teaspoon dried oregano leaves

⅛ teaspoon crushed red pepper flakes

⅛ teaspoon black pepper

1 (14-ounce) can no-salt-added diced tomatoes, undrained

3 cups Beef Stock (see recipe in this chapter)

1 cup water

3 corn tortillas, sliced

1 tablespoon olive oil

1 cup sour cream

¼ cup chopped fresh cilantro

1. Combine beef, onion, garlic, jalapeño, and bell peppers in 4-quart slow cooker and mix.

2. Add chili powder, paprika, cumin, oregano, red pepper flakes, and pepper and mix. Add tomatoes, beef stock, and water.

3. Cover and cook on low for 6–8 hours or until vegetables are tender.

4. Meanwhile, preheat oven to 400°F. Place sliced tortillas on a baking sheet and drizzle with olive oil. Bake for 8–13 minutes, turning once, until crisp and slightly browned. Remove from oven and cool on paper towels. Serve with the soup along with sour cream and cilantro.

PER SERVING: Calories: 245 | Total Fat: 12g | Saturated Fat: 5g | Cholesterol: 46mg | Protein: 22g | Sodium: 115mg | Potassium: 663mg | Fiber: 2g | Carbohydrates: 12g | Sugar: 3g

MUSHROOM AND BARLEY SOUP

Barley is a delicious chewy and nutty grain that is packed with fiber and nutrients. It contains a lot of insoluble fiber, which can lower cholesterol. Buy pearl barley, which has had the outer bran layer removed so it will cook evenly and more quickly.

SERVES 4

1 ounce dried porcini mushrooms

½ cup warm water

1 tablespoon unsalted butter

1 tablespoon olive oil

1 medium onion, chopped

3 cloves garlic, minced

1 (8-ounce) package cremini mushrooms, sliced

1 (8-ounce) package shiitake mushrooms, sliced

½ cup Duxelles (Chapter 4)

3 cups Beef Stock (see recipe in this chapter)

½ cup pearl barley

½ teaspoon dried oregano leaves

⅛ teaspoon pepper

1. In small bowl, combine dried mushrooms and water; let soak for 20 minutes. Drain mushrooms, reserving soaking water. Strain the soaking water. Coarsely chop the mushrooms.

2. In large pot, combine butter with olive oil over medium heat. Add the onion and garlic; cook and stir for 5 minutes.

3. Add the cremini mushrooms; cook and stir for another 5 minutes. Add shiitake mushrooms, dried mushrooms, reserved mushroom soaking liquid, duxelles, and the stock. Bring to a simmer; reduce heat and simmer for 10 minutes.

4. Add the barley, oregano, and pepper; bring to a simmer again. Partially cover pot, reduce heat to low, and simmer for 40–50 minutes or until the barley is tender.

PER SERVING: Calories: 383 | Total Fat: 22g | Saturated Fat: 9g | Cholesterol: 38mg | Protein: 14g | Sodium: 89mg | Potassium: 1,668mg | Fiber: 5g | Carbohydrates: 36g | Sugar: 6g

POTATO AND CARAMELIZED ONION SOUP

Potato soup is probably one of the most inexpensive recipes you can make. It is rich and filling and delicious served on a cold winter day. Without salt, this soup can be bland, but adding caramelized onions and garlic and lots of spices will pep things up.

SERVES 6

2 tablespoons olive oil

1 tablespoon unsalted butter

1 leek, chopped

4 cloves garlic, minced

5 large Yukon gold potatoes, peeled and diced

2 teaspoons chili powder

1 teaspoon smoked paprika

½ teaspoon ground cumin

½ teaspoon dried oregano leaves

¼ teaspoon white pepper

4 cups Chicken Stock (see recipe in this chapter)

1 cup Slow Cooker Caramelized Onions (Chapter 4)

2 cups frozen corn

1 cup whole milk or light cream

1. In large pot, heat oil and butter over medium heat. Add leek and garlic; cook and stir for 5 minutes.

2. Add potatoes, chili powder, paprika, cumin, oregano, and pepper; cook and stir for 4 minutes longer.

3. Add stock and bring to a simmer. Reduce heat to low, partially cover pot, and simmer for 12–15 minutes or until potatoes are tender.

4. Partially mash some of the potatoes using a potato masher or immersion blender.

5. Add onions and corn and bring to a simmer; simmer for 5 minutes. Stir in milk or cream and heat just to boiling, then serve.

PER SERVING: Calories: 291 | Total Fat: 12g | Saturated Fat: 3g | Cholesterol: 9mg | Protein: 8g | Sodium: 85mg | Potassium: 713mg | Fiber: 4g | Carbohydrates: 40g | Sugar: 8g

SHORT RIB CHILI

Beef short ribs are an excellent cut of meat to cook in the slow cooker. They add the most wonderful rich and intense flavor to this spicy chili recipe. You can buy short ribs either bone-in or boneless. The boneless ribs are easier to work with, but bone-in ribs offer more flavor. Since we aren't adding salt, bone-in is the way to go.

SERVES 6

3½ pounds bone-in beef short ribs

¼ cup flour

1 tablespoon chili powder

¼ teaspoon black pepper

2 tablespoons olive oil

2 medium onions, chopped

½ cup brewed coffee

2 medium red bell peppers, chopped

6 cloves garlic, minced

2 jalapeño peppers, minced

3 dried red chili peppers, crushed

1 bay leaf

1 teaspoon ground cumin

1 teaspoon dried oregano

3 cups Beef Stock (see recipe in this chapter)

1 (6-ounce) can no-salt-added tomato paste

1 (12-ounce) bottle beer

1 cup water

2 (15-ounce) cans no-salt-added black beans, rinsed and drained

1. Sprinkle ribs with flour, chili powder, and pepper. In large skillet, heat olive oil over medium heat. Add ribs; brown well on all sides, about 10 minutes total. Remove to 5-quart slow cooker.

2. Add onions to skillet; cook for 5 minutes, stirring to remove pan drippings. Add coffee; boil for 1 minute, then add to the slow cooker.

3. Add bell peppers, garlic, jalapeños, chili peppers, bay leaf, cumin, oregano, beef stock, tomato paste, beer, water, and beans to slow cooker and stir.

4. Cover and cook on low for 8–9 hours or until ribs are very tender.

5. Remove ribs from slow cooker. Remove meat from bones and add meat to slow cooker. Discard bones. Remove and discard bay leaf, stir, and serve chili.

PER SERVING: Calories: 413 | Total Fat: 14g | Saturated Fat: 4g | Cholesterol: 50mg | Protein: 30g | Sodium: 121mg | Potassium: 1,193mg | Fiber: 12g | Carbohydrates: 40g | Sugar: 4g

SUCCOTASH CHICKEN SOUP

Succotash is a summer garden staple made from lima beans and corn simmered together. You can make this soup in the winter with frozen corn. Serve with Garlic Toast (Chapter 6) and a green salad tossed with shredded carrots and mushrooms.

SERVES 6

4 ears fresh corn

3 (6-ounce) boneless, skinless chicken breasts, cut into strips

2 tablespoons flour

2 tablespoons olive oil

1 medium onion, chopped

2 cloves garlic, minced

1 tablespoon minced fresh ginger root

1 (14-ounce) package frozen baby lima beans

3 cups Chicken Stock (see recipe in this chapter)

1/8 teaspoon white pepper

3 tablespoons chopped fresh flat-leaf parsley

1. Cut the corn off the cob and reserve. Scrape the cobs with the back of a knife to remove milk and reserve. Sprinkle the chicken with flour.

2. In large pot, heat olive oil over medium heat. Add chicken to pot; cook and stir for 3 minutes.

3. Add onion, garlic, and ginger root; cook and stir for 3 minutes longer. Add corn, any liquid from the cobs, lima beans, chicken stock, and pepper to the pot.

4. Bring soup to a simmer, then reduce heat to low and simmer for 10 minutes or until chicken is tender. Sprinkle with parsley and serve.

PER SERVING: Calories: 328 | Total Fat: 8g | Saturated Fat: 1g | Cholesterol: 73mg | Protein: 36g | Sodium: 119mg | Potassium: 660mg | Fiber: 5g | Carbohydrates: 27g | Sugar: 2g

MINESTRONE

Minestrone is a rich and thick vegetable soup from Italy. It is usually made with pancetta, which is a cured but unsmoked type of Italian bacon that is very high in sodium. This version has veggies, beans, and pasta for a satisfying recipe. Add your favorite vegetables to make your own delicious version.

SERVES 6

2 tablespoons olive oil

1 medium onion, chopped

4 cloves garlic, minced

1 (8-ounce) package cremini mushrooms, sliced

3 stalks celery, sliced

¼ pound green beans, cut into 2" pieces

3 tablespoons no-salt-added tomato paste

1 (14-ounce) can no-salt-added diced tomatoes, undrained

1 (14-ounce) can no-salt-added kidney beans, rinsed and drained

1 (14-ounce) can no-salt-added navy beans, rinsed and drained

1 (14-ounce) can no-salt-added black beans, rinsed and drained

1 teaspoon dried oregano

1 teaspoon dried basil

¼ teaspoon pepper

5 cups Vegetable Broth (see recipe in this chapter)

½ cup small shell pasta

2 cups baby spinach leaves

¼ cup grated Parmesan cheese

1. In large pot, heat olive oil over medium heat. Add onion; cook and stir for 5 minutes or until crisp-tender.

2. Add garlic, mushrooms, and celery; cook and stir for another 3 minutes. Add green beans; cook and stir for 3 minutes longer. Add tomato paste; let paste brown in a few spots, then stir.

3. Add tomatoes, kidney beans, navy beans, black beans, oregano, basil, pepper, and broth. Bring to a simmer. Reduce heat and simmer for 30–40 minutes or until vegetables are tender.

4. Add pasta; simmer for 10–15 minutes or until the pasta is tender. Add spinach leaves and cook until wilted. Serve with Parmesan cheese sprinkled on top.

PER SERVING: Calories: 327 | Total Fat: 6g | Saturated Fat: 1g | Cholesterol: 2mg | Protein: 20g | Sodium: 135mg | Potassium: 1,218mg | Fiber: 13g | Carbohydrates: 50g | Sugar: 3g

SPICY FISH SOUP

The best types of fish for soup are firm fillets, such as cod, grouper, or halibut. Fish fillets cook in 10 minutes per inch of thickness, so they are added at the end of cooking time. Serve this soup with a cooling cucumber salad, some Roasted Garlic Crackers (Chapter 6), and a glass of white wine.

SERVES 4

1 tablespoon olive oil

1 tablespoon unsalted butter

1 leek, chopped

2 cloves garlic, minced

1 jalapeño pepper, minced

2 stalks celery, sliced

1 cup sliced button mushrooms

2 medium carrots, sliced

2 tablespoons no-salt-added tomato paste

1 (14-ounce) can no-salt-added diced tomatoes, undrained

3 cups Fish Stock (see recipe in this chapter)

½ teaspoon grated orange zest

1 teaspoon chili powder

1 teaspoon smoked paprika

⅛ teaspoon crushed red pepper flakes

1 pound firm white fish fillets, cubed

2 tablespoons chopped flat-leaf parsley

1. In large pot, heat olive oil and butter over medium heat. Add leek; cook and stir until crisp-tender, about 5 minutes.

2. Add garlic, jalapeño pepper, celery, mushrooms, and carrots. Cook and stir for 3 minutes longer.

3. Add tomato paste; let the paste brown in a few spots, then stir. Add tomatoes, fish stock, orange zest, chili powder, paprika, and red pepper flakes. Bring to a simmer, then reduce heat and simmer for 15 minutes.

4. Add fish fillets; simmer for 5–7 minutes longer or until fish is cooked and firm. Sprinkle with parsley and serve.

PER SERVING: Calories: 163 | Total Fat: 5g | Saturated Fat: 1g | Cholesterol: 37mg | Protein: 17g | Sodium: 131mg | Potassium: 823mg | Fiber: 2g | Carbohydrates: 11g | Sugar: 4g

SALMON CHOWDER

Salmon chowder is rich and thick and fragrant with lots of vegetables. Mushrooms, onions, fennel, and potatoes add flavor and texture to the soup. Just a bit of cheese is stirred in at the end for flavor. Fresh salmon fillets are crucial to the taste of this recipe; don't substitute canned salmon.

SERVES 10

2 tablespoons unsalted butter

1 medium onion, chopped

1 fennel bulb, thinly sliced

2 cloves garlic, minced

2 stalks celery, sliced

1 cup sliced mushrooms

2 Yukon gold potatoes, peeled and cubed

4 cups Fish Stock (see recipe in this chapter)

1 teaspoon dill seed

⅛ teaspoon pepper

2 cups frozen corn, thawed

4 (6-ounce) boneless, skinless salmon fillets, cubed

1 cup light cream

½ cup shredded Havarti cheese

2 tablespoons grated Parmesan cheese

¼ cup chopped fresh dill

1. In large pot, melt butter over medium heat. Add onion, fennel, garlic, celery, mushrooms, and potatoes; cook and stir for 7–9 minutes or until vegetables are almost tender.

2. Add fish stock, dill seed, and pepper and bring to a simmer. Simmer for 15 minutes or until vegetables are tender.

3. Add corn and salmon; bring to a simmer. Simmer for 5–6 minutes or until salmon is cooked through.

4. Stir in cream, Havarti, and Parmesan. Heat through, but do not boil. Garnish with fresh dill and serve immediately.

PER SERVING: Calories: 320 | Total Fat: 19g | Saturated Fat: 9g | Cholesterol: 73mg | Protein: 20g | Sodium: 129mg | Potassium: 693mg | Fiber: 2g | Carbohydrates: 17g | Sugar: 1g

CARIBBEAN-SEASONED PURÉED VEGETABLE SOUP

Many health food stores carry fresh-ground peanut butter. Once you taste peanut butter made fresh from dry-roasted nuts, you won't miss the salt, sugar, and other extra stuff that is added to commercial brands.

SERVES 6

1 tablespoon canola or grapeseed oil

1 large sweet onion, diced

2 cloves garlic, minced

1 large stalk celery, diced

½ teaspoon dried ginger

¼ teaspoon ground mustard

⅛ teaspoon ground allspice

½ teaspoon hot paprika

¼ teaspoon dried thyme

⅛ teaspoon fennel seed, crushed

⅛ teaspoon dried ground cloves

¼ teaspoon cayenne

¼ teaspoon freshly ground black pepper

4 medium carrots, peeled and diced

3 large potatoes, peeled and diced

1 medium-size sweet potato, peeled and diced

2 leeks, white parts only, washed well and diced

2 teaspoons low-sodium chicken base

4 cups water

½ cup smooth no-salt-added peanut butter

½ cup tahini

Optional: Minced fresh parsley, for garnish

Optional: Dried red pepper flakes, for garnish

Optional: Chopped scallions, for garnish

1. In a large saucepan, heat the oil and sauté the onion, garlic, and celery, stirring until the onions are transparent.

2. Add the spices and sauté for 1 minute.

3. Add the carrots, potatoes, leeks, chicken base, and water. Bring the soup to a boil; reduce the heat, cover, and simmer until the vegetables are tender, about 25 minutes.

4. Use a hand blender to stir in the peanut butter and tahini and to purée the vegetables. (Alternatively, transfer the soup to a blender or food processor to purée it.) Garnish with the optional ingredients, if desired, and serve.

PER SERVING: Calories: 372 | Total Fat: 24g | Saturated Fat: 3g | Cholesterol: 0mg | Protein: 11g | Sodium: 140mg | Potassium: 715mg | Fiber: 6g | Carbohydrates: 33g | Sugar: 8g

PUMPKIN AND GINGER SOUP

A tablespoon of dry white wine or vermouth per serving is an excellent, low-sodium way to punch up the flavor of soup. Just be sure to add it to the soup during the cooking process to allow enough time for the alcohol to evaporate.

SERVES 4

1 tablespoon canola or grapeseed oil

1 medium-size sweet onion, sliced

1 large stalk celery, sliced

2 bay leaves

¼ teaspoon dried thyme

¼ teaspoon dried oregano

4 medium carrots, sliced

2 cups pumpkin, cut into 1" cubes

3 tablespoons minced fresh ginger

4 cups water

Optional: ½ teaspoon cinnamon

Optional: Pinch each of ground cloves, allspice, and mace

Optional: Freshly ground black pepper, to taste

1. In a large saucepan, heat the oil and sauté the onion and celery, stirring until the onions are transparent.

2. Add the bay leaves, thyme, oregano, carrots, pumpkin, ginger, and water; bring to a boil. Reduce heat, cover, and simmer until the vegetables are tender, about 25 minutes.

3. Remove and discard the bay leaves. Use a hand blender to purée the soup. (Alternatively, transfer the soup to a blender or food processor to purée it.) Serve warm, sprinkled with cinnamon, spices, and freshly ground black pepper, if desired.

PER SERVING: Calories: 118 | Total Fat: 3g | Saturated Fat: 0g | Cholesterol: 0mg | Protein: 2g | Sodium: 75mg | Potassium: 676mg | Fiber: 4g | Carbohydrates: 20g | Sugar: 9g

GARLIC BROTH

A great way to store this and your other homemade stocks and broths is to make broth cubes. Most ice cube sections hold 2 tablespoons of liquid per cube, so 8 broth cubes will equal 1 cup of broth.

SERVES 8

9 cups water

4 cloves garlic, crushed

2 medium carrots, peeled and chopped

2 stalks celery, chopped

1 small sweet onion, quartered

5 black peppercorns

1 bay leaf

1. In a stockpot, bring the water to a boil. Add the remaining ingredients. Reduce the heat, cover, and simmer for 1 hour.

2. Pour the resulting stock through a strainer, pressing as much liquid as possible from the cooked vegetables; discard vegetables.

3. Cool the stock and refrigerate until needed, up to 3 days. Alternatively, freeze the broth in 1-cup portions so it's easily available to add to recipes.

PER SERVING: Calories: 4 | Total Fat: 0g | Saturated Fat: 0g | Cholesterol: 0mg | Protein: 0g | Sodium: 0mg | Potassium: 0mg | Fiber: 0g | Carbohydrates: 1g | Sugar: 0g

CHILLED CUCUMBER SOUP

Take a break from the traditional cold soup, gazpacho, and try this cool and refreshing cucumber soup. Its beautiful green hue will remind you of summer!

SERVES 4

2 large cucumbers, peeled, seeded, and chopped

1 tablespoon frozen apple juice concentrate

1 tablespoon red wine vinegar

1½ cups cold, cultured low-fat buttermilk

Optional: Dried dill weed

Optional: Lemon zest

1. Place the cucumbers, apple juice concentrate, and vinegar in a food processor. Process briefly, then add the buttermilk and process again until smooth.

2. Cover and refrigerate until ready to serve. Serve chilled with a pinch of dried dill weed and some lemon zest floating on top of each serving, if desired.

PER SERVING: Calories: 74 | Total Fat: 2g | Saturated Fat: 1g | Cholesterol: 7mg | Protein: 4g | Sodium: 82mg | Potassium: 372mg | Fiber: 0g | Carbohydrates: 9g | Sugar: 8g

RICH BLACK BEAN SOUP

If desired, serve peanut or almond butter at the table for those who want to have it with their soup. It adds delicious flavor and a creamy texture to this hearty dish.

SERVES 4

1 teaspoon peanut or canola oil

1 small sweet onion, minced

1 large green bell pepper, cored and diced

2 cloves garlic, minced

¼ teaspoon freshly ground black pepper

¼ teaspoon dried ground ancho pepper (or salt-free chili powder)

⅛ teaspoon ground cumin

⅛ teaspoon cinnamon

2 teaspoons unsweetened cocoa powder

1 tablespoon pepper jelly

1 cup water

1 (15-ounce) can no-salt-added black beans, rinsed and drained

4 teaspoons red wine vinegar

4 teaspoons extra-virgin olive oil

1. In a large, deep nonstick sauté pan, heat the oil over medium heat. Add the onion and green pepper; sauté until tender, about 5–7 minutes.

2. Add the garlic, black pepper, ancho pepper or chili powder, cumin, cinnamon, and cocoa; stir well, slightly sautéing the spices. Stir in the pepper jelly until dissolved.

3. Add the water and black beans. Heat over medium-low heat until steaming. Just prior to serving, add the red wine vinegar and olive oil, and stir well.

4. Divide into serving bowls and serve warm.

PER SERVING: Calories: 220 | Total Fat: 6g | Saturated Fat: 0g | Cholesterol: 0mg | Protein: 10g | Sodium: 5mg | Potassium: 492mg | Fiber: 10g | Carbohydrates: 32g | Sugar: 3g

HERB BROTH

Pouring boiling water over the dried herbs (see Step 2) releases the flavors more effectively than does bringing them to a boil in cold water.

SERVES 8

¼ cup dried thyme

¼ cup dried parsley

¼ cup dried minced onion

2 tablespoons dried oregano

20 black peppercorns

8 bay leaves

1 teaspoon dried lavender

Optional: 1 teaspoon dried lemon zest

9 cups boiling water

1. Place all the ingredients *except* the water in a stockpot. Bring the water to a boil in a separate pot.

2. Pour at least 2 cups of boiling water over the dried ingredients in the stockpot. Let sit for a few minutes. Add the remaining water to the stockpot and bring to a boil; reduce heat and simmer, uncovered, for 1 hour.

3. Pour the broth through a fine-mesh strainer. Add additional water, if necessary, to yield a total of 8 cups of broth. Refrigerate until needed, up to 3 days. You can also freeze the broth in 1-cup portions so it's easily available to add to recipes.

PER SERVING: Calories: 0 | Total Fat: 0g | Saturated Fat: 0g | Cholesterol: 0mg | Protein: 0g | Sodium: 0mg | Potassium: 0mg | Fiber: 0g | Carbohydrates: 0g | Sugar: 0g

ISLANDS CAULIFLOWER SOUP

This sublime soup offers the taste of paradise in just mere minutes. Now you can enjoy a warm lunch on the go.

SERVES 1

½ teaspoon low-sodium chicken base

½ cup boiling water

½ teaspoon Caribbean Spice Blend (Appendix A)

⅛ teaspoon freshly ground white or black pepper

1 cup diced (unseasoned) steamed cauliflower

1 tablespoon freeze-dried green onion

1. Prepare a 10-ounce, wide-mouth thermos by filling it with hot water.

2. Drain the hot water from the thermos and discard. In a medium bowl, stir the chicken base into the boiling water. Add the remaining ingredients and mix well. Pour the soup into the thermos and seal the lid.

3. At lunch, either stir the soup or shake the thermos a few times to combine the ingredients.

PER SERVING: Calories: 55 | Total Fat: 0g | Saturated Fat: 0g | Cholesterol: 0mg | Protein: 2g | Sodium: 108mg | Potassium: 257mg | Fiber: 3g | Carbohydrates: 9g | Sugar: 4g

BROCCOLI AND ROASTED POTATO SOUP

Who says you can't have a warm and satisfying lunch when you are on the run? This creamy concoction of potatoes and broccoli comes together in minutes and will warm you inside and out.

SERVES 1

3 potato wedges from Oven-Fried Potato Wedges (Chapter 13), chopped

½ cup boiling water

½ cup chopped (unseasoned) steamed broccoli florets

½ teaspoon low-sodium chicken base

Optional: Country Table Spice Blend (Appendix A), to taste

1. Prepare a 10-ounce, wide-mouth thermos by filling it with hot water.

2. Add the potatoes and broccoli to a microwave-safe bowl; cover and microwave on high until heated through. Drain the hot water from the thermos and discard. Put the heated potatoes and broccoli in the thermos.

3. Stir the chicken base into the boiling water; pour over the ingredients in the thermos, stir, and season to taste with the spice blend, if desired. Seal the lid. At lunch, either stir the soup or shake the thermos a few times to combine the ingredients.

PER SERVING: Calories: 171 | Total Fat: 0g | Saturated Fat: 0g | Cholesterol: 0mg | Protein: 6g | Sodium: 119mg | Potassium: 955mg | Fiber: 6g | Carbohydrates: 37g | Sugar: 2g

CHAPTER 6

SNACKS AND APPETIZERS

ROASTED GARLIC GUACAMOLE

Ripe avocados are sometimes difficult to find in the grocery store. Look for heavy avocados with smooth skin and no soft spots. Place them together in a bag on the kitchen counter for 1–3 days. When they yield to gentle pressure, they're ready. Lemon juice and roasted garlic eliminate the need for salt in this easy recipe.

SERVES 8

1 head Roasted Garlic (Chapter 4)

3 ripe avocados, halved and pitted

3 tablespoons lemon juice

⅛ teaspoon crushed red pepper flakes

1. Squeeze the cloves of garlic out of the papery husks and combine in medium bowl with avocados, lemon juice, and red pepper flakes.

2. Using a fork or a potato masher, mash the ingredients together until desired consistency. You can make the guacamole smooth or leave some chunks for more texture. Serve with baby carrots, unsalted tortilla chips, and celery sticks.

PER SERVING: Calories: 134 | Total Fat: 11g | Saturated Fat: 1g | Cholesterol: 0mg | Protein: 2g | Sodium: 6mg | Potassium: 406mg | Fiber: 5g | Carbohydrates: 9g | Sugar: 0g

CUCUMBER ROUNDS WITH SALSA

For this recipe, look for "seedless" English cucumbers that are unwaxed so you can serve them unpeeled. These cucumbers do have seeds, but they are very small and not bitter.

SERVES 8

1 English cucumber

2 cups Peach Raspberry Salsa (see recipe in this chapter)

Wash the cucumber and pat dry. Slice into ¼"-thick rounds. Top each round with about 2 teaspoons of the salsa. Serve immediately or cover and chill up to 2 hours before serving.

PER SERVING: Calories: 106 | Total Fat: 0g | Saturated Fat: 0g | Cholesterol: 0mg | Protein: 1g | Sodium: 5mg | Potassium: 276mg | Fiber: 3g | Carbohydrates: 26g | Sugar: 19g

BAKED POTATO CHIPS

The only trick with this recipe is to make sure that the potatoes are sliced very thinly and that they are dry before they go into the oven. You can use a mandoline to slice the potatoes, but an ordinary swivel-bladed vegetable peeler works quite well.

YIELDS 4 CUPS; SERVES 4–6

1 large russet potato, peeled if desired

2 tablespoons olive oil

⅛ teaspoon white pepper

½ teaspoon dried thyme or basil leaves

½ teaspoon paprika

1. Preheat oven to 400°F. Line two large baking sheets with sides with parchment paper and set aside.

2. Cut the potato into thin slices, crosswise, using a mandoline or a vegetable peeler. Place on paper towels and pat to remove moisture.

3. Arrange in a single layer on the prepared baking sheets. Brush with oil.

4. Bake for 12–17 minutes or until potatoes are golden and look like potato chips! Remove from oven and sprinkle with pepper, thyme, and paprika while hot. Cool and store in airtight container at room temperature up to 2 days.

PER SERVING (4 servings): Calories: 132 | Total Fat: 6g | Saturated Fat: 0g | Cholesterol: 0mg | Protein: 1g | Sodium: 10mg | Potassium: 417mg | Fiber: 1g | Carbohydrates: 16g | Sugar: 0g

CURRIED CHICKEN DIP

Curry powder is made of many different spices, including cinnamon, turmeric, peppers, cardamom, nutmeg, garlic, ginger, caraway, clove, and mustard seed. In India, every family has its own special blend. You can make your own or buy a good-quality brand for this recipe. Just make sure it's low in sodium!

YIELDS 2 CUPS; SERVING SIZE 2 TABLESPOONS

2 tablespoons olive oil

2 (6-ounce) boneless, skinless chicken breasts

½ cup Slow Cooker Caramelized Onions (Chapter 4)

1 tablespoon curry powder

4 ounces cream cheese, softened

⅔ cup sour cream

⅓ cup mascarpone cheese

2 tablespoons orange juice

½ cup finely chopped celery

1. Heat olive oil in medium pan over medium heat. Add chicken and cook, turning once, until thoroughly cooked to 160°F. Remove chicken from pan and let cool; cut into small pieces. Combine in medium bowl with caramelized onions and the curry powder.

2. In large bowl, beat cream cheese until smooth. Add sour cream and mascarpone cheese, beating well. Beat in orange juice and celery.

3. Stir chicken mixture into the cream-cheese mixture until combined. Cover and refrigerate for 1–2 hours to blend flavors before serving.

PER SERVING: Calories: 114 | Total Fat: 8g | Saturated Fat: 3g | Cholesterol: 33mg | Protein: 8g | Sodium: 53mg | Potassium: 111mg | Fiber: 0g | Carbohydrates: 2g | Sugar: 1g

CARAMELIZED ONION AND GARLIC DIP

This dip is far superior to any boxed mix you may have had in the past, and much lower in sodium. Caramelized onions are a cook's best friend; they can be used in so many ways. Adding some caramelized garlic to this recipe takes it to the next level.

YIELDS 2 CUPS; SERVING SIZE 2 TABLESPOONS

2 medium onions, chopped

2 tablespoons olive oil

1 tablespoon unsalted butter

5 cloves garlic, sliced

1 tablespoon brown sugar

1 tablespoon honey

3 ounces cream cheese, softened

½ cup sour cream

½ cup Mayonnaise (Chapter 4)

½ teaspoon dried thyme leaves

2 tablespoons chopped fresh parsley

1. In large saucepan, combine onions, olive oil, and unsalted butter over medium heat. Cook until the onions start to simmer, then turn heat to low and cook until onions are gold, about 15 minutes.

2. Add the garlic and cook, stirring frequently, until the garlic and onions are deep golden brown. Do not let the mixture burn. Add the brown sugar and honey and cook for another 4 minutes, stirring constantly. Remove from heat and let cool.

3. In medium bowl beat the cream cheese until smooth. Add sour cream, mayonnaise, thyme, and parsley. Stir in the onion-and-garlic mixture. Cover and refrigerate for 1–2 hours to let flavors blend. Serve with baked potato chips, baby carrots, zucchini slices, and celery sticks.

PER SERVING: Calories: 119 | Total Fat: 12g | Saturated Fat: 3g | Cholesterol: 20mg | Protein: 0g | Sodium: 24mg | Potassium: 33mg | Fiber: 0g | Carbohydrates: 2g | Sugar: 2g

AVOCADO DEVILED EGGS

Eggs used to be forbidden in a healthy diet; most recommendations were to eat two eggs a week. But the government agencies that issue these recommendations have withdrawn their warnings about dietary cholesterol. So go ahead and eat eggs—but in moderation.

SERVES 12

6 Hard-Cooked Eggs (Chapter 1)

1 medium ripe avocado

1 tablespoon chopped fresh chives

2 tablespoons Mayonnaise (Chapter 4)

1 tablespoon Grainy Mustard (Chapter 4)

1 tablespoon lemon juice

⅛ teaspoon crushed red pepper flakes

⅛ teaspoon white pepper

1. Peel the eggs and slice them in half lengthwise. Carefully remove the yolks; set the whites aside.

2. Place the yolks in a medium bowl and mash them with a potato masher. Add the avocado and mash until the mixture is smooth. Beat in the chives, mayonnaise, mustard, lemon juice, red pepper flakes, and white pepper and beat for 3 minutes until the mixture is very smooth.

3. Spoon or pipe the egg-yolk mixture back into the egg whites. Cover and refrigerate for 1–2 hours before serving.

PER SERVING: Calories: 89 | Total Fat: 7g | Saturated Fat: 1g | Cholesterol: 109mg | Protein: 3g | Sodium: 32mg | Potassium: 119mg | Fiber: 1g | Carbohydrates: 2g | Sugar: 0g

GARLIC BREAD

This recipe is special because it uses garlic cooked two ways. Use either homemade French Bread (Chapter 2) or Sourdough Bread (Chapter 2), because purchased bread is usually very high in sodium.

SERVES 6–8

1 head Roasted Garlic (Chapter 4)

⅓ cup unsalted butter, softened

2 tablespoons extra-virgin olive oil

2 cloves garlic, minced

1 teaspoon grated lemon zest

⅛ teaspoon white pepper

1 loaf French Bread (Chapter 2), split lengthwise

1. Remove roasted garlic from skins and mash. Add butter and olive oil and mix well.

2. Stir in minced garlic, lemon zest, and pepper and mix well. Spread on cut sides of French Bread.

3. Preheat broiler. Place bread on broiler pan, cut-side up, and broil until light golden brown and fragrant. Cut into pieces and serve immediately.

PER SERVING: Calories: 188 | Total Fat: 11g | Saturated Fat: 5g | Cholesterol: 20mg | Protein: 3g | Sodium: 27mg | Potassium: 67mg | Fiber: 0g | Carbohydrates: 18g | Sugar: 0g

CREAMY BROCCOLI DIP

Serve this dip with Baked Potato Chips (see recipe in this chapter), carrot and celery sticks, jicama slices, and toasted French bread slices for a great start to dinner.

YIELDS 2½ CUPS; SERVING SIZE 2 TABLESPOONS

1 tablespoon unsalted butter

1 medium onion, chopped

3 cloves garlic, minced

2 cups frozen broccoli florets, chopped

3 ounces cream cheese, softened

½ cup Mayonnaise (Chapter 4)

½ cup sour cream

¼ cup Greek yogurt

⅓ cup crumbled soft goat cheese

2 tablespoons lemon juice

2 tablespoons chopped fresh dill weed

⅛ teaspoon pepper

1. Preheat oven to 350°F. Spray a 1-quart casserole dish with cooking spray and set aside.

2. In medium saucepan, melt butter over medium heat. Add onion and garlic; cook and stir until vegetables start to turn golden, about 6–7 minutes. Add broccoli and cook for another 2–3 minutes. Remove from heat.

3. In large bowl, beat cream cheese until smooth. Beat in mayonnaise, sour cream, and yogurt until blended. Stir in goat cheese, lemon juice, dill, and pepper. Add the broccoli mixture.

4. Pour into prepared casserole dish. Bake for 20–25 minutes or until dip is bubbling around the edges and top begins to brown. Serve with crudités.

PER SERVING: Calories: 100 | Total Fat: 9g | Saturated Fat: 3g | Cholesterol: 19mg | Protein: 2g | Sodium: 44mg | Potassium: 53mg | Fiber: 0g | Carbohydrates: 1g | Sugar: 0g

LOADED POTATO SKINS

Bacon and cheese and lots of salt are usually used to prepare this recipe. But you can make a flavorful appetizer without much sodium! Just omit the bacon and cheese and add other ingredients such as onion, garlic, jalapeño peppers, horseradish, and sour cream.

SERVES 12

6 russet potatoes

3 tablespoons unsalted butter

1 medium onion, chopped

4 cloves garlic, minced

1 jalapeño pepper, minced

1 medium red bell pepper, chopped

⅔ cup sour cream

3 tablespoons Mustard (Chapter 4)

2 tablespoons horseradish

1 tablespoon lemon juice

¼ teaspoon black pepper

1. Preheat oven to 400°F. Scrub and dry the potatoes and prick each several times with a fork. Place directly on the oven rack and bake for 45–50 minutes or until potatoes are tender when gently squeezed. Remove to wire rack and cool for 30 minutes.

2. Meanwhile, melt butter in large saucepan over medium heat. Add onion and garlic; cook and stir for 6–7 minutes or until vegetables start to turn golden. Add jalapeño pepper and red bell pepper; cook and stir for another 3 minutes. Remove from heat and place in medium bowl; let cool 20 minutes.

3. Stir sour cream, mustard, horseradish, lemon juice, and black pepper into onion mixture.

4. Cut each potato in half lengthwise, then scoop out most of the flesh; reserve for another use. Cut each potato half in half again so you have 24 pieces. Arrange on a broiler pan.

5. Turn oven to broil. Top each potato slice with some of the sour-cream mixture. Broil 6" from the heat for 4–5 minutes or until mixture starts to brown. Serve immediately.

PER SERVING: Calories: 221 | Total Fat: 6g | Saturated Fat: 3g | Cholesterol: 14mg | Protein: 5g | Sodium: 40mg | Potassium: 912mg | Fiber: 4g | Carbohydrates: 35g | Sugar: 3g

HUMMUS

Hummus is a Greek spread or appetizer dip made with puréed chickpeas, also called garbanzo beans, and tahini, or sesame paste. You can find no-salt-added varieties of canned chickpeas that are worth looking for.

YIELDS 1 CUP; SERVING SIZE 2 TABLESPOONS

1 (16-ounce) can no-salt-added chickpeas, drained and rinsed

1 head Roasted Garlic (Chapter 4), cloves removed from skins

3 tablespoons tahini (sesame paste)

3 tablespoons lemon juice

½ teaspoon grated lemon zest

½ teaspoon dried thyme leaves

½ teaspoon dried oregano leaves

⅛ teaspoon white pepper

2 tablespoons water

3 tablespoons olive oil

2 tablespoons toasted sesame seeds

1. Combine chickpeas, garlic, tahini, lemon juice, zest, thyme, oregano, pepper, and water in blender or food processor; blend until desired consistency.

2. Scrape into serving bowl. Drizzle with olive oil and top with sesame seeds and serve immediately.

PER SERVING: Calories: 179 | Total Fat: 9g | Saturated Fat: 1g | Cholesterol: 0mg | Protein: 6g | Sodium: 11mg | Potassium: 220mg | Fiber: 4g | Carbohydrates: 19g | Sugar: 2g

ROASTED GARLIC CRACKERS

These crackers have an entire head of roasted garlic baked into the dough. And for even more flavor, chopped garlic is sprinkled on top halfway through the baking time, so it doesn't burn but toasts to a golden brown. Serve these with soup or a big salad, or with any appetizer dip recipe.

YIELDS 36 CRACKERS

1 head Roasted Garlic (Chapter 4)

½ cup unsalted butter, softened

1¼ cups flour

2 tablespoons sesame seeds

½ teaspoon dried thyme leaves

⅛ teaspoon white pepper

1 tablespoon cream, if needed

4 cloves garlic, minced

1. Remove the roasted garlic from the skin; discard skin. Place in food processor and add butter. Pulse until combined.

2. Add flour, sesame seeds, thyme, and pepper and pulse until a dough forms. You may need to add a little bit of cream or flour as needed for the dough to come together. Don't overwork.

3. Form dough into 2 logs and wrap in waxed paper. Refrigerate for 1–2 hours until dough is firm.

4. Preheat oven to 375°F. Cut the logs into ¼"-thick slices and place on parchment paper–lined cookie sheet. Bake for 10 minutes, then remove from oven and sprinkle with minced garlic. Bake for another 7–12 minutes or until the crackers are light golden brown and crisp. Cool completely on wire racks. Store in airtight containers at room temperature up to 5 days.

PER SERVING: Calories: 45 | Total Fat: 2g | Saturated Fat: 1g | Cholesterol: 7mg | Protein: 0g | Sodium: 1mg | Potassium: 18mg | Fiber: 0g | Carbohydrates: 4g | Sugar: 0g

STUFFED JALAPEÑOS

Most of the heat in these little peppers is contained in the seeds and the membranes. If you remove those, the recipe won't be quite as spicy. Serve these appetizers before a grilled meal or a meal of tacos and tostadas. For a cooling contrast, strawberry margaritas (with sugar instead of salt coating the rim) are a nice touch.

SERVES 8

8 small jalapeño peppers, cut in half

½ cup ricotta cheese

⅓ cup minced red bell pepper

2 tablespoons minced green onion

1 garlic clove, minced

1 tablespoon chopped fresh cilantro

1 tablespoon chopped fresh basil

1. Scrape seeds and membranes out of each jalapeño half if desired.

2. In small bowl, combine ricotta cheese, red bell pepper, green onion, garlic, cilantro, and basil and mix well. Stuff this mixture into the jalapeño peppers.

3. Cover and refrigerate for an hour or two before serving.

PER SERVING: Calories: 34 | Total Fat: 2g | Saturated Fat: 1g | Cholesterol: 7mg | Protein: 2g | Sodium: 13mg | Potassium: 68mg | Fiber: 0g | Carbohydrates: 1g | Sugar: 0g

PEACH RASPBERRY SALSA

Salsas can be made out of just about any fruit or vegetable, and they can be dressed up or down according to your taste. Use this recipe as a starting point to create your own custom blends. Make it as mild or spicy as you'd like by varying the number of chilies you use.

YIELDS 2 CUPS; SERVING SIZE ¼ CUP

4 medium peaches, peeled and chopped

3 tablespoons lemon juice

⅓ cup peach preserves

2 tablespoons honey

2 green onions, finely sliced

1 clove garlic, minced

1 jalapeño pepper, minced

2 cups fresh raspberries

1. In medium bowl, combine peaches with the lemon juice; toss to coat.

2. Add remaining ingredients except raspberries and stir gently to combine. Stir in raspberries, cover, and let stand for 10 minutes. Serve immediately or cover and refrigerate up to 1 day.

PER SERVING: Calories: 101 | Total Fat: 0g | Saturated Fat: 0g | Cholesterol: 0mg | Protein: 1g | Sodium: 4mg | Potassium: 221mg | Fiber: 3g | Carbohydrates: 25g | Sugar: 18g

CUCUMBER TOMATILLO SALSA

Use this as a topping for grilled fish or chicken, or as a dip with fresh vegetables or unsalted tortilla chips.

YIELDS 2 CUPS; SERVING SIZE 2 TABLESPOONS

1 pint tomatillos

1 large cucumber, peeled, seeded, and chopped

½ cup minced red onion

1 jalapeño pepper, minced

2 tablespoons lime juice

1 tablespoon honey or molasses

1 clove garlic, minced

2 tablespoons chopped flat-leaf parsley

2 tablespoons chopped fresh dill

1 teaspoon chopped fresh mint

½ teaspoon black pepper

⅛ teaspoon crushed red pepper flakes

1. Remove the husks from the tomatillos and rinse them thoroughly. Chop into ½" pieces.

2. Combine cucumber, tomatillos, red onion, and jalapeño pepper in a medium bowl and stir. Then add lime juice, honey, garlic, parsley, dill, mint, pepper, and red pepper flakes and stir gently.

3. Use immediately or cover and refrigerate up to 3 days.

PER SERVING: Calories: 10 | Total Fat: 0g | Saturated Fat: 0g | Cholesterol: 0mg | Protein: 0g | Sodium: 1mg | Potassium: 70mg | Fiber: 0g | Carbohydrates: 2g | Sugar: 1g

SPICY SALSA

The rule is: the smaller the pepper, the hotter it is. Remember that most of the capsaicin, the chemical that creates the burn in your mouth, is contained in the seeds and membranes. Remove those and the pepper will be much milder.

YIELDS 2 CUPS; SERVING SIZE ¼ CUP

4 large tomatoes, chopped

½ cup minced green bell pepper

½ cup minced red onion

1–3 jalapeño peppers, or hotter peppers such as Scotch bonnet, minced

2 cloves garlic, minced

2 tablespoons lemon juice

1 tablespoon lime juice

1 tablespoon sugar

2 tablespoons chopped cilantro or parsley

1 tablespoon chili powder

½ teaspoon cumin

⅛ teaspoon crushed red pepper flakes

⅛ teaspoon black pepper

Combine all ingredients in a medium bowl and mix gently. Cover and refrigerate up to 4 days.

PER SERVING: Calories: 27 | Total Fat: 0g | Saturated Fat: 0g | Cholesterol: 0mg | Protein: 0g | Sodium: 14mg | Potassium: 161mg | Fiber: 1g | Carbohydrates: 6g | Sugar: 4g

SPICY SNACK MIX

Most commercially made cereals have at least 200mg of sodium per cup. Nuts and popcorn come to the rescue! These snacks are high in protein and fiber, and low in sodium.

YIELDS 10 CUPS; 20 SERVINGS

4 cups unsalted dry-popped popcorn

2 cups unsalted dry-roasted peanuts

2 cups roasted unsalted cashews

1 cup roasted unsalted almonds

1 cup unsalted pretzel sticks

¼ cup unsalted butter

3 cloves garlic, minced

1 tablespoon chili powder

2 teaspoons Tabasco sauce

1 teaspoon dried oregano leaves

¼ teaspoon pepper

¼ teaspoon crushed red pepper flakes

1. Preheat oven to 350°F. Combine popcorn, peanuts, cashews, almonds, and pretzel sticks in a very large baking pan; toss to mix.

2. In small saucepan, melt butter over medium heat. Add garlic; cook for about 30 seconds until fragrant. Remove from heat and stir in chili powder, Tabasco sauce, oregano, pepper, and red pepper flakes.

3. Drizzle butter mixture over mixture in pan and stir to coat.

4. Bake, stirring every 10 minutes, for 40–50 minutes or until the mixture is crunchy and butter is absorbed. Cool, stirring occasionally, for 40–50 minutes. Store in airtight container at room temperature.

PER SERVING: Calories: 250 | Total Fat: 19g | Saturated Fat: 2g | Cholesterol: 5mg | Protein: 7g | Sodium: 41mg | Potassium: 245mg | Fiber: 2g | Carbohydrates: 14g | Sugar: 1g

STEAMER CLAMS IN GINGER SAUCE

Steamer clams are small clams with soft shells. They are meaty and tender and delicious. You can buy them canned; look online for best prices and availability. This easy recipe combines the clams with seasonings. Then you place a bit of the clam mixture on a crunchy cucumber and eat.

SERVES 7

2 teaspoons Bragg Liquid Aminos

1 teaspoon lemon juice

¼ cup thinly sliced spring onions

1 teaspoon white rice wine vinegar

4 teaspoons apple juice

1 teaspoon ground ginger

¼ teaspoon Oriental mustard powder

4 cloves garlic, minced, or 1 teaspoon garlic powder

1 teaspoon dried green onion flakes

¼ teaspoon granulated sugar

1 (15-ounce) can steamer cocktail clams, drained

1 large cucumber

1. In a bowl, combine all ingredients except the steamer clams and cucumber and mix thoroughly.

2. Add the drained clams and toss to mix.

3. Wash and slice the cucumber. Arrange the cucumber slices on a platter and divide the clam mixture among the slices, using a small spoonful for each. Chill until ready to serve.

PER SERVING: Calories: 100 | Total Fat: 0g | Saturated Fat: 0g | Cholesterol: 40mg | Protein: 16g | Sodium: 68mg | Potassium: 444mg | Fiber: 0g | Carbohydrates: 4g | Sugar: 0g

ONION DIP

Most people have had onion dip—you know, the kind made with boxed powdered onion mix. That is nothing like this dip. Plus, this recipe is low in sodium, while the boxed mix is packed with it.

SERVES 16

2 teaspoons onion powder

½ teaspoon dried green onion flakes

⅛ teaspoon dried granulated roasted garlic

⅛ teaspoon dried or freeze-dried chopped chives

⅛ teaspoon dried parsley

⅛ teaspoon celery seed

⅛ teaspoon dry mustard

½ cup plain nonfat yogurt

4 ounces cream cheese, at room temperature

1 tablespoon mayonnaise

1 teaspoon reduced-sodium Worcestershire sauce

Optional: 2–3 drops hot pepper sauce

Optional: Freshly ground pink or black pepper

Add all ingredients to a small bowl and mix to combine. Cover and refrigerate until needed.

PER SERVING: Calories: 34 | Total Fat: 2g | Saturated Fat: 1g | Cholesterol: 8mg | Protein: 0g | Sodium: 39mg | Potassium: 35mg | Fiber: 0g | Carbohydrates: 1g | Sugar: 1g

OPEN-FACED WILD MUSHROOM WONTONS

Great finger food for a party or perfect for an afternoon snack, these wontons are filled with the meaty flavor of mushrooms that will satisfy and delight.

SERVES 48

1 tablespoon olive or canola oil

1 tablespoon unsalted butter

½ cup sliced shallots

½ teaspoon freshly ground black pepper

¾ pound assorted wild mushrooms (such as chanterelle, wood ear, shiitake, morel), cleaned, stemmed, and thinly sliced

¾ cup water

¾ teaspoon low-sodium chicken base

¼ cup instant nonfat dry milk

½ cup ricotta cheese

½ teaspoon herbal seasoning blend of your choice

24 wonton wrappers

Olive oil spray

2 tablespoons grated Parmesan cheese

1. Preheat oven to 375°F.

2. In a large, heavy nonstick skillet, heat the oil and melt the butter over medium-high heat. Add the shallots and cook, stirring, for 1 minute. Add the pepper and mushrooms; sauté until the mushrooms become soft and most of the mushroom liquid is evaporated, about 8 minutes.

3. Add the water and heat until it begins to boil. Dissolve the chicken base in the water. Reduce heat and add the nonfat dry milk, whisking to combine with the mushroom mixture. Add the ricotta cheese and herbal seasoning, and mix to combine; cook until heated through. Remove from heat.

4. Line a baking sheet with nonstick aluminum foil. Prepare the wonton wrappers by lightly spraying one side of each with the spray oil. Place sprayed-side down on the foil. Evenly divide the mushroom mixture, placing a spoonful on each wonton wrapper. Top the mushroom mixture with the grated cheese.

5. Bake for 8–10 minutes or until the wontons are brown and crunchy and the cheese is melted and bubbly.

PER SERVING: Calories: 161 | Total Fat: 1g | Saturated Fat: 0g | Cholesterol: 3mg | Protein: 2g | Sodium: 100mg | Potassium: 61mg | Fiber: 0g | Carbohydrates: 10g | Sugar: 0g

SWEET STUFF GUACAMOLE DIP

The apple juice in this recipe gives this guacamole a slightly sweeter flavor that imparts a pleasant twist. Serve with unsalted tortilla chips.

SERVES 16

1 medium avocado

1½ teaspoons apple cider vinegar

1 clove garlic

1 teaspoon Bragg Liquid Aminos

½ teaspoon reduced-sodium Worcestershire sauce

2 teaspoons extra-virgin olive oil

2 tablespoons apple juice

½ cup plain nonfat yogurt

1 teaspoon fresh lemon juice

Put all ingredients in a food processor or blender and process until smooth.

PER SERVING: Calories: 30 | Total Fat: 2g | Saturated Fat: 0g | Cholesterol: 0mg | Protein: 0g | Sodium: 8mg | Potassium: 85mg | Fiber: 0g | Carbohydrates: 2g | Sugar: 0g

GARLIC TOAST

The ubiquitous garlic toast is a perfect complement to so many dishes that it would be almost impossible to name them all. This simple snack is great alongside pasta, meat, and vegetarian dishes, and also perfect on its own.

SERVES 4

Olive oil spray

4 (1-ounce) slices French Bread (Chapter 2)

1 clove garlic, cut in half lengthwise

1. Preheat oven to 350°F.

2. Using the spray oil (or an oil mister filled with extra-virgin olive oil), lightly spray both sides of each slice of bread. Arrange the bread slices on a baking sheet. Bake for 6–8 minutes.

3. Remove from oven. Handle the toasted bread slices carefully so that you don't burn your fingers, and rub the cut side of the garlic clove across the top of each slice. Serve warm.

PER SERVING: Calories: 79 | Total Fat: 0g | Saturated Fat: 0g | Cholesterol: 0mg | Protein: 2g | Sodium: 24mg | Potassium: 33mg | Fiber: 0g | Carbohydrates: 16g | Sugar: 0g

ROASTED GARLIC AND RED PEPPER HUMMUS

The ultimate dip and sandwich filling. This version calls for tahini, a smooth sesame butter sold in many supermarkets and natural food stores. If you can't find it, try substituting low-sodium peanut butter.

SERVES 16 (2 TABLESPOONS PER SERVING)

2 cloves Roasted Garlic (Chapter 4)

2 cups cooked no-salt-added chickpeas, drained

⅓ cup tahini

⅓ cup lemon juice

½ cup chopped roasted red peppers (see instructions for roasting peppers in Chapter 3)

¼ teaspoon dried basil

Freshly ground black pepper

1. In a food processor, combine the garlic, chickpeas, tahini, lemon juice, chopped red peppers, and basil. Process until the mixture is smooth.

2. Season to taste with freshly ground pepper. Transfer the hummus to a covered bowl and chill until ready to serve.

PER SERVING: Calories: 66 | Total Fat: 2g | Saturated Fat: 0g | Cholesterol: 0mg | Protein: 2g | Sodium: 6mg | Potassium: 96mg | Fiber: 2g | Carbohydrates: 6g | Sugar: 0g

EASY BREAD "STICKS"

Forget buying frozen or prepackaged breadsticks—make your own! You will cut down on preservatives, fat, and sodium when you bake your own breadsticks, and they taste better too.

SERVES 4

4 (1-ounce) thin slices French Bread (Chapter 2), cut in thirds lengthwise

Olive oil

1. Preheat over to 350°F.

2. Using an oil mister, lightly spray the breadsticks with olive oil. Arrange on a baking sheet.

3. Bake for 5–10 minutes. (Baking time will depend how crisp you want the bread "sticks.")

PER SERVING: Calories: 88 | Total Fat: 1g | Saturated Fat: 0g | Cholesterol: 0mg | Protein: 2g | Sodium: 24mg | Potassium: 30mg | Fiber: 0g | Carbohydrates: 16g | Sugar: 0g

HERBED PROVENCE-STYLE FLATBREAD (FOUGASSE)

Fougasse is a chewy type of bread from France that is shaped into a "leaf," by cutting the dough and pulling it apart in sections. If you are baking the fougasse on a bread stone, skip using the olive oil spray and dust your bread peel and the stone with cornmeal to prevent the flatbreads from sticking.

SERVES 24

Basic White Bread dough (Chapter 2)

½ teaspoon dried rosemary

¼ teaspoon dried French thyme

¼ teaspoon dried tarragon

¼ teaspoon dried basil

¼ teaspoon dried savory

¼ teaspoon dried fennel seeds

¼ teaspoon dried lavender

⅛ teaspoon dried marjoram

⅛ teaspoon freshly ground black pepper

2 tablespoons grated Parmesan cheese

2 tablespoons extra-virgin olive oil

1. Preheat oven to 450°F.

2. Remove the prepared basic bread dough from the refrigerator and punch it down. Lightly coat your hands with a bit of olive oil. Divide the dough into 24 equal pieces, shaping each piece into a ball. Set aside to rest for a few minutes.

3. Mix together the rosemary, thyme, tarragon, basil, savory, fennel seeds, lavender, marjoram, and pepper. Use a mortar and pestle or spice grinder to process into a coarse meal. Stir in the Parmesan cheese.

4. Using your hands, flatten each ball of dough to ⅓" thick. (Flatten into irregular shapes to give character to the bread.) Spray a baking sheet with olive oil spray and place the dough on the sheet. With a pastry scraper, *lame* (a tool used to slit the tops of bread loaves), or sharp knife, cut 3 or 4 lengthwise slashes all the way through the dough. Gently pull the dough apart where it was slashed to form oval holes. Cover with a clean towel, and let rest for 10 minutes.

5. Brush the breads lightly with 2 tablespoons olive oil, then sprinkle with the herb–Parmesan cheese topping. Bake until golden and crusty, about 15–18 minutes.

PER SERVING: Calories: 98 | Total Fat: 2g | Saturated Fat: 0g | Cholesterol: 0mg | Protein: 2g | Sodium: 103mg | Potassium: 27mg | Fiber: 0g | Carbohydrates: 16g | Sugar: 0g

SHRIMP TOASTS

Save yourself some time! There's no reason to remove the crusts from homemade bread slice by slice. Before you slice the bread, cut off the crusts. Then slice the bread into 1-ounce slices.

SERVES 48

1 pound peeled shrimp

¼ cup minced green onions

2 tablespoons minced fresh cilantro

1 teaspoon minced garlic

1 teaspoon minced jalapeño pepper

1 large egg white

1 tablespoon nonfat dry milk

4 ounces cream cheese, cut into pieces

½ cup plain nonfat yogurt

12 (1-ounce) slices Basic White Bread (Chapter 2), crusts removed

Olive oil spray

1. Preheat the oven to 375°F.

2. In a food processor, combine the shrimp, green onions, cilantro, garlic, jalapeño, egg white, and nonfat dry milk; process until smooth. Add cubes of cream cheese and pulse to incorporate. Add the yogurt and pulse just until incorporated, being careful not to overprocess.

3. To shorten the baking time and help ensure that the bread is crisp in the center, first toast it, then spray one side of each slice of bread with a light amount of the olive oil spray. Place slices (sprayed-side down) on a baking sheet treated with nonstick spray or covered with nonstick foil.

4. Evenly divide the shrimp mixture among the slices of bread, making sure to spread it to the edges of the bread.

5. Bake for 10–15 minutes, or until the bread is crisp and the shrimp topping bubbles and is lightly browned. Use a pizza cutter or serrated knife to cut each slice of bread into 4 equal pieces. Arrange on a tray or platter and serve immediately.

PER SERVING: Calories: 42 | Total Fat: 1g | Saturated Fat: 0g | Cholesterol: 17mg | Protein: 2g | Sodium: 50mg | Potassium: 40mg | Fiber: 0g | Carbohydrates: 4g | Sugar: 0g

HONEY-SPICED ALMONDS

Almonds are a delicious and healthy snack on their own, but when coated with a honey-spice mixture, they are even better. This recipe is also delicious added to a snack mix, or try it mixed with unsalted popcorn.

SERVES 12

2 tablespoons unsalted butter

½ teaspoon cinnamon

⅛ teaspoon ground cloves

⅛ teaspoon ground ginger

½ cup honey

½ teaspoon orange zest

3 cups raw almonds

1. Put the butter, spices, honey, and orange zest in a large microwave-safe bowl. Microwave on high for 1 minute or until the butter is melted. Stir well to combine.

2. Add the almonds to the honey mixture and stir well to combine. Microwave on high for 3 minutes; stir well. Microwave on high for another 3 minutes; stir. Spread the nuts on a nonstick foil-lined baking sheet to cool. Be careful—the mixture will be very hot!

PER SERVING: Calories: 266 | Total Fat: 20g | Saturated Fat: 2g | Cholesterol: 5mg | Protein: 7g | Sodium: 1mg | Potassium: 265mg | Fiber: 4g | Carbohydrates: 18g | Sugar: 13g

SWEET PEA GUACAMOLE

Frozen peas are sorted by size in saltwater baths. As a result, they'll already have a higher sodium content than fresh ones. If you use frozen peas, make sure you use a no-salt-added variety.

SERVES 8

3 tablespoons extra-virgin olive oil

2 tablespoons fresh lime juice

2 tablespoons minced fresh coriander

2 jalapeño peppers, seeded and minced

½ teaspoon ground cumin

½ teaspoon ground coriander

½ teaspoon ground black pepper

1 (16-ounce) package no-salt-added frozen peas, thawed and drained

2 plum tomatoes, peeled, seeded, and diced

1 small red onion, finely diced

Optional: Honey or jalapeño jelly, to taste

1. In the bowl of a food processor, combine the oil, lime juice, coriander, jalapeños, spices, and black pepper; process until smooth.

2. Add the peas. Pulse a few times to chop the peas and combine with the other ingredients.

3. Use a spatula to scrape the mixture into a serving bowl. Stir in the tomatoes and onion. Check seasoning and adjust if necessary, adding some honey or jalapeño jelly if a touch of sweetness is necessary to mellow the hotness of the peppers.

PER SERVING: Calories: 80 | Total Fat: 5g | Saturated Fat: 0g | Cholesterol: 0mg | Protein: 2g | Sodium: 4mg | Potassium: 179mg | Fiber: 2g | Carbohydrates: 6g | Sugar: 3g

TOMATO BUTTER TOASTS

To shorten the baking time and help ensure that the bread is crisp in the center, first toast it.

SERVES 48

¾ cup Tomato Butter (Chapter 4)

¼ cup minced green onions

2 tablespoons minced fresh basil

4 cloves garlic, minced

12 (1-ounce) slices Basic White Bread (Chapter 2), crusts removed

Olive oil spray

¾ cup grated Parmesan cheese

1. Preheat oven to 375°F.

2. In the bowl of a food processor, combine the tomato butter, green onions, basil, and garlic; process until mixed.

3. Spray one side of each slice of bread with a light amount of the olive oil spray and place (sprayed-side down) on a baking sheet treated with nonstick spray or covered with nonstick foil.

4. Evenly divide the tomato-butter mixture among the slices of bread, making sure to spread it to the edges of the bread. Evenly sprinkle 1 tablespoon of the Parmesan cheese over the top of each piece.

5. Bake for 10–12 minutes or until the bread is crisp and the topping bubbles and is lightly browned. Use a pizza cutter or serrated knife to cut each slice of bread into 4 equal pieces. Arrange on a tray or platter and serve immediately.

PER SERVING: Calories: 56 | Total Fat: 3g | Saturated Fat: 2g | Cholesterol: 8mg | Protein: 1g | Sodium: 67mg | Potassium: 39mg | Fiber: 0g | Carbohydrates: 4g | Sugar: 0g

GREEK YOGURT DIP

This dip is perfect for dunking your veggies or bite-sized pieces of your favorite bread. Put some out at your next party and watch it disappear.

SERVES 16

1 cup nonfat plain yogurt

1 tablespoon fresh lemon juice

1 tablespoon granulated sugar

2 teaspoons Greek Spice Blend (Appendix A)

Add all the ingredients to a small bowl and mix well. Cover and refrigerate overnight to allow the flavors to intensify. Stir again before serving.

PER SERVING: Calories: 11 | Total Fat: 0g | Saturated Fat: 0g | Cholesterol: 0mg | Protein: 0g | Sodium: 11mg | Potassium: 40mg | Fiber: 0g | Carbohydrates: 2g | Sugar: 1g

HONEY ALMOND SPREAD

Why use just peanut or almond butter on your toast when you can have this sweet and delicious spread instead? After trying it you'll never go back to the plain old stuff again.

SERVES 32 (1 TABLESPOON EACH)

2 tablespoons fresh orange juice

½ cup chopped raisins

1 tablespoon honey

4 ounces cream cheese

½ cup plain nonfat yogurt

¼ cup chopped Honey-Spiced Almonds (see recipe in this chapter)

1. Mix together the orange juice and raisins; set aside.

2. In a small bowl, mix together the honey, cream cheese, and yogurt. Stir the orange juice–chopped raisins mixture and almonds into the cream-cheese mixture. Cover, and chill in the refrigerator until ready to serve.

PER SERVING: Calories: 31 | Total Fat: 1g | Saturated Fat: 0g | Cholesterol: 4mg | Protein: 0g | Sodium: 14mg | Potassium: 42mg | Fiber: 0g | Carbohydrates: 3g | Sugar: 2g

PISSALADIÉRE (ONION TART)

This tart is perfect as a party food, for a brunch with guests, or even as a vegetarian meal along with a salad.

SERVES 24

¼ teaspoon dried lemon zest

¼ teaspoon mustard powder

1 tablespoon water

1 tablespoon extra-virgin olive oil

2 large sweet onions, thinly sliced

4 medium-size cloves garlic, finely chopped

1 fresh bay leaf

¼ teaspoon dried thyme, crushed

2 teaspoons dried parsley, crushed

¼ teaspoon freshly ground black pepper

Pinch dried red pepper flakes

½ recipe Basic White Bread dough (Chapter 2)

2 tablespoons grated Parmesan cheese

1. Preheat oven to 450°F with a rack set in the center position.

2. Add the lemon zest and mustard powder to a small microwave-safe bowl or coffee cup; spoon the water and oil over the top. Microwave on high for 30 seconds, then cover with plastic wrap and set aside.

3. Add the onions, garlic, and bay leaf to a microwave-safe bowl. Cover and microwave on high for 4 minutes. Turn the bowl and microwave on high for an additional 3 minutes. (Be careful not to burn the onions.) Carefully remove the cover (there will be lots of steam!). Discard the bay leaf and mix in the thyme, parsley, black pepper, and red pepper flakes; cover and set aside.

4. Treat a 13" × 18" rimmed baking sheet (jellyroll pan) with spray oil. Place the white bread dough on a lightly floured surface and roll into a 13" × 18" rectangle; transfer to the baking pan. Cover with a damp cotton towel or plastic wrap and let rest for 30 minutes to rise. (The dough may "shrink" away from the edges of the pan; if so, gently use the tips of your fingers to push it back to the edges.) Prick the dough all over with the tines of a fork. Uncover the lemon-granules mixture and whisk with a fork. Brush the mixture evenly over the dough.

5. Stir the Parmesan cheese into the cooked-onion mixture and spread the mixture evenly over the prepared dough. Bake for 12 minutes. Rotate the pan and bake until the crust is cooked through and the edges are lightly browned, about 12 minutes more. Remove from oven and transfer the tart to a serving board. Slice and serve warm or at room temperature.

PER SERVING: Calories: 51 | Total Fat: 1g | Saturated Fat: 0g | Cholesterol: 0mg | Protein: 1g | Sodium: 55mg | Potassium: 19mg | Fiber: 0g | Carbohydrates: 8g | Sugar: 0g

CARBONARA TART

Carbonara is an Italian pasta dish with cheese, eggs, and bacon. Here we take the essence of those ingredients and transform them into a delicious tart.

SERVES 24

¾ teaspoon bacon base

1 tablespoon water

1 tablespoon extra-virgin olive oil

2 large sweet onions, thinly sliced

4 medium-size cloves garlic, finely chopped

1 fresh bay leaf

¼ teaspoon dried thyme, crushed

2 teaspoons dried parsley, crushed

¼ teaspoon freshly ground black pepper

Pinch dried red pepper flakes

½ recipe Basic White Bread dough (Chapter 2)

4 large eggs, beaten

2 tablespoons grated Parmesan cheese

1. Preheat oven to 450°F with a rack set in the center position.

2. Add the bacon base to a small microwave-safe bowl or coffee cup; spoon the water and oil over the top. Microwave on high for 30 seconds, then cover with plastic wrap and set aside.

3. Add the onions, garlic, and bay leaf to a microwave-safe bowl. Cover and microwave on high for 4 minutes. Turn the bowl and microwave on high for an additional 3 minutes. (Be careful not to burn the onions.) Carefully remove the cover (there will be lots of steam!); discard the bay leaf and mix in the thyme, parsley, black pepper, and red pepper flakes; cover and set aside to cool.

4. Treat a 13" × 18" rimmed baking sheet (jellyroll pan) with spray oil. Place the white bread dough on a lightly floured surface and roll it into a 13" × 18" rectangle; transfer to the baking pan. Cover with a damp cotton towel or plastic wrap and let rest for 30 minutes to rise. (The dough may "shrink" away from the edges of pan; if so, gently use the tips of your fingers to push it back to the edges.) Prick the dough all over with the tines of a fork. Uncover the bacon-base mixture and whisk with a fork. Brush the mixture evenly over the dough.

5. Stir the eggs and Parmesan cheese into the cooked-onion mixture and spread the mixture evenly over the prepared dough. Bake for 12 minutes. Rotate the pan and bake until the crust is cooked through and the edges are lightly browned, about 12 minutes more. Remove from oven and transfer the tart to a serving board. Slice and serve warm or at room temperature.

PER SERVING: Calories: 71 | Total Fat: 1g | Saturated Fat: 0g | Cholesterol: 35mg | Protein: 2g | Sodium: 97mg | Potassium: 60mg | Fiber: 0g | Carbohydrates: 10g | Sugar: 1g

ITALIAN-STYLE BAKED STUFFED MUSHROOMS

These stuffed mushrooms are the perfect party food, easy to make, easy to grab, and easy to eat. Serve them warm from the oven.

SERVES 24

24 large button mushrooms

Olive oil spray

1 large sweet onion, chopped

1 clove garlic, minced

1 large tomato, peeled, seeded, and chopped

1 medium green bell pepper, seeded and minced

2 teaspoons fresh lemon juice

1 tablespoon extra-virgin olive oil

⅛ teaspoon freshly ground black pepper

⅛ teaspoon mustard powder

1 teaspoon Italian Spice Blend (Appendix A)

¼ cup shredded provolone cheese

¼ cup shredded whole-milk mozzarella cheese

¼ cup grated Parmesan cheese

½ cup bread crumbs

1. Preheat oven to 400°F.

2. Remove and chop the stems from the mushrooms; set aside. Lightly mist the tops and bottoms of the mushroom caps with the spray oil. Arrange in an oven-safe casserole dish or roasting pan, stem-side up.

3. Put the chopped mushroom stems, onion, garlic, tomato, green pepper, and lemon juice in a microwave-safe bowl. Cover and microwave on high for 3–5 minutes or until the onion is tender and transparent. Set aside to cool.

4. Stir the olive oil, black pepper, mustard powder, Italian Spice Blend, cheeses, and bread crumbs into the onion mixture. Evenly divide the mixture between the mushroom caps.

5. Lightly mist the stuffed mushroom caps with the spray oil. Bake for 20–25 minutes or until the mushrooms are tender and the cheese is melted and bubbling.

PER SERVING: Calories: 37 | Total Fat: 1g | Saturated Fat: 0g | Cholesterol: 2mg | Protein: 2g | Sodium: 38mg | Potassium: 108mg | Fiber: 0g | Carbohydrates: 4g | Sugar: 1g

GARLIC TOAST WITH A KICK

Garlic toast is practically perfect all on its own, but when you add this spice combination you take it to a new level of flavor. Serve this alongside your favorite pasta dish.

SERVES 4

Olive oil spray

8 (½-ounce) slices French Bread (Chapter 2)

2 teaspoons garlic powder

½ teaspoon onion powder

¼ teaspoon ground ginger

¼ teaspoon sweet paprika

⅛ teaspoon dried parsley, crushed

⅛ teaspoon oregano, crushed

⅛ teaspoon mustard powder

⅛ teaspoon cumin

1⁄16 teaspoon dried red pepper flakes, crushed

1⁄16 teaspoon cayenne

1. Preheat oven to 350°F.

2. Using the spray oil (or an oil mister filled with extra-virgin olive oil), lightly spray both sides of each slice of bread. Arrange the bread slices on a baking sheet.

3. In a medium bowl, combine all the remaining ingredients; mix well.

4. Sprinkle the spice mixture over the tops of the bread slices; press the seasoning into the bread and then lightly spray with the spray oil again. Bake for 6–8 minutes.

PER SERVING: Calories: 164 | Total Fat: 0g | Saturated Fat: 0g | Cholesterol: 0mg | Protein: 5g | Sodium: 50g | Potassium: 86mg | Fiber: 1g | Carbohydrates: 33g | Sugar: 0g

PIZZA-FLAVORED SOY NUTS

Instead of the Mrs. Dash Tomato Basil Garlic Seasoning Blend and oregano, you can substitute a bit of garlic powder, dried basil, and a pinch of salt.

SERVES 8

2 cups dried soybeans

8 cups water

Olive oil spray

1 teaspoon Mrs. Dash Tomato Basil Garlic Seasoning Blend

¼ teaspoon dried oregano

¼ teaspoon onion powder

1 or more (to taste) black peppercorns

Optional: ¼ teaspoon paprika

3 tablespoons grated Parmesan cheese

1. Put dried soybeans in a large bowl and pour the water over them. Cover and let soak overnight.

2. Preheat oven to 200°F. Drain the soybeans well and blot dry with a towel. Spread the soybeans in a single layer on a baking sheet treated with the spray oil. Bake for 2 hours, stirring occasionally.

3. Raise oven temperature to 375°F. Toast the soybeans for 5 minutes or until they're a deep golden brown.

4. While the soybeans bake, mix together the seasoning blend, oregano, onion powder, and black peppercorns; process to a fine powder in a spice grinder. Pour into a bowl large enough to hold the toasted soy nuts; stir in the paprika, if using it, and Parmesan cheese.

5. Remove the toasted soybeans from the oven and mist with the olive oil spray. Add the soybeans to the bowl with the seasonings; toss to mix. Serve warm from the oven or at room temperature. You can make this up to a week in advance if you store it in a covered container.

PER SERVING: Calories: 82 | Total Fat: 4g | Saturated Fat: 0g | Cholesterol: 1mg | Protein: 7g | Sodium: 29mg | Potassium: 225mg | Fiber: 2g | Carbohydrates: 4g | Sugar: 1g

MICROWAVE AIR-POPPED POPCORN

You defeat the purpose of healthful, air-popped popcorn if you drown it in butter and smother it with salt. Instead, squirt a little natural butter-flavored spray oil over it and sprinkle on your favorite herb seasoning blend.

YIELDS 4–16 CUPS

¼–1 cup popcorn kernels

1. To "air-pop" popcorn in the microwave, add the popcorn kernels to a brown paper bag large enough to hold the yield. Fold down the top. Spray the bag with water (or wet your hand and tap water onto the sides and bottom of the bag). Microwave on high for 3 minutes, or use the popcorn setting if your microwave has it.

2. If popping a smaller (¼-cup) batch, listen closely. Once you no longer hear popcorn popping every 2 seconds, stop the microwave; otherwise, the already-popped popcorn may burn. (There are almost always some unpopped kernels in each batch.)

PER SERVING (1 cup): Calories: 30 | Total Fat: 0g | Saturated Fat: 0g | Cholesterol: 0mg | Protein: 0g | Sodium: 0mg | Potassium: 24mg | Fiber: 1g | Carbohydrates: 6g | Sugar: 0g

PARTY MIX POPCORN

Be careful when you choose which pretzels to buy; many are made with unhealthy oils that are high in saturated fat. Try and find pretzel rounds made from certified organic unbleached wheat and rye flour, brown rice sweetener, barley malt, and sunflower oil.

SERVES 12

4 cups air-popped popcorn

8 ounces unsalted pretzels

1 cup unsalted dry-roasted peanuts

Olive oil spray

2 teaspoons Bragg Liquid Aminos

½ teaspoon garlic powder

¼ teaspoon onion powder

¼ teaspoon salt-free lemon pepper or Citrus Pepper (Appendix A)

⅛ teaspoon dried dill, crushed

⅛ teaspoon mustard powder

⅛ teaspoon dried lemon zest

1. Preheat oven to 300°F.

2. Mix together the popcorn, pretzels, and peanuts; spread on a nonstick jellyroll pan or baking sheet treated with the olive oil spray. Mist the top of the mixture with some additional spray oil and the liquid aminos.

3. In a small bowl mix together the remaining ingredients; sprinkle evenly over the popcorn mixture. Bake for 5 minutes. Toss the popcorn mixture and rotate the pan, then bake for an additional 5 minutes. Serve warm or at room temperature.

PER SERVING: Calories: 153 | Total Fat: 6g | Saturated Fat: 1g | Cholesterol: 0mg | Protein: 4g | Sodium: 135mg | Potassium: 117mg | Fiber: 1g | Carbohydrates: 19g | Sugar: 0g

CINNAMON SWEET POPCORN

Popcorn is a delicious and healthy snack. Did you know that popcorn is a whole grain? It's most often seasoned with cheese or other savory ingredients. Try this sweet recipe for a nice change of pace.

SERVES 4

Olive oil spray

4 cups air-popped popcorn

1 tablespoon granulated sugar

⅛ teaspoon ground cinnamon

Pinch ground nutmeg

Pinch ground cloves

Pinch ground allspice

⅛ teaspoon dried orange zest

1. Preheat oven to 300°F. Spray a jellyroll pan or baking sheet with the olive oil spray.

2. Spread the popcorn on the pan and lightly coat with the olive oil spray. Mix together the remaining ingredients; sprinkle over the popcorn.

3. Bake for 5 minutes. Toss the popcorn and rotate the pan, then bake for an additional 5 minutes. Serve warm or at room temperature.

PER SERVING: Calories: 42 | Total Fat: 0g | Saturated Fat: 0g | Cholesterol: 0mg | Protein: 0g | Sodium: 0mg | Potassium: 24mg | Fiber: 1g | Carbohydrates: 9g | Sugar: 3g

CORN TORTILLA CRISPS

This recipe calls for breaking the tortillas by hand into pieces after they are cooked. If you prefer equal-sized pieces, you can cut the tortillas before baking by stacking several together on a cutting board and cutting with a pizza cutter or serrated knife; if you do so, decrease the baking time by about a minute.

SERVES 4

4 Corn Tortillas (Chapter 2)

Olive oil spray

Mrs. Dash Extra Spicy Seasoning Blend, or lime juice and freshly ground pepper or salt

1. Preheat oven to 400°F. Lightly spray both sides of the tortillas with the spray oil.

2. Place the tortillas on a heavy baking sheet. Bake for 3–5 minutes, until crisp. (Be careful; they'll go from lightly browned to burned in a flash!) Season to taste and break each tortilla into 4 pieces.

PER SERVING: Calories: 66 | Total Fat: 2g | Saturated Fat: 0g | Cholesterol: 0mg | Protein: 1g | Sodium: 37mg | Potassium: 43mg | Fiber: 0g | Carbohydrates: 10g | Sugar: 0g

SAVORY STUFFED MUSHROOMS

While dried sage is a staple in most stuffing blends, its flavor is too strong for some tastes. If you prefer, you can omit the dried sage in the Stuffing Blend (Appendix A), increase the marjoram to 2 tablespoons, and add 1 tablespoon of dried thyme.

SERVES 12

24 large button mushrooms, cleaned, stems removed and chopped

Olive oil spray

¼ teaspoon low-sodium chicken base

¼ cup water

1 large sweet onion, chopped

⅛ teaspoon freshly ground black pepper

⅛ teaspoon mustard powder

½–1 teaspoon Stuffing Blend (Appendix A)

1 cup bread crumbs

2 large eggs, beaten

1. Preheat oven to 400°F.

2. Lightly mist the tops and bottoms of the mushroom caps with the spray oil. Arrange in an ovenproof casserole dish or roasting pan, stem-side up.

3. Put the base and water in a microwave-safe bowl; microwave on high for 30 seconds. Stir to mix the base with the water. Add the chopped mushroom stems and onion; cover and microwave on high for 3–5 minutes, until the onion is tender and transparent. Set aside to cool.

4. Stir the pepper, mustard powder, Stuffing Blend, bread crumbs, and eggs into the onion-broth mixture. Evenly divide the mixture between the mushroom caps, spooning approximately 2 teaspoons of the bread-crumb mixture into each cap. Lightly mist the stuffed mushroom caps with the spray oil. Bake for 20–25 minutes or until the mushrooms are tender when pierced with a fork.

PER SERVING: Calories: 60 | Total Fat: 1g | Saturated Fat: 0g | Cholesterol: 35mg | Protein: 3g | Sodium: 84mg | Potassium: 125mg | Fiber: 0g | Carbohydrates: 9g | Sugar: 2g

CHAPTER 7

PASTA DISHES

SPAGHETTI AGLIO E OLIO

This super simple recipe is usually drenched in Parmesan cheese, but we'll use toasted bread crumbs instead to lower the sodium content. Use a really good-quality pasta for this recipe, because that is crucial to its success. Serve with some rosé wine, a fruit salad, and some Garlic Bread (Chapter 6) on the side.

SERVES 8

4 slices French Bread (Chapter 2)

8 cloves garlic

1 pound spaghetti

¼ cup extra-virgin olive oil

2 tablespoons unsalted butter

¼ cup minced fresh basil leaves

2 tablespoons minced flat-leaf parsley

2 tablespoons grated Parmesan cheese

1. Toast the bread until crisp and golden brown. Let cool, then crush the bread to make crumbs; set aside. Slice half of the garlic cloves and finely mince the other half.

2. Bring a large pot of water to a boil. Cook the pasta until just al dente.

3. Meanwhile, in large skillet combine oil and butter; heat over medium-low heat until the butter melts. Add the sliced garlic; cook for 1 minute. Add the minced garlic; cook for 1 minute longer. Remove skillet from heat.

4. Drain the pasta, reserving about ⅔ cup pasta water. Add the pasta and pasta water to the skillet with the garlic and return to the heat. Cook mixture for 1–2 minutes or until sauce thickens slightly, tossing with tongs.

5. Sprinkle with the bread crumbs, basil, parsley, and Parmesan and toss over the heat for about a minute. Serve immediately.

PER SERVING: Calories: 355 | Total Fat: 11g | Saturated Fat: 3g | Cholesterol: 8mg | Protein: 10g | Sodium: 34mg | Potassium: 96mg | Fiber: 2g | Carbohydrates: 52g | Sugar: 0g

PASTA CACCIATORE

Cacciatore *is a term that means "hunter" in Italian. It is usually made with chicken cooked in a hearty red sauce rich with onions, herbs, and red wine. Let's turn it into a pasta sauce for a simple dinner that is ready in minutes. Use a sturdy pasta that will stand up well to a sauce, such as penne or ziti.*

SERVES 6

2 tablespoons olive oil

1 medium onion, chopped

1 (8-ounce) package mushrooms, sliced

4 cloves garlic, minced

1 medium zucchini, chopped

2 tablespoons no-salt-added tomato paste

½ cup dry red wine

1 (14-ounce) can no-salt-added diced tomatoes

1 (8-ounce) can no-salt-added tomato sauce

2 tablespoons Mustard (Chapter 4)

½ teaspoon dried oregano leaves

½ teaspoon dried basil leaves

½ teaspoon dried thyme leaves

¼ teaspoon crushed red pepper flakes

1 (16-ounce) package ziti or penne pasta

¼ cup chopped flat-leaf parsley

1. In a large skillet, heat olive oil over medium heat.

2. Add onion and mushrooms; cook, stirring occasionally, for 7–9 minutes or until mushrooms give up their liquid and the liquid evaporates.

3. Add garlic and zucchini; cook and stir for another 4 minutes.

4. Add tomato paste to skillet; let cook until the paste starts to brown in spots. Then add the wine, scraping the pan to remove drippings, and bring to a boil.

5. Add the tomatoes and tomato sauce, along with mustard, oregano, basil, thyme, and red pepper flakes. Stir and bring to a simmer. Lower heat and simmer for 10 minutes.

6. Bring a large pot of water to a boil. Add the pasta and cook until almost al dente, according to package directions.

7. When pasta is done, drain, reserving ½ cup pasta-cooking water.

8. Add the pasta and reserved cooking water to the skillet with the tomato sauce. Simmer for 1–2 minutes or until the pasta is cooked. Sprinkle with parsley and serve immediately.

PER SERVING: Calories: 407 | Total Fat: 7g | Saturated Fat: 1g | Cholesterol: 0mg | Protein: 14g | Sodium: 22mg | Potassium: 569mg | Fiber: 5g | Carbohydrates: 68g | Sugar: 6g

PASTA WITH PISTACHIO PESTO

A pesto made with pistachio nuts is unusual and very good. The nuts are rich and are a great substitute for cheese to reduce sodium. Toss with some hot cooked linguine for a quick and satisfying dinner.

SERVES 8

1 cup unsalted shelled pistachios

½ cup packed baby spinach leaves

½ cup packed fresh basil leaves

3 tablespoons minced flat-leaf parsley

2 tablespoons lemon juice

¼ cup extra-virgin olive oil

2 tablespoons water

⅛ teaspoon white pepper

1 pound linguine pasta

1. In food processor or blender, combine pistachios, spinach, basil, parsley, and lemon juice. Process or blend until finely chopped.

2. With the motor running, add the olive oil and blend until a sauce forms. Thin with water and season with pepper.

3. Bring a large pot of water to a boil. Add the pasta and cook until al dente. Drain pasta, reserving ½ cup pasta-cooking water.

4. Return pasta to the pot. Add pesto and reserved cooking water and stir until combined. Serve immediately.

PER SERVING: Calories: 370 | Total Fat: 15g | Saturated Fat: 2g | Cholesterol: 0mg | Protein: 11g | Sodium: 4mg | Potassium: 237mg | Fiber: 4g | Carbohydrates: 47g | Sugar: 2g

FRENCH ONION PASTA

This flavorful recipe is reminiscent of French onion soup, but doesn't take as long to make and is much easier to eat! The pasta is cooked in homemade beef stock for wonderful flavor. Caramelized onions and garlic mimic the flavor of the soup, and everything is topped with toasted bread crumbs for crunch.

SERVES 8

2 tablespoons olive oil

1 tablespoon unsalted butter

2 medium onions, chopped

5 cloves garlic, sliced

1 teaspoon dried marjoram leaves

1 (16-ounce) package spaghetti

4 cups Beef Stock (Chapter 5)

3 slices French Bread (Chapter 2), crisply toasted

¼ cup grated Parmesan cheese

1. In large skillet heat olive oil and butter over medium heat. Add onions and cook for 10 minutes, stirring frequently, until light golden brown. Add the garlic and lower the heat to low. Cook for 10–15 minutes, stirring frequently, until onions are deep golden brown. Stir in the marjoram.

2. Add the pasta to the skillet and stir. Then carefully add the beef stock (liquid may splatter). Make sure all of the pasta is under the surface of the liquid.

3. Bring to a simmer, then reduce heat to low and simmer, stirring frequently, until the pasta is al dente, about 8–12 minutes.

4. Crumble the toasted bread and sprinkle over each serving, along with the cheese, and serve immediately.

PER SERVING: Calories: 330 | Total Fat: 7g | Saturated Fat: 2g | Cholesterol: 6mg | Protein: 12g | Sodium: 95mg | Potassium: 199mg | Fiber: 3g | Carbohydrates: 51g | Sugar: 1g

MARINARA SAUCE

Serve this over al dente cooked pasta, or use it in other recipes. You can freeze it in 2-cup portions up to 4 months. Just thaw overnight in the fridge and use.

YIELDS 8 CUPS; SERVING SIZE ½ CUP

¼ cup extra-virgin olive oil

2 medium onions, chopped

3 cloves garlic, minced

2 stalks celery, diced

3 tablespoons minced celery leaves

3 tablespoons no-salt-added tomato paste

2 (14-ounce) cans no-salt-added diced tomatoes, undrained

1 (8-ounce) can no-salt-added tomato sauce

1 teaspoon dried basil leaves

1 bay leaf

¼ teaspoon white pepper

1. In a large pot, heat olive oil over medium heat. Add onions; cook and stir until tender, about 6–7 minutes.

2. Add garlic; cook and stir for 1 minute. Then stir in celery and celery leaves; cook and stir for 4 minutes longer.

3. Add tomato paste to the pot; let cook, undisturbed, for a few minutes until the paste starts to brown in spots. Then add the tomatoes, tomato sauce, basil, bay leaf, and pepper.

4. Bring to a simmer; reduce heat to low and simmer, stirring occasionally, for 30–60 minutes until sauce blends and thickens slightly. Cool, then remove and discard bay leaf. Store in the refrigerator up to 4 days or freeze up to 4 months.

PER SERVING: Calories: 49 | Total Fat: 3g | Saturated Fat: 0g | Cholesterol: 0mg | Protein: 0g | Sodium: 14mg | Potassium: 198mg | Fiber: 0g | Carbohydrates: 4g | Sugar: 2g

PENNE WITH VEGETABLE RAGOUT

A ragout is simply a mélange of vegetables and meat cooked until soft and tender. This recipe doesn't use meat, but relies on lots of veggies such as eggplant and mushrooms for a meaty taste. This ragout is delicious served with penne, a sturdy tubular pasta that can stand up to a rich and thick sauce.

SERVES 6

2 tablespoons extra-virgin olive oil

1 leek, chopped

1 medium onion, chopped

1 small eggplant, cubed

3 cloves garlic, minced

1 (8-ounce) package mushrooms, sliced

2 medium carrots, sliced

⅓ cup dry red wine

1 bay leaf

1 teaspoon dried oregano leaves

1 teaspoon dried thyme leaves

⅛ teaspoon pepper

1 (14-ounce) can no-salt-added diced tomatoes, undrained

½ cup water

1 (16-ounce) package penne pasta

1. In large skillet, heat olive oil over medium heat. Add leek and onion; cook and stir until crisp-tender, about 4–5 minutes.

2. Add eggplant, garlic, mushrooms, and carrots; cook, stirring occasionally, until crisp-tender, about 5 minutes.

3. Add wine; cook and stir until liquid is absorbed. Then add bay leaf, oregano, thyme, pepper, tomatoes, and water.

4. Bring to a simmer, reduce heat, partially cover, and simmer for 20–30 minutes or until sauce is thickened. Remove and discard bay leaf.

5. Bring a large pot of water to a boil. Add penne and cook until al dente. Drain pasta, reserving ½ cup cooking water.

6. Add pasta to the vegetables along with enough reserved cooking water to loosen sauce slightly. Cook for 1 minute, then serve.

PER SERVING: Calories: 394 | Total Fat: 6g | Saturated Fat: 1g | Cholesterol: 0mg | Protein: 13g | Sodium: 30mg | Potassium: 474mg | Fiber: 6g | Carbohydrates: 69g | Sugar: 5g

PASTA WITH ROASTED CAULIFLOWER

Cauliflower pairs well with pasta, especially when roasted with smoked paprika so it is meaty and rich. Some caramelized onions and roasted garlic round out the dish and add some sweetness. Serve with Garlic Bread (Chapter 6), a green salad tossed with dried cranberries and toasted walnuts, and a glass of white wine.

SERVES 4

1 head cauliflower, broken into small florets

2 tablespoons extra-virgin olive oil

2 teaspoons smoked paprika

¼ teaspoon pepper

2 tablespoons lemon juice

1 (16-ounce) package penne pasta

1 cup Slow Cooker Caramelized Onions (Chapter 4)

8 cloves Roasted Garlic (Chapter 4)

2 slices French Bread (Chapter 2), crisply toasted and crumbled

2 tablespoons grated Parmesan cheese

1. Preheat oven to 400°F. On a baking sheet with sides, toss cauliflower florets and olive oil. Sprinkle with paprika, pepper, and lemon juice and toss again.

2. Roast cauliflower for 10–15 minutes or until tender and light golden. Remove from oven.

3. Bring a large pot of water to a boil. Cook pasta until al dente. Drain, reserving ½ cup cooking water.

4. Return pasta to the pot along with the reserved water. Add cauliflower, onions, and garlic and cook over medium heat for 2 minutes.

5. Sprinkle with bread crumbs and Parmesan and serve immediately.

PER SERVING: Calories: 417 | Total Fat: 14g | Saturated Fat: 2g | Cholesterol: 2mg | Protein: 13g | Sodium: 75mg | Potassium: 480mg | Fiber: 7g | Carbohydrates: 6g | Sugar: 8g

ONION AND KALE PASTA

Kale is loaded with fiber, vitamin A, vitamin C, and B vitamins. It has a bitter taste and can be tough, but when cooked in chicken broth, it becomes smooth and rich. When combined with caramelized onions and pasta, along with just a bit of cheese, it makes an elegant main course served with a glass of red wine.

SERVES 4

1 large bunch kale

2 tablespoons olive oil

1 tablespoon unsalted butter

1 medium onion, chopped

4 cloves garlic, sliced

1 cup Chicken Stock (Chapter 5)

1 (16-ounce) package linguine pasta

1 teaspoon dried marjoram leaves

⅛ teaspoon pepper

2 tablespoons grated Romano cheese

1. Bring a large pot of water to a boil. Meanwhile, rinse kale well, trim off the tough center ribs, and chop.

2. Heat olive oil and butter in a large skillet over medium heat. Add onion; cook, stirring frequently, until onion is deep gold, about 9–11 minutes. Add garlic and stock; bring to a simmer.

3. Add kale to the skillet and cook until almost tender, about 3–4 minutes.

4. Meanwhile, add pasta to the pot of water and cook 2 minutes fewer than package directs. Drain pasta and add to skillet along with marjoram and pepper.

5. Simmer for 2 minutes or until pasta is al dente. Serve immediately with cheese.

PER SERVING: Calories: 249 | Total Fat: 5g | Saturated Fat: 1g | Cholesterol: 4mg | Protein: 9g | Sodium: 38mg | Potassium: 207mg | Fiber: 3g | Carbohydrates: 40g | Sugar: 1g

LEMON CHICKEN LINGUINE

Linguine is a long pasta like spaghetti, but it's thicker and has more substance. It holds a creamy sauce very well. When combined with lemon and chicken, linguine makes a very satisfying dinner. Serve with a green salad tossed with sliced mushrooms, cucumbers, and tomatoes, and a glass of white wine.

SERVES 8

2 tablespoons unsalted butter

2 tablespoons olive oil

4 (6-ounce) boneless, skinless chicken breasts, cut into 1" pieces

1 leek, chopped

3 cloves garlic, minced

1 cup Chicken Stock (Chapter 5)

3 tablespoons lemon juice

1 (16-ounce) package linguine pasta

½ cup heavy cream

2 teaspoons chopped fresh thyme leaves

1 teaspoon grated lemon zest

1. Bring a large pot of water to a boil.

2. Meanwhile, heat butter and olive oil over medium heat in a large skillet. Add chicken; cook, stirring frequently, until chicken is almost cooked through, about 5–7 minutes. Remove chicken from skillet and set aside.

3. Add leek and garlic to pan, stirring to remove pan drippings. Cook until crisp-tender, about 4–6 minutes.

4. Return chicken to skillet and add stock and lemon juice. Cook, stirring frequently, until sauce thickens slightly and chicken is cooked to 160°F as measured by a thermometer, about 8–10 minutes.

5. Cook linguine according to package directions until al dente. Drain pasta, reserving ½ cup cooking water.

6. Add drained pasta to skillet along with cream, thyme, and lemon zest. Cook, stirring and tossing with tongs, until pasta is coated. Add reserved cooking water as necessary to make a sauce. Serve immediately.

PER SERVING: Calories: 484 | Total Fat: 16g | Saturated Fat: 6g | Cholesterol: 101mg | Protein: 36g | Sodium: 78mg | Potassium: 303mg | Fiber: 2g | Carbohydrates: 46g | Sugar: 1g

SPAGHETTI BOLOGNESE

Bolognese sauce is simply a rich sauce made with ground beef. It is delicious on just about any pasta, but the classic "spag bol" is served with spaghetti. This dish is easy to make and very satisfying, especially on a cold winter night. Serve it with red wine and some Garlic Bread (Chapter 6) plus a spinach salad.

SERVES 6

1 pound lean ground beef

2 medium onions, chopped

1 (8-ounce) package mushrooms, sliced

5 cloves garlic, minced

¼ cup no-salt-added tomato paste

½ cup red wine

1 cup Beef Stock (Chapter 5)

2 (14-ounce) cans no-salt-added diced tomatoes, undrained

1 (8-ounce) can no-salt-added tomato sauce

¼ cup chopped fresh celery leaves

1 bay leaf

1 teaspoon dried oregano leaves

1 teaspoon dried basil leaves

2 tablespoons lemon juice

1 teaspoon sugar

¼ teaspoon pepper

1 (16-ounce) package spaghetti or linguine

¼ cup grated Parmesan cheese, if desired

1. In a large saucepan, cook beef with onions, stirring to break up meat, until meat is browned, about 6–8 minutes. Drain well.

2. Add mushrooms and garlic to pan; cook and stir for 4 minutes. Add tomato paste; let cook undisturbed for a few minutes so the paste browns in spots.

3. Add wine to pan; cook until it is absorbed, stirring frequently. Then stir in beef stock, diced tomatoes, tomato sauce, celery leaves, bay leaf, oregano, basil, lemon juice, sugar, and pepper and bring to a simmer.

4. Reduce heat to low and simmer for 30–40 minutes or until sauce thickens slightly. Remove and discard bay leaf.

5. Bring a large pot of water to a boil. Add the pasta; cook according to package directions until al dente. Drain pasta, place on serving platter, and top with sauce. Sprinkle with cheese, if using, and serve immediately.

PER SERVING: Calories: 357 | Total Fat: 7g | Saturated Fat: 2g | Cholesterol: 35mg | Protein: 21g | Sodium: 110mg | Potassium: 698mg | Fiber: 4g | Carbohydrates: 48g | Sugar: 5g

ASPARAGUS LEMON LINGUINE

You can add cooked chicken to this dish for a heartier meal, but it's good on its own. Lemon juice and lemon zest add lots of flavor. Serve with a spinach salad tossed with mushrooms and sliced tomatoes.

SERVES 8

1 pound fresh asparagus

2 tablespoons extra-virgin olive oil

¼ cup sliced green onions

3 tablespoons lemon juice

1 teaspoon grated lemon zest

½ cup light cream

2 large eggs, beaten

1 (16-ounce) package linguine pasta

1 tablespoon fresh thyme leaves

1. Bring a large pot of water to a boil. Hold asparagus spears with both hands and bend them until they snap. Discard the ends, and cut the tender part into 2" lengths.

2. In large saucepan, heat olive oil over medium heat. Add green onions; cook and stir for 2 minutes. Add asparagus pieces; cook and stir for 2–3 minutes longer.

3. Add lemon juice and zest to asparagus mixture and remove from heat.

4. In small bowl combine cream with eggs and mix until combined.

5. Cook pasta according to package directions until al dente. Drain, reserving ½ cup cooking water.

6. Return the saucepan with the asparagus to the heat. Add the pasta and immediately add the cream mixture. Toss with tongs until well coated, adding some reserved cooking water as needed to make a sauce.

7. Stir in the thyme and serve immediately.

PER SERVING: Calories: 327 | Total Fat: 10g | Saturated Fat: 4g | Cholesterol: 69mg | Protein: 11g | Sodium: 32mg | Potassium: 236mg | Fiber: 3g | Carbohydrates: 46g | Sugar: 1g

BAKED SPAGHETTI

Serve this wonderful dish with Garlic Bread (Chapter 6), and a fruit salad, Baked Pears with Rosemary (Chapter 14) for dessert.

SERVES 6

1 pound ground beef

1 medium onion, chopped

1 (8-ounce) package mushrooms, sliced

4 cloves garlic, minced

1 (14-ounce) can no-salt-added diced tomatoes, undrained

1 (8-ounce) can no-salt-added tomato sauce

1½ cups water

1 teaspoon dried basil leaves

½ teaspoon dried oregano leaves

½ teaspoon dried thyme leaves

⅛ teaspoon pepper

8 ounces spaghetti pasta, broken in half

¼ cup grated Parmesan cheese

1. Preheat oven to 350°F. Spray a 13" × 9" glass baking pan with nonstick cooking spray and set aside.

2. In large skillet, cook ground beef with onion over medium heat, stirring to break up meat, until beef is browned, about 8–9 minutes.

3. Add mushrooms and garlic; continue cooking for 3–4 minutes longer until tender. Drain well.

4. Return skillet to heat and add tomatoes, tomato sauce, water, basil, oregano, thyme, and pepper and bring to a simmer. Add uncooked pasta.

5. Transfer mixture to baking dish and cover with foil. Bake for 50 minutes, then uncover, sprinkle with cheese, and bake for 10–15 minutes longer or until pasta is tender and casserole is bubbling. Serve immediately.

PER SERVING: Calories: 367 | Total Fat: 13g | Saturated Fat: 5g | Cholesterol: 55mg | Protein: 23g | Sodium: 129mg | Potassium: 676mg | Fiber: 3g | Carbohydrates: 37g | Sugar: 4g

STUFFED SHELLS

Large pasta shells are easy to stuff with just about anything, and make a beautiful presentation. The serving size is 2 to 3 shells per person, depending on what else you're serving. This recipe uses chicken, onions, and a creamy mascarpone mixture seasoned with lots of herbs as the filling, and is baked in a white sauce.

SERVES 8

16 large pasta shells

2 tablespoons olive oil

1 medium onion, chopped

2 cloves garlic, minced

2 tablespoons all-purpose flour

¾ cup Chicken Stock (Chapter 5)

1⅓ cups whole milk

1½ cups chopped Poached Chicken Breasts (Chapter 8)

1 cup frozen baby peas, thawed and drained

½ cup mascarpone cheese

¼ cup grated Parmesan cheese

2 tablespoons chopped fresh basil leaves

1 tablespoon chopped fresh thyme leaves

1 tablespoon chopped flat-leaf parsley

⅛ teaspoon white pepper

2 slices French Bread (Chapter 2), crumbled

2 tablespoons unsalted butter

1. Bring a large pot of water to a boil. Cook the pasta shells until almost al dente according to package directions. Drain, rinse with cold water, and set aside.

2. In large saucepan, heat olive oil over medium heat. Add onion and garlic; cook and stir until tender, about 6 minutes.

3. Add flour to onion mixture; cook and stir for 2 minutes. Gradually add the chicken stock and milk, stirring until mixture thickens. Remove from heat.

4. In medium bowl, combine chicken breasts, peas, mascarpone, Parmesan, basil, thyme, parsley, and pepper and mix well. Add ⅔ cup of the sauce mixture and mix.

5. Stuff the pasta shells with the chicken mixture.

6. Place ½ cup of the sauce in the bottom of a 13" × 9" baking dish. Top with the stuffed shells and cover with remaining sauce.

7. Combine French bread crumbs and butter in a small bowl and mix well. Sprinkle over the shells.

8. Preheat oven to 375°F. Bake the shells for 25–30 minutes or until sauce is bubbling and the bread crumbs are golden brown. Serve immediately.

PER SERVING: Calories: 369 | Total Fat: 12g | Saturated Fat: 5g | Cholesterol: 42mg | Protein: 20g | Sodium: 109mg | Potassium: 261mg | Fiber: 2g | Carbohydrates: 43g | Sugar: 3g

CREAMY LASAGNA

This recipe uses a white sauce enriched with mascarpone cheese in place of most of the mozzarella cheese. It's rich and delicious. Serve with a green salad tossed with some zucchini slices and cherry tomatoes, and a glass of red wine. Garlic Bread (Chapter 6) on the side is essential.

SERVES 10–12

9 lasagna noodles

1½ pounds ground pork

1 medium onion, chopped

1 (8-ounce) package cremini mushrooms, sliced

4 cloves garlic, minced

1 (6-ounce) can no-salt-added tomato paste

1 (14-ounce) can no-salt-added diced tomatoes, undrained

1 (8-ounce) can no-salt-added tomato sauce

½ teaspoon dried oregano leaves

1 teaspoon dried basil leaves

1 teaspoon dried thyme leaves

⅛ teaspoon pepper

¼ cup unsalted butter

¼ cup all-purpose flour

½ cup Chicken Stock (Chapter 5)

1½ cups whole milk

½ cup mascarpone cheese

½ cup grated mozzarella cheese

¼ cup grated Parmesan cheese, divided

1. Preheat oven to 375°F. Bring a large pot of water to a boil.

2. Cook noodles until almost al dente according to package directions. Drain well, rinse with cold water, and set aside.

3. In large skillet, cook pork with onion and mushrooms, stirring to break up meat, until pork is browned, about 8–10 minutes. Drain well.

4. Add garlic and tomato paste to skillet; let tomato paste brown in spots, then stir well. Add undrained tomatoes, tomato sauce, oregano, basil, thyme, and pepper. Bring to a simmer, reduce heat, and simmer for 20 minutes.

5. Meanwhile, for white sauce, in a large saucepan, melt butter over medium heat. Add flour; cook and stir for 2 minutes. Gradually add chicken stock and milk; cook, stirring with a wire whisk, until sauce thickens.

6. Remove white sauce from heat and stir in mascarpone cheese, mozzarella cheese, and half of the Parmesan cheese.

7. In a 13" × 9" glass baking dish, place ½ cup of the meat sauce. Top with three lasagna noodles, then top with ⅓ of the white sauce. Repeat layers, ending with meat sauce. Sprinkle with remaining Parmesan cheese.

8. Bake for 25–35 minutes or until the lasagna is bubbling and hot. Let stand 5 minutes, then cut into squares to serve.

PER SERVING: Calories: 301 | Total Fat: 16g | Saturated Fat: 7g | Cholesterol: 51mg | Protein: 14g | Sodium: 127mg | Potassium: 572mg | Fiber: 2g | Carbohydrates: 23g | Sugar: 5g

CREAMY PESTO PASTA WITH VEGGIES

You can use any veggies you'd like in this simple and flavorful recipe. You can use light cream in place of the heavy cream; just reduce the amount to ⅔ cup. Serve with Flaky Crescent Rolls (Chapter 2) and a fruit salad made with apples, grapes, and oranges.

SERVES 6

2 tablespoons extra-virgin olive oil

1 medium onion, chopped

1 (8-ounce) package mushrooms, sliced

3 cloves garlic, minced

1 medium zucchini, sliced

12 ounces linguine pasta

1 cup grape tomatoes, cut in half

¾ cup Lemony Pesto (Chapter 4)

1 cup heavy cream

1. Bring a large pot of water to a boil.

2. Meanwhile, in large saucepan, heat olive oil over medium heat. Add onion and mushrooms; cook and stir until mushrooms give up their liquid and the liquid evaporates, about 10 minutes.

3. Add garlic and zucchini to pan; cook, stirring occasionally, for another 5 minutes.

4. Cook pasta according to package directions until al dente. Drain, reserving ½ cup pasta-cooking water.

5. Add tomatoes, pesto, and cream to pan with vegetables; simmer for 1 minute. Add pasta and enough reserved pasta water to form a sauce. Toss over medium heat for 1 minute, then serve.

PER SERVING: Calories: 553 | Total Fat: 34g | Saturated Fat: 12g | Cholesterol: 55mg | Protein: 12g | Sodium: 43mg | Potassium: 442mg | Fiber: 4g | Carbohydrates: 49g | Sugar: 3g

SALMON ALFREDO

Alfredo sauce is simply a white sauce, usually with Italian herbs such as oregano and basil added. The sauce is a great base for pasta, salmon, and some sautéed vegetables. You can use leftover cooked salmon fillets, or make some just for this recipe. You can also use cooked chopped chicken in place of the salmon.

SERVES 6

1 pound salmon fillets

1 tablespoon extra-virgin olive oil

1 teaspoon dried dill weed

1 tablespoon unsalted butter

1 shallot, minced

1½ cups light cream

2 tablespoons cornstarch

½ teaspoon grated lemon zest

2 cups frozen baby peas, thawed and drained

12 ounces linguine pasta

2 tablespoons grated Parmesan cheese

1. Brush salmon with olive oil and sprinkle with dill weed. Place on a broiler pan. Broil salmon 6" from heat source for 10–12 minutes or until salmon just flakes when tested with a fork. Let cool for 10 minutes, then break into large pieces, discarding skin. Set aside.

2. Bring a large pot of water to a boil.

3. In large saucepan, melt butter over medium heat. Add shallot; cook and stir until tender, about 3 minutes.

4. Add cream and cornstarch to pan with shallot; bring just to a simmer, stirring frequently with a wire whisk, until mixture thickens. Add lemon zest, peas, and salmon; remove from heat.

5. Cook pasta until al dente according to package directions. Drain and add to pan with salmon mixture. Toss over medium heat for 2 minutes, then sprinkle with cheese and serve.

PER SERVING: Calories: 581 | Total Fat: 29g | Saturated Fat: 14g | Cholesterol: 114mg | Protein: 27g | Sodium: 84mg | Potassium: 616mg | Fiber: 4g | Carbohydrates: 51g | Sugar: 3g

PASTITSIO

Pastitsio is a Greek pasta dish made of a meat sauce and a white sauce layered with penne or ziti pasta in a casserole dish. Lemon and herbs add flavor to this delicious recipe. Leftovers reheat beautifully.

SERVES 16

1 (16-ounce) package penne or ziti pasta

1 large egg, beaten

¼ cup heavy cream

1 pound ground beef

½ pound ground lamb

1 medium onion, chopped

4 cloves garlic, minced

3 tablespoons no-salt-added tomato paste

1 (8-ounce) can no-salt-added tomato sauce

1 teaspoon dried oregano

1 teaspoon dried marjoram

2 cups Beef Stock (Chapter 5), divided

⅓ cup unsalted butter

½ cup all-purpose flour

3 cups whole milk

3 ounces cream cheese, cut into cubes

⅓ cup grated Parmesan cheese

1. Bring a large pot of water to a boil. Add pasta; cook until al dente. Drain pasta, place in large bowl, and toss with beaten egg and heavy cream. Set aside.

2. In large skillet, cook beef and lamb with onion over medium heat, stirring to break up meat. Drain well.

3. Add garlic and tomato paste to pan with meat; let paste brown in spots for a few minutes. Then stir in tomato sauce, oregano, marjoram, and 1 cup beef stock; bring to a simmer, stirring to remove pan drippings. Let simmer while preparing white sauce.

4. In large saucepan, melt butter over medium heat. Add flour; cook and stir for 2 minutes. Add remaining 1 cup stock and milk; cook, stirring with wire whisk, until sauce thickens. Stir in cream cheese until blended.

5. Add ½ cup of the white sauce to the pasta and toss. Place pasta mixture in 13" × 9" glass baking dish.

6. Top with the meat sauce, remaining white sauce, and Parmesan cheese.

7. Preheat oven to 375°F. Bake for 40–50 minutes or until casserole is bubbling and cheese on top starts to brown. Let stand for 10 minutes, then cut into squares to serve.

PER SERVING: Calories: 343 | Total Fat: 17g | Saturated Fat: 8g | Cholesterol: 84mg | Protein: 16g | Sodium: 121mg | Potassium: 323mg | Fiber: 1g | Carbohydrates: 29g | Sugar: 4g

LASAGNA ROLL-UPS

Lasagna noodles are perfect for spreading with a filling and rolling up. You can use any filling you'd like in this recipe, but starting with ground pork and adding lots of herbs makes a very tasty dish. Serve with Garlic Bread (Chapter 6), steamed asparagus, and a green salad tossed with mushrooms and dried cranberries.

SERVES 6

12 lasagna noodles

1 pound ground pork

1 medium onion, chopped

2 (8-ounce) cans no-salt-added tomato sauce, divided

1 teaspoon dried basil leaves

½ teaspoon dried oregano leaves

⅛ teaspoon pepper

1½ cups ricotta cheese

1 large egg

2 tablespoons chopped flat-leaf parsley

1. Bring a large pot of water to a boil. Cook the lasagna noodles until al dente according to package directions. Drain, rinse with cold water, drain again, and set aside.

2. In large saucepan, cook pork with onion until the pork is browned, stirring to break up meat. Drain well.

3. Add one can of tomato sauce, basil, oregano, and pepper to the pork mixture; simmer for 5 minutes, stirring occasionally.

4. In medium bowl, combine ricotta, egg, and parsley; mix well.

5. Spread the lasagna noodles on a work surface. Spread each with 2 tablespoons of the ricotta mixture, then top with ¼ cup of the meat mixture. Roll up, starting from short end.

6. Place ½ cup of the remaining can of tomato sauce in a 13" × 9" baking dish. Top with the lasagna rolls, seam-side down. Drizzle remaining tomato sauce over all.

7. Preheat oven to 350°F. Bake for 25–30 minutes or until hot.

PER SERVING: Calories: 519 | Total Fat: 25g | Saturated Fat: 11g | Cholesterol: 121mg | Protein: 27g | Sodium: 117mg | Potassium: 691mg | Fiber: 2g | Carbohydrates: 42g | Sugar: 5g

SPINACH MUSHROOM PASTA SHELLS

Pasta shells come in all sizes. You can buy jumbo shells for stuffing, small shells for making casseroles, and medium shells that are perfect for holding a sauce. This recipe uses medium shells, in a rich spinach mushroom cream sauce. It's perfect for a quick dinner on a weeknight.

SERVES 6

½ ounce dried sliced porcini mushrooms

½ cup warm water

1 (16-ounce) package medium shell pasta

1 tablespoon unsalted butter

1 tablespoon olive oil

1 medium onion, chopped

2 cloves garlic, minced

1 (8-ounce) package cremini mushrooms, sliced

1 teaspoon dried marjoram leaves

Pinch nutmeg

3 cups baby spinach leaves

1 cup light cream

2 tablespoons cornstarch

2 tablespoons grated Parmesan cheese

1. In small bowl combine dried porcini mushrooms and warm water; let stand for 20 minutes. Drain mushrooms, discard stems, and chop tops. Strain soaking water and reserve.

2. Bring a large pot of water to a boil. Cook the pasta according to package directions until al dente; drain, rinse with cold water, and set aside.

3. In large saucepan, melt butter and olive oil over medium heat. Add onion, garlic, and cremini mushrooms; cook and stir for 8 minutes.

4. Add porcini mushrooms, marjoram, nutmeg, and spinach to the pan with vegetables; cook and stir until spinach wilts, about 2–3 minutes.

5. Add mushroom-soaking water, light cream, and cornstarch; bring just to a simmer, stirring frequently. Stir in pasta and Parmesan cheese; toss for 1–2 minutes until coated. Serve immediately.

PER SERVING: Calories: 488 | Total Fat: 18g | Saturated Fat: 9g | Cholesterol: 50mg | Protein: 14g | Sodium: 56mg | Potassium: 424mg | Fiber: 4g | Carbohydrates: 65g | Sugar: 1g

THREE-MUSHROOM PASTA

You can use any three varieties of mushrooms in this simple dish. The point is to use mushrooms that have different appearances and flavor to add interest. The type of pasta you use is also important. To stand up to the sauce, choose penne or ziti.

SERVES 6

1 ounce dried porcini mushrooms

½ cup warm water

2 tablespoons olive oil

1 tablespoon unsalted butter

2 shallots, minced

2 cloves garlic, minced

1 cup sliced shiitake mushrooms

1 cup sliced cremini mushrooms

1 (14-ounce) can no-salt-added diced tomatoes, undrained

1 cup Beef Stock (Chapter 5)

1 teaspoon dried marjoram leaves

⅛ teaspoon pepper

1 (12-ounce) box penne or ziti pasta

2 tablespoons grated Parmesan cheese

1. Bring a large pot of water to a boil. Combine dried mushrooms and the ½ cup warm water in a small bowl; set aside.

2. In large skillet, heat olive oil and butter. Add shallots and garlic; cook and stir for 4 minutes.

3. Add shiitake and cremini mushrooms to the skillet; cook, stirring occasionally, for another 6 minutes.

4. Meanwhile, drain dried mushrooms, reserving liquid. Remove stems from the mushrooms and discard; chop caps. Add caps and mushroom liquid to skillet along with diced tomatoes, stock, marjoram, and pepper.

5. Bring mushroom mixture to a boil, reduce heat, and simmer for 20 minutes, stirring occasionally, until sauce reduces.

6. Cook pasta until al dente according to package directions. Drain well and add to skillet. Cook for 1–2 minutes longer. Sprinkle with cheese and serve.

PER SERVING: Calories: 326 | Total Fat: 8g | Saturated Fat: 2g | Cholesterol: 6mg | Protein: 11g | Sodium: 48mg | Potassium: 440mg | Fiber: 4g | Carbohydrates: 51g | Sugar: 3g

MEATBALL ONE-POT PASTA

Did you know you can cook pasta right in the sauce you'll serve with it? Not only is this more efficient, with no pots of boiling water to lug around, but the pasta absorbs the flavors in the sauce so it's even more delicious than usual. Use homemade meatballs in this simple recipe. Serve with a green salad, garlic bread, and red wine.

SERVES 6

½ recipe Savory Meatballs (Chapter 9)

2 tablespoons olive oil

1 medium onion, chopped

3 cloves garlic, minced

¼ cup no-salt-added tomato paste

1 (8-ounce) can no-salt-added tomato sauce

3 cups Beef Stock (Chapter 5)

1 teaspoon dried basil leaves

½ teaspoon dried thyme leaves

⅛ teaspoon pepper

1 (12-ounce) package spaghetti pasta

½ cup heavy cream

1. Make the meatballs as directed and bake. Set aside.

2. In large skillet, heat olive oil over medium heat. Add onion and garlic; cook and stir until tender, about 7–9 minutes.

3. Add tomato paste, tomato sauce, beef stock, basil, thyme, and pepper and bring to a simmer.

4. Add pasta to the skillet. Stir to make sure the pasta is all underneath the liquid in the skillet. Bring to a simmer, then reduce heat to medium-low and cover skillet.

5. Cook, stirring occasionally, for 10 minutes. Then add the meatballs, cover again, and cook, stirring frequently, for another 5–8 minutes or until pasta is tender. Stir in the cream and heat for another 2 minutes, then serve immediately.

PER SERVING: Calories: 568 | Total Fat: 26g | Saturated Fat: 11g | Cholesterol: 103mg | Protein: 28g | Sodium: 119mg | Potassium: 850mg | Fiber: 4g | Carbohydrates: 53g | Sugar: 5g

LEMON AND GREENS PASTA

If you browse through the produce section of your supermarket you will be amazed at how many different kinds of greens there are. From kale to collards, from spinach to turnip greens and watercress, choose your favorites for this beautiful recipe. Just make sure to wash the greens really well—they can be quite sandy.

SERVES 6

1 (16-ounce) package linguine pasta

2 tablespoons olive oil

1 shallot, minced

4 cloves garlic, minced

1 cup sliced collard greens

1 cup sliced kale

1 cup sliced baby spinach leaves

1 cup watercress

1 cup Vegetable Broth (Chapter 5) or Chicken Stock (Chapter 5)

3 tablespoons lemon juice

1 teaspoon grated lemon zest

¼ cup sliced fresh basil leaves

⅓ cup grated Parmesan cheese

1. Bring a large pot of water to a boil. Cook the pasta according to package directions until al dente. Drain pasta, reserving ½ cup pasta-cooking water.

2. In large skillet, heat olive oil over medium heat. Add shallot and garlic; cook and stir until fragrant, about 2 minutes.

3. Add the collard greens and kale; sauté for 2–3 minutes. Add the spinach and watercress; sauté for another minute.

4. Add the broth or stock, lemon juice, and zest, and bring to a simmer. Simmer for 1–2 minutes or until greens are tender.

5. Add the basil and the pasta. Add enough reserved cooking water to make a sauce, if necessary; toss over medium heat for 1 minute. Sprinkle with cheese and serve.

PER SERVING: Calories: 386 | Total Fat: 8g | Saturated Fat: 2g | Cholesterol: 4mg | Protein: 15g | Sodium: 114mg | Potassium: 281mg | Fiber: 4g | Carbohydrates: 62g | Sugar: 1g

PENNE PESTO WITH MEATBALLS

Penne is a tubular pasta; the name means "quills" in Latin. The ends are pointed so it looks like a quill people used to write with. This pasta stands up to meatballs and robust pesto beautifully. So much flavor is packed into this recipe that you won't miss the salt at all.

SERVES 6

1 (16-ounce) package penne pasta

2 tablespoons olive oil

1 medium onion, chopped

2 cloves garlic, minced

½ recipe Savory Meatballs (Chapter 9)

½ cup Beef Stock (Chapter 5)

1 cup Lemony Pesto (Chapter 4)

2 tablespoons grated Parmesan cheese

1. Bring a large pot of water to a boil. Add the pasta; cook until al dente according to package directions. Drain, reserving ½ cup cooking water.

2. Meanwhile, in large skillet heat olive oil over medium heat. Add onion and garlic; cook, stirring frequently, for 8–9 minutes or until the onion starts to color.

3. Add the cooked meatballs to the onion mixture along with beef stock; simmer for 4–5 minutes.

4. Add the pasta, pesto, and cheese to the meatball mixture, along with enough cooking water to make a sauce, if necessary. Toss over heat for 1–2 minutes, then serve immediately.

PER SERVING: Calories: 716 | Total Fat: 38g | Saturated Fat: 9g | Cholesterol: 79mg | Protein: 30g | Sodium: 122mg | Potassium: 593mg | Fiber: 4g | Carbohydrates: 62g | Sugar: 2g

TOASTED WALNUT AND PARSLEY PESTO WITH NOODLES

Although this dish is delicious as it is, if you are feeling adventurous you could also sprinkle a spice blend over the top. You could use a traditional Italian spice mix or try something out of the ordinary, such as Chipotle Chili Powder Spice Blend (Appendix A) or salt-free chili powder blend.

SERVES 4

4 tablespoons chopped walnuts

4 cups cooked egg noodles (no salt added to cooking water)

4 tablespoons extra-virgin olive oil

¾ cup fresh parsley

2 tablespoons grated Parmesan cheese

1 clove garlic, crushed

2 teaspoons fresh lemon juice

Freshly ground black pepper, to taste

1. In a small nonstick saucepan over medium heat, toast the walnuts until they're light brown, being careful not to burn them. Set aside to cool.

2. Cook the noodles in unsalted water according to package directions. Drain.

3. While the noodles cook, add the oil, parsley, Parmesan cheese, crushed garlic, lemon juice, and half of the toasted walnuts to the bowl of a food processor. Process until smooth.

4. In a large serving bowl, toss the warm, drained cooked noodles with the pesto and the remaining chopped toasted walnuts. Grind the black pepper over the pasta and serve.

PER SERVING: Calories: 369 | Total Fat: 18g | Saturated Fat: 2g | Cholesterol: 48mg | Protein: 8g | Sodium: 52mg | Potassium: 140mg | Fiber: 2g | Carbohydrates: 41g | Sugar: 0g

CHICKEN BRUSCHETTA PASTA

Bruschetta is an Italian appetizer made of toasted bread rubbed with garlic, then topped with tomatoes, vinegar, and basil. Let's turn that into a pasta main course with some chicken and linguine. This fresh and gorgeous main dish is perfect for dinner in the summer. Make it only when tomatoes and basil are in season.

SERVES 8

1 pound linguine pasta

2 tablespoons olive oil

5 (6-ounce) boneless, skinless chicken breasts, cut into strips

¼ teaspoon pepper

¼ cup sliced green onion

4 cloves garlic, minced

4 large tomatoes, seeded and chopped

1 cup tomato juice

2 tablespoons balsamic vinegar

1 teaspoon sugar

¼ cup sliced fresh basil leaves

¼ cup grated Parmesan cheese

1. Bring a large pot of water to a boil. Cook the linguine pasta according to package directions until al dente. Drain, reserving ½ cup cooking water.

2. Heat olive oil over medium heat in large skillet. Sprinkle chicken with pepper and add to skillet. Cook, stirring frequently, until chicken is done at 160°F. Remove from skillet and set aside.

3. Add green onions and garlic to skillet and cook, stirring to remove pan drippings, until tender, about 2 minutes.

4. Add tomatoes and tomato juice to skillet; simmer for 4–5 minutes or until tomatoes start to break down.

5. Add chicken back to skillet along with vinegar, sugar, and pasta. Toss over medium heat for a few minutes, adding reserved pasta-cooking water as necessary. Sprinkle with basil and cheese and serve.

PER SERVING: Calories: 474 | Total Fat: 9g | Saturated Fat: 2g | Cholesterol: 94mg | Protein: 44g | Sodium: 132mg | Potassium: 592mg | Fiber: 3g | Carbohydrates: 50g | Sugar: 5g

SWEET-AND-SOUR PORK PENNE

Sweet and sour aren't flavors usually served with pasta, but this recipe is delicious. You can also make this recipe with chicken, or use ziti or medium shell pasta. Serve with red wine and a green salad.

SERVES 6

1 cup Chicken Stock (Chapter 5)

½ cup pineapple juice

½ cup Easy Homemade Ketchup (Chapter 4)

2 tablespoons Mustard (Chapter 4)

3 tablespoons lemon juice

3 tablespoons sugar

2 tablespoons apple cider vinegar

3 tablespoons water

2 tablespoons cornstarch

1½ pounds pork tenderloin, cut into strips

1 (16-ounce) package penne pasta

3 tablespoons olive oil

1 medium onion, chopped

2 medium red bell peppers, cut into strips

3 cloves garlic, minced

1. In large bowl, combine chicken stock, pineapple juice, ketchup, mustard, lemon juice, sugar, vinegar, water, and cornstarch. Add pork and stir. Let stand for 20 minutes.

2. Meanwhile, bring a large pot of water to a boil. Cook the pasta until al dente according to package directions. Drain and reserve.

3. Remove pork from marinade; reserve marinade. Heat oil in large skillet over medium-high heat.

4. Add pork to skillet; stir-fry until done, about 2–4 minutes. Remove pork from skillet.

5. Add onion, red bell peppers, and garlic to the skillet; stir-fry until tender, about 4–6 minutes.

6. Add pork and reserved marinade to skillet; stir-fry until sauce thickens and bubbles. Stir in pasta, stir-fry for 1 minute, then serve.

PER SERVING: Calories: 578 | Total Fat: 11g | Saturated Fat: 2g | Cholesterol: 73mg | Protein: 36g | Sodium: 81mg | Potassium: 790mg | Fiber: 4g | Carbohydrates: 79g | Sugar: 16g

CURRIED CHICKEN PASTA WITH DRIED CRANBERRIES

Curry powder is a piquant combination of many different spices. Buy the best you can afford for the most intense color and flavor. It's delicious sautéed with chicken and vegetables and served with pasta. Dried cranberries are an unusual ingredient in this recipe, but they add a punch of color and flavor.

SERVES 4

1 (12-ounce) package gemelli pasta

3 (6-ounce) boneless, skinless chicken breasts, cut into strips

3 tablespoons flour

2–3 teaspoons curry powder

⅛ teaspoon pepper

2 tablespoons olive oil

1 medium onion, chopped

½ cup sliced celery

2 cloves garlic, minced

1 cup Chicken Stock (Chapter 5)

½ cup light cream

⅓ cup dried cranberries

1. Bring a large pot of water to a boil. Cook pasta until al dente according to package directions. Drain and set aside.

2. Meanwhile, sprinkle chicken with flour, curry powder, and pepper. Heat oil in large skillet over medium heat; cook chicken, stirring frequently, until light brown and done to 160°F, about 4–6 minutes. Remove chicken from skillet.

3. Add onion, celery, and garlic to skillet; cook, stirring to remove pan drippings, until tender, about 5–7 minutes.

4. Add stock to skillet; bring to a simmer. Return chicken to skillet along with pasta, cream, and cranberries; simmer for 2–3 minutes until sauce coats the ingredients. Serve immediately.

PER SERVING: Calories: 767 | Total Fat: 23g | Saturated Fat: 8g | Cholesterol: 142mg | Protein: 56g | Sodium: 133mg | Potassium: 520mg | Fiber: 5g | Carbohydrates: 80g | Sugar: 8g

SAUSAGE FETTUCCINE AND BROCCOLI RABE

Broccoli rabe is an interesting vegetable. It looks like broccoli, but has flowers and leggier stems. The heads are smaller than regular broccoli stems. When cooked, it becomes silky and tender with a slightly bitter flavor, the perfect foil for sausage, pasta, and pesto. Serve with a fruit salad and some brownies for dessert.

SERVES 8

1 (12-ounce) package fettuccine pasta

1 tablespoon olive oil

½ recipe Spicy Sausage (Chapter 10)

1 medium onion, chopped

2 cloves garlic, minced

1 pound broccoli rabe, trimmed

1 cup Chicken Stock (Chapter 5)

½ cup Lemony Pesto (Chapter 4)

1. Bring a large pot of water to a boil. Cook the pasta according to package directions until al dente. Drain, reserving ½ cup pasta-cooking water.

2. Meanwhile, heat olive oil in large saucepan over medium heat. Add sausage; cook, stirring to break up meat, until sausage is done. Drain well.

3. Add onion, garlic, and broccoli rabe to sausage in saucepan. Cook, stirring frequently, for 4 minutes.

4. Add the stock to the broccoli rabe and bring to a simmer. Simmer for 4–6 minutes, stirring occasionally, until broccoli rabe is tender.

5. Add pesto and pasta to the saucepan and toss over medium heat, adding reserved cooking water as needed to make a sauce. Serve immediately.

PER SERVING: Calories: 331 | Total Fat: 15g | Saturated Fat: 3g | Cholesterol: 19mg | Protein: 13g | Sodium: 140mg | Potassium: 298mg | Fiber: 3g | Carbohydrates: 35g | Sugar: 1g

PORCINI PESTO PASTA

Porcini mushrooms can be very large with a very thick stem. They are almost always sold dry and can be expensive. But their rich and meaty flavor is incomparable. Pesto, onions, garlic, and pasta complete this simple but hearty dish. It's best served with red wine and a spinach salad tossed with tomatoes.

SERVES 8

2 ounces dried porcini mushrooms

1 cup warm water

1 (16-ounce) package penne pasta

2 tablespoons olive oil

1 medium onion, chopped

3 cloves garlic, minced

1 cup Lemony Pesto (Chapter 4)

⅓ cup ricotta cheese

1. Combine mushrooms and water in a medium bowl; let stand for 20 minutes. Drain, reserving soaking water. Strain the soaking water to remove any grit. Chop mushrooms.

2. Bring a large pot of water to a boil. Cook the pasta according to package directions until al dente. Drain, reserving ½ cup cooking water; set aside.

3. In large saucepan, heat olive oil over medium heat. Add onion and garlic; cook and stir for 5–7 minutes or until almost tender. Add mushrooms; cook for 2 minutes.

4. Add mushroom-soaking liquid and bring to a simmer.

5. Add pasta, pesto, ricotta cheese, and enough reserved cooking water to make a sauce. Toss over medium heat until ingredients are coated. Serve.

PER SERVING: Calories: 425 | Total Fat: 20g | Saturated Fat: 3g | Cholesterol: 6mg | Protein: 11g | Sodium: 33mg | Potassium: 251mg | Fiber: 3g | Carbohydrates: 50g | Sugar: 1g

VEGGIE PASTA STIR-FRY

A stir-fry is a great way to serve pasta. The vegetables stay bright and crisp-tender, making them the perfect complement to the tender pasta. Use your favorite veggies; just choose ones that cook in about the same amount of time so they are all tender and finished at the same time.

SERVES 6

1 (12-ounce) package linguine or spaghetti

2 tablespoons olive oil

1 cup sliced leeks

1 medium onion, chopped

1 cup sliced mushrooms

1 medium red bell pepper, sliced

2 cloves garlic, minced

1 large tomato, chopped

1 cup sliced zucchini

1 cup frozen baby peas, thawed

½ teaspoon dried thyme leaves

½ teaspoon dried basil leaves

⅓ cup light cream

2 tablespoons grated Parmesan cheese

1. Bring a large pot of water to a boil. Cook the pasta according to package directions until al dente. Drain, reserving ½ cup pasta-cooking water.

2. In large skillet, heat olive oil over medium heat. Add leeks, onion, and mushrooms; stir-fry for 5 minutes.

3. Add red bell pepper and garlic; stir-fry for another 2 minutes. Then add tomato and zucchini; stir-fry for 2–3 minutes longer.

4. Add pasta, peas, thyme, basil, and cream, along with enough reserved pasta-cooking water to make a sauce. Toss over medium heat until combined. Sprinkle with cheese and serve immediately.

PER SERVING: Calories: 348 | Total Fat: 10g | Saturated Fat: 3g | Cholesterol: 16mg | Protein: 11g | Sodium: 38mg | Potassium: 370mg | Fiber: 4g | Carbohydrates: 52g | Sugar: 5g

SIMPLE TOMATO SAUCE

This sauce is so simple to make but tastes as if you toiled all day in the kitchen over it. If you are not using all the sauce immediately, allow it to cool completely and pour 1- or 2-cup portions into freezer containers; it will keep in the freezer for up to 6 months.

SERVES 12

½ cup extra-virgin olive oil

1 large sweet onion, chopped

2 cloves garlic, minced

1 large stalk celery, finely chopped

1 large carrot, peeled and grated

¼ teaspoon freshly ground black pepper

⅛ teaspoon mustard powder

1 (14-ounce) can no-salt-added diced
   tomatoes

¼ teaspoon (or to taste) granulated sugar

⅛ teaspoon grated lemon zest

1 (15-ounce) can no-salt-added tomato sauce

1 (28-ounce) can no-salt-added tomato purée

2 dried bay leaves

½ teaspoon dried oregano, crushed

½ teaspoon dried basil, crushed

Pinch red pepper flakes

Optional: 1 teaspoon onion powder

Optional: 1 teaspoon garlic powder

Optional: 4 tablespoons unsalted butter or
   extra-virgin olive oil

1. In a large, deep nonstick sauté pan, heat the oil over medium-high heat. Add the onion and garlic; sauté until soft and translucent, about 5–10 minutes.

2. Add the celery, carrot, black pepper, and mustard powder; mix well. Sauté for 5 minutes.

3. Drain the juice from the diced tomatoes and reserve. Add the drained tomatoes to the pot; sauté until all the vegetables are soft, about 5–10 minutes. Add the sautéed tomato mixture to the bowl of a food processor; process until smooth. Return to the pan.

4. Add the reserved juice from the tomatoes, the sugar, lemon zest, tomato sauce, tomato purée, bay leaves, oregano, basil, and red pepper flakes; reduce heat and simmer, uncovered, for 45 minutes.

5. Remove the bay leaves and discard; check sauce for seasoning, adding the onion and garlic powders at this time, if desired. Simmer for an additional 15 minutes or until thick. If the sauce tastes too acidic, add a little bit more sugar or some fresh or dried thyme, a pinch at a time; you can also mellow the flavor by whisking in some unsalted butter, 1 tablespoon at a time.

PER SERVING: Calories: 139 | Total Fat: 9g | Saturated Fat: 1g | Cholesterol: 0mg | Protein: 2g | Sodium: 36mg | Potassium: 556mg | Fiber: 2g | Carbohydrates: 13g | Sugar: 7g

LOW-FAT TOMATO SAUCE

As you are making this sauce, remember that a pinch of sugar is a wonderful flavor enhancer and will help cut the acidity in this (or any other) cooked tomato sauce.

SERVES 12

Olive oil spray

1 large sweet onion, chopped

2 cloves garlic, minced

1 large stalk celery, finely chopped

1 large carrot, peeled and grated

1 dried bay leaf

1 (14-ounce) can no-salt-added diced tomatoes

½ teaspoon dried oregano, crushed

½ teaspoon dried basil, crushed

Pinch red pepper flakes

¼ teaspoon freshly ground black pepper

⅛ teaspoon mustard powder

1 teaspoon (or to taste) granulated sugar

⅛ teaspoon dried lemon granules, crushed

1 (15-ounce) can no-salt-added tomato sauce

1 (28-ounce) can no-salt-added tomato purée

1 teaspoon onion powder

1 teaspoon garlic powder

2 teaspoons extra-virgin olive oil

1. In a large, covered microwave-safe casserole dish treated with the olive spray oil, add the onion, garlic, celery, carrot, and bay leaf. Drain the juice from the diced tomatoes and reserve. Add the drained tomatoes to the dish; mix well. Cover and microwave on high for 5 minutes, turning the dish halfway through the cooking time.

2. Carefully remove the cover and stir in the oregano, basil, red pepper flakes, black pepper, mustard powder, sugar, and lemon granules. Cover and let rest for 3 minutes. Carefully remove the cover and check that the onion is transparent. If not, microwave on high for additional 1-minute increments until all the vegetables are cooked and soft.

3. Remove the bay leaf and discard; add the tomato mixture to the bowl of a food processor; process until smooth.

4. Bring a large, deep nonstick sauté pan treated with the spray oil to temperature over low heat. Add the puréed tomato-vegetable mixture, reserved juice from the tomatoes, tomato sauce, and tomato purée; reduce heat and simmer, uncovered, for 45 minutes.

5. Add the onion and garlic powders; simmer for an additional 15 minutes or until thick. Whisk in the extra-virgin olive oil. If the sauce tastes too acidic, add a little bit more sugar or thyme, a pinch at a time.

6. If you are not using all the sauce immediately, allow it to cool completely and pour 1- to 2-cup portions into freezer containers; it will keep in the freezer for up to 6 months.

PER SERVING: Calories: 67 | Total Fat: 1g | Saturated Fat: 0g | Cholesterol: 0mg | Protein: 2g | Sodium: 33mg | Potassium: 545mg | Fiber: 2g | Carbohydrates: 13g | Sugar: 7g

EASY CHICKEN LO MEIN

If you prefer to serve the stir-fry over brown rice—or another grain, like quinoa—simply add some lemon juice and mustard powder to the cooking water instead of the salt suggested on the package.

SERVES 8

⅛ teaspoon chicken base

½ cup water

2 (10-ounce) packages frozen stir-fry vegetables

1 tablespoon freeze-dried shallots

1 pound cooked dark- and light-meat chicken

⅛ cup (or to taste) no-salt-added ginger stir-fry sauce

1 pound no-salt-added oat bran pasta

1 teaspoon lemon juice

⅛ teaspoon mustard powder

1 teaspoon cornstarch

¼ teaspoon toasted sesame oil

Optional: 4 thinly sliced scallions

Optional: Bragg Liquid Aminos or other low-sodium soy sauce

1. Add the chicken base and water to a large microwave-safe bowl; microwave on high for 30 seconds. Stir to dissolve the base into the water.

2. Add the vegetables and freeze-dried shallots to the bowl; microwave on high for 3–5 minutes, depending on how you prefer your vegetables cooked. (Keep in mind that the vegetables will continue to steam for a minute or so while the cover remains on the dish.) Drain ¼ cup of the broth into a small nonstick sauté pan and set aside.

3. Add the chicken and stir-fry sauce to the vegetables; stir well. Cover and set aside.

4. Bring a large pot of water to a boil. Add the pasta, lemon juice, and mustard powder.

5. While the pasta cooks, in a small cup or bowl add a tablespoon of water to the cornstarch and whisk to make a slurry. Bring the reserved broth in the sauté pan to a boil over medium-high heat. Whisk in the slurry; cook for at least 1 minute, stirring constantly.

6. Once the mixture thickens, remove from heat; add the toasted sesame oil to the broth mixture, then whisk again. Pour the thickened broth mixture over the vegetables and chicken; toss to mix. Cover and microwave the chicken-vegetable mixture at 70 percent power for 2 minutes or until the chicken is heated through.

7. Drain the pasta; add it to the chicken-vegetable mixture and stir to combine. Divide among 4 plates. Garnish with chopped scallion, and liquid aminos, if using.

PER SERVING: Calories: 370 | Total Fat: 5g | Saturated Fat: 1g | Cholesterol: 47mg | Protein: 25g | Sodium: 65mg | Potassium: 286mg | Fiber: 5g | Carbohydrates: 52g | Sugar: 3g

CHAPTER 8

POULTRY MAIN DISHES

CURRIED CHICKEN MEATBALL AND RICE SKILLET

Chicken meatballs are delicate, tender, and delicious, especially when flavored with curry powder. Accompany with a crisp green salad and some fresh fruit for a cooling contrast.

SERVES 6

1 slice Basic White Bread (Chapter 2), made into crumbs

4 teaspoons curry powder, divided

1 large egg

1 tablespoon chopped fresh chives

1 pound ground chicken

2 tablespoons unsalted butter

1 tablespoon olive oil

1 medium onion, chopped

2 cloves garlic, minced

1⅓ cups basmati rice

2 cups Chicken Stock (Chapter 5)

⅓ cup water

⅓ cup mango chutney

1 tablespoon lemon juice

1. In medium bowl, combine bread crumbs, 2 teaspoons curry powder, egg, and chives and mix well. Add ground chicken and mix gently to coat. Form into 16 meatballs.

2. Combine unsalted butter and olive oil in a large saucepan over medium heat. When this mixture melts, add the meatballs and cook until browned, about 5 minutes, turning gently. Remove meatballs from skillet.

3. Add onion and garlic to skillet; cook and stir to remove brown bits. Cook for another 5–6 minutes or until tender.

4. Add rice and stir; cook for 1 minute longer. Add chicken stock, water, chutney, lemon juice, and remaining 2 teaspoons curry powder, and bring to a simmer.

5. Return meatballs to skillet and cover; reduce heat to low. Simmer for 18–22 minutes or until rice is tender and the meatballs are done to 165°F. Serve immediately.

PER SERVING: Calories: 305 | Total Fat: 9g | Saturated Fat: 3g | Cholesterol: 87mg | Protein: 19g | Sodium: 121mg | Potassium: 158mg | Fiber: 0g | Carbohydrates: 33g | Sugar: 1g

GUACAMOLE-STUFFED CHICKEN

Guacamole is delicious on its own, of course, but it's simply fabulous stuffed inside a tender chicken breast. The creamy guacamole is the perfect complement to the succulent chicken. And the crispy coating is a wonderful finishing touch.

SERVES 4

4 (6-ounce) boneless, skinless chicken breasts

1 cup Roasted Garlic Guacamole (Chapter 6)

¼ cup flour

⅛ teaspoon pepper

1 large egg, beaten

2 slices French Bread (Chapter 2), crumbled

2 tablespoons grated Parmesan cheese

1. Preheat oven to 375°F. Place chicken breasts on waxed paper and cover with more waxed paper. Using a rolling pin, pound until about ⅓" thick, being careful not to tear the meat. Peel off the top piece of waxed paper.

2. Divide guacamole among the chicken breasts and roll up, tucking in the ends. Secure with toothpicks.

3. On plate, combine flour and pepper. Roll chicken in this mixture and shake off excess.

4. Place egg in shallow bowl. Dip each piece of chicken into the egg.

5. On plate, combine bread crumbs and cheese. Dip chicken into this mixture to coat and place in baking dish.

6. Bake chicken for about 30–35 minutes or until a meat thermometer registers 160°F. Make sure you are not putting the thermometer tip in the guacamole in the center of the chicken. Let rest for 5 minutes, then remove toothpicks and serve.

PER SERVING: Calories: 291 | Total Fat: 10g | Saturated Fat: 2g | Cholesterol: 120mg | Protein: 31g | Sodium: 140mg | Potassium: 597mg | Fiber: 3g | Carbohydrates: 16g | Sugar: 0g

APPLE CHICKEN

Chicken breasts are mild and tender and pair well with lots of different ingredients. Apples are a nice pairing with this meat, especially when you add pecans and lemon juice. This easy recipe can be multiplied to serve more people; just use a larger pan! Serve with a chopped vegetable salad and some heated dinner rolls.

SERVES 4

4 (6-ounce) boneless, skinless chicken breasts

¼ cup flour

½ teaspoon dried thyme leaves

⅛ teaspoon white pepper

2 tablespoons unsalted butter

1 tablespoon olive oil

2 unpeeled Granny Smith apples, thickly sliced

1½ cups apple juice

2 tablespoons lemon juice

3 tablespoons Honey Mustard (Chapter 4)

3 tablespoons sliced green onions

½ cup chopped toasted pecans

1. Sprinkle chicken breasts with flour, thyme, and pepper.

2. In large skillet, heat butter and olive oil over medium heat until melted. Add chicken; cook, turning once, until golden brown, about 5–7 minutes. Remove chicken from skillet.

3. To drippings remaining in skillet, add apples; sauté for 2 minutes. Add apple juice, lemon juice, and honey mustard to skillet and bring to a simmer.

4. Return chicken to skillet; reduce heat to low and simmer for another 7–9 minutes or until chicken is thoroughly cooked to 160°F. Sprinkle with green onions and toasted pecans and serve.

PER SERVING: Calories: 739 | Total Fat: 37g | Saturated Fat: 7g | Cholesterol: 161mg | Protein: 60g | Sodium: 125mg | Potassium: 779mg | Fiber: 6g | Carbohydrates: 42g | Sugar: 25g

PINEAPPLE CURRY CHICKEN

Curry powder is a wonderful complement to chicken, as is pineapple. So combine them for a delicious and easy dish! When made in the slow cooker, this easy recipe will perfume your house all day.

SERVES 4

1 medium onion, chopped

1 cup baby carrots

3 cloves garlic, minced

4 (6-ounce) boneless, skinless chicken breasts, cut into strips

2 (8-ounce) cans pineapple tidbits, drained, reserving juice

1 tablespoon curry powder

1 (13-ounce) can coconut milk

½ cup Chicken Stock (Chapter 5)

2 tablespoons cornstarch

2 tablespoons water

1. In 4- to 5-quart slow cooker, place onion, carrots, and garlic. Top with chicken breasts, then add pineapple.

2. In small bowl, combine curry powder with reserved pineapple liquid; pour into slow cooker. Add coconut milk and stock.

3. Cover and cook on low for 7–8 hours or until chicken is tender and thoroughly cooked to 160°F.

4. In small bowl, combine cornstarch and water and mix until smooth. Stir into slow cooker; cover and cook on high for 10–15 minutes or until sauce is thickened. Serve over hot cooked rice.

PER SERVING: Calories: 416 | Total Fat: 21g | Saturated Fat: 17g | Cholesterol: 65mg | Protein: 29g | Sodium: 119mg | Potassium: 798mg | Fiber: 3g | Carbohydrates: 29g | Sugar: 17g

CHICKEN AND MUSHROOM RISOTTO

Risotto is an Italian dish, made by cooking short-grain rice in stock while stirring frequently. The stirring action helps the rice release starch as it cooks, which makes the finished dish creamy. For best results, use short-grain Arborio rice for this recipe—although I have made it with long-grain rice and it's delicious that way, too.

SERVES 6

1 ounce dried mushrooms

½ cup warm water

3 (6-ounce) boneless, skinless chicken breasts

2 tablespoons unsalted butter

1 tablespoon olive oil

1 medium onion, chopped

4 cloves garlic, minced

1 (8-ounce) package button mushrooms, sliced

1½ cups uncooked Arborio or long-grain rice

½ cup dry white wine

3–4 cups Chicken Stock (Chapter 5)

⅓ cup crumbled soft goat cheese

2 tablespoons minced fresh chives

1. Place dried mushrooms in a small bowl and cover with water; let stand until softened. Drain mushrooms, reserving liquid. Cut stems off mushrooms and discard; chop mushrooms. Strain liquid and set aside.

2. Cut chicken into 1" cubes and set aside.

3. Heat unsalted butter and olive oil in a large saucepan over medium heat. Add onion and garlic; cook for 3 minutes.

4. Add button mushrooms; cook for 5–7 minutes longer or until mushrooms give up their liquid and the liquid evaporates. Stir in chicken; cook for 3 minutes. Add rehydrated dried mushrooms.

5. Add the rice; cook and stir for 2 minutes. Then add the reserved mushroom soaking liquid and wine; cook over medium heat, stirring frequently, until liquid is absorbed.

6. Add the chicken stock, one ladle at a time, stirring after each addition, until the rice is tender. This should take about 20–25 minutes. Add the goat cheese and chives.

7. Cover and remove from heat; let stand for 3–4 minutes. Stir and serve immediately.

PER SERVING: Calories: 413 | Total Fat: 14g | Saturated Fat: 6g | Cholesterol: 94mg | Protein: 37g | Sodium: 135mg | Potassium: 592mg | Fiber: 1g | Carbohydrates: 28g | Sugar: 1g

CHICKEN CARBONARA

The trick to this recipe is to add the egg mixture off the heat, so the eggs cook when they come into contact with the hot pasta but don't scramble. This dish must be served immediately while it's hot so that you get the wonderful contrast of tender chicken, creamy sauce, and al dente pasta.

SERVES 8

4 (6-ounce) boneless, skinless chicken breasts, cubed

⅛ teaspoon white pepper

2 tablespoons unsalted butter

1 (16-ounce) package spaghetti

1 tablespoon olive oil

1 medium onion, chopped

1 medium red bell pepper, chopped

3 cloves garlic, minced

4 large eggs, beaten

⅔ cup whole milk

¼ cup grated Parmesan cheese

1. Bring a large pot of water to a boil over high heat.

2. Sprinkle chicken with pepper. In large skillet, melt butter over medium heat. Add chicken; cook, stirring frequently, until chicken registers 160°F on a meat thermometer. Remove chicken from skillet and set aside.

3. Add pasta to water; cook according to package directions until al dente, or just barely tender to the bite.

4. Meanwhile, add olive oil to skillet; cook onion, bell pepper, and garlic until tender, about 4–5 minutes. Return chicken to skillet and remove from heat.

5. In medium bowl, beat eggs with milk and cheese.

6. Reserve ½ cup pasta-cooking water. Drain pasta and immediately add to skillet with chicken and vegetables.

7. Pour egg mixture over hot pasta and chicken mixture and toss with tongs until coated, adding some of the reserved pasta-cooking water if needed to form a smooth sauce. Serve immediately.

PER SERVING: Calories: 472 | Total Fat: 12g | Saturated Fat: 4g | Cholesterol: 191mg | Protein: 40g | Sodium: 125mg | Potassium: 346mg | Fiber: 3g | Carbohydrates: 45g | Sugar: 2g

CHICKEN CHUTNEY STIR-FRY

Stir-fries are simple to make, if you follow one rule: Have all of the ingredients prepared before you start to cook. Once the cooking process starts, you can't stop to chop a bell pepper or find the curry powder. Once you start cooking, this delicious recipe will be ready for the table in about 15 minutes.

SERVES 4

3 (6-ounce) boneless, skinless chicken breasts, cubed

2 teaspoons curry powder

⅛ teaspoon white pepper

¾ cup coconut milk

¼ cup mango chutney

1 tablespoon cornstarch

2 tablespoons safflower oil

1 medium onion, chopped

1 large carrot, cut into ¼" rounds

1 medium yellow bell pepper, chopped

2 cloves garlic, minced

½ cup chopped unsalted peanuts

1. In bowl, combine chicken, curry powder, and white pepper; mix until coated. Set aside for 10 minutes.

2. In another bowl, combine coconut milk, chutney, and cornstarch and mix well.

3. In wok or skillet, heat safflower oil over medium-high heat. Add chicken; stir-fry until chicken is almost done. Remove chicken from wok to a plate.

4. Add onion to wok; stir-fry until crisp-tender, about 4 minutes. Add carrot; stir-fry for another 3 minutes. Add bell pepper and garlic; stir-fry for 2 minutes longer.

5. Return chicken to wok. Add coconut-milk mixture; stir-fry until sauce is thickened and chicken is cooked to 160°F, about 3 minutes. Sprinkle with peanuts and serve with hot rice.

PER SERVING: Calories: 394 | Total Fat: 26g | Saturated Fat: 10g | Cholesterol: 49mg | Protein: 25g | Sodium: 76mg | Potassium: 640mg | Fiber: 3g | Carbohydrates: 17g | Sugar: 5g

MUSTARD-BRAISED CHICKEN

Braising is cooking meat for a fairly long time, covered, in a liquid. Because of this long cooking time, chicken breasts will not work, so you'll need to use chicken thighs. And they're cooked on the bone for more flavor.

SERVES 4

8 bone-in, skin-on chicken thighs

⅛ teaspoon pepper

1 teaspoon dry mustard powder

1 teaspoon dried basil leaves

1 tablespoon unsalted butter

1 tablespoon olive oil

1 medium onion, chopped

3 cloves garlic, sliced

2 russet potatoes, cut into 1½" pieces

1½ cups Chicken Stock (Chapter 5)

6 tablespoons Grainy Mustard (Chapter 4), divided

2 tablespoons chopped chives

1. Sprinkle chicken with pepper, mustard powder, and basil; rub into skin and set aside for 10 minutes.

2. Combine butter and olive oil in a large skillet with a lid over medium heat. Add chicken, skin-side down; cook until browned, about 5–6 minutes. Remove chicken to plate.

3. Add onion and garlic to skillet; cook, stirring to remove pan drippings, until onion is crisp-tender, about 5–6 minutes.

4. Return chicken to skillet and place potatoes around chicken.

5. In small bowl, combine stock and 4 tablespoons mustard; mix well. Pour into skillet.

6. Bring to a simmer over medium heat, then reduce heat to low. Cover and simmer until chicken registers 160°F on a thermometer and potatoes are tender. Stir in remaining mustard, then sprinkle with chives and serve.

PER SERVING: Calories: 564 | Total Fat: 28g | Saturated Fat: 7g | Cholesterol: 122mg | Protein: 37g | Sodium: 128mg | Potassium: 1,190mg | Fiber: 4g | Carbohydrates: 37g | Sugar: 3g

COBB PITA SANDWICH

Cobb salads are made of chicken, bacon, blue cheese, and vegetables all combined in a creamy dressing. Let's turn that great recipe into a sandwich using your own homemade pita breads.

SERVES 4

2 (6-ounce) boneless, skinless chicken breasts

½ teaspoon dried thyme leaves

⅛ teaspoon white pepper

¼ cup lemon juice, divided

2 tablespoons olive oil

⅓ cup sour cream

2 tablespoons Mayonnaise (Chapter 4)

2 tablespoons Honey Mustard (Chapter 4)

2 Hard-Cooked Eggs (Chapter 1), peeled and chopped

1 medium avocado, peeled and chopped

½ cup chopped fresh mushrooms

2 whole Pita Breads (Chapter 2)

1 cup torn butter lettuce

1. Sprinkle chicken breasts with thyme and pepper and 1 tablespoon lemon juice; set aside for 10 minutes.

2. Heat olive oil in medium saucepan over medium heat. Sauté chicken, turning once, until light brown and thoroughly cooked to 160°F, about 8–9 minutes. Remove from pan, cover with foil, and let stand for 10 minutes.

3. In large bowl, combine remaining lemon juice, sour cream, mayonnaise, and honey mustard and mix well.

4. Cut chicken into cubes and add to dressing in bowl. Add eggs, avocado, and mushrooms.

5. Cut the pita breads in half and open pockets. Line each pocket with lettuce and fill with chicken mixture; serve immediately.

PER SERVING: Calories: 450 | Total Fat: 6g | Saturated Fat: 30g | Cholesterol: 157mg | Protein: 21g | Sodium: 97mg | Potassium: 569mg | Fiber: 4g | Carbohydrates: 25g | Sugar: 5g

GREEK CHICKEN

Greek flavors include lemon, garlic, mint, and oregano, and these ingredients are delicious when cooked with tender chicken. Serve this dish with some hot cooked brown rice or Creamy Brown Rice Pilaf (Chapter 13) and some sliced tomatoes and cucumbers.

SERVES 4

4 (6-ounce) boneless, skinless chicken breasts

3 tablespoons olive oil

3 tablespoons lemon juice

2 cloves garlic, minced

1 tablespoon chopped fresh oregano

2 tablespoons chopped fresh mint

1 cup grape tomatoes, cut in half

½ cup Chicken Stock (Chapter 5)

1 tablespoon unsalted butter

1. Place chicken in a resealable plastic bag. Add olive oil, lemon juice, garlic, oregano, and mint to the bag and seal. Massage chicken in the bag. Then place the bag in a baking dish and refrigerate at least 8 hours or overnight.

2. When you're ready to eat, heat a large saucepan over medium heat. Remove chicken from marinade; reserve marinade.

3. Add chicken to pan and cook, turning once, until cooked to 160°F, about 9–10 minutes. Remove chicken from pan and cover to keep warm.

4. Add tomatoes, reserved marinade, and chicken stock to pan and bring to a simmer. Simmer for 3–4 minutes until slightly reduced.

5. Remove pan from heat and swirl in butter. Place chicken on serving platter, pour sauce over, and serve immediately.

PER SERVING: Calories: 258 | Total Fat: 14g | Saturated Fat: 3g | Cholesterol: 73mg | Protein: 27g | Sodium: 85mg | Potassium: 449mg | Fiber: 0g | Carbohydrates: 3g | Sugar: 1g

TURKEY BURGERS

When you make these burgers, combine all of the ingredients that go into the turkey first, then add the turkey and mix gently so the burgers are tender. Serve with roasted red peppers and avocado for a fabulous meal.

SERVES 4

1 tablespoon olive oil

1 small onion, diced

3 cloves garlic, minced

2 tablespoons Chicken Stock (Chapter 5) or water

2 tablespoons Honey Mustard (Chapter 4)

1 tablespoon lemon juice

1¼ pounds ground turkey

1 large red bell pepper

¼ cup Mayonnaise (Chapter 4)

4 Hamburger Buns (Chapter 2), split and toasted

2 medium avocados, sliced

1. In small saucepan, heat olive oil over medium heat. Add onion; cook for 5 minutes, stirring frequently. Add garlic; cook for another 1–2 minutes until vegetables are tender. Remove from heat and place in large bowl.

2. Add chicken stock, honey mustard, and lemon juice to vegetables and stir. Add turkey and mix with hands. Form into 4 burgers; cover and refrigerate.

3. Hold the red bell pepper over a gas flame, or broil it, until the skin is blackened. Put the pepper into a paper bag and close; let stand 5 minutes. Peel skin off pepper and discard. Cut pepper into strips and remove seeds.

4. Prepare and preheat grill. Cook burgers for 7–9 minutes, turning once, until they register 165°F on a meat thermometer. Remove from grill.

5. To assemble burgers, spread mayonnaise on the hamburger buns. Place turkey burgers on bun bottoms, then add bell pepper strips, and avocado. Add bun tops and serve immediately.

PER SERVING: Calories: 801 | Total Fat: 48g | Saturated Fat: 6g | Cholesterol: 122mg | Protein: 36g | Sodium: 129mg | Potassium: 734mg | Fiber: 10g | Carbohydrates: 64g | Sugar: 12g

CURRIED TURKEY BURGERS

Curry powder is a great addition to turkey burgers. This simple recipe has so much flavor, with very little sodium. Make sure you read the label on the curry powder you buy so you know that it's low in sodium. Top these burgers with a spread made from sour cream and chutney, and serve on toasted homemade buns.

SERVES 4

1 tablespoon olive oil

2 scallions, minced

2 cloves garlic, minced

1 tablespoon minced fresh ginger root

2½ teaspoons curry powder, divided

1¼ pounds ground turkey

⅓ cup sour cream

⅓ cup Mango Chutney (Chapter 4)

1 tablespoon lemon juice

⅛ teaspoon white pepper

4 Hamburger Buns (Chapter 2), split and toasted

4 leaves butter lettuce

½ cup sliced cucumbers

1. In small saucepan, heat olive oil over medium heat. Add scallions, garlic, and ginger root; cook and stir for 3–4 minutes until fragrant. Add 2 teaspoons curry powder and cook for 30 seconds; remove to large bowl and let cool.

2. Add turkey to vegetables and mix with your hands. Form into 4 patties and refrigerate.

3. In small bowl, combine sour cream, chutney, lemon juice, remaining ½ teaspoon curry powder, and white pepper and refrigerate.

4. When ready to eat, prepare and preheat grill. Grill burgers, turning once, until they register 165°F on a meat thermometer, about 8–10 minutes.

5. Spread the chutney mixture on the bottom half of the hamburger buns. Add lettuce, cucumbers, turkey burgers, and bun tops, then serve immediately.

PER SERVING: Calories: 562 | Total Fat: 23g | Saturated Fat: 4g | Cholesterol: 102mg | Protein: 30g | Sodium: 137mg | Potassium: 244mg | Fiber: 3g | Carbohydrates: 58g | Sugar: 14g

CHICKEN IN ORANGE SAUCE

Orange sauce is usually served with duck, because its sharp sweetness pierces through the rich fattiness of the meat. But this sauce is also delicious with chicken. Serve this over hot cooked noodles, quinoa, or basmati rice, along with a mixed fruit salad and some toasted French bread.

SERVES 4

4 (6-ounce) boneless, skinless chicken breasts, cut into 1"-wide strips

⅛ teaspoon white pepper

¾ cup orange juice, divided

2 tablespoons olive oil

1 tablespoon unsalted butter

1 tablespoon minced fresh ginger root

1 medium onion, finely chopped

1 teaspoon dried thyme leaves

2 tablespoons honey

2 tablespoons white wine vinegar

1 teaspoon grated orange zest

½ cup Chicken Stock (Chapter 5)

2 tablespoons cornstarch

2 tablespoons minced fresh chives

1. Place chicken in bowl and sprinkle with white pepper and 2 tablespoons orange juice; toss to coat and set aside for 15 minutes.

2. Meanwhile, heat olive oil and butter in large saucepan over medium heat. Add ginger root and onion; cook and stir until tender, about 6–7 minutes.

3. In small bowl, combine remaining orange juice, thyme, honey, vinegar, orange zest, stock, and cornstarch and mix well; set aside.

4. Add chicken to skillet; cook, stirring frequently, until chicken is almost cooked through, about 5 minutes.

5. Stir orange-juice mixture and add to skillet. Cook, stirring constantly, until sauce thickens and bubbles and chicken is thoroughly cooked to 160°F. Sprinkle with chives and serve immediately.

PER SERVING: Calories: 288 | Total Fat: 11g | Saturated Fat: 3g | Cholesterol: 73mg | Protein: 27g | Sodium: 86mg | Potassium: 432mg | Fiber: 0g | Carbohydrates: 18g | Sugar: 12g

ROMAN CHICKEN

Serve this recipe with hot cooked noodles, a glass of rosé or red wine, and a green salad made with romaine lettuce, chopped mushrooms, and green onions.

SERVES 4

8 (6-ounce) boneless, skinless chicken thighs

2 tablespoons flour

¼ teaspoon black pepper

2 tablespoons olive oil

1 medium onion, chopped

4 cloves garlic, sliced

1 medium red bell pepper, chopped

3 tablespoons no-salt-added tomato paste

1 (14-ounce) can no-salt-added diced tomatoes, undrained

⅓ cup rosé or white wine

½ cup Chicken Stock (Chapter 5)

2 teaspoons fresh marjoram leaves

2 teaspoons fresh basil leaves

2 tablespoons lemon juice

1. Sprinkle chicken with flour and pepper and set aside.

2. In large skillet, heat olive oil over medium heat. Add chicken and cook, turning once, until almost cooked through, about 7–9 minutes. Remove chicken from skillet and set aside.

3. Add onion and garlic to pan; cook and stir to remove pan drippings. Cook until tender, about 5 minutes. Add red bell pepper to pan; cook for 2 minutes longer.

4. Add tomato paste to skillet; cook for 2 minutes. Then add the undrained tomatoes, wine, and chicken stock and bring to a simmer.

5. Return chicken to pan and bring back to a simmer. Reduce heat to low, cover, and simmer for 20 minutes or until chicken is cooked to 165°F.

6. Stir in marjoram, basil, and lemon juice and serve immediately.

PER SERVING: Calories: 238 | Total Fat: 10g | Saturated Fat: 1g | Cholesterol: 68mg | Protein: 19g | Sodium: 104mg | Potassium: 641mg | Fiber: 2g | Carbohydrates: 13g | Sugar: 5g

CHICKEN WITH PINEAPPLE RAISIN SAUCE

Chicken blends well with just about any other ingredient, because it's so mild. This sauce is sweet, with a hint of sharpness from the onions and the ginger. Canned pineapple is a low-sodium food and it's easy to use. Keep a few cans in the pantry, along with some golden and regular raisins to make this simple dish for dinner.

SERVES 4

1 tablespoon olive oil

2 tablespoons unsalted butter

4 (6-ounce) boneless, skinless chicken breasts

3 tablespoons flour

½ teaspoon dried tarragon leaves

⅛ teaspoon pepper

1 medium onion, chopped

2 tablespoons minced fresh ginger root

2 (8-ounce) cans pineapple tidbits in juice

2 tablespoons lemon juice

2 tablespoons honey

⅓ cup golden raisins

⅓ cup raisins

1. Melt olive oil and butter in large skillet over medium heat.

2. Meanwhile, sprinkle chicken with flour, tarragon, and pepper. Add to skillet and brown, about 3–4 minutes on each side, turning once, until almost cooked. Remove from skillet.

3. Add onion and ginger root to skillet; cook, stirring to scrape up pan drippings, for 4–5 minutes until tender.

4. Add undrained pineapple, lemon juice, honey, golden raisins, and raisins and bring to a simmer. Simmer for 4–5 minutes.

5. Return chicken to skillet and cover with sauce. Cover skillet and simmer over low heat for 8–12 minutes or until chicken is cooked to 160°F.

PER SERVING: Calories: 370 | Total Fat: 10g | Saturated Fat: 4g | Cholesterol: 80mg | Protein: 28g | Sodium: 79mg | Potassium: 584mg | Fiber: 1g | Carbohydrates: 42g | Sugar: 31g

TANDOORI CHICKEN

For this dish the meat is marinated in a mixture of yogurt and spices such as curry powder, cumin, ginger, peppers, and garlic. The marinade makes the meat very tender, and so flavorful you don't need to add any salt.

SERVES 4

4 (6-ounce) boneless, skinless chicken breasts

¾ cup plain yogurt

2 tablespoons lemon juice

1 tablespoon minced ginger root

1 tablespoon curry powder

3 cloves garlic, minced

½ teaspoon ground turmeric

½ teaspoon ground cumin

⅛ teaspoon pepper

⅛ teaspoon crushed red pepper flakes

1. Place chicken in a glass baking dish. In medium bowl, combine yogurt, lemon juice, ginger root, curry powder, garlic, turmeric, cumin, pepper, and red pepper flakes and mix well. Pour over chicken and turn to coat.

2. Cover and refrigerate for 8–12 hours.

3. When ready to eat, preheat oven to 375°F. Remove chicken from marinade and place on a baking sheet with sides.

4. Roast chicken until a meat thermometer registers 160°F, about 25–30 minutes. Serve immediately.

PER SERVING: Calories: 164 | Total Fat: 3g | Saturated Fat: 1g | Cholesterol: 71mg | Protein: 28g | Sodium: 96mg | Potassium: 414mg | Fiber: 0g | Carbohydrates: 4g | Sugar: 2g

CRUNCHY FLAXSEED CHICKEN

Flaxseed is one of the new "superfoods." This tiny seed is packed full of protein, omega-3 essential fatty acids, lignans, and fiber. When ground, they make an excellent coating for chicken that cooks up crunchy and nutty-tasting. Serve this dish with some Scalloped Potatoes (Chapter 13) and a green salad.

SERVES 4

4 (6-ounce) boneless, skinless chicken breasts

½ cup ground flaxseed

3 tablespoons sesame seeds

3 tablespoons flour

½ teaspoon dried marjoram leaves

⅛ teaspoon white pepper

3 tablespoons Mayonnaise (Chapter 4)

1 tablespoon Mustard (Chapter 4)

1 egg white

2 tablespoons unsalted butter

1 tablespoon olive oil

1. Place chicken breasts on a platter. On another platter, combine flaxseed, sesame seeds, flour, marjoram, and white pepper. On a shallow plate, combine mayonnaise, mustard, and egg white and beat well.

2. Dip the chicken into the mayonnaise mixture, shake off excess, then dip into the flaxseed mixture to coat well. Refrigerate chicken for 15 minutes.

3. When ready to eat, melt butter and olive oil in a large skillet over medium heat. Add chicken and cook for 10–14 minutes, turning once, until a meat thermometer registers 160°F. Serve immediately.

PER SERVING: Calories: 460 | Total Fat: 31g | Saturated Fat: 7g | Cholesterol: 94mg | Protein: 32g | Sodium: 97mg | Potassium: 506mg | Fiber: 6g | Carbohydrates: 12g | Sugar: 0g

SLOW COOKER CHICKEN PAPRIKASH

Sweet paprika is made of several pepper varieties and has a mild flavor. Smoked paprika is made from dried chilies that are smoked over oak and adds a rich flavor to recipes. Both are used in this flavorful dish that cooks in the slow cooker.

SERVES 4

8 (4-ounce) boneless, skinless chicken thighs, cut into 1" strips

1 (8-ounce) package mushrooms, sliced

1 medium onion, chopped

4 cloves garlic, sliced

1 tablespoon sweet paprika

1 tablespoon smoked paprika

3 tablespoons tomato paste

1 (14-ounce) can no-salt-added fire-roasted diced tomatoes, undrained

½ cup Chicken Stock (Chapter 5)

2 tablespoons lemon juice

2 tablespoons flour

⅔ cup sour cream

1. In 4- to 5-quart slow cooker, combine chicken, mushrooms, onion, and garlic and mix. Sprinkle with both kinds of paprika and toss to coat.

2. In medium bowl, combine tomato paste, diced tomatoes, chicken stock, and lemon juice and mix well. Pour into slow cooker.

3. Cover and cook on low for 6–8 hours or until chicken is cooked to 165°F and is tender.

4. In small bowl, combine flour and sour cream and mix with wire whisk. Ladle ⅓ cup of the liquid from the slow cooker into the sour-cream mixture and mix well. Stir into slow cooker; cover and cook on high for about 10 minutes or until sauce is thickened. Serve over hot cooked rice or noodles.

PER SERVING: Calories: 246 | Total Fat: 11g | Saturated Fat: 5g | Cholesterol: 87mg | Protein: 21g | Sodium: 136mg | Potassium: 872mg | Fiber: 3g | Carbohydrates: 16g | Sugar: 6g

CHICKEN WITH MOSTARDA

Mostarda is an Italian condiment that is made from mustard and fruit. Some of the liquid from the Mostarda is brushed on the chicken as it grills to add wonderful flavor, then more of the condiment is served on the side. Serve with a cucumber salad for cooling contrast, and dinner rolls.

SERVES 4

4 (6-ounce) boneless, skinless chicken breasts

⅛ teaspoon white pepper

½ teaspoon grated lemon zest

1¼ cups Mostarda (Chapter 4)

1. Prepare and preheat grill. Sprinkle chicken with pepper and lemon zest.

2. Pound the chicken breasts until they are an even thickness, about ⅓" thick.

3. Drain off some of the liquid from the Mostarda and place in a small cup.

4. Place chicken on grill over medium-high heat and brush with liquid from Mostarda. Grill for 2–3 minutes on each side, turning once and brushing again with the liquid, until done to 160°F.

5. Remove chicken from grill. Serve with remaining Mostarda.

PER SERVING: Calories: 377 | Total Fat: 3g | Saturated Fat: 0g | Cholesterol: 65mg | Protein: 29g | Sodium: 85mg | Potassium: 746mg | Fiber: 5g | Carbohydrates: 58g | Sugar: 48g

ROASTED LEMON CHICKEN

Lemon and garlic are tucked under the skin and roasted along with the chicken in this delicious and flavorful recipe. Chicken that is roasted on the bone will always be more flavorful, and the skin helps keep the meat moist. You can remove the skin before you eat the chicken; the lemon and garlic are edible.

SERVES 6

6 (10-ounce) bone-in, skin-on chicken breasts

1 medium lemon

3 cloves garlic, thinly sliced

3 tablespoons Mustard (Chapter 4)

1 teaspoon dried thyme leaves

¼ teaspoon white pepper

1. Preheat oven to 400°F. Loosen skin from the chicken, leaving it attached. Thinly slice half of the lemon to get 6 slices.

2. Carefully stuff a lemon slice and a few garlic slices under the skin of each piece; smooth skin back over the meat.

3. Squeeze juice from remaining lemon half into a dish and mix in mustard; spread each chicken breast with this mixture, then sprinkle with thyme and pepper. Place chicken in roasting pan.

4. Roast chicken for 30–40 minutes or until a meat thermometer registers 160°F. Let stand for 5 minutes, then serve.

PER SERVING: Calories: 145 | Total Fat: 2g | Saturated Fat: 0g | Cholesterol: 65mg | Protein: 27g | Sodium: 74mg | Potassium: 325mg | Fiber: 0g | Carbohydrates: 2g | Sugar: 0g

POACHED CHICKEN BREASTS

Poaching is a technique that cooks food in a liquid that is almost simmering. This method results in very tender and moist meat. You can poach boneless, skinless chicken pieces or bone-in, skin-on pieces. Just test each piece with a food thermometer to make sure it's 160°F before you remove it from the poaching liquid.

SERVES 6–8

8 (6-ounce boneless or 10-ounce bone-in) chicken breast halves

1 bay leaf

½ teaspoon black peppercorns

1 teaspoon mustard seeds

2 sprigs marjoram

1 square cheesecloth

1. Place chicken in a large pot or saucepan. Place bay leaf, peppercorns, mustard seeds, and marjoram on a square of cheesecloth and tie with kitchen string; add to pot with chicken.

2. Cover everything in the pot with water. Bring to a simmer over medium heat, then reduce heat to medium-low. No bubbles should form in the center of the pot.

3. Cook the bone-in, skin-on chicken breasts for 18–22 minutes; cook boneless, skinless chicken breasts for 12–15 minutes until 160°F.

4. Remove pan from heat; remove chicken from pan and place in glass baking dish. Remove and discard the cheesecloth bundle. Pour some of the poaching liquid over the chicken; reserve the rest for another use.

5. Cover the pan and refrigerate the chicken until cold. Remove bones and skin, if using bone-in breasts, and cube the meat. You can freeze the meat up to 4 months; to thaw, let stand overnight in the refrigerator.

PER SERVING: Calories: 144 | Total Fat: 2g | Saturated Fat: 0g | Cholesterol: 72mg | Protein: 27g | Sodium: 59mg | Potassium: 180mg | Fiber: 0g | Carbohydrates: 0g | Sugar: 0g

SLOW COOKER CHICKEN RISOTTO

You can cook risotto in the slow cooker; this method doesn't save you much time, but you don't have to stand at the stove stirring while you add broth or stock. The chicken is browned before it's added to the rice mixture to add a little more flavor to this dish.

SERVES 4

2 tablespoons olive oil

2 (6-ounce) boneless, skinless chicken breasts, cut into cubes

1 medium onion, finely chopped

3 cloves garlic, minced

1¾ cups Arborio or other short-grain rice

4⅔ cups Chicken Stock (Chapter 5)

½ pound asparagus

2 tablespoons minced chives

2 tablespoons unsalted butter

2 tablespoons grated Parmesan cheese

1. In skillet, heat olive oil over medium-high heat. Add chicken breasts; cook until lightly browned on all sides, about 3–4 minutes. Remove to plate.

2. Add onion and garlic to skillet; cook and stir to remove pan drippings. Add rice to skillet; cook for 1 minute longer. Remove to 4-quart slow cooker.

3. Add chicken to slow cooker. Pour chicken stock over all and stir. Cover and cook on high for 2 hours or until rice is almost tender; stir.

4. Rinse asparagus and slice into 1" pieces; add to slow cooker and stir. Cover and cook on high for another 25–35 minutes or until rice is tender, chicken is 160°F, and asparagus is tender.

5. Stir in chives, butter, and cheese; let stand 5 minutes, then serve.

PER SERVING: Calories: 517 | Total Fat: 16g | Saturated Fat: 6g | Cholesterol: 51mg | Protein: 26g | Sodium: 140mg | Potassium: 583mg | Fiber: 1g | Carbohydrates: 65g | Sugar: 1g

CAJUN-STYLE CHICKEN

When you are buying chicken, it's important to read the label. Some chickens and chicken parts are injected with a tenderizing solution that can be very high in sodium. If the label reads "contains up to 10% chicken broth" or another indication, such as more than 70mg of sodium per serving, pass it up.

SERVES 4

4 (4-ounce) boneless, skinless chicken breasts

2 teaspoons olive oil

½ teaspoon paprika

½ teaspoon cayenne pepper

¼ teaspoon onion powder

¼ teaspoon garlic powder

¼ teaspoon freshly ground black pepper

¼ teaspoon freshly ground white pepper

⅛ teaspoon dried oregano

⅛ teaspoon dried thyme

⅛ teaspoon dried basil

⅛ teaspoon dried rosemary

Optional: ¼ teaspoon brown sugar

1. Put the chicken breasts and olive oil in a heavy-duty, sealable plastic bag. Turn the bag to completely coat the chicken in the oil.

2. In a medium bowl, mix together the remaining ingredients. Dip the top half of each chicken breast in the dried seasoning mixture.

3. Heat a nonstick skillet or grill pan on medium-high. Place the chicken breasts in the skillet, spice-coated-side down. Cook for 2–3 minutes or until the top half of the chicken begins to lose its pinkish color and the spiced side of the chicken is browned well. Use tongs to turn the chicken. Cook for 2–3 minutes longer or until the chicken is done to 160°F.

PER SERVING: Calories: 147 | Total Fat: 3g | Saturated Fat: 0g | Cholesterol: 65mg | Protein: 26g | Sodium: 73mg | Potassium: 305mg | Fiber: 0g | Carbohydrates: 0g | Sugar: 0g

STEAMED CHILI-PEPPERED CHICKEN

If steaming a meat entrée and vegetables, consult the estimated steaming times for both; you may need to add the vegetables to the steamer sometime after you start steaming the entrée. Be sure to add an additional 1–2 minutes to the cooking time to compensate for opening the steamer.

SERVES 4

¼ teaspoon ground ancho pepper

¼ teaspoon ground chipotle pepper

⅛ teaspoon dried marjoram

Pinch ground cumin

¼ teaspoon dried Mexican oregano

⅛ teaspoon dried thyme

⅛ teaspoon ground cloves

1 teaspoon garlic powder

1 tablespoon white wine vinegar

4 (4-ounce) boneless, skinless chicken thighs

1. In a small bowl, mix together the ancho pepper, chipotle pepper, marjoram, cumin, oregano, thyme, cloves, and garlic powder.

2. In a separate bowl, pour the vinegar over the chicken, turning the chicken to evenly coat it in the vinegar.

3. Cut out four 16" squares of parchment paper. Dip the vinegar-coated chicken in the seasoning mixture, coating both sides. Place each thigh in the center of a parchment-paper square. Bring the 4 corners together and tie closed with string. Place in a steamer and steam over simmering water for 1 hour or until chicken is cooked to 160°F.

PER SERVING: Calories: 52 | Total Fat: 1g | Saturated Fat: 0g | Cholesterol: 34mg | Protein: 8g | Sodium: 38mg | Potassium: 108mg | Fiber: 0g | Carbohydrates: 0g | Sugar: 0g

CHICKEN CACCIATORE

This is a simple and satisfying low-sodium chicken recipe, with a hearty full-bodied wine sauce and amazingly tender meat.

SERVES 4

4 teaspoons olive oil

1 large sweet onion, diced or sliced

4 (4-ounce) boneless, skinless chicken breasts

¼ teaspoon freshly ground black pepper

2 tablespoons dry red wine

1 (15-ounce) can no-salt-added tomato sauce

1 teaspoon garlic powder

½ teaspoon dried basil

¼ teaspoon dried oregano

¼ teaspoon dried parsley

⅛ teaspoon mustard powder

Pinch grated lemon zest

Pinch dried red pepper flakes

1 teaspoon lemon juice

¼ teaspoon granulated sugar

Optional: 4 tablespoons grated Parmesan cheese

1. Heat a deep nonstick skillet over medium heat. Add the olive oil and chopped onion; sauté the onion until transparent. Push to the edges of the pan.

2. Add the chicken breasts. Sprinkle the pepper over the chicken. Pan-fry for 2 minutes on each side. Use tongs to transfer the chicken breasts to a bowl or platter; set aside.

3. Add the wine to the pan. Bring to a boil and cook for 2 minutes, stirring the wine into the onion and using a spoon or spatula to scrape (deglaze) the bottom of the pan.

4. Add the tomato sauce, garlic powder, basil, oregano, parsley, mustard powder, lemon zest, red pepper flakes, lemon juice, and sugar to the pan; stir to combine.

5. Add the chicken back to the pan, spooning some of the tomato sauce over the top of the chicken. Reduce heat. Simmer, covered, for 25–35 minutes or until chicken is cooked to 160°F. Serve immediately, topped with freshly grated Parmesan cheese if desired.

PER SERVING: Calories: 247 | Total Fat: 6g | Saturated Fat: 1g | Cholesterol: 65mg | Protein: 28g | Sodium: 92mg | Potassium: 799mg | Fiber: 2g | Carbohydrates: 16g | Sugar: 10g

RED AND GREEN BELL PEPPER CHICKEN

Bell peppers are sweet and juicy and the perfect complement to chicken. When cooked in a tomato-wine sauce, as in this recipe, they become even sweeter. You could add onion or shallots to this recipe for even more flavor.

SERVES 4

4 teaspoons olive oil

1 medium green bell pepper, seeded and chopped

1 medium red bell pepper, seeded and chopped

2 cloves garlic, minced

4 (4-ounce) boneless, skinless chicken thighs

¼ teaspoon freshly ground black pepper

2 tablespoons dry red or white wine

1 (14.5-ounce) can no-salt-added diced tomatoes

1 teaspoon dried basil

½ teaspoon dried parsley

⅛ teaspoon dried marjoram or oregano

1 teaspoon lemon juice

¼ teaspoon granulated sugar

1. Heat a deep nonstick skillet over medium heat. Add the olive oil and chopped bell peppers; sauté until tender. Add the garlic and sauté for 1 minute, being careful not to burn the garlic. Push the mixture to the edges of the pan.

2. Add the chicken thighs. Sprinkle the pepper over the chicken. Pan-fry for 2 minutes on each side. Use tongs to transfer the chicken to a bowl or platter; set aside.

3. Add the wine to the pan. Bring to a boil and cook for 2 minutes, stirring the wine into the vegetables and using a spoon or spatula to scrape (deglaze) the bottom of the pan.

4. Add the tomatoes, basil, parsley, marjoram or oregano, lemon juice, and sugar to the pan; stir to combine.

5. Add the chicken back to the pan, spooning some of the tomatoes over the top of the chicken. Reduce heat. Simmer, covered, for 20–25 minutes or until chicken registers 165°F. Serve immediately.

PER SERVING: Calories: 217 | Total Fat: 9g | Saturated Fat: 1g | Cholesterol: 94mg | Protein: 23g | Sodium: 110mg | Potassium: 584mg | Fiber: 2g | Carbohydrates: 8g | Sugar: 4g

OLIVE OIL AND LEMON HERBED CHICKEN

Using a butter-flavored margarine in this recipe doesn't significantly drop the overall fat content of the recipe; however, it does drop the less healthful saturated fat content. Using unsalted butter, the saturated fat for the recipe would be 4.13g.

SERVES 4

4 (4-ounce) boneless, skinless chicken thighs

4 teaspoons olive oil

⅛ teaspoon dried marjoram or oregano

¼ teaspoon dried parsley

⅛ teaspoon dried rosemary

⅛ teaspoon dried thyme or lemon thyme

¼ teaspoon garlic powder

2 tablespoons dry white wine

½ teaspoon cornstarch

2 tablespoons fresh lemon juice

4 teaspoons margarine

1. Add the chicken thighs and olive oil to a heavy-duty, sealable plastic bag. Close the bag and turn it to coat each chicken piece completely.

2. In a small bowl, mix together the marjoram or oregano, parsley, rosemary, thyme, and garlic powder.

3. Heat a nonstick skillet or grill pan over medium-high heat. Remove chicken from marinade; reserve marinade. Dip the top of the chicken in the herb seasoning mixture. Add marinade from the baggie to the skillet. Place the chicken in the skillet, herb-coated-side down.

4. Fry the chicken for 2–3 minutes on each side or until the juices run clear and temperature registers 160°F. Transfer the cooked chicken to a serving platter and keep warm.

5. Add the wine to the skillet, stirring and scraping the bottom of the pan (deglazing) to remove any chicken "bits." Add any herbs remaining in the bowl to the pan. Bring the wine to a boil.

6. Stir the cornstarch into the lemon juice, whisking to remove any lumps. Add the lemon-juice mixture to the wine and bring to a boil. Reduce heat, stirring constantly, simmering the mixture until it thickens.

7. Remove the pan from the heat and whisk in the margarine. Pour over the chicken and serve immediately.

PER SERVING: Calories: 101 | Total Fat: 6g | Saturated Fat: 1g | Cholesterol: 32mg | Protein: 8g | Sodium: 34mg | Potassium: 104mg | Fiber: 0g | Carbohydrates: 1g | Sugar: 0g

JAVA CHICKEN PAPRIKA

Coffee lovers, this recipe is for you! The moist and flavorful recipe will leave you wanting more. Although boneless chicken breasts are used here, you can substitute whatever chicken parts you have on hand; just remember to adjust the cooking time accordingly.

SERVES 4

1 pound boneless, skinless chicken breasts

½ cup fresh lemon juice

¼ teaspoon freshly ground black pepper

1 tablespoon olive oil

1 large sweet onion, sliced

2 teaspoons paprika

½ teaspoon salt-free chili powder

½ teaspoon instant espresso powder

¼ cup water

1 tablespoon cornstarch

1 tablespoon instant nonfat dry milk

½ cup skim milk

Optional: Additional paprika, for garnish

1. Place the chicken breasts between pieces of waxed paper or plastic wrap. Pound the breasts into thin pieces using a wooden mallet or rolling pin. Divide into 4 equal-sized pieces.

2. Place the chicken breasts in a small bowl. Pour the lemon juice over the chicken and season with the freshly ground black pepper. Marinate for at least 5 minutes. Drain and pat dry, reserving the lemon juice.

3. In a large nonstick skillet, heat the olive oil over medium heat. Add the onion and sauté until transparent, about 5–7 minutes. Remove the onion with a slotted spoon and set aside.

4. Increase the heat to medium-high. Add the chicken breasts to the pan. Quick-fry the chicken breasts for about 1 minute on each side. Transfer the chicken to a serving platter and keep warm.

5. Add the onion back to the pan and reheat. Add the paprika and chili powder; stir well. Add the espresso powder and water; bring to a boil.

6. In a small bowl, whisk together the cornstarch, nonfat dry milk, and skim milk. Add the milk mixture and the reserved lemon juice to the pan; bring to a boil. Reduce heat and simmer, stirring until thickened.

7. Spoon the sauce over the chicken. Sprinkle with additional paprika, if desired. Serve immediately.

PER SERVING: Calories: 214 | Total Fat: 5g | Saturated Fat: 0g | Cholesterol: 66mg | Protein: 28g | Sodium: 111mg | Potassium: 549mg | Fiber: 1g | Carbohydrates: 13g | Sugar: 7g

HERBED CHICKEN PAPRIKASH

You can alter the flavor of a dish by getting one of the paprika varieties from a specialty shop. Varieties include Budapest Exquisite Sweet, California (mild with a deep red color), Hungarian Sweet, Hungarian Half Sharp (slightly spicier), Smoked Spanish Sweet, and Smoked Spanish Hot paprikas.

SERVES 6

4 (8-ounce) chicken leg quarters, skin removed

Olive oil spray

¼ teaspoon dried marjoram or oregano

¼ teaspoon dried thyme

¼ teaspoon dried basil

⅛ teaspoon dried rosemary

⅓ cup dry white wine

⅓ cup low-sodium chicken broth

⅔ cup fresh button mushrooms, sliced

1 clove garlic, minced

¼ cup finely grated carrots

2 tablespoons unbleached all-purpose flour

2 tablespoons water

1 teaspoon paprika

2 tablespoons plain nonfat yogurt

Optional: Additional paprika, for garnish

1. Bring a deep nonstick skillet to temperature over medium heat. Spray both sides of the chicken with the olive oil spray. Sprinkle the chicken with the marjoram or oregano, thyme, basil, and rosemary. Add the chicken to the skillet and cook for 2 minutes on each side or until browned.

2. Add the wine and chicken broth to pan; bring to a boil. Reduce heat, cover, and simmer for 20 minutes. Add the mushrooms, garlic, and carrots, cover, and simmer for an additional 10 minutes or until chicken registers 160°F. Use tongs to transfer the chicken to a serving plate. Keep warm.

3. In a small bowl, mix together the flour and water, whisking to remove any lumps. Add the mixture to the pan and increase heat to medium; bring to a boil, stirring constantly. Continue to cook over medium heat, stirring until the mixture thickens.

4. Stir in the paprika. Remove from heat and stir in the yogurt. Pour the sauce over the chicken. Sprinkle with additional paprika, if desired.

PER SERVING: Calories: 209 | Total Fat: 5g | Saturated Fat: 1g | Cholesterol: 120mg | Protein: 31g | Sodium: 137mg | Potassium: 412mg | Fiber: 0g | Carbohydrates: 3g | Sugar: 0g

SEASONED CHICKEN

A heart-healthy menu calls for smaller meat entrées. When you plan your meals to include lots of grains, vegetables, and fruit, 3–4 ounces is usually a sufficient serving of meat.

Parts of chicken, with skin, either white or dark meat

Seasoning blend of your choice from the following recipes

1. Preheat oven to 375°F.

2. Mix together the ingredients from the seasoning blend to make a paste.

3. Wash chicken pieces under cold running water. Pat dry with a paper towel. Carefully pull back the skin, using the tip of a boning knife, if necessary, to loosen the membrane under the skin from the meat. Evenly rub the seasoning paste directly on the meat. Pull the skin back to cover the meat. Place a roasting rack inside a roasting pan and treat with nonstick spray. Arrange the chicken pieces on the rack so that they aren't touching. (Juices that drain from the meat and the baked "bits" that adhere to the roasting pan can be used in sauces or gravy, provided you first drain off any fat.)

4. Bake until the juices run clear—about 40 minutes for legs or thighs and about 50 minutes for whole chicken breasts. Reduce baking times by 10 minutes if using boneless, skin-on chicken pieces. Remove from the oven and allow the meat to rest on the rack for 5–10 minutes. Pull the skin away from the meat, using a boning knife, if necessary, to cut away the still-attached end. (The skin can usually just be torn off.) Serve immediately.

PER SERVING (1-ounce boneless, skinless chicken breast (white meat): Calories: 31 | Total Fat: 0g | Saturated Fat: 0g | Cholesterol: 16mg | Protein: 6g | Sodium: 18mg | Potassium: 72mg | Fiber: 0g | Carbohydrates: 0g | Sugar: 0g

PER SERVING (1-ounce boneless, skinless chicken breast (dark meat): Calories: 33 | Total Fat: 1g | Saturated Fat: 0g | Cholesterol: 23mg | Protein: 5g | Sodium: 24mg | Potassium: 65mg | Fiber: 0g | Carbohydrates: 0g | Sugar: 0g

Fines Herbes Chicken Seasoning

1 teaspoon lemon juice

¼ teaspoon dried parsley

¼ teaspoon dried chervil

¼ teaspoon dried tarragon

¼ teaspoon freeze-dried chives

1/16 teaspoon dried orange granules, crushed, if desired

PER SERVING: Calories: 2 | Total Fat: 0g | Saturated Fat: 0g | Cholesterol: 0mg | Protein: 0g | Sodium: 0mg | Potassium: 34mg | Fiber: 0g | Carbohydrates: 0g | Sugar: 0g

Spiced Orange Chicken Seasoning

1 teaspoon frozen orange juice concentrate

¼ teaspoon honey

¼ teaspoon garlic powder

⅛ teaspoon freshly ground black pepper

1/16 teaspoon ground cinnamon

Pinch ground cloves

Pinch ground allspice

Pinch ground mace

PER SERVING: Calories: 20 | Total Fat: 0g | Saturated Fat: 0g | Cholesterol: 0mg | Protein: 0g | Sodium: 0mg | Potassium: 54mg | Fiber: 0g | Carbohydrates: 5g | Sugar: 3g

Zesty Lemon Herb Chicken Seasoning

2 teaspoons lemon juice

2 teaspoons freeze-dried shallots or chives

¼ teaspoon marjoram

¼ teaspoon thyme

¼ teaspoon rosemary

⅛ teaspoon salt-free chili powder

2 drops lemon oil

PER SERVING: Calories: 14 | Total Fat: 0g | Saturated Fat: 0g | Cholesterol: 0mg | Protein: 0g | Sodium: 4mg | Potassium: 65mg | Fiber: 0g | Carbohydrates: 3g | Sugar: 1g

Chili-Jalapeño Chicken Seasoning

2 teaspoons jalapeño jelly

¼ teaspoon onion powder

¼ teaspoon garlic powder

¼ teaspoon (hot or sweet) paprika

¼ teaspoon chili pepper

⅛ teaspoon oregano

⅛ teaspoon thyme

Pinch ground cumin

Pinch ground coriander

Pinch cayenne

1/16 teaspoon dried lemon granules, crushed, if desired

PER SERVING: Calories: 50 | Total Fat: 0g | Saturated Fat: 0g | Cholesterol: 0mg | Protein: 0g | Sodium: 5mg | Potassium: 62mg | Fiber: 1g | Carbohydrates: 12g | Sugar: 7g

Herbes de Provence Chicken Seasoning

¼ teaspoon dried basil

¼ teaspoon dried marjoram

¼ teaspoon dried thyme

⅛ teaspoon dried mint

⅛ teaspoon dried rosemary

⅛ teaspoon fennel seeds

⅛ teaspoon dried lavender

1/16 teaspoon dried lemon granules, crushed, if desired

1 teaspoon dry white wine (or enough to form a paste)

PER SERVING: Calories: 7 | Total Fat: 0g | Saturated Fat: 0g | Cholesterol: 0mg | Protein: 0g | Sodium: 0mg | Potassium: 17mg | Fiber: 0g | Carbohydrates: 0g | Sugar: 0g

Chili-Bourbon Chicken Seasoning

2 teaspoons bourbon

1 teaspoon reduced-sodium Worcestershire sauce

1 teaspoon no-salt-added tomato paste

2 teaspoons freeze-dried green onion

¼ teaspoon garlic powder

⅛ teaspoon freshly ground black pepper

⅛ teaspoon chili powder

Pinch cayenne pepper

Optional: Salt-free hickory smoke or mesquite base (powder), to taste

PER SERVING: Calories: 39 | Total Fat: 0g | Saturated Fat: 0g | Cholesterol: 0mg | Protein: 0g | Sodium: 9mg | Potassium: 106mg | Fiber: 0g | Carbohydrates: 3g | Sugar: 1g

Apple Jalapeño Chicken Seasoning

1 tablespoon applesauce

1 teaspoon apple cider vinegar

1 tablespoon freeze-dried shallots or chives

1 teaspoon jalapeño jelly

¼ teaspoon garlic powder

⅛ teaspoon freshly ground black pepper

Optional: ⅛ teaspoon chipotle powder

Optional: ¼ teaspoon brown sugar

PER SERVING: Calories: 45 | Total Fat: 0g | Saturated Fat: 0g | Cholesterol: 0mg | Protein: 0g | Sodium: 3mg | Potassium: 108mg | Fiber: 0g | Carbohydrates: 1g | Sugar: 6g

Jamaican Jerk Roasted Chicken Seasoning

⅛ teaspoon dried lime granules, crushed

⅛ teaspoon ground ginger

¼ teaspoon onion powder

⅛ teaspoon ground allspice

¼ teaspoon garlic powder

⅛ teaspoon sweet paprika

⅛ teaspoon dried thyme

⅛ teaspoon freshly ground black pepper

Pinch dried cloves

Pinch cayenne

1 teaspoon jalapeño jelly

PER SERVING: Calories: 25 | Total Fat: 0g | Saturated Fat: 0g | Cholesterol: 0mg | Protein: 0g | Sodium: 2mg | Potassium: 28mg | Fiber: 0g | Carbohydrates: 6g | Sugar: 3g

YOGURT "FRIED" CHICKEN

Each head of garlic usually has 10–15 cloves. As a rule, 1 minced clove of garlic will yield ½ teaspoon. When substituting garlic powder, use ⅛ teaspoon of powder (not garlic salt) for each clove of garlic, or vice versa.

SERVES 4

Olive oil spray

4 (1-ounce) slices French Bread (Chapter 2)

1 pound boneless, skinless chicken breasts (trimmed of fat)

1 teaspoon garlic powder

1 teaspoon paprika

¼ teaspoon mustard powder

¼ teaspoon dried thyme

2 teaspoons Citrus Pepper (Appendix A)

1 cup nonfat plain yogurt

1. Preheat oven to 350°F. Treat a baking pan with the olive oil spray.

2. Place the bread in the bowl of a food processor or in a blender; process to make bread crumbs.

3. Cut the chicken breasts into 8 equal-sized strips.

4. In a medium-size bowl, combine the garlic powder, paprika, mustard powder, thyme, and Citrus Pepper with the yogurt and mix well.

5. Add the chicken to the yogurt mixture, stirring to make sure all sides of the strips are covered. Lift the chicken strips out of the yogurt mixture and dredge all sides in the bread crumbs. Lightly mist the breaded chicken pieces with the spray oil and arrange in the pan.

6. Bake for 10 minutes. Use a spatula or tongs to turn the chicken pieces. Optional: For the last 5 minutes of cooking, place the pan under the broiler to give the chicken a deep golden color. Watch closely to ensure the chicken "crust" doesn't burn.

PER SERVING: Calories: 244 | Total Fat: 2g | Saturated Fat: 0g | Cholesterol: 66mg | Protein: 31g | Sodium: 136mg | Potassium: 501mg | Fiber: 0g | Carbohydrates: 21g | Sugar: 5g

INDOOR-GRILLED CHICKEN BREAST

For maximum impact allow the chicken to steep in the marinade as long as possible, even overnight. This marinade will work equally well with any cut of chicken.

SERVES 4

1 teaspoon cider vinegar

1 teaspoon garlic powder

4 teaspoons salt-free honey mustard

1 teaspoon brown sugar

1 teaspoon Citrus Pepper (Appendix A)

2 teaspoons olive oil

4 (4-ounce) boneless, skinless chicken breast cutlets

1. In a medium-size bowl, combine the cider vinegar, garlic powder, honey mustard, brown sugar, and Citrus Pepper. Slowly whisk in the olive oil to thoroughly combine and make a paste.

2. Rinse the chicken cutlets and dry between paper towels. If necessary to ensure a uniform thickness of the cutlets, put them between sheets of plastic wrap or waxed paper and pound to flatten them.

3. Pour the marinade into a heavy-duty (freezer-style) sealable plastic bag. Add the chicken cutlets, moving them around in the mixture to coat all sides. Seal the bag, carefully squeezing out as much air as possible. Refrigerate and allow the chicken to marinate for at least 1 hour, or as long as overnight.

4. Preheat an indoor (George Foreman–style) grill. When the grill is heated, place the chicken on the grill. Close the grill lid and cook the cutlets for 3–4 minutes or until a food thermometer registers 160°F.

PER SERVING: Calories: 163 | Total Fat: 4g | Saturated Fat: 0g | Cholesterol: 65mg | Protein: 26g | Sodium: 74mg | Potassium: 311mg | Fiber: 0g | Carbohydrates: 3g | Sugar: 2g

CHICKEN CURRY

This quick and easy chicken curry tastes terrific and will leave your house smelling incredible. Serve over cooked basmati rice.

SERVES 4

4 teaspoons olive or canola oil

4 (4-ounce) boneless, skinless chicken breast fillets

1 large Vidalia onion, chopped

2 teaspoons curry powder

¼ teaspoon freshly ground black pepper

⅛ cup unbleached all-purpose flour

⅛ cup unsweetened, no-salt-added applesauce

1 cup skim milk

1. Bring a large, deep nonstick sauté pan to temperature over medium heat. Add the oil.

2. Add the chicken to the pan and sauté for 2 minutes on each side. Remove from the pan and keep warm.

3. Add the onion and sauté until transparent, about 5 minutes. Add the curry powder and pepper; mix with the onion. Stir in the flour and applesauce to create a roux. Increase the heat to medium-high.

4. Gradually whisk in the milk, and bring to a boil.

5. Reduce heat to medium-low to maintain a simmer. Add the chicken back to the pan. Cover and simmer for 5 minutes or until the chicken is cooked through to 160°F and the sauce is thickened.

PER SERVING: Calories: 208 | Total Fat: 6g | Saturated Fat: 1g | Cholesterol: 67mg | Protein: 28g | Sodium: 107mg | Potassium: 433mg | Fiber: 0g | Carbohydrates: 7g | Sugar: 4g

QUICK INDOOR-GRILLED CHICKEN BREAST

In a rush? This recipe will have your dinner on the table in under ten minutes! Serve with some rice or a hearty green salad.

SERVES 4

4 (4-ounce) boneless, skinless chicken breasts

1 teaspoon frozen apple juice concentrate

4 tablespoons sodium-free honey mustard sauce

1 teaspoon lemon juice

1 teaspoon Citrus Pepper (Appendix A)

1. Plug in indoor grill. Add chicken. Close the lid. Grill for 4–5 minutes or until the chicken is cooked to 160°F.

2. While the chicken grills, add the remaining ingredients to a small microwave-safe bowl. Immediately before serving, microwave on high for 30 seconds to heat the sauce. Evenly divide over the grilled chicken breasts and serve immediately.

PER SERVING: Calories: 141 | Total Fat: 1g | Saturated Fat: 0g | Cholesterol: 65mg | Protein: 26g | Sodium: 74mg | Potassium: 312mg | Fiber: 0g | Carbohydrates: 2g | Sugar: 1g

GRILLED JERK CHICKEN

Jerk Spice Blend seasoning is already spicy hot. You can tone down the heat in this recipe by omitting the jalapeño and sugar, and substituting 1 teaspoon of jalapeño jelly instead. Another alternative is to omit the jalapeño and double the amount of scallions.

SERVES 4

1 teaspoon Jerk Spice Blend (Appendix A)

1 teaspoon Bragg Liquid Aminos

2 teaspoons fresh lime juice

1 teaspoon olive or canola oil

1 jalapeño, seeded and chopped

2 scallions, white and green parts chopped

1 teaspoon granulated sugar

Pinch mustard powder

4 (4-ounce) boneless, skinless chicken breasts

1. Preheat a George Foreman–style indoor grill.

2. Add all ingredients except the chicken to a small food processor or blender and purée.

3. Rub both sides of the chicken with the spice mixture. Grill for 4–6 minutes, until the chicken is cooked through to 160°F. Serve immediately.

PER SERVING: Calories: 141 | Total Fat: 2g | Saturated Fat: 0g | Cholesterol: 65mg | Protein: 26g | Sodium: 133mg | Potassium: 315mg | Fiber: 0g | Carbohydrates: 1g | Sugar: 1g

EASY ITALIAN-SEASONED TURKEY SAUSAGE

Convert this Easy Italian-Seasoned Turkey Sausage to a hot Italian-style turkey sausage recipe by adding some dried red pepper flakes or substituting some dried basil, thyme, and oregano for some of the Italian seasoning.

SERVES 8

1 pound lean ground turkey

1½ teaspoons salt-free seasoning blend

1. In a mixing bowl, combine the ground turkey with your choice of seasoning blend until well mixed. Form into 8 equal-sized patties.

2. Pan-fry in a nonstick grill pan or prepare in a covered indoor grill (such as a George Foreman–style indoor grill). The sausage is done when the temperature registers 165°F.

PER SERVING: Calories: 75 | Total Fat: 3g | Saturated Fat: 0g | Cholesterol: 0mg | Protein: 11g | Sodium: 40mg | Potassium: 0mg | Fiber: 0g | Carbohydrates: 0g | Sugar: 0g

EASY CHICKEN BARBECUE

This is a quick chicken dish full of barbecue goodness. Serve with some grilled corn on the cob, baked potatoes, and grilled veggies for a fantastic summer meal.

SERVES 4

1 tablespoon water or chicken broth or lemon juice

1 small sweet onion, chopped

1 clove garlic, chopped

1 pound Seasoned Chicken (see recipe in this chapter)

¼ cup no-salt-added honey barbecue sauce and marinade

1. In a medium-size microwave-safe bowl, combine the water, onion, and garlic; microwave on high for 3 minutes or until the onion is transparent.

2. Add the chicken and barbecue sauce to the bowl; mix well. Cover and microwave at 70 percent power for 2 minutes or until the chicken is heated through; stir and serve.

PER SERVING: Calories: 138 | Total Fat: 4g | Saturated Fat: 1g | Cholesterol: 90mg | Protein: 22g | Sodium: 107mg | Potassium: 267mg | Fiber: 0g | Carbohydrates: 0g | Sugar: 0g

EASY GINGER CASHEW CHICKEN AND BROCCOLI

The spicy bite of ginger works beautifully with the crisp fresh taste of broccoli and the nutty crunch of cashews. Serve this dish over cooked rice.

SERVES 4

1 tablespoon water or chicken broth or lemon juice

1 small sweet onion, chopped

1 clove garlic, chopped

4 cups broccoli florets

1 pound cooked dark-meat chicken, chopped

6 tablespoons salt-free ginger stir-fry sauce

¼ cup unsalted dry-roasted cashew pieces

Optional: Candied ginger, minced

1. In a large microwave-safe bowl, combine the water, onion, garlic, and broccoli. Cover and microwave on high for 4 minutes or until the broccoli is crisp-tender.

2. Add the chicken and stir-fry sauce; stir well. Microwave at 70 percent power for 2 minutes or until the mixture is heated through.

3. Serve over cooked rice; top each serving with 1 tablespoon of the cashews, and minced candied ginger, if desired.

PER SERVING: Calories: 235 | Total Fat: 9g | Saturated Fat: 2g | Cholesterol: 90mg | Protein: 26g | Sodium: 118mg | Potassium: 542mg | Fiber: 0g | Carbohydrates: 13g | Sugar: 2g

CHAPTER 9

BEEF MAIN DISHES

MARINATED FLANK STEAK

Flank steak is a cut that is relatively new to the market. It is cut from the abdominal muscles of the cow. The grain is very evident because the muscle is used a lot as the cow moves around. Flank steak is only tender when cut against the grain, or across the lines in the meat.

SERVES 4

1½ pounds flank steak

3 cloves garlic, minced

¼ cup minced onion

1 teaspoon ground black pepper

2 teaspoons green peppercorn, crushed

1 jalapeño pepper, minced

3 tablespoons lemon juice

2 tablespoons olive oil

1. In a large glass baking dish, place the flank steak. In small bowl, combine remaining ingredients and mix well; pour over steak.

2. Cover dish and refrigerate for 8–24 hours.

3. When ready to eat, prepare and preheat grill. Remove steak from marinade; reserve marinade.

4. Grill steak 6" from medium coals for 8–9 minutes per side, turning once and brushing occasionally with reserved marinade, until a meat thermometer registers at least 140°F for rare. Do not overcook flank steak or it will be tough; the meat should be medium at most. Discard remaining marinade.

5. Remove steak from the grill, place on platter, and tent with foil. Let stand for 10 minutes, then slice thinly against the grain.

PER SERVING: Calories: 323 | Total Fat: 17g | Saturated Fat: 5g | Cholesterol: 71mg | Protein: 37g | Sodium: 98mg | Potassium: 632mg | Fiber: 0g | Carbohydrates: 2g | Sugar: 0g

DIRTY RICE

Dirty rice is simply rice cooked with other ingredients so it isn't just one color. This main-dish recipe is a one-dish meal; just add a green salad and dinner is ready.

SERVES 6

1¼ pounds ground beef

1 medium onion, chopped

1 medium red bell pepper, chopped

4 cloves garlic, minced

2 cups long-grain brown rice

4½ cups Beef Stock (Chapter 5)

1 tablespoon chili powder

1 teaspoon ground cumin

½ teaspoon crushed red pepper flakes

⅛ teaspoon black pepper

1. In large saucepan, cook ground beef with onion over medium heat, stirring to break up meat, until beef is browned, about 7–8 minutes. Drain off most of the fat.

2. Add red bell pepper and garlic to the saucepan; cook for 2 minutes longer, stirring occasionally.

3. Stir in rice and cook for 1 minute, then add beef stock, chili powder, cumin, red pepper flakes, and pepper, and bring to a simmer.

4. Reduce heat to low, cover pot, and simmer for 20–25 minutes until the rice is tender. Serve immediately.

PER SERVING: Calories: 427 | Total Fat: 12g | Saturated Fat: 4g | Cholesterol: 61mg | Protein: 28g | Sodium: 140mg | Potassium: 629mg | Fiber: 4g | Carbohydrates: 49g | Sugar: 1g

MARINATED HANGER STEAK

Hanger steak used to be called "butcher's steak" because butchers wouldn't sell it, but saved it for themselves because it has such rich flavor. Ask the butcher to remove the membrane and cut the steak in half lengthwise. When marinated, grilled, and sliced thinly against the grain, this cut is tender and flavorful.

SERVES 6

3 tablespoons Grainy Mustard (Chapter 4)

4 cloves garlic, minced

1 teaspoon dried oregano leaves

2 tablespoons red wine or beef broth

2 tablespoons lemon juice

1 tablespoon honey

2 tablespoons olive oil

¼ teaspoon pepper

2 pounds hanger steak, trimmed

1. In large resealable plastic bag, combine mustard, garlic, oregano, wine, lemon juice, honey, olive oil, and pepper. Add the steak and seal bag; massage with your hands to mix the marinade with the meat. Place in large pan and refrigerate at least 8 hours or overnight.

2. When ready to eat, prepare and preheat grill. Remove steak from marinade; discard marinade.

3. Grill steaks over medium coals for 5–7 minutes on each side until the minimum temperature is 140°F. Remove from grill, cover with foil, and let stand for 5 minutes. Slice against the grain and serve.

PER SERVING: Calories: 282 | Total Fat: 12g | Saturated Fat: 3g | Cholesterol: 51mg | Protein: 33g | Sodium: 80mg | Potassium: 555mg | Fiber: 0g | Carbohydrates: 5g | Sugar: 3g

SLOW COOKER ROAST BEEF DINNER

The slow cooker is the best way to cook large chunks of meat. The beef becomes meltingly tender using this method, since all of the moisture released during cooking stays in the pot. Choose an inexpensive cut of chuck or round steak for this recipe, and add all the veggies you want.

SERVES 12

1 (4-pound) beef chuck roast, trimmed

¼ cup flour

1 teaspoon dried marjoram leaves

1 teaspoon dried thyme leaves

¼ teaspoon pepper

2 tablespoons olive oil

2 medium onions, chopped

6 cloves garlic, sliced

3 tablespoons no-salt-added tomato paste

1 cup Beef Stock (Chapter 5)

4 large carrots, sliced

1 parsnip, peeled and cubed

2 stalks celery, sliced

1. Sprinkle the beef with flour, marjoram, thyme, and pepper.

2. In large skillet, heat olive oil over medium heat. Add beef and brown well, without moving, until the meat releases from the pan, about 5 minutes. Turn meat over and brown on the other side, for about 5 minutes. Remove from pan.

3. Add onions and garlic to pan; cook and stir to remove pan drippings. Cook for 3 minutes.

4. Add tomato paste to pan; cook, stirring occasionally, until the tomato paste starts to brown in spots. Add beef stock; scrape to remove pan drippings, and simmer for 1 minute; remove from heat.

5. Place carrots, parsnip, and celery in 5- to 6-quart slow cooker. Top with beef. Pour mixture from skillet over all.

6. Cover slow cooker and cook on low for 8–10 hours or until beef and vegetables are tender. Serve meat with vegetables and sauce.

PER SERVING: Calories: 259 | Total Fat: 8g | Saturated Fat: 2g | Cholesterol: 66mg | Protein: 34g | Sodium: 140mg | Potassium: 733mg | Fiber: 1g | Carbohydrates: 8g | Sugar: 2g

SLOW COOKER BRAISED LEMON SHORT RIBS

Short ribs are cut from the rib section of the cow. They can be purchased bone-in or boneless. For this recipe, buy bone-in ribs, since we're trying to get as much flavor as possible out of the meat without using salt. Serve with mashed potatoes and some glazed carrots for a filling and delicious meal.

SERVES 12

5 pounds bone-in beef short ribs

⅓ cup flour

1 teaspoon dried marjoram leaves

1 teaspoon dried oregano leaves

1 tablespoon grated lemon zest, divided

3 tablespoons olive oil

½ teaspoon crushed red pepper flakes

1 medium onion, chopped

4 cloves garlic, minced

2 unpeeled whole lemons, quartered, seeds removed

1 cup Beef Stock (Chapter 5)

1. The short ribs should be cut crosswise by the butcher so they are about 3" long. Sprinkle with flour, marjoram, oregano, and 1 teaspoon lemon zest.

2. Heat olive oil in large skillet. Brown the ribs, a few at a time, until brown, about 3–4 minutes per side. As the ribs brown, remove them to a 5- to 6-quart slow cooker.

3. When ribs are all browned, sprinkle evenly with remaining 2 teaspoons lemon zest and crushed red pepper flakes.

4. Add onion and garlic to the skillet; cook and stir to remove pan drippings. Cook for 4 minutes.

5. Add lemons to skillet; cook for 1 minute. Then add beef stock and bring just to a simmer. Pour over meat in slow cooker.

6. Cover and cook on low for 8–9 hours or until the meat is very tender. Discard lemon quarters. Skim fat off liquid and discard; serve liquid with ribs.

PER SERVING: Calories: 374 | Total Fat: 22g | Saturated Fat: 8g | Cholesterol: 111mg | Protein: 36g | Sodium: 129mg | Potassium: 703mg | Fiber: 0g | Carbohydrates: 3g | Sugar: 0g

SLOW COOKER POT ROAST WITH CREAMER POTATOES

Creamer potatoes are tiny white potatoes with very thin skins. They are usually cooked quickly, but you can cook them in the slow cooker if an acid such as lemon juice or vinegar is added to keep them firm. Put a little dish of Grainy Mustard (Chapter 4) on the table when you serve this meal.

SERVES 12

2 pounds creamer potatoes

4 pounds chuck roast, trimmed

¼ cup flour

1 teaspoon dried basil leaves

1 teaspoon dried marjoram leaves

¼ teaspoon pepper

2 tablespoons unsalted butter

1 tablespoon olive oil

1 medium onion, chopped

6 cloves garlic, sliced

1 cup Beef Stock (Chapter 5)

3 tablespoons apple cider vinegar

¼ cup honey

1. Wash potatoes and place them in the bottom of a 5-quart slow cooker.

2. Sprinkle roast with flour, basil, marjoram, and pepper.

3. Melt butter and olive oil in a large skillet over medium heat. Add beef and cook, turning once, until browned, about 7–9 minutes. Place meat on top of potatoes in slow cooker.

4. Add onion and garlic to the skillet; cook and stir for 4 minutes to remove pan drippings. Add stock, vinegar, and honey to skillet and bring to a simmer. Simmer 1 minute, then pour over meat in slow cooker.

5. Cover and cook on low for 8–10 hours or until meat is tender. Remove meat and potatoes and place on serving plate. Skim fat from liquid and discard; serve liquid with the meat and potatoes.

PER SERVING: Calories: 324 | Total Fat: 9g | Saturated Fat: 3g | Cholesterol: 71mg | Protein: 35g | Sodium: 123mg | Potassium: 943mg | Fiber: 1g | Carbohydrates: 22g | Sugar: 6g

BEEF AND BEAN ENCHILADAS

It's easy to create a low-sodium version of this classic Mexican dish; the spicy peppers make up for the lack of salt. Serve with a fruit salad for a cooling contrast, and lots of cold, cold beer.

SERVES 8

1 pound ground beef

1 medium onion, chopped

4 cloves garlic, minced

1 jalapeño pepper, minced

2 cups Refried Beans (Chapter 13)

½ cup Spicy Salsa (Chapter 6)

2 (8-ounce) cans no-salt-added tomato sauce

2 teaspoons chili powder

½ teaspoon ground cumin

¼ teaspoon black pepper

12 corn tortillas

1 cup shredded low-sodium Colby cheese

1. Preheat oven to 350°F. Spray a 13" × 9" glass baking dish with nonstick cooking spray; set aside.

2. In large skillet, cook ground beef with onion and garlic, stirring to break up meat, about 7–9 minutes. When meat is browned, drain well.

3. Add jalapeño pepper and beans to ground beef; mix well. Add the salsa and set aside.

4. In medium bowl, combine the tomato sauce with chili powder, cumin, and pepper and mix well. Pour ½ cup of this sauce into the baking dish.

5. Divide the ground beef mixture among the tortillas and roll up. Place on the sauce in the baking dish; top with remaining sauce and sprinkle with cheese.

6. Bake for 25–30 minutes or until cheese is melted and casserole is bubbly. Serve immediately.

PER SERVING: Calories: 374 | Total Fat: 15g | Saturated Fat: 6g | Cholesterol: 51mg | Protein: 22g | Sodium: 119mg | Potassium: 772mg | Fiber: 5g | Carbohydrates: 36g | Sugar: 4g

SAVORY MEATBALLS

When you don't add salt to meatballs, they can taste flat. You can fix that by adding an ingredient that has umami, the meaty taste described in Japanese cooking. Mushrooms have lots of it, especially when cooked until deep brown, and all the more when minced and mixed with other savories in a condiment known as duxelles.

SERVES 8

2 tablespoons unsalted butter

1 cup diced onion

2 cloves garlic, minced

1 cup Duxelles (Chapter 4)

1 large egg, beaten

2 tablespoons Mustard (Chapter 4)

1 teaspoon dried marjoram

1 teaspoon dried basil

1 teaspoon dried thyme

½ teaspoon black pepper

2 pounds lean ground beef

1. Preheat oven to 400°F.

2. In medium skillet, melt butter over medium heat. Add onion and garlic to skillet; cook and stir until crisp-tender, about 4 minutes. Place in large bowl with the duxelles.

3. Add egg, mustard, marjoram, basil, thyme, and pepper to mushroom mixture and mix well. Add beef and mix with your hands just until combined.

4. Form beef into 1" meatballs. Arrange meatballs on a large baking sheet with sides. Bake for 20–25 minutes or until the meatballs register 165°F on a meat thermometer. Drain well, then use in recipes or freeze in 2-cup portions.

PER SERVING: Calories: 290 | Total Fat: 18g | Saturated Fat: 8g | Cholesterol: 115mg | Protein: 25g | Sodium: 89mg | Potassium: 604mg | Fiber: 0g | Carbohydrates: 3g | Sugar: 1g

MEATBALL STROGANOFF

Substitute your own meatballs for the strips of beef in this recipe to cut lots of preparation time and money. This easy dish is wholesome and delicious.

SERVES 6

½ recipe Savory Meatballs (see recipe in this chapter)

2 tablespoons unsalted butter

1 medium onion, chopped

1 cup sliced mushrooms

4 cloves garlic, minced

3 tablespoons flour, divided

½ teaspoon dried dill weed

½ teaspoon celery seed

⅛ teaspoon pepper

2 cups Beef Stock (Chapter 5)

½ cup sour cream

1. Prepare the meatballs and bake; drain and set aside.

2. In large skillet, melt butter over medium heat. Add onion, mushrooms, and garlic; cook and stir for 6–7 minutes until tender.

3. Sprinkle vegetables with 2 tablespoons flour, dill weed, celery seed, and pepper; cook for 1 minute. Then add the stock and bring to a simmer.

4. Add meatballs to the skillet; simmer until sauce is thickened, about 10 minutes.

5. Mix sour cream with remaining 1 tablespoon flour in small bowl. Add ½ cup liquid from the skillet to the sour-cream mixture and stir well.

6. Add the sour-cream mixture to the skillet, and heat through (do not boil). Serve with hot cooked egg noodles.

PER SERVING: Calories: 294 | Total Fat: 20g | Saturated Fat: 10g | Cholesterol: 96mg | Protein: 19g | Sodium: 100mg | Potassium: 520mg | Fiber: 0g | Carbohydrates: 7g | Sugar: 1g

GUACAMOLE BURGERS

Guacamole makes a great addition to the classic burger. Always cook all ground meat to 165°F or you risk making someone sick. Use an instant-read food thermometer to check the temperature. The burger will still be moist and juicy because of the panade, or milk-and-bread combination, mixed into the meat.

SERVES 4

2 ripe avocados, chopped

2 tablespoons lemon juice

2 tablespoons sour cream

1 tablespoon chopped fresh cilantro

1 garlic clove, minced

¼ teaspoon pepper, divided

1 slice French Bread (Chapter 2), crumbled

3 tablespoons milk

2 tablespoons minced green onions

½ teaspoon dried basil leaves

1¼ pounds lean ground beef

4 Hamburger Buns (Chapter 2), split and toasted

¼ cup Mayonnaise (Chapter 4)

4 leaves butter lettuce

4 slices tomato

1. In small bowl, combine avocados, lemon juice, sour cream, cilantro, garlic, and ⅛ teaspoon pepper and mash until chunky. Divide in half; put half in the refrigerator.

2. In large bowl, combine bread crumbs, milk, green onions, basil, and remaining ⅛ teaspoon pepper and mix well. Add ground beef; mix with your hands until combined. Then form into 8 patties.

3. Place 4 patties on work surface; spread each with about 2 tablespoons of the reserved guacamole mixture. Top with the other four patties, and press edges to seal.

4. Refrigerate hamburger patties while you prepare and preheat grill.

5. When ready, grill burgers over medium coals, turning once, until thoroughly cooked to 165°F as tested with a meat thermometer.

6. Place bottoms of hamburger buns on work surface. Top with mayonnaise, then burgers, then some reserved guacamole, then lettuce and tomato. Add bun tops and serve immediately.

PER SERVING: Calories: 870 | Total Fat: 52g | Saturated Fat: 12g | Cholesterol: 142mg | Protein: 32g | Sodium: 140mg | Potassium: 1,166mg | Fiber: 10g | Carbohydrates: 64g | Sugar: 4g

SLOPPY JOES

This mixture is delicious served on split and toasted hamburger buns. Some Baked Potato Chips (Chapter 6), a cool green salad, and some ice cream for dessert are all you need for a satisfying meal.

SERVES 4

1 pound ground beef

1 medium onion, chopped

½ cup chopped mushrooms

2 cloves garlic, minced

½ cup chopped celery

2 tablespoons no-salt-added tomato paste

2 (8-ounce) cans no-salt-added tomato sauce

1 tablespoon lemon juice

1 tablespoon honey

½ teaspoon dried basil leaves

½ teaspoon dried oregano leaves

⅛ teaspoon pepper

4 split, toasted Hamburger Buns (Chapter 2)

1. In large skillet, cook ground beef and onion over medium heat, stirring frequently to break up meat, until beef starts to brown.

2. Add mushrooms, garlic, and celery; cook, stirring occasionally, until meat is browned and vegetables are tender. Drain well.

3. Return skillet to heat and add tomato paste; cook and stir for 4 minutes until paste begins to brown.

4. Add tomato sauce, lemon juice, honey, basil, oregano, and pepper and bring to a simmer. Simmer for 10 minutes or until slightly thickened.

5. Serve beef mixture on hamburger buns.

PER SERVING: Calories: 592 | Total Fat: 21g | Saturated Fat: 6g | Cholesterol: 101mg | Protein: 32g | Sodium: 139mg | Potassium: 1,081mg | Fiber: 5g | Carbohydrates: 67g | Sugar: 19g

STEAK WITH CHIMICHURRI

You could use a flank or hanger steak for this recipe, or a sirloin tip or skirt steak. The steak should be sliced thinly against the grain, piled onto a serving platter, and drizzled with more sauce before serving.

SERVES 4

1 (1½–1¾-pound) hanger or skirt steak

¼ teaspoon pepper

1 cup Chimichurri (Chapter 4), divided

1. The day before you want to serve this recipe, place the steak in a large resealable plastic bag. Top with pepper and ½ cup of the Chimichurri; seal bag and rub with your hands to mix.

2. Place bag in a large baking dish and refrigerate at least 8 hours or overnight.

3. When ready to eat, prepare and preheat grill.

4. Remove steak from marinade; discard excess marinade. Grill steak for 15–20 minutes, turning once, until steak reaches desired doneness (at least 140°F for food safety reasons).

5. Remove steak from grill, cover with foil, and let stand 5 minutes. Then carve steak against the grain and put on a serving plate. Drizzle with remaining Chimichurri and serve immediately.

PER SERVING: Calories: 562 | Total Fat: 40g | Saturated Fat: 9g | Cholesterol: 100mg | Protein: 45g | Sodium: 135mg | Potassium: 585mg | Fiber: 0g | Carbohydrates: 2g | Sugar: 0g

STUFFED PEPPERS

You can use any color peppers you'd like in this recipe; a combination of several different colors is pretty. You'll need about a cup of cooked rice for this recipe; that's ⅓ cup uncooked. Cover the rice with water and cook for 20 minutes, then drain off the excess water and use in the recipe.

SERVES 4

4 large bell peppers

1 pound ground beef

1 medium onion, chopped

2 cloves garlic, minced

2 medium tomatoes, chopped

1 cup cooked rice

1 (8-ounce) can no-salt-added tomato sauce

1 tablespoon lemon juice

1 teaspoon sugar

½ teaspoon dried marjoram leaves

½ cup water

1. Preheat oven to 350°F. Cut off the top ½" of each bell pepper. Remove seeds and membranes from inside the pepper; set aside.

2. In large skillet, cook ground beef with onion and garlic, stirring to break up meat, until the meat is browned and cooked. Drain well.

3. Stir in the tomatoes; cook for 4–5 minutes, stirring frequently. Then add the rice, tomato sauce, lemon juice, sugar, and marjoram leaves. Simmer for 3 minutes longer.

4. Stuff the beef mixture into the peppers, mounding over the top. Place peppers in a 2-quart baking dish. Pour water around peppers and cover with foil.

5. Bake for 25 minutes, then uncover and bake another 5–10 minutes or until peppers are tender. Serve immediately.

PER SERVING: Calories: 321 | Total Fat: 11g | Saturated Fat: 4g | Cholesterol: 73mg | Protein: 26g | Sodium: 89mg | Potassium: 1,012mg | Fiber: 4g | Carbohydrates: 26g | Sugar: 9g

STUFFED CABBAGE

Stuffed cabbage is originally from Hungary. This frugal dish is very good for you and so delicious, especially on a cold winter night. This recipe stretches a pound of ground beef to serve six people, so it's easy on your budget as well as your health.

SERVES 6; SERVING SIZE 2 ROLLS

1 large head green cabbage

1 pound lean ground beef

1 medium onion, chopped

4 cloves garlic, minced

1 medium tomato, chopped

2 large eggs, beaten

¼ cup Mustard (Chapter 4)

2 tablespoons olive oil

1 (14-ounce) can no-salt-added diced tomatoes, undrained

1 (6-ounce) can no-salt-added tomato paste

2 tablespoons brown sugar

2 tablespoons lemon juice

1 bay leaf

2 teaspoons paprika

2 teaspoons caraway seeds

⅛ teaspoon black pepper

⅛ teaspoon cayenne pepper

1. Bring a large pot of water to a boil. Add cabbage; cook for a few minutes or until outer leaves loosen. Remove cabbage from pot, rinse with cold water, and remove 12 outer leaves. Chop remaining cabbage and set aside.

2. In large skillet, cook ground beef with onion and garlic, stirring to break up meat, until ground beef is cooked. Add chopped tomato and reserved chopped cabbage and cook until crisp-tender, about 5 minutes. Drain well. Remove ground beef mixture to a bowl.

3. Add eggs and mustard to ground beef mixture and mix well; set aside.

4. Return skillet to medium heat; add olive oil. Add diced tomatoes, tomato paste, brown sugar, lemon juice, bay leaf, paprika, caraway seeds, pepper, and cayenne pepper and bring to a simmer. Reduce heat to low and simmer while preparing cabbage rolls.

5. Cut the large tough section of each cabbage leaf away and discard. Divide beef mixture among the cabbage leaves and roll up, tucking in ends.

6. Preheat oven to 350°F. Remove bay leaf from tomato sauce and discard. Place about 1 cup of the tomato-sauce mixture in the bottom of a Dutch oven. Add the cabbage rolls, seam-side down. Pour remaining tomato-sauce mixture over all.

7. Cover and bake for 45–55 minutes or until cabbage is tender and sauce is bubbling. Serve immediately.

PER SERVING: Calories: 320 | Total Fat: 15g | Saturated Fat: 4g | Cholesterol: 119mg | Protein: 22g | Sodium: 137mg | Potassium: 1,123mg | Fiber: 8g | Carbohydrates: 25g | Sugar: 14g

PEPPER STEAK

Bell peppers are loaded with vitamin C and fiber, and the different colors make a lovely sight. It is cooked as a stir-fry, so be sure to have all of the ingredients prepared and ready to go before you start cooking. Once the cooking starts, the recipe will be ready in about 15 minutes. Serve over hot cooked brown rice.

SERVES 4

3 tablespoons lemon juice

1 tablespoon honey

1 tablespoon molasses

½ teaspoon dried thyme leaves

½ teaspoon dried oregano leaves

⅛ teaspoon black pepper

1 pound round or sirloin steak

2 tablespoons olive oil

1 medium onion, chopped

1 tablespoon minced ginger root

3 cloves garlic, sliced

3 large bell peppers, cut into strips

¾ cup Beef Stock (Chapter 5), divided

2 tablespoons cornstarch

1. In shallow bowl, combine lemon juice, honey, molasses, thyme, oregano, and pepper and mix well.

2. Cut the steak into thin strips against the grain and add to the lemon mixture; toss to coat and set aside.

3. In large skillet or wok, heat olive oil over medium heat. Add onion, ginger root, and garlic; stir-fry for 3–4 minutes until crisp-tender.

4. Drain marinade from meat; reserve marinade. Add beef to skillet; stir-fry for 2–3 minutes or until at least 140°F.

5. Add bell peppers to skillet along with reserved marinade and ½ cup beef stock. Bring to a simmer; simmer for 4–6 minutes or until beef and vegetables are tender.

6. Combine remaining ¼ cup stock and cornstarch in a small bowl and stir well. Add to skillet; cook for 1–2 minutes longer or until sauce is thickened. Serve immediately.

PER SERVING: Calories: 299 | Total Fat: 11g | Saturated Fat: 2g | Cholesterol: 47mg | Protein: 27g | Sodium: 84mg | Potassium: 749mg | Fiber: 2g | Carbohydrates: 20g | Sugar: 11g

GOULASH

Goulash is usually served over egg noodles, but in this recipe the pasta is cooked right in the sauce for ease. Cooking pasta in sauce also adds flavor and ensures that the pasta doesn't overcook, since the acid in the tomatoes slows softening. Serve with a green salad and some Dinner Rolls (Chapter 2).

SERVES 10

1½ pounds lean sirloin steak

¼ cup flour

4 teaspoons paprika, divided

½ teaspoon dried marjoram leaves

½ teaspoon dried oregano leaves

¼ teaspoon pepper

2 tablespoons olive oil

2 medium onions, chopped

6 cloves garlic, minced

2 (14-ounce) cans no-salt-added diced tomatoes, undrained

3 (8-ounce) cans no-salt-added tomato sauce

1¼ cups Beef Stock (Chapter 5)

1 tablespoon lemon juice

2 teaspoons caraway seeds

4 cups penne pasta

1. Cube the steak and toss with flour, 2 teaspoons paprika, marjoram, oregano, and pepper.

2. In very large skillet, heat olive oil over medium heat. Add beef in batches; stir to brown, about 4 minute for each batch. Remove all beef from skillet.

3. Add onions and garlic to skillet; cook, stirring to remove pan drippings, for 5–6 minutes until tender.

4. Add undrained tomatoes, tomato sauce, beef stock, lemon juice, caraway seeds, and remaining 2 teaspoons paprika. Bring to a simmer.

5. Add beef to skillet. Bring to a simmer. Simmer, uncovered, stirring frequently, for 10 minutes.

6. Add pasta to skillet and stir, making sure pasta is submerged in sauce. Simmer for about 15–18 minutes, stirring frequently, until pasta is tender but still firm to the bite. Serve immediately.

PER SERVING: Calories: 375 | Total Fat: 12g | Saturated Fat: 3g | Cholesterol: 45mg | Protein: 28g | Sodium: 135mg | Potassium: 1,242mg | Fiber: 5g | Carbohydrates: 37g | Sugar: 10g

CHUTNEY MEATBALLS

Adding chutney to the meat transforms plain meatballs into something special. You could look for a low-sodium chutney, but they are hard to find. Your best bet is to make your own Mango Chutney (Chapter 4) and use it in this delicious recipe. Serve over hot cooked rice or couscous.

SERVES 4

1 slice French Bread (Chapter 2), crumbled

2 tablespoons milk

1 cup Mango Chutney (Chapter 4), divided

1 large egg, beaten

2 tablespoons minced parsley

1 clove garlic, minced

2 teaspoons curry powder, divided

1 pound ground beef

2 tablespoons olive oil

1 medium onion, chopped

2 tablespoons no-salt-added tomato paste

1 (8-ounce) can no-salt-added tomato sauce

1 cup Beef Stock (Chapter 5)

1. In large bowl, combine bread crumbs, milk, ¼ cup chutney, egg, parsley, garlic, and 1 teaspoon curry powder; mix well. Add ground beef; mix with your hands until blended. Form into 30 meatballs.

2. Heat olive oil in skillet over medium heat. Add meatballs; brown on all sides, about 4–6 minutes total; do not cook through. Remove meatballs to a plate as they brown.

3. When meatballs are browned, drain pan but do not wipe out. Add onion to skillet. Cook, stirring to remove pan drippings, for 4–5 minutes or until crisp-tender.

4. Add tomato paste to skillet; cook without stirring until paste just begins to brown. Add tomato sauce, beef stock, and remaining 1 teaspoon curry powder and bring to a simmer, stirring frequently.

5. Return meatballs to skillet. Simmer for 15–20 minutes or until meatballs are thoroughly cooked to 165°F, stirring occasionally. Stir remaining ¾ cup chutney into the skillet and heat for a few minutes. Serve immediately.

PER SERVING: Calories: 414 | Total Fat: 20g | Saturated Fat: 6g | Cholesterol: 127mg | Protein: 28g | Sodium: 137mg | Potassium: 873mg | Fiber: 2g | Carbohydrates: 30g | Sugar: 19g

SALISBURY STEAK WITH MUSHROOM GRAVY

Salisbury steak is actually ground beef mixed with eggs and bread crumbs and formed into patties. The patties are sautéed, then simmered in a rich gravy.

SERVES 4

⅓ cup Duxelles (Chapter 4)

2 tablespoons minced green onions

1 large egg, beaten

3 tablespoons bread crumbs

1 tablespoon Mustard (Chapter 4)

¼ teaspoon pepper, divided

1 pound lean ground beef

1 tablespoon olive oil

1 medium onion, chopped

3 cloves garlic, minced

1 (8-ounce) package mushrooms, sliced

2 tablespoons flour

2 cups Beef Stock (Chapter 5)

½ teaspoon dried marjoram

1. In large bowl, combine duxelles, green onions, egg, bread crumbs, mustard, and ⅛ teaspoon pepper and mix well. Add beef and mix with hands until incorporated. Form into 4 patties.

2. In large saucepan, heat olive oil over medium heat. Add patties; brown about 4 minutes on each side, turning once. Remove patties from saucepan; drain saucepan, but do not wipe out.

3. Add onion, garlic, and sliced mushrooms to saucepan and cook until tender, stirring frequently to remove pan drippings. Sprinkle flour into saucepan and cook for 1 minute.

4. Add beef stock, marjoram, and remaining ⅛ teaspoon pepper to saucepan and bring to a simmer. Return patties to saucepan and simmer for 8–10 minutes or until meat is thoroughly cooked to 165°F.

PER SERVING: Calories: 371 | Total Fat: 19g | Saturated Fat: 6g | Cholesterol: 131mg | Protein: 31g | Sodium: 136mg | Potassium: 824mg | Fiber: 2g | Carbohydrates: 17g | Sugar: 2g

OVEN BBQ MEATLOAF

This recipe is packed full of flavor. The most important trick with meatloaf is to let it stand, covered with foil, for 5–10 minutes after it comes out of the oven. That will make it easier to slice and will allow the juices to redistribute. Serve with mashed potatoes and steamed corn.

SERVES 6

1 tablespoon olive oil

1 medium onion, finely chopped

1 cup minced mushrooms

2 cloves garlic, minced

1¼ cups BBQ Sauce (Chapter 4), divided

¼ teaspoon pepper

1½ pounds lean ground beef

1. Preheat oven to 350°F.

2. In medium skillet, heat olive oil over medium heat. Add onion, mushrooms, and garlic; cook and stir until the mixture begins to brown, about 7–9 minutes. Transfer mixture to large bowl.

3. Add ¾ cup BBQ sauce and pepper to onion mixture and let cool for 10 minutes. Then add beef, mixing with your hands until incorporated. Form into a rectangular loaf and place on a broiler pan.

4. Top the meatloaf with the remaining BBQ sauce. Bake for 50–60 minutes until internal temperature reaches 165°F. Cover with foil and let stand for 5 minutes, then slice and serve.

PER SERVING: Calories: 255 | Total Fat: 14g | Saturated Fat: 5g | Cholesterol: 73mg | Protein: 23g | Sodium: 88mg | Potassium: 531mg | Fiber: 0g | Carbohydrates: 6g | Sugar: 4g

CURRIED SLOW COOKER POT ROAST

Choose chuck, brisket, or round roast for this recipe; these inexpensive cuts become very tender in the slow cooker. This is a one-dish meal, so all you need is a green salad and a lemon pie for dessert.

SERVES 6–8

4 medium carrots, sliced

1 pound new potatoes

2 pounds boneless beef roast

¼ cup flour

2 tablespoons curry powder, divided

¼ teaspoon pepper

3 tablespoons olive oil

2 medium onions, chopped

3 cloves garlic, sliced

1 tablespoon minced fresh ginger root

½ cup pineapple juice

1 cup Beef Stock (Chapter 5)

½ cup Mango Chutney (Chapter 4)

1. Place carrots and potatoes in a 5- to 6-quart slow cooker. Sprinkle the roast with flour, 1 tablespoon curry powder, and pepper.

2. In large skillet, heat olive oil over medium-high heat. Add the roast and brown on both sides, turning once, about 4–6 minutes total. Remove from skillet and place in slow cooker over vegetables.

3. Add onions, garlic, and ginger root to skillet. Cook, stirring to remove pan drippings, for 5 minutes. Deglaze the pan with pineapple juice and beef stock and bring to a simmer. Stir in chutney and pour over meat in slow cooker.

4. Cover and cook on low for 8–9 hours or until meat is tender. Serve meat and vegetables with sauce.

PER SERVING: Calories: 304 | Total Fat: 10g | Saturated Fat: 2g | Cholesterol: 49mg | Protein: 28g | Sodium: 128mg | Potassium: 843mg | Fiber: 3g | Carbohydrates: 24g | Sugar: 7g

LIME-MARINATED GRILLED STEAK

If you like spicy hot flavors, substitute a salt-free Thai seasoning or jerk seasoning blend for the spices in this recipe. Both go well with lime juice.

SERVES 4

2 tablespoons canola or olive oil

½ cup fresh lime juice

Pinch dried red pepper flakes

½ teaspoon garlic powder

½ teaspoon onion powder

¼ teaspoon ground ginger

⅛ teaspoon dried thyme

⅛ teaspoon salt-free chili powder

Pinch each of ground cinnamon, allspice, and cloves

1 (18-ounce) boneless round steak, fat removed

2 teaspoons freshly ground black pepper

1. In a noncorrosive dish large enough to allow the meat to lie flat, combine the oil, lime juice, red pepper flakes, garlic powder, onion powder, ground ginger, thyme, chili powder, cinnamon, allspice, and cloves. Add steak to the dish, turning it to coat it in the marinade. Cover and refrigerate for 8 hours or overnight. (Turn the meat a few times during this marinating process.)

2. Preheat grill coals to medium-hot (350°F to 400°F).

3. Remove the meat from the marinade and sprinkle with the black pepper. Grill over direct heat for 4 minutes on one side. Turn and grill for another 2–4 minutes, until the meat is cooked to the desired doneness, at least 140°F. Transfer to a cutting board or platter and allow the meat to rest for 10 minutes. (Tent with aluminum foil if necessary to maintain meat temperature.) To serve, slice thinly against the grain.

PER SERVING: Calories: 313 | Total Fat: 15g | Saturated Fat: 4g | Cholesterol: 126mg | Protein: 39g | Sodium: 81mg | Potassium: 399mg | Fiber: 0g | Carbohydrates: 3g | Sugar: 0g

ROAST BEEF

To impart the rich flavor of the pan juices to potatoes and vegetables, roast the potatoes and vegetables on a separate baking sheet. Then, once you've skimmed the fat from the pan juices, toss them with the juices. Return the potatoes and vegetables to the oven for 10–20 minutes while the roast rests.

SERVES 8

2–2¼-pound lean boneless beef roast, visible fat removed

1 tablespoon olive or canola oil

1 teaspoon freshly ground black pepper

½ teaspoon garlic powder

⅛ teaspoon salt-free chili powder

Pinch dried thyme

1 small white onion, sliced

1 medium carrot, peeled and sliced

1 large stalk celery, sliced

¼ cup dry red wine

¼ cup water

1. Preheat oven to 350°F. Treat a roasting pan with nonstick spray.

2. Pat the roast dry with paper towels. Add the oil, pepper, garlic powder, chili powder, and thyme to a small bowl and mix well. Rub the oil mixture onto the meat.

3. Place the meat in the center of the prepared pan and arrange the onion, carrot, and celery around it. Pour the wine and water over the vegetables. Insert the probe of a meat thermometer into the center of thickest part of the roast. Roast, uncovered, to desired doneness. For rare, cook until internal temperature is 135°F; for well done, cook to 165°F—approximately 1–1¼ hours cooking time.

4. Remove the roast from pan to a cutting board or serving platter. Tent with aluminum foil and allow to rest for 10–20 minutes.

5. Remove the vegetables from pan juices with a slotted spoon and discard. Skim off the fat from the pan juices. Serve the juices over the roast.

PER SERVING: Calories: 229 | Total Fat: 9g | Saturated Fat: 3g | Cholesterol: 66mg | Protein: 30g | Sodium: 77mg | Potassium: 455mg | Fiber: 0g | Carbohydrates: 1g | Sugar: 0g

VEAL AND SPINACH IN LEMON SAUCE

Tender veal is accented with tart lemon and tangy spinach. Serve with roasted potatoes and fresh corn for a spectacular meal.

SERVES 8

3 tablespoons olive or canola oil

1½ pounds lean veal, cut into cubes

1 large white onion, chopped

¼ cup water

1 tablespoon lemon juice

¼ teaspoon freshly ground black pepper

¼ teaspoon fennel seeds, crushed

¼ teaspoon garlic powder

⅛ teaspoon salt-free chili powder

3 green onions, white and green parts chopped

2 (10-ounce) packages frozen spinach, thawed and drained

Optional: 1 lemon, cut into 6 wedges

1. Bring oil to temperature over medium-high heat in a large, deep nonstick sauté pan; brown the veal. Add the onion and sauté until transparent.

2. Add the water, lemon juice, pepper, fennel seeds, garlic powder, and chili powder. Bring to a boil, then reduce heat; cover and simmer for 1 hour or until the veal is tender, stirring occasionally and adding more water, if necessary.

3. Add the green onions and spinach. Cover and simmer for 10 minutes. Serve immediately. Garnish with lemon wedges, if desired.

PER SERVING: Calories: 257 | Total Fat: 14g | Saturated Fat: 3g | Cholesterol: 98mg | Protein: 28g | Sodium: 128mg | Potassium: 483mg | Fiber: 2g | Carbohydrates: 4g | Sugar: 0g

BEEF FILLET

Be sure your oven is very clean when you set it to use high temperatures like the ones called for in this recipe; otherwise, the high temperatures will cause it to smoke.

SERVES 8

1 (2-pound) fillet of beef, trimmed and tied

1½ teaspoons unsalted butter, at room temperature

1½ teaspoons olive oil

1½ teaspoons coarsely ground black pepper

2 teaspoons sweet paprika

2 tablespoons garlic powder

1½ teaspoons onion powder

½ teaspoon cayenne pepper

⅓ teaspoon dried oregano

⅓ teaspoon dried thyme

1. Preheat the oven to 500°F. Treat a baking sheet or a roasting rack set in a roasting pan with nonstick spray.

2. Pat the outside of the meat dry with a paper towel. Place the meat on a piece of heavy-duty aluminum foil large enough to hold the fillet. Set aside to come to room temperature while you prepare remaining ingredients.

3. In a small bowl, mix together the unsalted butter and olive oil.

4. In another small bowl, combine all the remaining dry ingredients; mix well.

5. Use your hands to spread the butter–olive oil mixture over the entire surface of the meat. Sprinkle the dry seasoning mixture evenly over the entire surface of the meat, patting it into the meat. Move the fillet to the prepared baking sheet or roasting rack. Insert the probe of a meat thermometer into the center of thickest part of the fillet. Roast, uncovered, to desired doneness: 140°F for rare, 150°F for medium, and 165°F for well done. (Keep in mind that the temperature of the fillet will rise by a few degrees while it rests.)

6. Remove the beef from the oven, and place it under an aluminum foil "tent" that is crimped tightly to the pan. Allow the meat to rest at room temperature for 20 minutes. Remove the tent and the strings holding the meat together; use a serrated knife to slice the fillet into 16 equal-sized pieces.

PER SERVING: Calories: 241 | Total Fat: 9g | Saturated Fat: 3g | Cholesterol: 114mg | Protein: 34g | Sodium: 72mg | Potassium: 359mg | Fiber: 0g | Carbohydrates: 2g | Sugar: 0g

QUICK SEASONED JUMBO HAMBURGERS

These three meats combine so well and create such a flavorful burger, you'll never go back to an all-beef burger again! Serve with Baked Potato Chips (Chapter 6) and a side salad for a filling and delicious meal.

SERVES 4

½ pound lean ground sirloin

¼ pound ground boneless, skinless chicken breast

¼ pound ground boneless, skinless turkey breast

1 teaspoon salt-free steak seasoning

¼ teaspoon brown sugar

1. In a mixing bowl, combine all the ingredients until well mixed. Form into 4 equal-sized patties.

2. Pan-fry in a nonstick grill pan or prepare in a covered indoor grill (such as a George Foreman–style indoor grill) until the temperature registers 165°F on a meat thermometer.

PER SERVING: Calories: 167 | Total Fat: 7g | Saturated Fat: 2g | Cholesterol: 68mg | Protein: 22g | Sodium: 75mg | Potassium: 182mg | Fiber: 0g | Carbohydrates: 0g | Sugar: 0g

EASY SLOW-COOKED "ROAST" BEEF

Adding a low-sodium beef base will provide a hearty beef broth in this recipe. Strain any fat from that broth— or, even better, refrigerate the broth overnight and then remove and discard the hardened fat. The broth can be kept for 1 or 2 days in the refrigerator, or frozen for up to 3 months.

SERVES 8

2¼-pound London broil roast, trimmed of fat and cut into pieces

Water, as needed

½ teaspoon low-sodium beef base

⅛ teaspoon roasted mirepoix flavor concentrate

½ tablespoon dried minced onion

½ teaspoon dried minced garlic

1. Put the roast and all other ingredients into a 3 to 4-quart slow cooker, add enough water to cover the roast, and cook on low for 6–8 hours or until meat is tender.

2. Remove the meat from the slow cooker and discard the resulting broth (or save it for later use). Remove any remaining fat from the meat and discard that as well. Weigh the meat and separate it into 4-ounce servings. The meat can be kept for 1 or 2 days in the refrigerator, or freeze portions for use later.

PER SERVING: Calories: 178 | Total Fat: 5g | Saturated Fat: 2g | Cholesterol: 66mg | Protein: 29g | Sodium: 97mg | Potassium: 335mg | Fiber: 0g | Carbohydrates: 0g | Sugar: 0g

LIVERWURST

If you don't have a meat grinder available, you can cut the meat into cubes and freeze it for 20 minutes, then add the semifrozen cubes to the bowl of your food processor and pulse until ground.

SERVES 6

Unbleached muslin

1 pound fresh pork liver

1 pound lean beef round steak, trimmed of any fat

1 large sweet white onion, finely diced

3 tablespoons nonfat dry milk

1 teaspoon freshly fine-ground white pepper

2 teaspoons paprika

1 teaspoon granulated sugar

½ teaspoon marjoram

½ teaspoon finely ground coriander

¼ teaspoon mace

¼ teaspoon ground allspice

¼ teaspoon ground cardamom

¼ teaspoon mustard powder

⅛ teaspoon grated lemon zest

1. In place of casings, prepare a piece of unbleached muslin about 12" long and 8" wide. Fold the muslin lengthwise and tightly stitch a seam across one of the short ends and continue along the open side. Leave a seam of about ⅛" from the edge of the material. Turn the muslin casing so that the stitching is on the inside. Set it aside until you are ready to stuff it.

2. Run the liver and round steak through a meat grinder with the fine disk. Mix well to combine the liver and beef. Transfer the ground meat to a bowl, sprinkle the remaining ingredients over the ground meat, and mix thoroughly.

3. Pack the mixture into the muslin casing. (It's easier to get the meat packed to the bottom of the casing if you first fold the open end down over itself a few inches.) Firmly pack the meat into the casing. Either stitch the open end closed or secure it with a wire twist tie, butcher's twine, or cotton cord.

4. In a large kettle, bring enough water to a boil to cover the liverwurst in the muslin packet by 2"–3". Add the liverwurst. Place a weight—such as a heavy plate—on the liverwurst to keep it submerged. Bring the water to a boil again; reduce the heat, cover, and simmer for 3 hours.

5. Either transfer the muslin packet to a pan of ice water or drain the hot water from the pan and replace it with an equal quantity of ice water. Let the liverwurst cool, then refrigerate it for at least 8 hours or overnight. Remove the muslin casing and slice the liverwurst into 4-ounce portions to serve.

PER SERVING: Calories: 244 | Total Fat: 6g | Saturated Fat: 2g | Cholesterol: 278mg | Protein: 34g | Sodium: 133mg | Potassium: 616mg | Fiber: 1g | Carbohydrates: 9g | Sugar: 5g

SLOW COOKER BEEF BARBECUE

The main ingredients in Worcestershire sauce are malt vinegar, sugar, molasses, tamarind, onions, anchovies, and salt, making it, as you can imagine, pretty high in sodium. Luckily there are several low-sodium varieties of Worcestershire sauce on the market today.

SERVES 6

1½ pounds Easy Slow-Cooked "Roast" Beef (see recipe in this chapter)

1 cup water

½ cup dry white wine

½ cup low-salt ketchup

1 tablespoon red wine vinegar

2 teaspoons reduced-sodium Worcestershire sauce

2 teaspoons mustard powder

1 tablespoon dried minced onion

1 teaspoon dried minced garlic

1 teaspoon cracked black pepper

1 tablespoon brown sugar

¼ teaspoon salt-free chili powder

Pinch dried red pepper flakes, crushed

1. Add the cooked beef to the slow cooker. Mix together all the remaining ingredients and pour over the beef. Add additional water, if necessary, to completely cover the meat.

2. Cover and cook on high for 2–3 hours or until mixture simmers. Adjust the seasonings, if necessary.

PER SERVING: Calories: 228 | Total Fat: 6g | Saturated Fat: 2g | Cholesterol: 66mg | Protein: 30g | Sodium: 101mg | Potassium: 442mg | Fiber: 0g | Carbohydrates: 8g | Sugar: 6g

CHAPTER 10

PORK, LAMB, AND VENISON MAIN DISHES

SPICY SAUSAGE

Making your own sausage is a snap, and you can flavor it the way you like. This is a bulk sausage recipe. You can mix the pork and seasonings and form the mixture into patties; freeze, uncooked, up to 4 months. Or you can cook the mixture as you would ground beef, then freeze it in 1-cup portions for use in recipes.

YIELDS 4 POUNDS; 16 SERVINGS

4 pounds ground pork

2 tablespoons brown sugar

8 cloves garlic, minced

1–4 jalapeño peppers, minced

1 teaspoon black pepper

1 teaspoon cayenne pepper

2 teaspoons smoked paprika

1 teaspoon dried marjoram leaves

1. Combine all ingredients in a large bowl and mix with hands until combined. Form into 32 patties and freeze. To use, thaw overnight in the refrigerator. Sauté in a large skillet until the pork registers 165°F on a meat thermometer, about 7–10 minutes, turning once. Drain and serve.

2. Or freeze the raw pork mixture in 1-cup portions up to 4 months. To use, thaw overnight in the refrigerator, then cook as you would ground beef to use in recipes.

PER SERVING: Calories: 307 | Total Fat: 24g | Saturated Fat: 8g | Cholesterol: 81mg | Protein: 19g | Sodium: 64mg | Potassium: 349mg | Fiber: 0g | Carbohydrates: 2g | Sugar: 1g

LAMB CHOPS WITH BERRY-MINT COMPOTE

Lamb has a particularly cloying fat that has a very rich mouthfeel. Because of this, the meat is usually served with something that will cut through that fat, such as mint, a tart jelly, or lemon. This elegant entrée should be served with some scalloped potatoes, steamed asparagus, and a fruit salad.

SERVES 4

12 lamb loin chops

½ teaspoon dried mint leaves

⅛ teaspoon pepper

1 cup sliced strawberries

1 cup blueberries

⅓ cup water

¼ cup honey

3 tablespoons chopped fresh mint leaves

1 cup raspberries

2 tablespoons olive oil

1. Sprinkle lamb with dried mint and pepper and refrigerate.

2. For compote, combine strawberries, blueberries, water, and honey in a medium saucepan. Bring to a simmer; simmer until berries are tender, about 3–4 minutes. Remove from heat and add fresh mint and raspberries; cool for 1 hour.

3. Heat olive oil in a large skillet over medium heat and sauté the lamb for 6–9 minutes, turning once, until medium, about 145°F. Remove to a plate and tent with aluminum foil for 5 minutes. Serve the lamb with the compote.

PER SERVING: Calories: 282 | Total Fat: 7g | Saturated Fat: 3g | Cholesterol: 72mg | Protein: 24g | Sodium: 88mg | Potassium: 541mg | Fiber: 3g | Carbohydrates: 30g | Sugar: 24g

PORK MEDALLIONS WITH CRANBERRY SAUCE

Pork medallions are cut from boneless pork tenderloin, which is the most tender cut of this meat. Slice the tenderloin across, then press down to flatten. These medallions cook very quickly, and are topped with a bright and beautiful cranberry sauce. This is an excellent recipe for a holiday dinner party.

SERVES 6–8

2 (1-pound) pork tenderloins

⅓ cup flour

1 teaspoon dried marjoram leaves

¼ teaspoon white pepper

2 tablespoons butter

2 tablespoons olive oil

1 medium onion, chopped

2 cloves garlic, minced

1 cup whole cranberries

¼ cup dry red wine

1 cup Chicken Stock (Chapter 5)

⅔ cup dried cranberries

3 tablespoons sour cream

1. Cut the pork tenderloins into 2" pieces crosswise. Place on a work surface and press down with a drinking glass to make the tenderloins about 1–½" thick. Sprinkle with flour, marjoram, and pepper, and set aside.

2. In large skillet, melt butter with olive oil over medium heat. Add the pork and cook until browned on each side, turning once, about 4–5 minutes. Remove the pork from the pan as it browns. You may need to do this in two batches.

3. When pork is browned, add onion and garlic to the pan. Cook and stir for 5–7 minutes or until crisp-tender, stirring to remove pan drippings.

4. Add whole cranberries and wine to the pan; bring to a boil. Reduce heat and simmer for 1–2 minutes.

5. Add chicken stock and bring to a simmer again. Simmer for 5–9 minutes or until cranberries soften.

6. Return pork medallions to skillet along with the dried cranberries. Simmer for 3–5 minutes longer or until the pork registers at least 145°F on a meat thermometer. Stir in the sour cream and serve.

PER SERVING: Calories: 276 | Total Fat: 11g | Saturated Fat: 4g | Cholesterol: 84mg | Protein: 26g | Sodium: 69mg | Potassium: 498mg | Fiber: 1g | Carbohydrates: 14g | Sugar: 7g

OVEN BBQ LAMB

Lamb ribs may be a cut you have to order from your butcher, so plan ahead. The ribs are smothered in your own homemade barbecue sauce, which you can make as mild or spicy as you'd like. Serve with lots of beer and napkins, and a green salad with tomatoes and cucumbers.

SERVES 8

5 pounds lamb ribs, defrosted if frozen

½ teaspoon white pepper

1 teaspoon grated lemon zest

3 cups BBQ Sauce (Chapter 4)

1. Preheat oven to 350°F. Sprinkle ribs with pepper and lemon zest; rub into the meat.

2. Place ribs on a rack on a baking sheet with sides, rib-side down. Bake for 30 minutes.

3. Drain off any accumulated fat, and cover with ¾ of the BBQ sauce. Bake for 30 minutes longer.

4. Remove from oven and top with remaining barbecue sauce. Bake for 10–15 minutes longer or until ribs are tender and glazed.

PER SERVING: Calories: 210 | Total Fat: 8g | Saturated Fat: 3g | Cholesterol: 86mg | Protein: 24g | Sodium: 78mg | Potassium: 366mg | Fiber: 1g | Carbohydrates: 0g | Sugar: 5g

PORK TENDERLOIN WITH CHIMICHURRI

Pork tenderloin is a long, fairly thin muscle cut from underneath the pig. It is very tender with very little fat. Tenderloin cooks quickly and is complemented by just about every flavor and cuisine on the planet. In this recipe, it's marinated for a bit, then grilled until tender and served with Chimichurri.

SERVES 4

1 pound pork tenderloin

2 tablespoons Mustard (Chapter 4)

2 tablespoons lemon juice

1 tablespoon chopped fresh parsley

¼ teaspoon white pepper

1 cup Chimichurri (Chapter 4)

1. Place pork tenderloin in a large resealable plastic food bag. Add mustard, lemon juice, parsley, and pepper. Close bag and massage pork. Place in a large baking dish and refrigerate for 2–8 hours.

2. When ready to eat, prepare and preheat grill. Grill pork for 14–18 minutes, turning every few minutes, until a meat thermometer registers 145°F.

3. Remove the pork from the grill, place on serving platter, and tent with foil. Let stand 5 minutes.

4. Slice pork against the grain and serve with Chimichurri.

PER SERVING: Calories: 393 | Total Fat: 30g | Saturated Fat: 4g | Cholesterol: 73mg | Protein: 25g | Sodium: 69mg | Potassium: 587mg | Fiber: 1g | Carbohydrates: 5g | Sugar: 1g

SLOW COOKER PORK CACCIATORE

Pork loin is best slow-cooked, which makes this recipe perfect. Serve with lots of garlic bread and a green salad.

SERVES 6

1 (2-pound) boneless pork loin roast

1 teaspoon dried oregano leaves

¼ teaspoon pepper

3 tablespoons olive oil

2 medium onions, chopped

1 (8-ounce) package cremini mushrooms, sliced

4 cloves garlic, minced

3 tablespoons no-salt-added tomato paste

⅓ cup dry red wine

1 (28-ounce) can no-salt-added tomato purée, undrained

2 tablespoons Mustard (Chapter 4)

1 teaspoon dried basil leaves

1 teaspoon dried thyme leaves

1. Sprinkle the pork with oregano and pepper. In large skillet, heat olive oil over medium heat. Add pork and brown on all sides, turning occasionally, for 6–8 minutes. Remove pork to 5-quart slow cooker.

2. Add onions and mushrooms to skillet; cook and stir to remove pan drippings, until mushrooms give up their liquid and the liquid evaporates.

3. Add garlic; cook for 1 minute. Then add tomato paste; let cook until the paste browns in spots.

4. Add wine and tomato purée; stir well to scrape the pan. Simmer for 5 minutes or until slightly thickened.

5. Add mustard, basil, and thyme to sauce. Pour over pork in slow cooker, lifting pork so some sauce goes underneath.

6. Cover slow cooker and cook for 7–9 hours on low or until pork is tender. Slice pork and serve with mushroom sauce.

PER SERVING: Calories: 385 | Total Fat: 17g | Saturated Fat: 4g | Cholesterol: 83mg | Protein: 37g | Sodium: 116mg | Potassium: 1,502mg | Fiber: 3g | Carbohydrates: 17g | Sugar: 8g

PINEAPPLE CURRY PORK

Combining a curry and a stir-fry is a great way to experience the cuisines of two regions at once. India is famous for its curries, and stir-fry recipes are the norm in Asian countries. This fresh and bright recipe is packed full of flavor, with very little sodium.

SERVES 6

4 boneless pork loin chops

2 egg whites

1 tablespoon lemon juice

¼ cup cornstarch

3 tablespoons safflower or peanut oil

1 medium onion, chopped

3 cloves garlic, minced

2 medium carrots, thinly sliced

1 tablespoon curry powder

3 tablespoons apple cider vinegar

½ cup Chicken Stock (Chapter 5)

1 (20-ounce) can pineapple tidbits, drained, reserving juice

½ cup reserved pineapple juice

¼ cup Easy Homemade Ketchup (Chapter 4)

2 tablespoons brown sugar

1. Cut the chops into 1" pieces. Beat egg whites with lemon juice until foamy; stir pork into this mixture. Remove pork, shake to drain slightly, and dredge in cornstarch. Cover and refrigerate for 30 minutes.

2. When ready to cook, heat oil in wok or large skillet over medium heat. Add pork cubes, stirring to separate; stir-fry for 2–4 minutes or until the pork turns white. Remove from wok and set aside.

3. Add onion, garlic, and carrots to wok; stir-fry for 4–6 minutes or until crisp-tender. Add curry powder; stir-fry for 1 minute longer.

4. In small bowl, combine vinegar, chicken stock, pineapple juice, ketchup, and brown sugar and mix well. Add to wok along with pork and the drained pineapple.

5. Stir-fry until pork is cooked to 145°F and sauce has thickened slightly, about 4–6 minutes. Serve immediately over hot cooked rice.

PER SERVING: Calories: 243 | Total Fat: 11g | Saturated Fat: 2g | Cholesterol: 32mg | Protein: 15g | Sodium: 72mg | Potassium: 530mg | Fiber: 1g | Carbohydrates: 20g | Sugar: 12g

PORK PICCATA

This recipe is a great one for entertaining. The pork cooks quickly and the sauce is bright with lemon, garlic, and peppercorns. Piccata is usually made with capers, which are very salty. Peppercorns make an admirable substitute.

SERVES 4

1 pound pork tenderloin, sliced 1" thick

3 tablespoons flour

1 teaspoon grated lemon zest

2 tablespoons unsalted butter

1 tablespoon olive oil

1 leek, chopped

3 cloves garlic, sliced

1 cup Chicken Stock (Chapter 5)

3 tablespoons lemon juice

1 tablespoon green peppercorns

1. Sprinkle the sliced pork with flour and lemon zest; rub into pork.

2. In a large skillet heat butter with olive oil over medium heat. When foamy, add the pork slices. Cook pork in batches for 2–3 minutes on each side until cooked to 145°F. Remove to plate and tent with foil.

3. Add leek and garlic to skillet; cook until tender, about 6–8 minutes, stirring to remove pan drippings.

4. Add stock and lemon juice to skillet and bring to a simmer. Simmer for 5 minutes or until slightly thickened.

5. Return pork to skillet and add peppercorns. Simmer for 1–2 minutes or until pork is heated. Serve immediately.

PER SERVING: Calories: 251 | Total Fat: 12g | Saturated Fat: 5g | Cholesterol: 89mg | Protein: 26g | Sodium: 82mg | Potassium: 563mg | Fiber: 0g | Carbohydrates: 9g | Sugar: 1g

PORK WITH SPINACH AND LEMON

Pork loin chops are one of the more tender cuts of this meat. Cook them with lemon and some spinach for a fresh and tasty recipe for dinner anytime. Serve this one-dish recipe with a fruit salad, and perhaps some bread, along with Toffee Squares (Chapter 14) for dessert.

SERVES 4

4 boneless pork loin chops, about 1" thick

¼ cup flour

½ teaspoon dried thyme leaves

½ teaspoon grated lemon zest

⅛ teaspoon white pepper

2 tablespoons unsalted butter

1 tablespoon olive oil

1 scallion, minced

2 cloves garlic, minced

4 cups baby spinach leaves

½ cup Chicken Stock (Chapter 5)

3 tablespoons lemon juice

1. Sprinkle the chops with flour, thyme, lemon zest, and white pepper.

2. Melt butter with olive oil in large skillet over medium heat. Add the pork chops. Cook, turning once, until browned, about 5–7 minutes total. Remove pork from skillet and set aside.

3. Add scallion and garlic to drippings in pan; cook, stirring well, until fragrant, about 2 minutes.

4. Add spinach to pan and sauté for 30 seconds. Then add chicken stock and bring to a simmer.

5. Return pork to skillet and cook, stirring, until meat registers 145°F on a meat thermometer, about 2 minutes longer.

6. Add lemon juice to skillet, stir, and serve immediately.

PER SERVING: Calories: 254 | Total Fat: 13g | Saturated Fat: 5g | Cholesterol: 78mg | Protein: 23g | Sodium: 84mg | Potassium: 602mg | Fiber: 1g | Carbohydrates: 9g | Sugar: 0g

MAPLE-ORANGE–GLAZED PORK TENDERLOIN

When you buy maple syrup, look for grade B. That is a less expensive type of syrup, but it is darker and richer and has more flavor. The pork is roasted whole, then sliced before serving. It's delicious with potatoes and steamed green beans.

SERVES 4

1 (1-pound) pork tenderloin

⅓ cup maple syrup

3 tablespoons orange juice

1 tablespoon water

1 teaspoon dried marjoram leaves

1 teaspoon grated orange zest

1 clove garlic, minced

⅛ teaspoon pepper

1. Place pork tenderloin in a resealable plastic food storage bag. Add maple syrup, orange juice, water, marjoram, orange zest, garlic, and pepper. Massage pork to rub marinade into the meat. Seal bag, place in large dish, and refrigerate for 2–8 hours.

2. When ready to cook, preheat oven to 350°F. Remove pork from marinade and place the meat on a roasting pan; reserve marinade.

3. Roast pork for 20 minutes, then remove from oven and cover with marinade. Return to oven and roast for 15–20 minutes longer, basting once with marinade in the pan, until pork registers at least 145°F. Let stand 10 minutes, then slice to serve.

PER SERVING: Calories: 200 | Total Fat: 2g | Saturated Fat: 0g | Cholesterol: 73mg | Protein: 24g | Sodium: 62mg | Potassium: 536mg | Fiber: 0g | Carbohydrates: 19g | Sugar: 16g

PORK BLACK BEAN SKILLET

Black beans, also known as turtle beans, are black on the outside and white and creamy within. When cooked with Mexican seasonings and tender pork, they make a satisfying meal. Serve this dish with some cooked brown rice, a salad made of mesclun and butter lettuce with grape tomatoes, and fresh fruit.

SERVES 4

2 tablespoons olive oil

1 medium onion, chopped

3 cloves garlic, minced

1 jalapeño pepper, minced

3 boneless pork loin chops, cut into 1" cubes

2 teaspoons chili powder

½ teaspoon ground cumin

⅛ teaspoon white pepper

1 (14-ounce) can no-salt-added black beans, rinsed and drained

1 cup Spicy Salsa (Chapter 6)

½ cup Chicken Stock (Chapter 5)

2 tablespoons minced fresh cilantro

1. In large skillet, heat olive oil over medium heat. Add onion, garlic, and jalapeño pepper; cook and stir until crisp-tender, about 5 minutes.

2. In a large bowl, sprinkle pork with chili powder, cumin, and white pepper and toss to coat. Add to skillet; cook and stir for 3–4 minutes until pork turns white.

3. Add beans, salsa, and chicken stock and bring to a simmer. Simmer for 5–10 minutes or until pork is cooked and sauce has thickened slightly. Sprinkle with cilantro and serve immediately.

PER SERVING: Calories: 327 | Total Fat: 12g | Saturated Fat: 2g | Cholesterol: 32mg | Protein: 24g | Sodium: 66mg | Potassium: 840mg | Fiber: 10g | Carbohydrates: 30g | Sugar: 3g

SLOW COOKER MOROCCAN LAMB

Lamb shoulder is an inexpensive cut of this tender meat. It cooks very well in the slow cooker along with flavors from the Middle East, including garlic, lemon, ginger, and cinnamon. Serve this rich and spicy dish with some hot cooked couscous, a fruit salad for a cooling contrast, and Pita Bread (Chapter 2).

SERVES 6

1¾ pounds boneless lamb shoulder

3 tablespoons flour

1 teaspoon paprika

½ teaspoon ground cumin

½ teaspoon ground cinnamon

⅛ teaspoon cardamom

⅛ teaspoon pepper

2 tablespoons olive oil

1 medium onion, chopped

3 cloves garlic, finely minced

1 tablespoon grated fresh ginger root

1 teaspoon grated lemon zest

1 cup Chicken Stock (Chapter 5)

2 tablespoons honey

2 tablespoons lemon juice

1 cup chopped dried apricots

1 cup chopped pitted dates

½ cup toasted pine nuts

¼ cup chopped flat-leaf parsley

1. Cut the lamb into 2" pieces, trimming excess fat. In small bowl, combine flour, paprika, cumin, cinnamon, cardamom, and pepper and mix well. Sprinkle over lamb and toss to coat.

2. In large skillet, heat olive oil over medium heat. Add lamb and brown briefly on all sides, about 3 minutes total. Remove lamb to 4- to 5-quart slow cooker.

3. Add onion and garlic to skillet; cook, stirring to remove pan drippings, until crisp-tender. Add ginger root, lemon zest, chicken stock, honey, and lemon juice and bring to a simmer. Pour over lamb in slow cooker.

4. Stir apricots and dates into slow cooker. Cover and cook on low for 6–8 hours or until lamb is tender.

5. Sprinkle with pine nuts and parsley and serve immediately.

PER SERVING: Calories: 426 | Total Fat: 19g | Saturated Fat: 3g | Cholesterol: 84mg | Protein: 30g | Sodium: 108mg | Potassium: 831mg | Fiber: 3g | Carbohydrates: 35g | Sugar: 27g

PORK WITH MOSTARDA

Mostarda makes an excellent marinade for pork, and more of this spicy and sweet mixture is served on the side. Serve this recipe with a salad made of cucumbers, zucchini, and mint and some homemade rolls on the side.

SERVES 4

4 bone-in pork loin chops

⅛ teaspoon pepper

1½ cups Mostarda (Chapter 4), divided

⅓ cup water

2 tablespoons olive oil

1. Sprinkle pork chops with pepper and place in a large resealable plastic food bag. Add ½ cup of the Mostarda and water.

2. Seal bag and massage the pork. Place bag in a baking dish and refrigerate for 2–4 hours.

3. When ready to cook, remove pork from marinade; discard marinade. Preheat oven to 375°F.

4. Heat olive oil in a large ovenproof skillet over medium heat. Add the pork and brown on both sides, about 2–3 minutes total. Place skillet in oven.

5. Roast the chops for 8–13 minutes or until a meat thermometer registers 145°F. Let the chops stand for 5 minutes, then serve with remaining Mostarda on the side.

PER SERVING: Calories: 528 | Total Fat: 9g | Saturated Fat: 2g | Cholesterol: 122mg | Protein: 42g | Sodium: 117mg | Potassium: 1,192mg | Fiber: 6g | Carbohydrates: 70g | Sugar: 58 g

SLOW COOKER APRICOT BBQ PORK CHOPS

Pork chops cook beautifully in the slow cooker. You can brown them before cooking for a richer flavor, but you don't have to. The barbecue sauce and apricot preserves give the chops a beautiful color and even better taste. The chops will be very tender, and the sauce rich, sweet, and spicy.

SERVES 6

6 boneless pork loin chops

⅛ teaspoon pepper

2 cups BBQ Sauce (Chapter 4)

½ cup apricot preserves

1 medium onion, chopped

1. Sprinkle chops with pepper. In small bowl, combine BBQ sauce, apricot preserves, and onion; mix well.

2. Place ½ cup of the sauce mixture in a 4- to 5-quart slow cooker. Top with half of the chops in a single layer, then add more sauce. Repeat layers, ending with all of the sauce.

3. Cover and cook on low for 7–9 hours or until the chops are very tender. Serve immediately.

PER SERVING: Calories: 251 | Total Fat: 7g | Saturated Fat: 2g | Cholesterol: 48mg | Protein: 20g | Sodium: 65mg | Potassium: 562mg | Fiber: 1g | Carbohydrates: 25g | Sugar: 18g

LAMB CHOPS WITH HERB SAUCE

Lamb chops are usually very tiny, so plan on two or three per serving. This tender meat is very rich and should be served with a simple and flavorful sauce for contrast. This elegant recipe is delicious served with roasted small potatoes, steamed asparagus, and a lemony fruit salad for a great spring dinner.

SERVES 4

8–12 lamb chops, trimmed

2 cloves garlic, cut into slivers

⅛ teaspoon pepper

¼ cup extra-virgin olive oil

1 tablespoon lemon juice

¼ cup fresh mint leaves

¼ cup fresh flat-leaf parsley, chopped

1 tablespoon fresh whole thyme leaves

1 tablespoon agave nectar

1 tablespoon safflower or peanut oil

1. Cut small slits in the lamb chops right next to the bone, and insert garlic slivers. Set aside.

2. In food processor or blender, combine pepper, olive oil, lemon juice, mint, parsley, thyme, and agave nectar and process or blend until combined. Set aside.

3. Heat safflower oil in large skillet over medium-high heat. Add lamb; cook for 3 minutes, then turn. Cook for 2–4 minutes longer or until the lamb reaches desired doneness, at least 145°F. Remove lamb to plate and tent with foil; let stand 5 minutes. Serve lamb with sauce.

PER SERVING: Calories: 316 | Total Fat: 22g | Saturated Fat: 4g | Cholesterol: 72mg | Protein: 23g | Sodium: 95mg | Potassium: 443mg | Fiber: 0g | Carbohydrates: 4g | Sugar: 2g

MANGO PORK

Tender and mild pork combines really well with mango, curry powder, and chutney in this easy recipe. Serve with hot cooked rice or couscous to soak up the wonderful sauce. You can serve this like a typical curry, with all the condiments on the side: chutney, peanuts, toasted coconut, and cilantro.

SERVES 4

2 ripe mangoes

1 pound pork tenderloin

¼ cup flour

1 tablespoon curry powder

⅛ teaspoon pepper

2 tablespoons butter

1 tablespoon olive oil

1 medium onion, chopped

2 cloves garlic, minced

1 cup Chicken Stock (Chapter 5)

¼ cup pineapple juice

½ cup Mango Chutney (Chapter 4)

2 tablespoons heavy cream

⅓ cup coarsely chopped roasted unsalted cashews

1. To prepare mangoes, stand each on end. Cut down with a sharp knife to remove pieces, slicing around the large pit in the center. Score the flesh in cubes, then cut it off of the skin. Set mango cubes aside.

2. Cut the pork into 1½" pieces. Toss with flour, curry powder, and pepper.

3. In a large saucepan, heat butter with oil over medium heat. Add pork cubes; cook and stir until lightly browned, about 4–5 minutes. Remove pork from saucepan and set aside.

4. Add onion and garlic to pan; cook for 3–5 minutes, stirring to remove pan drippings, until crisp-tender. Add chicken stock and pineapple juice and bring to a simmer.

5. Return pork to pan and simmer over low heat for 3–4 minutes or until pork is cooked.

6. Add mango, chutney, and cream to pan; stir to combine. Heat through, but do not boil. Sprinkle with cashews and serve immediately.

PER SERVING: Calories: 450 | Total Fat: 20g | Saturated Fat: 7g | Cholesterol: 99mg | Protein: 28g | Sodium: 88mg | Potassium: 845mg | Fiber: 3g | Carbohydrates: 40g | Sugar: 25g

STUFFED PORK TENDERLOIN

This is a recipe for a special occasion; it would be delicious as an alternative Thanksgiving entrée. Serve it with scalloped potatoes, Citrus-Glazed Carrots (Chapter 13), and Lemon Meringue Angel Food Dessert (Chapter 14) for a spectacular finish.

SERVES 6

2 (1-pound) pork tenderloins

1 teaspoon dried thyme leaves

¼ teaspoon white pepper

¼ cup Mustard (Chapter 4)

2 tablespoons unsalted butter

1 medium onion, chopped

1 cup sliced mushrooms

2 cloves garlic, minced

2 cups baby spinach leaves

4 cups cubed Cornbread (Chapter 2)

¼ cup chopped fresh celery leaves

2 tablespoons olive oil

1. Preheat oven to 400°F. Place the pork tenderloins on a work surface. Cut a lengthwise slit down the center of each tenderloin to within ½" of the bottom. Spread open each tenderloin and cover with parchment paper. Pound the tenderloins until they are ½" thick overall. Sprinkle with thyme and pepper and spread with mustard; set aside.

2. In medium skillet, melt butter over medium heat. Add onion, mushrooms, and garlic; cook and stir until the mushrooms give up their liquid and the liquid evaporates, about 8–9 minutes. Add spinach; sauté until wilted, about 3–4 minutes. Remove to large bowl.

3. Add cornbread and celery leaves to spinach mixture.

4. Divide mixture on top of one tenderloin placed mustard-side up. Top with the other tenderloin, mustard-side down. Tie the bundle together with kitchen string at 2" intervals. Brush with olive oil.

5. Roast for 25–35 minutes or until a meat thermometer registers 145°F. Be sure the thermometer isn't poking into the stuffing. Remove roast from oven, cover with foil, and let stand 5 minutes, then remove string and slice to serve.

PER SERVING: Calories: 453 | Total Fat: 18g | Saturated Fat: 7g | Cholesterol: 151mg | Protein: 37g | Sodium: 137mg | Potassium: 882mg | Fiber: 2g | Carbohydrates: 33g | Sugar: 9g

PORK TENDERLOIN BRUSCHETTA

This recipe uses grilled pork tenderloin slices instead of the bread for a twist. The recipe takes only minutes to prepare, so is ideal for last-minute entertaining. Serve with a fruit salad, some grilled corn on the cob, and Lemon Curd Ice Cream (Chapter 14) for dessert.

SERVES 4

1 pound pork tenderloin

1 tablespoon olive oil

1 teaspoon dried basil leaves

¼ teaspoon pepper

2 beefsteak tomatoes, seeded and chopped

1 shallot, minced

1 clove garlic, minced

⅓ cup sliced fresh basil leaves

2 tablespoons lemon juice

2 tablespoons extra-virgin olive oil

1. Slice the tenderloin into 4 pieces, slicing across the tenderloin but at an angle. Press on the pieces until they are about 1" thick. Brush with olive oil and sprinkle with dried basil and pepper.

2. In medium bowl, combine tomatoes, shallot, garlic, basil, lemon juice, and extra-virgin olive oil; mix well and refrigerate.

3. Prepare and preheat grill. Grill the tenderloin slices 6" from medium coals for 4–6 minutes per side, turning once, until a meat thermometer registers at least 145°F. Top each piece with some of the cold tomato mixture and serve immediately.

PER SERVING: Calories: 222 | Total Fat: 12g | Saturated Fat: 2g | Cholesterol: 73mg | Protein: 24g | Sodium: 62mg | Potassium: 549mg | Fiber: 0g | Carbohydrates: 2g | Sugar: 1g

HONEY MUSTARD PORK ROAST

Pork and mustard are natural partners. The mustard mellows as it cooks and creates a flavorful crust on the meat. This excellent roast recipe is perfect for company. Serve with Scalloped Potatoes (Chapter 13), Steamed Green Beans and Asparagus (Chapter 13), and your own homemade Dinner Rolls (Chapter 2).

SERVES 6

1 (2½-pound) pork loin roast

4 cloves garlic, cut into slivers

⅓ cup Honey Mustard (Chapter 4)

2 tablespoons brown sugar

1 teaspoon white pepper

1 teaspoon dried marjoram leaves

½ cup Chicken Stock (Chapter 5)

1. Preheat oven to 350°F. Place the pork on a roasting pan and cut slits in the surface. Push garlic slivers into the slits.

2. In small bowl, combine honey mustard, brown sugar, pepper, and marjoram and rub over the roast. Pour chicken stock around the roast.

3. Roast the meat for 50–60 minutes or until a meat thermometer reaches 145°F. Cover with foil and let stand for 10 minutes, then slice to serve.

PER SERVING: Calories: 338 | Total Fat: 13g | Saturated Fat: 4g | Cholesterol: 103mg | Protein: 42g | Sodium: 93mg | Potassium: 858mg | Fiber: 0g | Carbohydrates: 8g | Sugar: 6g

GINGER PORK STIR-FRY

Pork is usually stir-fried with vegetables. Let's switch things up and stir-fry this tender and mild meat with fruit instead. Fruit does stir-fry well, but it's added at the last minute just so it's heated through. This unusual and refreshing dish is loaded with vitamin C and vitamin A. Serve over hot cooked brown rice or quinoa.

SERVES 4

1 pound pork tenderloin

2 tablespoons cornstarch

¼ teaspoon ground ginger

1 cup Chicken Stock (Chapter 5)

⅓ cup peach preserves

1 tablespoon lemon juice

⅛ teaspoon white pepper

2 tablespoons safflower or peanut oil

1 medium onion, chopped

1 tablespoon grated fresh ginger root

1 medium firm pear, sliced

2 medium firm peaches, peeled and sliced

2 tablespoons toasted sliced almonds

1. Cut the pork tenderloin into ½"-thick slices; cut slices in quarters and set aside.

2. In small bowl, combine cornstarch, ground ginger, chicken stock, peach preserves, lemon juice, and pepper, and mix well; set aside.

3. In wok or large skillet, heat oil over medium-high heat. Add pork; stir-fry for 2–3 minutes until just barely browned; remove pork from wok.

4. Add onion; stir-fry for 4 minutes. Add ginger root; stir-fry for another 2 minutes. Add the pear and stir-fry for 1 minute, then add the peaches; stir-fry for 2 minutes longer.

5. Stir the chicken stock mixture and add to the wok along with the pork; stir-fry for 1–2 minutes until sauce is thickened. Top with the almonds and serve immediately.

PER SERVING: Calories: 374 | Total Fat: 12g | Saturated Fat: 1g | Cholesterol: 73mg | Protein: 27g | Sodium: 89mg | Potassium: 204mg | Fiber: 3g | Carbohydrates: 39g | Sugar: 22g

LAMB PICCATA

Piccata is any dish cooked with lemons, wine, and capers. Capers are simply too salty for a low-sodium diet, so they are omitted. We'll use green peppercorns instead. The lemon and peppercorns cut through the unctuous fat of the lamb chops, adding a wonderful layer of flavor.

SERVES 4

4 (6–8-ounce) boneless lamb loin chops

½ teaspoon dried thyme leaves

⅛ teaspoon white pepper

⅓ cup flour

2 tablespoons unsalted butter

2 tablespoons olive oil

¼ cup white wine

¼ cup lemon juice

1 cup Chicken Stock (Chapter 5)

1 tablespoon whole green peppercorns

1 teaspoon grated lemon zest

1. Place lamb chops on waxed paper; cover with more waxed paper. Gently pound the lamb until about ¼" thick.

2. Sprinkle lamb with thyme and pepper; coat with flour.

3. In large skillet, melt butter and olive oil over medium heat. Add lamb and cook, turning once, until browned, about 2–4 minutes per side. The lamb should be at least 140°F. Remove from pan and tent with foil to keep warm.

4. Add wine, lemon juice, and chicken stock to the pan; bring to a boil over high heat. Simmer for 3 minutes, scraping up pan drippings, until sauce is slightly reduced.

5. Return lamb to the pan along with any accumulated juices. Add peppercorns and lemon zest; heat through, and serve immediately.

PER SERVING: Calories: 398 | Total Fat: 21g | Saturated Fat: 8g | Cholesterol: 124mg | Protein: 37g | Sodium: 128mg | Potassium: 666mg | Fiber: 0g | Carbohydrates: 10g | Sugar: 0g

COFFEE PULLED PORK

Coffee adds a deep and nutty flavor to the pork, and just a bit of cocoa powder deepens the flavor even more. This recipe is excellent piled on your own homemade Ciabatta Rolls (Chapter 2), and topped with Zippy Coleslaw (Chapter 3).

SERVES 8

1 (2½-pound) pork butt roast

3 tablespoons espresso powder

1 tablespoon cocoa powder

2 tablespoons brown sugar

1 teaspoon dried marjoram leaves

¼ teaspoon white pepper

¼ teaspoon crushed red pepper flakes

3 tablespoons safflower oil

3 medium onions, sliced

5 cloves garlic, sliced

½ cup Chicken Stock (Chapter 5)

1 cup strong brewed coffee

1 cup BBQ Sauce (Chapter 4)

1. Sprinkle the roast with espresso powder, cocoa powder, brown sugar, marjoram, white pepper, and crushed red pepper flakes; rub into the meat. Set aside for 20 minutes.

2. Heat oil in large skillet over medium-high heat. Brown meat on all sides, about 8 minutes total.

3. Place onions and garlic in bottom of 5-quart slow cooker. Top with the roast. Pour chicken stock, brewed coffee, and BBQ sauce over all.

4. Cover and cook on low for 8–10 hours or until the meat is very tender.

5. Remove meat from slow cooker and shred using two forks.

6. Skim fat from the top of the liquid in the slow cooker. Stir pork back into the liquid. Cover and cook on low for another 30 minutes.

PER SERVING: Calories: 268 | Total Fat: 13g | Saturated Fat: 3g | Cholesterol: 85mg | Protein: 27g | Sodium: 105mg | Potassium: 638mg | Fiber: 0g | Carbohydrates: 7g | Sugar: 4g

FIVE-SPICE PORK ROAST

Five-spice powder is a classic in Asian cooking. It's composed of cloves, star anise, cinnamon, pepper, and fennel seeds. You can buy the mixture at most large grocery stores, or make your own. If you do make your own, buy whole spices and grind them in a spice blender, then store in an airtight container in a dark, cool cupboard.

SERVES 6

1 tablespoon unsalted butter

2 medium onions, sliced

1 (2½-pound) boneless loin pork roast

3 cloves garlic, slivered

1 tablespoon toasted sesame oil

4 teaspoons five-spice powder

2 tablespoons honey

⅓ cup water

1. Heat butter in large pan over medium heat. Add onions; cook, stirring occasionally, until the onions are tender, about 7–8 minutes. Place onions in a large roasting pan.

2. Add the pork roast to the roasting pan and cut slits in the meat. Push garlic slivers into the cuts.

3. Rub the pork with the sesame oil and sprinkle with five-spice powder; rub into meat. Drizzle with honey and pour water into the pan around the pork. Let stand 20 minutes.

4. Preheat oven to 325°F. Roast the meat for 50–60 minutes or until a meat thermometer registers 145°F. Cover roast and let stand for 10 minutes, then slice to serve.

PER SERVING: Calories: 351 | Total Fat: 16g | Saturated Fat: 5g | Cholesterol: 109mg | Protein: 41g | Sodium: 87mg | Potassium: 823mg | Fiber: 0g | Carbohydrates: 7g | Sugar: 5g

BRAISED HERB-SEASONED PORK CHOPS

Braising just means cooking at a fairly low heat with liquid. The pork becomes very tender when cooked this way. The combination of herbs and spices is very delicious; but you could use your own favorite seasonings.

SERVES 4

4 (4-ounce) lean, boneless pork loin chops

1 teaspoon olive oil

½ teaspoon marjoram

¼ teaspoon garlic powder

⅛ teaspoon onion powder

⅛ teaspoon freshly ground black pepper

⅛ teaspoon salt-free chili powder

½ cup water

1. Pat the pork chops dry with a paper towel. In a small bowl, mix together the oil, marjoram, garlic powder, onion powder, pepper, and chili powder to form a paste. Rub the mixture onto all sides of the chops.

2. Bring a deep nonstick skillet to temperature over medium-high heat. Add the chops and brown on both sides, cooking for 2–3 minutes per side. Add the water and bring to a boil. Reduce heat, cover, and simmer for 30 minutes. Serve immediately.

PER SERVING: Calories: 238 | Total Fat: 7g | Saturated Fat: 2g | Cholesterol: 122mg | Protein: 39g | Sodium: 103mg | Potassium: 651mg | Fiber: 0g | Carbohydrates: 0g | Sugar: 0g

SLOW-ROASTED PORK RIBS

Spare ribs are the ribs of a pig that are the least expensive cut. There isn't a lot of meat on the bones, but that meat is very flavorful. Slow roasting ensures that the meat is tender. This make-ahead recipe is perfect for entertaining. Cook the pork the day before, refrigerate it overnight, then grill it when you're ready to eat.

SERVES 6

1 teaspoon garlic powder

1 teaspoon onion powder

2 teaspoons ground cumin, divided

4 teaspoons salt-free chili powder, divided

2 teaspoons dark brown sugar

1 tablespoon freshly cracked pepper

1/3 teaspoon dried oregano

1 teaspoon dried cilantro, divided

2 teaspoons frozen orange juice concentrate

1 tablespoon plus 1 teaspoon water

2 tablespoons freshly squeezed lime juice, divided

Dash (or more, to taste) low-sodium hot red pepper sauce

2 teaspoons olive oil

2-pound rack pork spare ribs

1 tablespoon molasses

2 tablespoons plus 2 teaspoons low-sodium ketchup

1/3 teaspoon salt-free hickory smoke or mesquite base (powder)

1. Preheat oven to 300°F.

2. In the bowl of a food processor fitted with a steel blade or in the jar of a blender, combine the garlic powder, onion powder, 1 teaspoon cumin, 2 teaspoons chili powder, brown sugar, pepper, oregano, 1/3 teaspoon cilantro, orange juice concentrate, water, 2 teaspoons lime juice, hot red pepper sauce, and olive oil; blend until smooth.

3. Dry the ribs with paper towels, then rub them thoroughly with the paste. Place the ribs on a rack in a large roasting pan and cook for 3 hours or until the meat is tender and pulls easily from the bone. (Ribs can be cooled for 30 minutes and then refrigerated, covered, up to 2 days.)

4. In a small bowl, combine the molasses, ketchup, remaining 1 tablespoon plus 1 teaspoon lime juice, 1 teaspoon cumin, remaining 2/3 teaspoon cilantro, remaining 2 teaspoons chili powder, and hickory smoke or mesquite base.

5. Place a rack 3" from the broiler. Heat broiler to high. Place the ribs on a baking sheet. Broil for 3–5 minutes per side, or until a light crust forms on the surface. Brush the ribs with the molasses mixture and broil for an additional 30 seconds. Use tongs to carefully turn over the ribs and brush that side with the molasses mixture; broil for an additional 30 seconds. To serve, cut the ribs apart between the bones.

PER SERVING: Calories: 207 | Total Fat: 8g | Saturated Fat: 2g | Cholesterol: 83mg | Protein: 24g | Sodium: 97mg | Potassium: 532mg | Fiber: 0g | Carbohydrates: 8g | Sugar: 5g

APRICOT AND JALAPEÑO-GRILLED LAMB STEAKS

Lamb steaks are a cut that is more common in the UK than in the United States. You may have to order them from the butcher. But they are tender and juicy with a rich flavor. They pair perfectly with this sweet, tart, and spicy marinade.

SERVES 8

1 (16-ounce) can apricots in juice

1 tablespoon white wine vinegar

2 teaspoons cornstarch

2 tablespoons seeded and finely minced jalapeño peppers

1 clove garlic, minced

½ cup 100% fruit (no-sugar-added) apricot preserves

2 teaspoons frozen orange juice concentrate

2 tablespoons water

¼ teaspoon mustard powder

8 (5-ounce) lamb sirloin steaks (¾" thick)

Olive oil spray

1. Add the juice from the canned apricots, the vinegar, and cornstarch to a small saucepan. Whisk well to remove any lumps. Bring to a boil over medium-high heat. Reduce heat and simmer, stirring constantly for 1 minute or until the mixture thickens. Remove from heat. Finely chop the apricots and add them to the sauce along with the jalapeño and garlic. Set aside until ready to serve.

2. Preheat grill coals to medium-hot (350°F–400°F).

3. Add the apricot preserves, orange juice concentrate, water, and mustard powder to a microwave-safe bowl; microwave on high for 30 seconds. Whisk the mixture. If it's not yet melted to a spreadable consistency, microwave on high for additional 10-second intervals, stirring after each interval.

4. Pat the steaks dry with paper towels. Lightly spray each side with the olive oil spray. Place the steaks on a grill rack over direct heat. Grill for 3 minutes each side. Baste with the apricot–orange juice mixture and grill for an additional 2 minutes per side, or until cooked to desired doneness, at least 140°F. Discard remaining apricot-orange juice mixture. Serve with the apricot-jalapeño sauce.

PER SERVING: Calories: 208 | Total Fat: 6g | Saturated Fat: 2g | Cholesterol: 90mg | Protein: 30g | Sodium: 89mg | Potassium: 522mg | Fiber: 0g | Carbohydrates: 4g | Sugar: 2g

INDOOR-GRILLED GARLIC SAUSAGE

Making your own sausage can be fun. And you can control what goes into these savory patties. Add your own favorite seasonings to the mix; dried marjoram and basil would be a nice option.

SERVES 6

1 pound lean ground pork

½ pound ground beef sirloin

½ teaspoon garlic powder

1 teaspoon salt-free seasoning blend

Pinch ground cloves

Optional: Pinch dried red pepper flakes

½ teaspoon freshly ground black pepper, divided

1. Preheat indoor grill or bring a large, deep nonstick sauté pan or grill pan to temperature over medium-high heat.

2. Place all the ingredients except ¼ teaspoon of the black pepper in a bowl and mix well. Shape into 6 patties. Place the patties on the grill, sprinkling the tops of the patties with the remaining pepper, and close the lid. Grill for 3–4 minutes or until a meat thermometer registers 165°F.

PER SERVING: Calories: 187 | Total Fat: 9g | Saturated Fat: 4g | Cholesterol: 80mg | Protein: 22g | Sodium: 65mg | Potassium: 123mg | Fiber: 0g | Carbohydrates: 0g | Sugar: 0g

SWEET AND SPICY KIELBASA

Kielbasa is usually sold as a link sausage. It usually contains beef and pork, as in this recipe. Forming the meat into patties is a bit different and fun, but it's worth it to be able to eat this savory sausage on a low-sodium diet.

SERVES 6

1 teaspoon bourbon

Pinch dried red pepper flakes

1 pound ground pork shoulder

½ pound ground beef chuck

1 teaspoon freshly ground black pepper, divided

½ teaspoon ground allspice

1 teaspoon garlic powder

⅛ teaspoon ground mustard

1 teaspoon brown sugar

1. Preheat indoor grill or bring a large, deep nonstick sauté pan or grill pan to temperature over medium-high heat.

2. In a large bowl, combine bourbon with all the remaining ingredients except ¼ teaspoon of the black pepper; mix well. Shape into 6 patties. Place the patties on the grill, sprinkling the tops of the patties with the remaining pepper, and close the lid. Grill for 3–4 minutes or until a meat thermometer registers 165°F.

PER SERVING: Calories: 200 | Total Fat: 11g | Saturated Fat: 4g | Cholesterol: 71mg | Protein: 21g | Sodium: 73mg | Potassium: 373mg | Fiber: 0g | Carbohydrates: 0g | Sugar: 0g

GRILLED LAMB STEAKS

Lamb steaks are tender and juicy. Serve them with something sweet and tart to cut through the rich fat: a salad made from mixed berries, or a green salad tossed with a sharp vinaigrette, mushrooms, and grape tomatoes.

SERVES 4

4 (5-ounce) lean lamb sirloin steaks (¾" thick)

2 teaspoons olive oil

1 clove garlic, crushed

1. Preheat grill coals to medium-hot (350°F–400°F).

2. Pat the lamb steaks dry with a paper towel. Add the olive oil and garlic to a microwave-safe bowl; microwave on high for 20 seconds. Rub the garlic-infused olive oil into all sides of the steaks. Rub the softened garlic clove across the top of each steak.

3. Place the steaks on grill rack over direct heat. Grill for 5 minutes on each side or to desired doneness, at least 140°F. (The direct heat is important at first to sear the meat, but if it starts to char, use tongs to move the steaks to indirect heat or to a spot on the grill that is less hot.)

PER SERVING: Calories: 212 | Total Fat: 9g | Saturated Fat: 3g | Cholesterol: 90mg | Protein: 29g | Sodium: 115mg | Potassium: 470mg | Fiber: 0g | Carbohydrates: 0g | Sugar: 0g

SOUTH OF THE BORDER SAUSAGE

This spicy sausage is perfect for breakfast if you enjoy Tex Mex food. The combination of spices and herbs is savory and hot, but remember that you can change the proportions or add your own favorite Tex Mex ingredients.

SERVES 16

2 pounds ground pork shoulder

1 teaspoon ground black pepper

1 teaspoon dried parsley

1 teaspoon salt-free chili powder

1 teaspoon garlic powder

1 teaspoon onion powder

½ teaspoon paprika

⅛ teaspoon dried red pepper flakes, crushed

⅛ teaspoon Mexican oregano, crushed

Pinch ground cinnamon

Pinch ground cloves

Optional: ⅛ teaspoon unsweetened cocoa powder

Add all ingredients to a bowl and mix until well blended. The traditional preparation method calls for putting the sausage mixture in casings; however, it works equally well when it's shaped into 16 small sausage patties and broiled or grilled to 165°F, or sautéed to be combined with the ingredients in other dishes.

PER SERVING: Calories: 93 | Total Fat: 4g | Saturated Fat: 2g | Cholesterol: 42mg | Protein: 11g | Sodium: 33mg | Potassium: 10mg | Fiber: 0g | Carbohydrates: 0g | Sugar: 0g

SLOW-COOKED VENISON

Most cooked meats wrapped in foil or placed in sealable plastic freezer bags can be stored in the freezer for 3 months, or up to 2 years if frozen in vacuum-sealed plastic containers.

SERVES 8

1 (2¼-pound) lean venison roast, trimmed of fat and cut into pieces

Water, as needed

¼ teaspoon low-sodium beef base

⅛ teaspoon roasted mirepoix flavor concentrate

1 tablespoon cider vinegar

1. Put the venison in a 4-quart slow cooker, add enough water to cover the roast, and set the cooker on high. Dissolve the bases in the vinegar and add to the cooker. Once the mixture begins to boil, reduce temperature to low. Allow the meat to simmer for 8 hours or until tender.

2. Drain off and discard the resulting broth from the meat. Remove any remaining fat from the meat and discard that as well. Weigh the meat and separate it into 4-ounce servings. The meat can be kept for 1 or 2 days in the refrigerator, or freeze portions for use later.

PER SERVING: Calories: 140 | Total Fat: 3g | Saturated Fat: 0g | Cholesterol: 100mg | Protein: 25g | Sodium: 117mg | Potassium: 445mg | Fiber: 0g | Carbohydrates: 0g | Sugar: 0g

SWEET PEPPER AND FENNEL SAUSAGE

A touch of sugar or other sweet ingredients added to sausage before it's cooked not only sweetens the meat, it also aids in the caramelization process that takes place when meat is seared at high temperatures. The "sugar" in such recipes can be honey or fruit, or another sweet low-sodium condiment.

SERVES 8

1 teaspoon fennel seeds, crushed

⅛ teaspoon salt-free chili powder

2 pounds ground pork butt

½ teaspoon freshly ground black pepper

⅛ teaspoon mustard powder

Pinch cayenne pepper

2 teaspoons crushed garlic

¼ cup finely minced roasted red pepper, skin removed (see instructions for roasting peppers in Chapter 3)

½ teaspoon honey

1. Toast the fennel seeds in a nonstick skillet over medium heat until the seeds just begin to darken, about 2 minutes, stirring constantly. Cool, then grind using a spice grinder or mortar and pestle.

2. Add ground seeds to a large bowl along with the remaining ingredients and mix until well blended. Shape into 8 patties. Prepare by grilling, broiling, or sautéing, cooking until a meat thermometer registers 165°F.

PER SERVING: Calories: 155 | Total Fat: 6g | Saturated Fat: 2g | Cholesterol: 68mg | Protein: 21g | Sodium: 74mg | Potassium: 405mg | Fiber: 0g | Carbohydrates: 1g | Sugar: 0g

SAUSAGE GRAVY

Sausage gravy is a classic southern recipe, typically served over biscuits for breakfast, or over mashed potatoes for a barbecue. The sausage and mustard provide the flavor in this classic recipe.

SERVES 6

1 cup nonfat cottage cheese

1 cup skim milk

¼ cup instant nonfat dry milk

⅛ pound Peppery Turkey Sausage (Chapter 1)

⅛ teaspoon mustard powder

Pinch grated lemon zest

2 teaspoons olive oil

1 tablespoon unbleached all-purpose flour

1. In a blender or food processor container, combine the cottage cheese, skim milk, and dry milk; process until smooth. Set aside.

2. In a large, deep nonstick sauté pan, fry the sausage until done, breaking it into small pieces with a heat-safe spatula as you fry it.

3. Add the mustard powder, lemon zest, and olive oil; mix well and heat until sizzling.

4. Add the flour, stirring constantly to create a roux (the thickening agent). Gradually stir in some of the cottage-cheese mixture, using the back of a spatula or a whisk to blend it with the roux; stir constantly to avoid lumps. Once you have about ½ cup of the cottage-cheese mixture blended into the roux, you can add the remaining amount.

5. Continue to cook, stirring constantly, until the mixture begins to steam. Lower the heat and allow the mixture to simmer (being careful that it doesn't come to a boil) until the gravy reaches the desired consistency.

PER SERVING: Calories: 80 | Total Fat: 2g | Saturated Fat: 0g | Cholesterol: 8mg | Protein: 7g | Sodium: 135mg | Potassium: 192mg | Fiber: 0g | Carbohydrates: 7g | Sugar: 5g

SEASONED PORK ROAST

Pork loin roast is a juicy and flavorful cut. It is not the same as a pork tenderloin, so don't confuse the two. A pork loin should be cooked for a long period of time so it becomes tender, while a tenderloin is typically quickly grilled or broiled.

SERVES 4

1 (1-pound) pork loin roast

1 cup dry white wine

2 tablespoons lemon juice

2 teaspoons olive oil

¼ cup sodium-free honey mustard sauce

2 tablespoons minced shallots

1 teaspoon onion powder

½ teaspoon garlic powder

½ teaspoon dried thyme

¼ teaspoon ground black pepper

1. Pat the pork loin with paper towels to remove any excess moisture.

2. In a heavy, freezer-style, sealable plastic bag, combine all the remaining ingredients; turn the bag until the ingredients are well mixed. Add the meat to the marinade and turn the bag to coat the meat evenly. Place the bag in the refrigerator. Marinate at least 8 hours, up to 24 hours.

3. Preheat oven to 350°F. Spray a roasting pan with rack with nonstick cooking spray.

4. Remove the meat from marinade and place it on the prepared rack in the roasting pan. Roast until a meat thermometer reads 145°F–170°F, depending on your preference, about 20–35 minutes. Tent the roast with aluminum foil and let "rest" for 10 minutes before carving.

PER SERVING: Calories: 246 | Total Fat: 8g | Saturated Fat: 1g | Cholesterol: 62mg | Protein: 24g | Sodium: 52mg | Potassium: 506mg | Fiber: 0g | Carbohydrates: 2g | Sugar: 0g

VENISON AND VEGGIE STOVETOP CASSEROLE

Venison, or deer meat, is naturally low in fat and very flavorful. It's delicious combined with potatoes and vegetables in a rich sauce made from tomatoes, wine, and red currant jelly.

SERVES 4

1 teaspoon olive oil

1 teaspoon butter

1 small sweet onion, chopped

½ cup no-salt-added tomato purée

2 cloves garlic, minced

¼ teaspoon low-sodium beef base

¾ cup dry red wine

2 tablespoons red currant jelly

½ cup water

⅛ cup lemon juice

1 tablespoon cornstarch

Optional: ¼ teaspoon granulated sugar

¼ teaspoon dried parsley

⅛ teaspoon salt-free chili powder

⅛ teaspoon mustard powder

⅛ teaspoon freshly ground black pepper

Pinch dried thyme

Pinch dried basil

1 (16-ounce) package frozen hash brown potatoes, thawed

1 (10-ounce) frozen vegetable blend, thawed

1 pound Slow-Cooked Venison, cubed (see recipe in this chapter)

Optional: Fresh parsley sprigs

1. Heat the olive oil and butter in a large, deep nonstick sauté pan. Add the onion and sauté until transparent; stir in the tomato purée and sauté for 2 minutes. Add the garlic and sauté for 1 minute. Add the beef base; stir to dissolve and mix it with the other ingredients.

2. In a mixing cup, whisk together the wine, jelly, water, lemon juice, and cornstarch. Add to the pan and bring to a boil.

3. Add the sugar, if using, parsley, chili powder, mustard powder, pepper, thyme, basil, and hash browns; stir to coat. Reduce heat, cover, and simmer for 30 minutes.

4. Add the thawed vegetables and meat; simmer for 5–10 minutes longer until heated through. Serve immediately, garnished with fresh parsley, if desired.

PER SERVING: Calories: 364 | Total Fat: 6g | Saturated Fat: 1g | Cholesterol: 90mg | Protein: 27g | Sodium: 133mg | Potassium: 985mg | Fiber: 5g | Carbohydrates: 41g | Sugar: 5g

PORK LOIN DINNER IN ADOBO SAUCE

You can substitute puréed canned chipotle peppers in adobo sauce for the homemade kind from Chapter 4. On average, this ingredient will add about 15 calories per serving and increase the sodium content.

SERVES 4

1 large sweet onion, thinly sliced

2 tart apples, peeled, cored, and thinly sliced

4 medium-size potatoes, peeled and thinly sliced

1 tablespoon apple cider vinegar

4 teaspoons unsalted butter

4 (5-ounce) pork medallions, cut from boneless loin

2 teaspoons olive or peanut oil

½ teaspoon freshly ground pepper

½ cup Chipotle Peppers in Adobo Sauce (Chapter 4)

¼ teaspoon low-sodium chicken base

½ cup water

1. Preheat oven to 200°F.

2. In a microwave-safe dish, combine the onion, apples, and potatoes. Top with the vinegar and butter. Cover and microwave on high for 5 minutes or until tender. Leave covered and allow the mixture to "steam" while preparing the pork medallions.

3. Pat the pork medallions dry with paper towels. Rub the oil onto the pork and season with the pepper.

4. Heat a sauté pan treated with nonstick spray over medium heat for 2 minutes. Add the pork and sauté for 3–4 minutes on each side until a meat thermometer registers 140°F. Remove the pork from the pan, set the pan aside, and place the meat on a baking sheet. Cover and put the pork in the preheated oven.

5. Once the pork is moved to the warm oven, remove the lid to the potato mixture (being careful not to burn yourself with the steam) and test for doneness. Microwave on high for another 2 minutes, if necessary, or until the onion is transparent and the apples and potatoes are tender. Set the dish in the preheated oven to keep warm.

6. Pour off the oil from the sauté pan used for the pork and add the chipotle peppers in adobo sauce. Over high heat, bring the sauce to a boil while stirring. Add the chicken base and stir until dissolved. Add the water and, while continuing to stir, cook over high heat for 2–3 minutes or until the sauce is thick enough to coat the back of a spoon. Set aside and keep warm.

7. Spoon the apples, onions, and potatoes onto the centers of 4 serving plates. Place the sautéed pork medallions atop each and divide the sauce among each serving. Serve immediately.

PER SERVING: Calories: 384 | Total Fat: 9g | Saturated Fat: 3g | Cholesterol: 102mg | Protein: 32g | Sodium: 114mg | Potassium: 1,202mg | Fiber: 4g | Carbohydrates: 41g | Sugar: 8g

EASY SLOW-COOKED PORK

Once the meat has been removed from the resulting broth in this recipe, strain the broth; once cooled, cover and refrigerate the broth overnight. Remove and discard the hardened fat. The broth can be kept for 1 or 2 days in the refrigerator, or frozen up to 3 months.

SERVES 12

1 (4½-pound) bone-in lean pork roast

1 teaspoon pork base

¼ teaspoon roasted mirepoix flavor concentrate

1 tablespoon dried minced onion

1 teaspoon dried minced garlic

Water, as needed

1. Put the roast and all the other ingredients in a 4 to 5-quart slow cooker, adding enough water to cover the roast. Cover and cook on low for 8–10 hours until very tender.

2. Separate the meat from the resulting broth; discard the broth (or refrigerate it for a later use). Remove any remaining fat from the meat and take the meat off the bone; discard the fat and bone. Weigh the meat and separate it into 4-ounce servings. The meat can be kept for 1 or 2 days in the refrigerator, or freeze portions for use later.

PER SERVING: Calories: 145 | Total Fat: 4g | Saturated Fat: 1g | Cholesterol: 71mg | Protein: 23g | Sodium: 128mg | Potassium: 419mg | Fiber: 0g | Carbohydrates: 0g | Sugar: 0g

PEPPED-UP PORK SANDWICHES

Leftover pork makes delicious sandwiches. In this recipe, the tender meat is combined with colorful bell peppers, garlic, and onion. Serve on toasted bread, or on Ciabatta Rolls (Chapter 2).

SERVES 4

1 large white or yellow onion, chopped

1 large red bell pepper, seeded and chopped

1 large green bell pepper, seeded and chopped

1 clove garlic, minced

3 tablespoons pork or chicken broth

1 tablespoon salt-free steak sauce and marinade

½ pound cooked pork, shredded

8 slices thinly sliced low-salt bread, toasted if desired

1. In a medium-size microwave-safe bowl, combine the onion, peppers, garlic, and broth. Microwave on high for 5 minutes or until the onion is transparent and the peppers are soft.

2. Add the steak sauce and pork; stir to combine. Cover and microwave at 70 percent power for 2 minutes or until the mixture is heated through. Taste and add more steak sauce, if desired.

3. Let the pork mixture stand for 3 minutes, then make sandwiches with the meat mixture and the bread. Serve immediately.

PER SERVING: Calories: 276 | Total Fat: 6g | Saturated Fat: 2g | Cholesterol: 49mg | Protein: 21g | Sodium: 53mg | Potassium: 492mg | Fiber: 3g | Carbohydrates: 30g | Sugar: 5g

EASY SWEET-AND-SOUR PORK

If you've ever ordered sweet-and-sour pork from your local Asian take-out restaurant, you know how good it is. But you probably don't know that it's loaded with sodium. This easy and quick recipe replicates the flavors in a much healthier version.

SERVES 4

1 large white or yellow onion, cut into large dice

1 large green bell pepper, seeded and chopped

1 clove garlic, minced

⅛ cup (2 tablespoons) dry sherry or chicken broth

¼ cup salt-free sweet-and-sour marinade

½ pound cooked pork, shredded

1. In a medium-size microwave-safe bowl, combine the onion, pepper, garlic, and sherry; microwave on high for 3 minutes or until the vegetables are crisp-tender.

2. Add the sweet-and-sour marinade and pork; stir to combine. Cover and microwave at 70 percent power for 2 minutes or until the mixture is heated through. Taste and add more sweet-and-sour marinade, if desired.

PER SERVING: Calories: 107 | Total Fat: 1g | Saturated Fat: 0g | Cholesterol: 36mg | Protein: 12g | Sodium: 33mg | Potassium: 324mg | Fiber: 0g | Carbohydrates: 8g | Sugar: 6g

WARM PORK SALAD

A salad doesn't have to be cold! This delicious recipe is super easy and quick to make. You can use slow-cooked chicken or even beef if you'd like, for a change of pace.

SERVES 2

¼ pound Easy Slow-Cooked Pork (see recipe in this chapter)

2 tablespoons salt-free honey mustard sauce and marinade

1 Granny Smith or Golden Delicious apple, sliced

2 slices red onion

2 cups coleslaw mix

4 drops toasted sesame oil

Dash freshly ground black pepper

1. In a small nonstick sauté pan treated with nonstick spray, stir-fry the leftover pork until warm. Add the honey mustard sauce; mix until well-blended.

2. Add the apple, onion, and coleslaw mix; stir, then cover and cook for 2 minutes or until the vegetables are crisp-tender.

3. Top the salads with 2 drops each of the sesame oil and some freshly ground black pepper.

PER SERVING: Calories: 272 | Total Fat: 12g | Saturated Fat: 1g | Cholesterol: 35mg | Protein: 15g | Sodium: 57mg | Potassium: 505mg | Fiber: 4g | Carbohydrates: 25g | Sugar: 19g

PORK BARBECUE SANDWICHES

Barbecue sandwiches are a wonderful treat no matter the season. You can make this recipe with leftover grilled pork too; just shred the meat before you mix it with the rest of the ingredients. It's also delicious served on Ciabatta Rolls (Chapter 2).

SERVES 4

Nonstick cooking spray

2 teaspoons canola oil

1 small Granny Smith or Golden Delicious apple, peeled, cored, and grated

1 small sweet onion, finely minced

2 tablespoons salt-free honey mustard sauce and marinade

2 tablespoons salt-free honey mustard BBQ sauce and marinade

⅛ teaspoon freshly ground black pepper

½ pound Easy Slow-Cooked Pork (see recipe in this chapter)

8 (1-ounce) slices Old-Style Whole-Wheat Bread (Chapter 2)

1. Bring a nonstick sauté pan treated with spray oil to temperature over medium heat. Add the oil, apple, and onion; sauté until the onion is transparent.

2. Add the sauces and pepper; mix well. Add the pork and simmer with the sauces, stirring until heated through.

3. Evenly divide the pork mixture over 4 slices of the bread; top with the remaining 4 slices. Serve immediately.

PER SERVING: Calories: 288 | Total Fat: 5g | Saturated Fat: 1g | Cholesterol: 35mg | Protein: 17g | Sodium: 78mg | Potassium: 303mg | Fiber: 2g | Carbohydrates: 41g | Sugar: 7g

BAKED PORK TENDERLOIN DINNER

Sweet, spicy, and delicious, this easy dish bakes up wonderfully and can even be doubled for a no-fuss dinner party.

SERVES 4

4 small Yukon gold potatoes, scrubbed, peeled, and sliced

4 (2-ounce) pieces trimmed boneless pork loin, pounded flat

4 Granny Smith or Golden Delicious apples, peeled, cored, and sliced

1 large sweet onion, sliced

1 tablespoon minced shallot

⅛ cup apple cider or apple juice

⅛ teaspoon mustard powder

⅛ teaspoon grated lemon zest

⅛ teaspoon freshly ground black pepper

1. Preheat oven to 350°F. Spray an ovenproof casserole dish with nonstick spray.

2. Layer the potato slices from 2 of the potatoes across the bottom of the prepared dish. Top with 2 pieces of the flattened pork loin. Arrange the apple and onion slices over the top of the loin. Sprinkle the shallot over the apples and onion. Top with the remaining flattened pork loins, then the remaining potatoes.

3. In a small bowl, mix together the apple cider (or juice), mustard powder, lemon zest, and pepper. Drizzle the apple-cider mixture over the top of the casserole. Cover and bake for 45 minutes or everything is tender. Leave the casserole covered and let rest for 10 minutes before serving.

PER SERVING: Calories: 133 | Total Fat: 1g | Saturated Fat: 0g | Cholesterol: 36mg | Protein: 13g | Sodium: 35mg | Potassium: 509mg | Fiber: 1g | Carbohydrates: 16g | Sugar: 0g

CHAPTER 11

FISH AND SEAFOOD MAIN DISHES

PESTO FISH SWIRLS

Tender fillets of fish are supple enough that they can be filled and rolled up to make pretty pinwheels. You will need to find thin and flat fillets of sole or orange roughy for this recipe.

SERVES 4

2 tablespoons minced green onion

1 clove garlic, minced

⅓ cup Lemony Pesto (Chapter 4)

¼ cup sun-dried tomatoes in oil, minced

4 (6-ounce) thin white fish fillets

2 tablespoons lemon juice

1. In small bowl, combine green onion, garlic, pesto, and sun-dried tomatoes and mix well.

2. Place fish fillets on work surface. Spread each with ¼ of the pesto mixture and roll up with the pesto mixture inside. Place in 9" square glass microwave-safe baking dish. Pour lemon juice around fish.

3. Cover and microwave on high for 8–10 minutes or until the fish just flakes when tested with a fork. Let stand on solid surface so the heat redistributes for 4 minutes, then serve.

PER SERVING: Calories: 259 | Total Fat: 11g | Saturated Fat: 1g | Cholesterol: 97mg | Protein: 33g | Sodium: 139mg | Potassium: 699mg | Fiber: 0g | Carbohydrates: 3g | Sugar: 0g

FISH WITH TRIPLE BERRY SAUCE

Fruit can be delicious with fish. Its sweet-and-sour flavor really complements tender and mild white fish fillets. This sauce could also be used over pork or chicken. You could use boysenberries or blackberries as a substitute for any of the berries in this recipe.

SERVES 4

3 tablespoons unsalted butter, divided

2 green onions, minced

½ cup blueberries

½ cup sliced strawberries

1 tablespoon lemon juice

¼ teaspoon grated lemon zest

½ cup raspberries

1 egg white

4 (6-ounce) white fish fillets

½ cup finely chopped pecans

1. In small saucepan, melt 1 tablespoon butter over medium heat. Add green onions; cook and stir for 2 minutes.

2. Add blueberries and strawberries; cook and stir for 3–4 minutes until berries soften. Add lemon juice and zest. Simmer until berries start to release juice. Stir in raspberries and remove from heat.

3. In shallow bowl, beat egg white until frothy. Dip fish into egg white, then into pecans.

4. Melt remaining 2 tablespoons butter in large skillet. Add fish; cook, turning once, until fish just flakes when tested with fork, about 6–8 minutes. Remove from skillet, top with berry sauce, and serve immediately.

PER SERVING: Calories: 476 | Total Fat: 31g | Saturated Fat: 7g | Cholesterol: 132mg | Protein: 40g | Sodium: 137mg | Potassium: 823mg | Fiber: 4g | Carbohydrates: 10g | Sugar: 4g

SALMON CAKES

There are low-sodium varieties of canned salmon, but they can be hard to find. Make your salmon cakes with fresh salmon instead for a wonderful taste and texture. When you grill salmon fillets for dinner, make two extra and save them for this recipe.

SERVES 8

3 (6-ounce) cooked salmon fillets, flaked

2 slices French Bread (Chapter 2), crumbled

1 large egg, beaten

¾ cup Mayonnaise (Chapter 4), divided

1 tablespoon Honey Mustard (Chapter 4)

2 tablespoons minced green onions

2 tablespoons chopped flat-leaf parsley

2 teaspoons fresh thyme leaves

⅛ teaspoon white pepper

2 tablespoons sour cream

2 tablespoons milk

1 shallot, minced

1 tablespoon chopped fresh dill weed

2 tablespoons flour

2 tablespoons olive oil

1 tablespoon unsalted butter

1. Break the salmon into flakes and set aside.

2. In large bowl, combine bread crumbs, egg, ¼ cup mayonnaise, honey mustard, green onions, parsley, thyme, and pepper and mix well. Add salmon and mix gently to combine.

3. Form salmon mixture into 4 patties, then cover and refrigerate.

4. In small bowl, combine remaining ½ cup mayonnaise, sour cream, milk, shallot, and dill; mix well and refrigerate.

5. When ready to eat, coat salmon patties with flour. Heat olive oil and butter in large saucepan over medium heat.

6. Sauté salmon patties, turning once, for about 4 minutes on each side until golden brown. Serve immediately with the dill sauce.

PER SERVING: Calories: 554 | Total Fat: 41g | Saturated Fat: 8g | Cholesterol: 166mg | Protein: 37g | Sodium: 102mg | Potassium: 925mg | Fiber: 0g | Carbohydrates: 6g | Sugar: 1g

GRILLED MUSTARD SALMON TACOS

Salmon tacos are a delicious change of pace from shredded chicken or ground beef tacos. When you buy salmon, make sure you read the nutrition labels. The salmon varieties with the lowest sodium content are sockeye, wild coho, and Chinook. Make sure the salmon has not been brined or flavored.

SERVES 4

3 tablespoons Mustard (Chapter 4)

1 tablespoon honey

¼ teaspoon white pepper

2 (6-ounce) salmon fillets

1 avocado, cut in half, pit removed

2 large plum tomatoes, cut in half

1 jalapeño pepper

½ medium red onion, peeled

2 tablespoons lemon juice

2 tablespoons sour cream

4 low-sodium taco shells

1½ cups shredded red cabbage

1. Prepare and preheat grill. In small bowl, combine mustard, honey, and pepper. Coat salmon with this mixture.

2. Grill salmon, turning once, until the fish just flakes when tested with a fork. Remove from grill and set aside.

3. Grill the avocado halves, plum tomato halves, jalapeño pepper, and red onion until grill marks form. Chop the avocado and tomatoes, and mince the jalapeño pepper. Chop the red onion.

4. Combine with lemon juice and sour cream in medium bowl. Break salmon into chunks.

5. Heat taco shells, if desired. Make tacos with salmon, avocado mixture, and cabbage and serve immediately.

PER SERVING: Calories: 331 | Total Fat: 18g | Saturated Fat: 3g | Cholesterol: 49mg | Protein: 20g | Sodium: 56mg | Potassium: 848mg | Fiber: 6g | Carbohydrates: 22g | Sugar: 7g

CURRIED GRILLED SALMON

Curry is a wonderful partner with salmon. The sweet spiciness of the curry powder brings out the meatiness of the salmon. Serve with curry condiments—shredded coconut, chopped unsalted peanuts, Mango Chutney (Chapter 4), and chopped green onions—for an elegant meal.

SERVES 4

4 (6-ounce) salmon fillets

1 tablespoon curry powder

1 clove garlic, minced

2 tablespoons sour cream

1 tablespoon lemon juice

⅛ teaspoon white pepper

1. Place salmon fillets in a baking dish.

2. In small bowl, combine curry powder, garlic, sour cream, lemon juice, and pepper and mix well. Brush onto salmon.

3. Cover and refrigerate salmon for at least 2 hours to marinate.

4. When ready to eat, prepare and preheat grill. Grill salmon 6" from medium coals for 9–12 minutes or until the fish flakes when tested with fork. Serve with chutney, coconut, and other accompaniments as desired.

PER SERVING: Calories: 260 | Total Fat: 12g | Saturated Fat: 2g | Cholesterol: 96mg | Protein: 34g | Sodium: 80mg | Potassium: 874mg | Fiber: 0g | Carbohydrates: 1g | Sugar: 0g

BAKED ORANGE ROUGHY IN WHITE WINE

Fish always makes a fresh, light, and easy main course, and it's naturally very low in sodium! This bright and tangy dish would be perfect served alongside some rice pilaf and a green salad.

SERVES 4

4 (4-ounce) orange roughy fillets

2 tablespoons dry white wine

1 tablespoon lemon juice

1 teaspoon dried basil

½ teaspoon grated lemon zest

Optional: Freshly ground white or black pepper

1. Preheat oven to 425°F. Treat a baking dish with nonstick spray.

2. Pat fillets dry with a paper towel. Pour the wine and lemon juice into the prepared dish. Arrange the fillets in the dish, tucking under any thin ends if necessary so the fillets are of an even thickness. Sprinkle the basil and lemon zest evenly over the fish. Season with pepper, if desired.

3. Cover the dish with foil. Bake until the fish flakes when tested with a fork, about 12–18 minutes, depending on the thickness of the fillets. Serve immediately.

PER SERVING: Calories: 94 | Total Fat: 0g | Saturated Fat: 0g | Cholesterol: 68mg | Protein: 18g | Sodium: 81mg | Potassium: 200mg | Fiber: 0g | Carbohydrates: 0g | Sugar: 0g

JERK SALMON

Jerk seasoning was first developed in Jamaica. Jerk seasoning is typically very spicy, and is delicious with tender and mild salmon. Serve a fruit salad as a cooling contrast to this flavorful meal.

SERVES 4

3 cups flavored wood chips (pimento, pear, or mesquite)

1 tablespoon olive oil

1 tablespoon Jerk Spice Blend (Appendix A)

2 tablespoons orange juice

1 tablespoon brown sugar

1 clove garlic, minced

¼ teaspoon black pepper

⅛ teaspoon cayenne pepper

4 (6-ounce) salmon fillets

1. Soak the wood chips in enough water to cover for at least 1 hour.

2. In small bowl, combine olive oil, jerk spice blend, orange juice, brown sugar, garlic, pepper, and cayenne pepper and mix well. Brush this mixture onto the salmon fillets.

3. Cover fillets and refrigerate for 1 hour. Meanwhile, prepare and preheat grill.

4. Place the wood chips on the charcoal or in a metal tin as directed for your gas grill.

5. Grill the salmon, covered, about 6" from medium coals for 7–10 minutes or until the fish flakes when tested with a fork. Let stand 5 minutes, then serve.

PER SERVING: Calories: 292 | Total Fat: 14g | Saturated Fat: 2g | Cholesterol: 93mg | Protein: 33g | Sodium: 75mg | Potassium: 883mg | Fiber: 0g | Carbohydrates: 3g | Sugar: 3g

SPICY SALMON TOSTADAS

Tostadas are like flat tacos. Tortillas are fried or grilled until crisp, then topped with meats, vegetables, sauce, and cheese. Serve lots of beer and fresh fruit with this Mexican entrée.

SERVES 6

3 (6-ounce) salmon fillets

1 tablespoon chili powder

2 tablespoons lemon juice

1 (16-ounce) can no-salt-added cannellini beans, drained and rinsed

½ cup Spicy Salsa (Chapter 6)

⅓ cup safflower or peanut oil

6 (8-inch) low-sodium flour tortillas

2 medium tomatoes, seeded and chopped

2 medium avocados, peeled and chopped

1 cup sour cream

1. Place salmon fillets in a glass baking dish.

2. In small bowl, combine chili powder and lemon juice; rub onto salmon. Refrigerate for 30 minutes.

3. Meanwhile, put the drained beans into a bowl and mash. Mix in the salsa, then put into a medium skillet; heat over low heat, stirring occasionally.

4. Preheat oven to 400°F. Roast the salmon for 14–18 minutes or until the flesh flakes when tested with a fork. Remove from oven and let cool for 10 minutes.

5. In large skillet, heat the oil to 375°F. Fry the tortillas, one at a time, until they are crisp and slightly puffy. Remove to paper towels to drain.

6. To serve, top the crisp tortillas with the bean mixture, then salmon, tomatoes, avocados, and sour cream. Serve immediately.

PER SERVING: Calories: 663 | Total Fat: 40g | Saturated Fat: 8g | Cholesterol: 75mg | Protein: 32g | Sodium: 110mg | Potassium: 1,560mg | Fiber: 13g | Carbohydrates: 46g | Sugar: 4g

SALMON BURGERS WITH SLAW

Salmon burgers are a nice change of pace from regular beef or turkey burgers. The delicate flesh of the salmon is delicious when mixed with mustard and sour cream, then formed into patties. The burgers are topped with a simple slaw for crunch and texture and flavor contrast.

SERVES 4

¼ cup sour cream

3 tablespoons Mayonnaise (Chapter 4)

3 tablespoons Grainy Mustard (Chapter 4)

1¼ pounds boneless salmon fillets

1 slice French Bread (Chapter 2), crumbled

1 large egg, beaten

1 tablespoon lime juice

⅛ teaspoon white pepper

2 tablespoons olive oil

4 Hamburger Buns (Chapter 2), split and toasted

2 cups Zippy Coleslaw (Chapter 3)

1. In small bowl, combine sour cream, mayonnaise, and mustard and mix well. Set aside.

2. Cut the raw salmon into cubes. Mash ½ cup of the cubes until smooth using a potato masher or in a food processor. Stir the cubed and mashed salmon together in a medium bowl.

3. Add bread crumbs and egg to salmon mixture and mix well. Stir in ¼ cup of the sour cream mixture, lime juice, and pepper.

4. Form salmon mixture into 4 patties and refrigerate for 15 minutes.

5. When ready to eat, heat olive oil in a large skillet. Cook the patties in the oil, turning once, until cooked through to 160°F.

6. Spread remaining sour cream mixture on both top and bottom buns. Add the salmon burgers to the bottom halves of buns and top with the slaw and the top halves of buns. Serve immediately.

PER SERVING: Calories: 854 | Total Fat: 50g | Saturated Fat: 9g | Cholesterol: 180mg | Protein: 35g | Sodium: 140mg | Potassium: 950mg | Fiber: 5g | Carbohydrates: 64g | Sugar: 13g

SPICED RUBBED SALMON WITH CITRUS SALSA

Citrus fruits make an excellent and flavorful salsa and are delicious served with spicy grilled salmon. You can roast this salmon in the oven or grill it for more flavor. Use a grill basket to make it easier to turn the fish. It's delicious served with some steamed broccoli and a green salad tossed with mushrooms and cherry tomatoes.

SERVES 4

1 tablespoon brown sugar

1 teaspoon paprika

1 teaspoon chili powder

¼ teaspoon black pepper

¼ teaspoon crushed red pepper flakes

2 cloves garlic, minced

2 tablespoons lime juice, divided

2 tablespoons olive oil

4 (6-ounce) salmon fillets

1 cup chopped peeled orange

½ cup chopped peeled grapefruit

2 tablespoons minced green onion

½ teaspoon grated lemon zest

1 jalapeño pepper, minced

1. In small bowl, combine brown sugar, paprika, chili powder, pepper, crushed red pepper flakes, garlic, 1 tablespoon lime juice, and olive oil and mix well.

2. Coat the salmon with this mixture and place in glass baking dish. Cover and refrigerate for 30 minutes.

3. Meanwhile, in medium bowl combine orange, grapefruit, green onion, remaining 1 tablespoon lime juice, lemon zest, and jalapeño pepper. Mix and chill.

4. When ready to eat, prepare and preheat grill or preheat oven to 400°F. Grill salmon for 4–5 minutes on each side, turning once, until done. Or roast salmon for 14–18 minutes or until it flakes when tested with a fork. Serve the salmon with the salsa.

PER SERVING: Calories: 349 | Total Fat: 17g | Saturated Fat: 2g | Cholesterol: 93mg | Protein: 34g | Sodium: 82mg | Potassium: 1,006mg | Fiber: 2g | Carbohydrates: 12g | Sugar: 6g

LEMON COD EN PAPILLOTE

Cooking fish en papillote means it's wrapped in parchment paper and baked in the oven. The paper holds in all the flavors and the fish gently steams with the lemon and dill. The packets are served to guests right on their dinner plates. Each diner opens the packet (warn them to be careful of the steam!) and digs in.

SERVES 4

4 (6-ounce) cod fillets

⅛ teaspoon pepper

4 sprigs fresh dill

1 lemon, thinly sliced

2 green onions, sliced

2 tablespoons unsalted butter

1. Preheat oven to 400°F. Cut four large pieces of parchment paper about 12" × 18". Fold in half and crease, then unfold.

2. Place each piece of cod on a piece of parchment paper, about 2" from the center crease. Top with the pepper, dill, lemon slices, and green onions. Top each with about 2 teaspoons butter.

3. Fold the parchment paper over the fish and other ingredients, and crimp the edges tightly. Place the bundles on two baking sheets.

4. Bake fish for 10–17 minutes or until the fish flakes when tested with a fork. If the fillets are 1" thick, they should cook for 10 minutes. Cook longer depending on the thickness.

5. To serve, place bundles on plates, cut the top with scissors, and open.

PER SERVING: Calories: 192 | Total Fat: 6g | Saturated Fat: 3g | Cholesterol: 88mg | Protein: 30g | Sodium: 93mg | Potassium: 721mg | Fiber: 0g | Carbohydrates: 0g | Sugar: 0g

SALMON PICCATA

The word piccata *means that meat of some type is cooked with lemon, white wine, and capers. But because capers are high in salt, let's substitute a few pink peppercorns instead, along with some dill for flavor. This simple dish is perfect for company. Serve it with some steamed green beans and a fruit salad.*

SERVES 4

4 (6-ounce) salmon fillets

2 tablespoons flour

½ teaspoon dried dill weed

2 tablespoons unsalted butter

1 tablespoon olive oil

1 shallot, minced

2 cloves garlic, minced

¼ cup dry white wine

½ cup Fish Stock (Chapter 5)

3 tablespoons lemon juice

½ teaspoon grated lemon zest

1½ tablespoons pink peppercorns, slightly crushed

1 tablespoon minced fresh dill weed

1. Coat salmon on both sides with flour and dried dill weed.

2. In large skillet, melt butter with olive oil over medium heat. Add salmon fillets; cook, turning once, until the salmon is lightly browned, about 5–6 minutes. Remove salmon to platter.

3. Add shallot and garlic to pan; cook and stir to remove pan drippings. Add wine and fish stock and bring to a simmer.

4. Return salmon to the pan and add lemon juice and zest. Simmer for 2–3 minutes or until salmon is cooked.

5. Sprinkle with pink peppercorns and fresh dill weed and serve salmon immediately with the sauce.

PER SERVING: Calories: 357 | Total Fat: 20g | Saturated Fat: 5g | Cholesterol: 108mg | Protein: 34g | Sodium: 85mg | Potassium: 887mg | Fiber: 0g | Carbohydrates: 4g | Sugar: 0g

SALMON SCAMPI

Serve this wonderful dish over cooked pasta, with a green salad tossed with mushrooms, green onions, and cherry tomatoes and topped with Avocado Salad Dressing (Chapter 3), and Lemon Raspberry Eton Mess (Chapter 14) for dessert.

SERVES 4

4 (6-ounce) salmon fillets

3 tablespoons unsalted butter

1 tablespoon olive oil

3 cloves garlic, sliced

2 tablespoons sliced green onions

3 tablespoons lemon juice

3 tablespoons white wine

1 tablespoon Mustard (Chapter 4)

½ teaspoon grated lemon zest

⅛ teaspoon white pepper

1. Preheat oven to 400°F. Place salmon fillets in a glass baking dish and set aside.

2. In medium saucepan, melt butter with olive oil over medium heat. Add garlic; cook until fragrant, about 1 minute, stirring constantly.

3. Add green onions; cook for 1 minute, stirring constantly. Add lemon juice and white wine and bring to a simmer. Remove from heat and add mustard, lemon zest, and pepper and stir with a wire whisk until blended.

4. Pour sauce over salmon in dish. Roast for 14–19 minutes or until salmon just flakes when tested with a fork. Serve immediately with the sauce.

PER SERVING: Calories: 372 | Total Fat: 23g | Saturated Fat: 7g | Cholesterol: 116mg | Protein: 34g | Sodium: 34mg | Potassium: 877mg | Fiber: 0g | Carbohydrates: 2g | Sugar: 0g

ORANGE-STEAMED FISH

This fish is simply steamed to create a dish that melts in your mouth. The combination of citrus tang, sweetness, and spice is amazing. So much flavor—and it's low in sodium!

SERVES 4

4 (4-ounce) orange roughy or other mild fish fillets

½ cup sliced celery

¼ cup orange juice

⅛ teaspoon onion powder

⅛ teaspoon garlic powder

⅛ teaspoon freshly ground white or black pepper

Pinch each of dried basil, mustard powder, oregano, and thyme

4 thin orange slices

1. Pat fillets dry with a paper towel. Arrange the sliced celery on the steaming tray of a steamer or on steaming insert for a traditional stovetop pan. Place the fish fillets on top of the celery.

2. In a small bowl, mix the orange juice with the seasonings and then spoon evenly over the fish. Top with the orange slices.

3. Set the steaming tray over the boiling water and cover tightly with the lid. Steam the fish until the fish flakes when tested with a fork about 6–10 minutes, depending on the thickness of the fillet and the steaming method. Use a spatula to transfer the steamed fish, celery, and orange slices to individual plates and serve immediately.

PER SERVING: Calories: 100 | Total Fat: 0g | Saturated Fat: 0g | Cholesterol: 68mg | Protein: 18g | Sodium: 93mg | Potassium: 275mg | Fiber: 0g | Carbohydrates: 3g | Sugar: 2g

CITRUS FISH TACOS

Tacos made with fish are popular in Mexico and in California, and they are a nice change of pace from the traditional beef or chicken tacos. Oranges and grapefruit add a wonderful freshness and tang to the fish, tomatoes, and lettuce that are stuffed into a crisp tortilla shell.

SERVES 4

1 medium grapefruit, peeled and chopped

1 large orange, peeled and chopped

¼ cup chopped green onions

1 clove garlic, minced

1 jalapeño pepper, minced

2 tablespoons lemon juice

1¼ pounds sole fillets

3 tablespoons flour

2 teaspoons chili powder

⅛ teaspoon pepper

2 tablespoons olive oil

4 low-sodium taco shells, warmed

3 cups torn butter lettuce

1 medium tomato, chopped

½ cup sour cream

1. In small bowl, combine grapefruit, orange, green onions, garlic, jalapeño pepper, and lemon juice and set aside.

2. Sprinkle the sole fillets with flour, chili powder, and pepper.

3. Heat olive oil in a large skillet. Sauté the fish, turning once, until it just flakes when tested with a fork, about 4–5 minutes. Remove from heat and flake into large pieces.

4. Make tacos with the taco shells, fish, citrus mixture, butter lettuce, tomato, and sour cream and serve immediately.

PER SERVING: Calories: 346 | Total Fat: 17g | Saturated Fat: 5g | Cholesterol: 82mg | Protein: 22g | Sodium: 128mg | Potassium: 1,919mg | Fiber: 4g | Carbohydrates: 27g | Sugar: 9g

GINGER ORANGE FISH STIR-FRY

Mild fish fillets take well to just about any flavor and any ethnic cuisine. Ginger is traditionally used in Asian stir-fry recipes. Let's add some orange for a pop of flavor and color. This delicious recipe can be served over hot cooked brown or white rice, with a green salad on the side and a nice glass of white wine.

SERVES 4

⅔ cup orange juice

2 tablespoons lemon juice

⅓ cup Easy Homemade Ketchup (Chapter 4)

2 tablespoons brown sugar

2 tablespoons arrowroot

½ teaspoon ground ginger

½ teaspoon grated orange zest

⅛ teaspoon white pepper

2 tablespoons olive oil

1¼ pounds sole or orange roughy fillets, cut into 1½" pieces

1 medium onion, chopped

1 tablespoon minced fresh ginger

1 clove garlic, minced

2 medium carrots, thinly sliced

2 cups torn kale

1. In small bowl, combine orange juice, lemon juice, ketchup, brown sugar, arrowroot, ground ginger, orange zest, and pepper and mix well.

2. Heat oil in wok or large skillet over medium-high heat. Add fish; cook on both sides, turning once, until fish is just cooked through, about 4–5 minutes; remove from wok and flake into large pieces.

3. Add onion to skillet; stir-fry for 4 minutes. Add fresh ginger and garlic; stir-fry for 2 minutes longer.

4. Add carrots; stir-fry for 3 minutes. Add the kale; stir-fry for 2 minutes.

5. Add the fish and the orange sauce to the skillet. Stir-fry for 1–3 minutes or until the sauce thickens and bubbles. Serve immediately.

PER SERVING: Calories: 268 | Total Fat: 8g | Saturated Fat: 1g | Cholesterol: 54mg | Protein: 23g | Sodium: 134mg | Potassium: 849mg | Fiber: 2g | Carbohydrates: 25g | Sugar: 14g

ALMOND-CRUSTED FISH

Ground almonds make a fabulous coating for mild fish fillets. Because the fillets are delicate and the coating is too, be careful when you're cooking the fish. A nonstick skillet and nonstick spatula are necessities for the prettiest presentation.

SERVES 4

4 (6-ounce) orange roughy or tilapia fillets

¾ cup ground almonds

1 slice French Bread (Chapter 2), crumbled

2 tablespoons minced flat-leaf parsley

½ teaspoon grated lemon zest

¼ cup flour

½ teaspoon dried thyme leaves

⅛ teaspoon white pepper

1 egg white, slightly beaten

2 tablespoons unsalted butter

2 tablespoons olive oil

1. Place the fillets on a plate.

2. In shallow bowl, combine almonds, bread crumbs, parsley, and lemon zest. On a plate, combine flour, thyme, and pepper. Place egg white in another shallow bowl.

3. Dip the fillets into the flour mixture, then into the egg white. Dip them into the almond mixture to coat on both sides. Return to plate.

4. Melt butter and olive oil over medium-low heat in a large nonstick skillet. Add the fillets. Cook on one side for 3 minutes, carefully turn, and cook on the other side for 2–3 minutes longer or until the fish just flakes when tested with a fork. Serve immediately.

PER SERVING: Calories: 483 | Total Fat: 29g | Saturated Fat: 7g | Cholesterol: 100mg | Protein: 42g | Sodium: 110mg | Potassium: 749mg | Fiber: 3g | Carbohydrates: 15g | Sugar: 1g

CRISP MUSTARD-BAKED FISH

Even people who don't like fish will love this recipe! This super simple and unusual dish is perfect for entertaining guests; serve with steamed asparagus, some rolls from Chapter 2, and a green salad.

SERVES 4

4 (8-ounce) ½" thick cod fillets

2 tablespoons Mustard (Chapter 4)

2 tablespoons Mayonnaise (Chapter 4)

1 tablespoon lemon juice

½ teaspoon grated lemon zest

1 cup crushed Baked Potato Chips (Chapter 6)

2 teaspoons minced fresh basil leaves

2 teaspoons minced fresh flat-leaf parsley

1 teaspoon minced fresh thyme leaves

⅛ teaspoon white pepper

1. Preheat oven to 400°F. Place fillets on a baking sheet with sides.

2. In small bowl, combine mustard, mayonnaise, lemon juice, and lemon zest and mix well. Spread over the fish.

3. In small bowl, combine potato-chip crumbs, basil, parsley, thyme, and pepper and mix well. Place on the fish, spreading evenly and pressing down lightly.

4. Bake for 10–14 minutes or until the crust is crisp and the fish flakes when tested with a fork. Serve immediately.

PER SERVING: Calories: 307 | Total Fat: 11g | Saturated Fat: 1g | Cholesterol: 106mg | Protein: 42g | Sodium: 127mg | Potassium: 1,116mg | Fiber: 1g | Carbohydrates: 7g | Sugar: 0g

FISH AND SLAW SANDWICHES

Fish makes a delicious sandwich, especially when the tender fillets are breaded and baked and crisp and hot. Pair them with a creamy and spicy cold and crunchy coleslaw on homemade buns for a real treat. This is the type of food that should be served outdoors with a cold beer.

SERVES 4

3 slices French Bread (Chapter 2)

2 tablespoons grated Parmesan cheese

1 teaspoon dried thyme leaves

¼ teaspoon white pepper

2 egg whites, slightly beaten

4 (6-ounce) cod fillets

4 Hamburger Buns (Chapter 2), split and toasted

¼ cup Mayonnaise (Chapter 4)

1⅓ cups Zippy Coleslaw (Chapter 3)

1. Preheat oven to 400°F. Spray a cookie sheet with nonstick cooking spray and set aside.

2. Toast the bread until very crisp. Let cool, then crumble. Combine on a plate with the Parmesan, thyme, and pepper.

3. Place egg whites in shallow bowl.

4. Dip the fillets into the egg whites, then into the crumb mixture, pressing to coat. Place on prepared cookie sheet.

5. Bake the fish for 12–17 minutes or until it flakes when tested with a fork. Remove from the cookie sheet and make sandwiches with the buns, mayonnaise, and coleslaw. Serve immediately.

PER SERVING: Calories: 371 | Total Fat: 16g | Saturated Fat: 3g | Cholesterol: 66mg | Protein: 22g | Sodium: 113mg | Potassium: 505mg | Fiber: 2g | Carbohydrates: 33g | Sugar: 5g

GRILLED LEMON FILLETS

Grilling fish can be tricky, since delicate fillets tear and break apart easily. You can solve this problem by placing a sheet of heavy-duty foil on the grill and grilling the fish on that. Poke a few holes in the foil to let the smoke through so the fish is well flavored.

SERVES 4

3 tablespoons unsalted butter

1 shallot, minced

2 cloves garlic, minced

3 tablespoons lemon juice

½ teaspoon grated lemon zest

4 (6-ounce) mahi mahi or red snapper fillets

⅛ teaspoon white pepper

1. In small saucepan, melt butter over medium-low heat. Add shallot and garlic; cook and stir until fragrant, about 2–3 minutes. Remove from heat and add lemon juice and zest. Spoon half of this mixture into a small bowl to brush on the fish while it grills.

2. Prepare and preheat grill for medium coals. Place fillets on work surface and sprinkle with pepper.

3. Place a sheet of heavy-duty foil on the grill and poke holes in it with a knife. Add the fish, brush with a bit of the reserved butter mixture, and grill for 2–4 minutes or until the edges look opaque.

4. Flip the fish and brush with remaining reserved portion of the butter mixture. Grill for another 2–3 minutes or until the fish flakes when tested with a fork. Remove to serving plate and pour other half of the butter mixture over all and serve immediately.

PER SERVING: Calories: 195 | Total Fat: 10g | Saturated Fat: 5g | Cholesterol: 64mg | Protein: 23g | Sodium: 74mg | Potassium: 500mg | Fiber: 0g | Carbohydrates: 1g | Sugar: 0g

SESAME SNAPPER

Fish contains high amounts of omega-3 fatty acids, which lower blood pressure and improve blood circulation.

SERVES 4

1 tablespoon nonfat yogurt

1 teaspoon mayonnaise

1 teaspoon olive or canola oil

¼ cup unseasoned bread crumbs

2 tablespoons white sesame seeds

¼ teaspoon coarsely ground white or black pepper

⅛ teaspoon grated lemon zest

⅛ teaspoon grated orange zest

⅛ teaspoon garlic powder

⅛ teaspoon onion powder

4 (4-ounce) snapper fillets

Nonstick spray

1. In a shallow bowl, combine the yogurt, mayonnaise, and oil.

2. In another shallow bowl, combine the bread crumbs with the sesame seeds. Put the pepper, lemon and orange zests, and garlic and onion powders into a spice grinder or use a mortar and pestle to grind and mix well. Add to the bread-crumb mixture and stir to combine.

3. Pat fillets dry with paper towel. Brush the skinless side of each fillet with the yogurt blend and then press into the bread-crumb mixture.

4. Treat a large, nonstick, oven-safe skillet with nonstick spray. Heat the skillet over moderate heat. (Be careful not to get the skillet too hot or the sesame seeds will burn.) Add the fillets to the pan, crumb-side down, and sauté until golden brown, about 2–3 minutes. Turn the fillets and sauté until cooked through, about 2 minutes.

PER SERVING: Calories: 205 | Total Fat: 5g | Saturated Fat: 0g | Cholesterol: 42mg | Protein: 26g | Sodium: 88mg | Potassium: 501mg | Fiber: 1g | Carbohydrates: 12g | Sugar: 1g

STOVETOP POACHED HALIBUT WITH HERBED LEMON SAUCE

Lemon juice, lemon zest, and mustard powder are used often in the recipes in this book. They enhance the flavor in a way similar to salt without increasing the sodium content of the dish.

SERVES 4

4 (4-ounce) halibut fillets

1 medium lemon

⅓ cup mixture fresh herb sprigs (parsley, dill, chives, and/or chervil) and/or celery leaves

¼ teaspoon black peppercorns

1 bay leaf

1. Pat the fish fillets dry.

2. Put 2–3" of water in a pan broad enough to hold the fillets without overlapping them.

3. Cut the lemon in half. Squeeze the juice from 1 half and reserve for later. Thinly slice the remaining half lemon, reserving 2 slices to cut in half for garnish.

4. Add the lemon slices, herbs, peppercorns, and bay leaf to the water and bring to a boil. Reduce the heat and add the fillets; simmer until the fish is opaque through the thickest part (cut to test) and cooked to 145°F, or for about 8–10 minutes for fillets that are 1" thick. Transfer the fish to a plate and cover with foil to keep warm.

5. Strain and discard all but 1 cup of the poaching liquid. Bring the reserved poaching liquid to a boil over high heat until it is reduced by half, about 1–2 minutes. Stir in the reserved lemon juice. Arrange the halibut on 4 plates and spoon the lemon-herb sauce over the fish. Serve immediately, garnished with the reserved lemon slices.

PER SERVING: Calories: 126 | Total Fat: 2g | Saturated Fat: 0g | Cholesterol: 36mg | Protein: 23g | Sodium: 64mg | Potassium: 537mg | Fiber: 0g | Carbohydrates: 0g | Sugar: 0g

PAN-SEARED FLOUNDER FILLETS

To serve, transfer the flounder to a serving dish and place on top of mixed greens. Spoon your favorite salsa or fruit vinaigrette on top of the fish. If you prefer the flavor of a milder condiment to mellow the Cajun spices used on the fish, serve with some fruit, chutney, or a dollop of plain nonfat yogurt and lemon juice.

SERVES 4

4 teaspoons olive oil

4 (4-ounce) flounder fillets

1–2 teaspoons Cajun Spice Blend (Appendix A)

1. In a cast-iron skillet, heat the olive oil until smoking.

2. Coat both sides of the flounder with the Cajun spice blend. Place the coated flounder in the pan and cook for 2–3 minutes per side (depending on thickness) until cooked through.

PER SERVING: Calories: 143 | Total Fat: 5g | Saturated Fat: 0g | Cholesterol: 54mg | Protein: 21g | Sodium: 92mg | Potassium: 409mg | Fiber: 0g | Carbohydrates: 0g | Sugar: 0g

MICROWAVE POACHED SALMON

Salmon is best prepared without a lot of fanfare so you can enjoy its clean flavor. So here is a quick and healthy salmon dinner for a weeknight when you are short on time.

SERVES 4

4 (4-ounce) center-cut salmon fillets

1 tablespoon white wine or 1 teaspoon frozen white grape juice concentrate mixed with 2 teaspoons water

3 tablespoons water

½ teaspoon lemon pepper

⅛ teaspoon fennel seeds

1. Place the salmon fillets in a deep, microwave-safe casserole dish. Add the wine or grape juice mixture and water. Evenly divide the lemon pepper and fennel seeds over the fillets.

2. Cover and microwave on high for 6 minutes or until the fish just turns opaque throughout and flakes easily when tested with a fork. Let the fish stand on a solid surface for 3 minutes, then serve.

PER SERVING: Calories: 164 | Total Fat: 7g | Saturated Fat: 1g | Cholesterol: 62mg | Protein: 22g | Sodium: 50mg | Potassium: 556mg | Fiber: 0g | Carbohydrates: 0g | Sugar: 0g

ORANGE ROUGHY WITH ITALIAN ROASTED VEGETABLES

This hearty and filling dish can be served all on its own or with a side of rice or roasted potatoes for a satisfying dinner. If you can't find orange roughy, tilapia or mahi mahi fillets would work equally well.

SERVES 4

Olive oil spray

¾ pound orange roughy or other mild, firm white fish fillets

1 (10-ounce) package frozen mixed vegetables

1 (14.5-ounce) can no-salt-added diced tomatoes

1 teaspoon roasted garlic powder

½ teaspoon dried minced onion

½ teaspoon dried basil

¼ teaspoon dried parsley

⅛ teaspoon dried oregano

⅛ teaspoon granulated sugar

1 tablespoon grated Parmesan cheese

1. Preheat oven to 375°F. Treat a 2- to 3-quart baking pan or casserole dish with the olive spray oil.

2. Pat fillets dry with a paper towel.

3. Place the frozen vegetables in an even layer across the bottom of the prepared pan. Place the fish on the vegetables. Pour the tomatoes and juice evenly over the top. Spray tomatoes with a thin layer of the olive oil spray.

4. Sprinkle the garlic powder, minced onion, basil, parsley, oregano, and sugar over the tomatoes.

5. Cover the baking pan with aluminum foil or a lid and bake for 30 minutes. Remove the cover (being careful not to burn yourself on the steam). Sprinkle with cheese. Bake for an additional 5–10 minutes or until the cheese is melted and the fish flakes when tested with a fork.

PER SERVING: Calories: 136 | Total Fat: 1g | Saturated Fat: 0g | Cholesterol: 52mg | Protein: 17g | Sodium: 115mg | Potassium: 472mg | Fiber: 4g | Carbohydrates: 14g | Sugar: 4g

TUNA CAKES

You can substitute low-sodium chicken base for the crab base in this recipe and lower the sodium content even further.

SERVES 9

2 teaspoons olive oil

2 teaspoons unsalted butter

1 small red onion, chopped

1 small green or red bell pepper, seeded and chopped

Optional: 1 jalapeño pepper, seeded and finely chopped

2 cloves garlic, minced

¼ teaspoon dried rosemary

1 teaspoon sweet paprika

1 teaspoon dried basil

1 teaspoon dried parsley

½ teaspoon dried tarragon

½ teaspoon fresh ground white pepper

¼ teaspoon crab base

½ cup water

1 tablespoon lemon juice

½ cup nonfat cottage cheese

1 large egg

1 (6-ounce) can low-sodium canned tuna, drained

1 cup bread crumbs, divided

Olive oil spray

1. Preheat oven to 375°F.

2. Heat olive oil and butter over medium heat in a nonstick saute pan until melted. Add the onion, bell pepper, and jalapeño, if using; sauté until the onion is transparent. Add the garlic and sauté for 1 minute, being careful not to burn the garlic. Add the rosemary, paprika, basil, parsley, tarragon, and pepper; stir well. Add the crab base; stir well to dissolve into the sautéed vegetable mixture. Add the water and lemon juice to the pan and bring to a boil.

3. Place cottage cheese and egg in a blender or food processor and pulse to mix. Whisk the cottage-cheese mixture into the boiling vegetable mixture in the pan. Reduce heat and simmer until the mixture thickens and the egg is cooked, stirring constantly.

4. Remove from heat and stir in the drained tuna and ¾ cup of the bread crumbs. Spray a square baking pan with the olive oil spray. Pour the mixture into the pan, spreading it out evenly along the bottom. Evenly top with the remaining bread crumbs. Spray the crumbs with the olive oil spray.

5. Bake for 25–30 minutes or until the mixture is set and the bread crumbs on top are browned. Cut into 9 pieces.

PER SERVING: Calories: 107 | Total Fat: 3g | Saturated Fat: 1g | Cholesterol: 32mg | Protein: 8g | Sodium: 136mg | Potassium: 122mg | Fiber: 0g | Carbohydrates: 10g | Sugar: 1g

BAKED SEASONED BREAD CRUMB–CRUSTED FISH

Choose your favorite white-fleshed fish for this dish, either haddock (as used here) or pollock or cod. Serve with some Oven-Fried Potato Wedges (Chapter 13) and some malt vinegar and salt-free ketchup.

SERVES 6

Olive oil spray

2 large lemons

¼ cup dried bread crumbs

¼ teaspoon onion powder

¼ teaspoon ground fennel seeds

¼ teaspoon freshly ground black pepper

⅛ teaspoon celery seeds

⅛ teaspoon dried lemon thyme or thyme

⅛ teaspoon dried parsley

⅛ teaspoon salt-free chili powder

1½ pounds halibut fillets

1. Preheat the oven to 375°F. Spray a baking dish with the olive oil spray.

2. Wash the lemons and cut 1 into thin slices; set aside. Grate 1 tablespoon of zest from the second lemon, then juice it into a shallow dish; set aside the juice. Combine the grated zest, bread crumbs, onion powder, fennel seeds, black pepper, celery seeds, thyme, parsley, and chili powder in a small bowl and stir to mix; set aside.

3. Arrange the lemon slices in the bottom of the prepared baking dish. Dip the fish pieces in the lemon juice and set them on the lemon slices in the baking dish. Sprinkle the bread-crumb mixture evenly over the fish pieces. Spray the bread-crumb topping with a light coating of the olive oil spray. Bake until the crumbs are lightly browned and the fish is just opaque through and flakes easily when tested with a fork, about 10–15 minutes. (Baking time will depend on the thickness of the fish.) Serve immediately, using the lemon slices as garnish.

PER SERVING: Calories: 145 | Total Fat: 2g | Saturated Fat: 0g | Cholesterol: 36mg | Protein: 24g | Sodium: 94mg | Potassium: 532mg | Fiber: 0g | Carbohydrates: 4g | Sugar: 0g

SWEET ONION SOLE FILLETS

In this recipe the Vidalia onions caramelize and create a kind of crust for the sole fillets, making a sweet and delicious meal. Vidalia onions are sweeter than the regular yellow or white onions we use in recipes. They are grown in Georgia.

SERVES 4

2 cups medium-sliced Vidalia onions

1 tablespoon balsamic vinegar

2 teaspoons brown sugar

1 pound sole fillets

Olive oil spray

1 teaspoon salt-free lemon pepper blend

1. Preheat oven to 375°F.

2. Put the onions into a covered, microwave-safe dish and microwave on high for 5 minutes or until the onions are transparent. Carefully remove the cover (being careful not to burn yourself on the steam) and stir in the vinegar and brown sugar. Cover and microwave on high for an additional 30 seconds. Let stand for several minutes so the onions absorb the flavors. Remove the lid and microwave on high for an additional 30–60 seconds to evaporate any excess moisture, watching the onions carefully so they don't burn.

3. Pat fish dry using paper towels. Arrange the fillets on baking sheet treated with the olive oil spray. Lightly spray the top of the fillets too. Evenly sprinkle the lemon pepper over the fish. Spoon the caramelized onions over the tops of the fillets, pressing the onions to form a light "crust" over the surface of the fish. Bake for 12–15 minutes or until the fish flakes with a fork and the onions darken and caramelize further.

PER SERVING: Calories: 128 | Total Fat: 1g | Saturated Fat: 0g | Cholesterol: 54mg | Protein: 22g | Sodium: 101mg | Potassium: 553mg | Fiber: 1g | Carbohydrates: 6g | Sugar: 3g

EASY OVEN-ROASTED SALMON STEAKS

Baked salmon with a kick! The seasoning in this recipe is tangy and sweet and the fish is juicy and delicious.

SERVES 4

2 teaspoons extra-virgin olive oil

4 (5-ounce) salmon steaks, skin on

1 teaspoon Citrus Pepper (Appendix A)

1. Preheat the oven to 350°F.

2. Rub ½ teaspoon of the olive oil into the flesh side of each salmon steak. Sprinkle the Citrus Pepper over the olive oil–treated flesh and press it into the fish.

3. Spray an oven-safe baking dish with nonstick spray. Place the steaks skin-side down in the dish. Roast for 25 minutes or until the salmon flakes when tested with a fork.

PER SERVING: Calories: 221 | Total Fat: 11g | Saturated Fat: 1g | Cholesterol: 77mg | Protein: 28g | Sodium: 62mg | Potassium: 694mg | Fiber: 0g | Carbohydrates: 0g | Sugar: 0g

EASY-BAKED COD

This dish is simple and easy, yet not short on flavor. Serve with Scalloped Potatoes (Chapter 13) or Creamy Brown Rice Pilaf (Chapter 13) for a spectacular low-sodium meal.

SERVES 4

1 pound cod fillets

Olive oil spray

1 teaspoon salt-free lemon pepper or seasoning blend

1. Preheat oven to 375°F.

2. Pat fish dry with paper towels. Arrange the fillets on a baking sheet treated with the olive oil spray. Lightly spray the tops of the fillets with the olive oil spray. Evenly sprinkle the lemon pepper over the fish.

3. Bake for 7–10 minutes or until the fish flakes with a fork.

PER SERVING: Calories: 93 | Total Fat: 0g | Saturated Fat: 0g | Cholesterol: 48mg | Protein: 20g | Sodium: 61mg | Potassium: 468mg | Fiber: 0g | Carbohydrates: 0g | Sugar: 0g

BAKED RED SNAPPER AMANDINE

Baking times given for fish dishes assume the fillet is about 1" thick at the thickest part. Fold "tails" or thinner sections under the fish to create an even thickness throughout to help ensure even baking times. That way, you'll avoid ending up with some of the fish dry and overdone.

SERVES 4

1 pound red snapper fillets

4 teaspoons unbleached all-purpose flour

¼ teaspoon freshly ground white or black pepper

¼ teaspoon salt-free chili powder

⅛ teaspoon dried parsley

⅛ teaspoon grated lemon zest

⅛ teaspoon garlic powder

⅛ teaspoon onion powder

¹⁄₁₆ teaspoon ground coriander

2 teaspoons olive oil

2 tablespoons ground raw almonds

2 teaspoons unsalted butter

1 tablespoon lemon juice

1. Preheat oven to 375°F.

2. Pat fish dry with paper towels. Add the flour, white or black pepper, chili powder, parsley, lemon zest, garlic powder, onion powder, and coriander to a small bowl; mix to combine. Sprinkle the fillets with the seasoned flour, front and back.

3. In an ovenproof nonstick skillet over medium heat, sauté the fillets in the olive oil until they are browned on both sides. Combine the ground almonds and butter in a microwave-safe dish and microwave on high for 30 seconds or until the butter is melted; stir to combine. Pour the almond-butter mixture and lemon juice over the fillets. Bake for 3–5 minutes or until the almonds are nicely browned and the fish flakes when tested with a fork.

PER SERVING: Calories: 188 | Total Fat: 8g | Saturated Fat: 2g | Cholesterol: 47mg | Protein: 24g | Sodium: 76mg | Potassium: 521mg | Fiber: 0g | Carbohydrates: 3g | Sugar: 0g

ITALIAN-SEASONED BAKED FISH

Part of the secret of enhancing flavors without salt is to use a variety of complementary seasonings, such as the combination of dried ingredients and powders used in this recipe. The sweeter flavors of the powders provide a nice contrast with the chunkier textures created by the dried minced ingredients.

SERVES 4

1 pound cod fillets

1 (14.5-ounce) can no-salt-added diced tomatoes

¼ teaspoon dried minced onion

¼ teaspoon onion powder

¼ teaspoon dried minced garlic

¼ teaspoon garlic powder

¼ teaspoon dried basil

¼ teaspoon dried parsley

⅛ teaspoon dried oregano

⅛ teaspoon granulated sugar

⅛ teaspoon grated lemon zest

¹⁄₁₆ teaspoon salt-free chili powder

Optional: Pinch dried red pepper flakes

1 tablespoon grated Parmesan cheese

1. Preheat the oven to 375°F. Treat a 2- to 3-quart baking pan or casserole dish with nonstick cooking spray.

2. Pat cod dry with paper towels.

3. Add all the ingredients except the fish to the prepared baking pan and stir to mix. Arrange the fillets over the tomatoes, folding thin tail ends under to give the fillets even thickness; spoon some of the tomato mixture over the fillets. For fillets about 1" thick, bake uncovered for 20–25 minutes or until the fish is opaque and flakes when tested with a fork.

PER SERVING: Calories: 118 | Total Fat: 1g | Saturated Fat: 0g | Cholesterol: 49mg | Protein: 21g | Sodium: 91mg | Potassium: 675mg | Fiber: 1g | Carbohydrates: 4g | Sugar: 2g

BAKED ORANGE ROUGHY WITH SPICED RASPBERRY SAUCE

You may decide you only want to use half the sauce called for in this recipe, or you may want to add additional water or fruit juice to the sauce to mellow the flavor.

SERVES 4

Olive oil spray

1 pound orange roughy fillets

1 bay leaf

1 clove garlic, crushed

1 medium apple, peeled, cored, and cubed

½ teaspoon grated fresh ginger

½ teaspoon minced candied ginger

1 small red onion, chopped

3 tablespoons water, divided

2 teaspoons frozen raspberry juice concentrate

1 teaspoon frozen apple juice concentrate

1 teaspoon reduced-sugar orange marmalade

½ teaspoon reduced-sodium Worcestershire sauce

¼ teaspoon honey

⅛ teaspoon grated lemon zest

1 teaspoon lemon juice

½ teaspoon rice wine vinegar

⅛ teaspoon ground ginger

⅛ teaspoon crushed anise seeds

⅛ teaspoon dry mustard

⅛ teaspoon ground cinnamon

Pinch ground cloves

Pinch dried red pepper flakes

1⅓ cups cooked brown rice

1. Preheat oven to 400°F. Spray a baking dish with the olive oil spray.

2. Pat fish dry with paper towels. Lightly spray both sides of the fish with the olive spray oil, then arrange in 1 layer in the dish.

3. In a microwave-safe bowl, mix together the bay leaf, garlic, apple, grated fresh and minced candied ginger, onion, and 1 tablespoon water. Cover and microwave on high for 2 minutes or until the apple is tender and the onion is transparent. Stir, discard the bay leaf, and top the fillets with the apple mixture. Bake uncovered for 15–18 minutes or until the fish is opaque.

4. While the fish bakes, combine all the remaining ingredients except the rice in a microwave-safe bowl; microwave on high for 30 seconds. Stir, add a little water if needed to thin mixture, and microwave for 15 seconds or until heated through. Cover until ready to serve. (If necessary, bring back to temperature by microwaving the mixture for another 15 seconds just prior to serving.)

5. To serve, divide the cooked rice evenly among 4 serving plates. Top the rice with the baked fish and apple mixture. Evenly divide the sauce between the 4 servings, drizzling it atop the fish, or serve it on the side.

PER SERVING: Calories: 202 | Total Fat: 1g | Saturated Fat: 0g | Cholesterol: 68mg | Protein: 20g | Sodium: 95mg | Potassium: 318mg | Fiber: 1g | Carbohydrates: 26g | Sugar: 9g

TUNA AND FRESH TOMATO PIZZA

Tuna on pizza? You bet. This combination may seems a bit odd, but the flavor will win you over!

SERVES 4–6

Pizza Crust

1 cup warm water

¼ teaspoon granulated sugar

1 teaspoon active dry yeast

1 teaspoon olive oil

1 cup unbleached all-purpose flour

Optional: ½ teaspoon sea salt

Pizza Topping

2 medium-size tomatoes

½ teaspoon garlic powder

½ teaspoon dried basil

¼ teaspoon dried parsley

⅛ teaspoon dried oregano

1 (6-ounce) can 50% less sodium chunk light tuna, drained

1 cup nonfat cottage cheese

1 teaspoon potato flour or all-purpose flour

4 teaspoons grated Parmesan cheese

CRUST PER SERVING:
Calories: 127 | Total Fat: 1g | Saturated Fat: 0g | Cholesterol: 0mg | Protein: 3g | Sodium: 2mg | Potassium: 53mg | Fiber: 1g | Carbohydrates: 24g | Sugar: 0g

PIZZA PER SERVING:
Calories: 146 | Total Fat: 1g | Saturated Fat: 0g | Cholesterol: 11mg | Protein: 13g | Sodium: 117mg | Potassium: 192mg | Fiber: 1g | Carbohydrates: 19g | Sugar: 1g

For pizza crust:

1. Mix the water, sugar, and yeast together in a small bowl and set aside for 5–10 minutes to allow the yeast to proof.

2. Once the yeast is bubbling, add to it the olive oil, flour, and sea salt. Stir together with a fork, working the dough until it pulls away from the side of the bowl. It's important that the dough be worked enough to form a ball in the bowl; however, it will still be very sticky.

3. Turn the dough out onto a lightly floured surface and, using a knife or pastry cutter, divide it into 4 sections. Next, oil your hands by rubbing ¼ teaspoon of olive oil over your palms. Shape each of the 4 dough sections into a ball, then one by one, flatten each ball until it forms a "crust" about 6" in diameter. Place each crust on a jellyroll baking sheet treated with nonstick spray. At that size, you should be able to arrange all 4 crusts on 1 sheet. Using the tines of a fork, prick each crust a few times. (This prevents them from rising too high during baking and creating pita-style bread instead.)

For pizza:

1. Preheat oven to 400°F.

2. Clean and peel the tomatoes. Slice or dice them and arrange them evenly over the pizza crusts.

3. In a small bowl, combine the garlic powder, basil, parsley, and oregano; sprinkle over the tomatoes. Spread the drained tuna over the pizzas.

4. Mix together the cottage cheese, flour, and Parmesan cheese in a medium bowl, then divide evenly over the pizzas.

5. Bake until the cheese bubbles and the crusts are done. The amount of baking time—anywhere from 3 to 8 minutes or more—will vary considerably, depending on how thin you've made your crusts, which affects how thickly you've topped those crusts. (Prebaked crusts will also take less time.)

CITRUS PEPPER ORANGE ROUGHY

Orange roughy is such a versatile fish that it can handle almost any seasoning you choose. Substitute the Citrus Pepper in this recipe for your favorite spice blend and enjoy.

SERVES 4

4 teaspoons olive oil

4 (4-ounce) orange roughy fillets

2 teaspoons Citrus Pepper (Appendix A)

1. Pat fish dry with paper towels.

2. Bring a large, deep nonstick sauté pan to temperature over medium-high heat. Rub ½ teaspoon of olive oil on each side of each fish fillet. Sprinkle the Citrus Pepper over the curved (or most attractive) side of the fillets. Place the coated fish in the pan, seasoned-side down. Cook for 2–3 minutes per side (depending on thickness) until cooked through and fish flakes when tested with a fork.

PER SERVING: Calories: 126 | Total Fat: 5g | Saturated Fat: 0g | Cholesterol: 68mg | Protein: 18g | Sodium: 81mg | Potassium: 189mg | Fiber: 0g | Carbohydrates: 0g | Sugar: 0g

CHAPTER 12

VEGETARIAN MAIN DISHES

HUMMUS PIZZA

Since the hummus is so creamy and rich you don't need much cheese with this pizza, which saves on the sodium content. You can look for a low-sodium hummus for this pizza, but try making your own using no-salt-added chickpeas for a fresh taste.

SERVES 6

1 recipe Pizza Crust (Chapter 2)

1 cup Hummus (Chapter 6)

1 tablespoon olive oil

1 medium red onion, chopped

1 medium red bell pepper, sliced

1 medium yellow summer squash, cubed

1 cup baby spinach leaves

½ cup shredded mozzarella cheese

1. Preheat oven to 400°F. Roll the pizza dough to a 14" circle and place on a pizza plate or stone. Prebake the pizza crust for 5 minutes; remove from oven. Prepare hummus.

2. In large skillet, heat olive oil over medium heat. Add onion, bell pepper, and squash and cook, stirring frequently, until tender, about 7–9 minutes. Add spinach, cover pan, and remove from heat. Set aside for 3 minutes.

3. Meanwhile, spread hummus on the pizza crust. Top with the vegetable mixture and the cheese.

4. Bake for 15–25 minutes or until the crust is deep golden brown and the cheese is melted and beginning to brown. Serve immediately.

PER SERVING: Calories: 475 | Total Fat: 20g | Saturated Fat: 3g | Cholesterol: 7mg | Protein: 15g | Sodium: 112mg | Potassium: 520mg | Fiber: 8g | Carbohydrates: 59g | Sugar: 5g

BARLEY RISOTTO

Barley is a whole grain that is packed with fiber, selenium, and vitamin B_1. It is chewy and nutty and very delicious. Use it instead of rice to make a super simple risotto that doesn't need to be stirred while it's cooking.

SERVES 4

1 tablespoon butter

1 tablespoon olive oil

1 medium onion, finely chopped

3 cloves garlic, minced

1 cup sliced carrots

1 cup sliced baby portobello mushrooms

2 cups barley

2 teaspoons fresh thyme leaves

4½ cups Vegetable Broth (Chapter 5)

2 cups baby spinach leaves

2 tablespoons grated Parmesan cheese

1. In a large heavy saucepan with a tight-fitting lid, melt butter with olive oil over medium heat. Add onion, garlic, and carrots; cook and stir for 4–5 minutes or until crisp-tender.

2. Add mushrooms; cook and stir for 4 minutes longer. Then add barley; cook and stir for 3–4 minutes or until toasted.

3. Add the thyme and all of the vegetable broth and bring to a simmer. Lower the heat, clamp on the lid, and simmer for 20–25 minutes, stirring occasionally, until the barley has absorbed the liquid and is tender.

4. Stir in the spinach and cheese, cover, and let stand for 5 minutes. Stir gently to combine and serve immediately.

PER SERVING: Calories: 389 | Total Fat: 7g | Saturated Fat: 2g | Cholesterol: 7mg | Protein: 14g | Sodium: 130mg | Potassium: 652mg | Fiber: 13g | Carbohydrates: 69g | Sugar: 2g

SOUTHWEST BLACK BEAN PIZZA

Lots of black beans, spices, and vegetables make this rich pizza wonderful. A combination of salsa and tomato sauce makes the tasty sauce. You can use any of your favorite vegetables in this easy recipe, and make it as hot or mild as you like. Serve with some cold beer and fresh fruit with cookies for dessert.

SERVES 6

1 Pizza Crust (Chapter 2)

1 (8-ounce) can no-salt-added tomato sauce

1 jalapeño pepper, minced

½ cup Spicy Salsa (Chapter 6)

1 tablespoon chili powder

1 (15-ounce) can no-salt-added black beans, rinsed and drained

2 cloves garlic, minced

3 green onions, sliced

1 cup frozen corn, thawed

1 cup cherry tomatoes, cut in half

½ cup shredded mozzarella cheese

1. Preheat oven to 400°F. Prepare pizza crust and roll out to 14" circle; place on pizza stone or pizza pan. Bake for 5 minutes; remove from oven.

2. In small bowl, combine tomato sauce, jalapeño pepper, salsa, and chili powder. Spread over pizza crust.

3. Top with beans, garlic, green onions, thawed corn, cherry tomatoes, and mozzarella cheese.

4. Bake for 15–25 minutes or until crust is deep golden brown, vegetables are tender, and cheese is melted and beginning to brown. Cut into wedges and serve immediately.

PER SERVING: Calories: 353 | Total Fat: 6g | Saturated Fat: 1g | Cholesterol: 7mg | Protein: 15g | Sodium: 115mg | Potassium: 655mg | Fiber: 10g | Carbohydrates: 61g | Sugar: 5g

FRIED RICE

Soy sauce is a key component in this recipe, and it adds a wonderful rich and savory taste to the dish. We'll use darkly sautéed mushrooms in place of the soy sauce for an even better flavor, and add sesame oil for a toasted, nutty flavor.

SERVES 4

3 tablespoons safflower or peanut oil, divided

½ cup minced cremini mushrooms

1 medium onion, chopped

2 cloves garlic, minced

1 tablespoon minced fresh ginger root

1 teaspoon five-spice powder

3 cups cold cooked white rice

2 large eggs, beaten

⅓ cup Vegetable Broth (Chapter 5)

1 cup frozen peas, thawed

1 tablespoon sesame oil

1. In wok or large skillet, heat 1 tablespoon oil. Add the mushrooms; cook over low heat, stirring frequently, until the mushrooms are deep brown. Remove from wok and set aside.

2. Add remaining 2 tablespoons oil to wok. Stir-fry the onion, garlic, and ginger root until crisp-tender, about 5 minutes.

3. Sprinkle the food with the five-spice powder and add the rice to the wok; stir-fry until the rice is hot and slightly toasted.

4. Add the beaten eggs; stir-fry until the eggs are cooked and broken into small pieces. Add the vegetable broth, peas, mushrooms, and sesame oil; stir-fry until hot and serve immediately.

PER SERVING: Calories: 335 | Total Fat: 16g | Saturated Fat: 2g | Cholesterol: 105mg | Protein: 9g | Sodium: 48mg | Potassium: 297mg | Fiber: 2g | Carbohydrates: 37g | Sugar: 2g

BLACK BEAN CHILI

You can let this chili cook all day in your slow cooker, and come home to a house that smells wonderful and dinner that is only minutes away. Serve with hot Cornbread (Chapter 2) right out of the oven.

SERVES 6

2 tablespoons safflower or peanut oil

2 medium onions, chopped

3 cloves garlic, minced

1 jalapeño pepper, minced

3 (14-ounce) cans no-salt-added black beans, rinsed and drained

2 (14-ounce) cans no-salt-added diced tomatoes, undrained

1 cup Spicy Salsa (Chapter 6)

1 tablespoon chili powder

1 teaspoon ground cumin

1 teaspoon smoked paprika

1 teaspoon dried oregano leaves

½ cup sour cream

1. In medium saucepan, heat oil over medium heat. Add onions and garlic; cook and stir until tender, about 6 minutes. Place in 4- to 5-quart slow cooker.

2. Add jalapeño, beans, tomatoes, and salsa to the slow cooker and stir well. Add chili powder, cumin, paprika, and oregano and stir.

3. Cover and cook on low for 7–9 hours or until chili is bubbling. Serve topped with the sour cream.

PER SERVING: Calories: 133 | Total Fat: 9g | Saturated Fat: 2g | Cholesterol: 10mg | Protein: 3g | Sodium: 49mg | Potassium: 439mg | Fiber: 3g | Carbohydrates: 12g | Sugar: 6g

REFRIED BEAN PIZZA

Refried beans make a fabulous pizza sauce. The rich flavor and meaty texture of the beans is perfect on a crisp pizza crust. Top with lots of veggies and just a bit of cheese if you like for a satisfying dinner that is much better than take-out. Serve with a green salad and lots of cold beer.

SERVES 6

1 recipe Pizza Crust (Chapter 2)

2 tablespoons olive oil

1 medium onion, chopped

4 cloves garlic, sliced

1 jalapeño pepper, minced

1 medium red bell pepper, sliced

1 medium yellow bell pepper, sliced

1 cup Refried Beans (Chapter 13) made with Vegetable Broth (Chapter 5)

1 beefsteak tomato, seeded and chopped

2 teaspoons chili powder

1 teaspoon ground cumin

⅛ teaspoon black pepper

⅛ teaspoon crushed red pepper flakes

½ cup shredded CoJack cheese, if desired

1. Preheat oven to 400°F. Roll the pizza dough to a 14" circle and place on a pizza pan or stone. Prebake the pizza crust for 5 minutes; remove from oven.

2. In large saucepan, heat olive oil over medium heat. Add onion and garlic; cook and stir for 4–5 minutes or until crisp-tender. Add jalapeño pepper, red pepper, and yellow pepper and sauté for another 3 minutes. Remove from heat.

3. In medium bowl, combine refried beans with the chopped tomato, chili powder, cumin, pepper, and crushed red pepper flakes. Mix well and spread on pizza crust.

4. Top with vegetables and sprinkle with cheese, if using. Bake for 15–25 minutes or until the crust is golden brown and toppings are hot.

PER SERVING: Calories: 337 | Total Fat: 12g | Saturated Fat: 3g | Cholesterol: 9mg | Protein: 11g | Sodium: 108mg | Potassium: 414mg | Fiber: 5g | Carbohydrates: 46g | Sugar: 1g

CURRIED VEGGIE COUSCOUS

Vegetables and couscous together make a satisfying dish. Add some curry powder for flavor. This recipe is very healthy and delicious, as well as colorful. Serve with some toasted Pita Breads (Chapter 2).

SERVES 4

2 tablespoons olive oil

1 medium onion, chopped

1 leek, cleaned and chopped

3 cloves garlic, minced

1 cup sliced mushrooms

1 medium zucchini, seeded and chopped

1 medium tomato, seeded and chopped

1 cup frozen edamame, thawed

2 teaspoons curry powder

¼ teaspoon turmeric

1 cup couscous

2 cups Vegetable Broth (Chapter 5)

⅓ cup chopped flat-leaf parsley

1. In large saucepan, heat olive oil over medium heat. Add onion, leek, and garlic; cook and stir for 5 minutes.

2. Add mushrooms to pan; cook and stir for 4 minutes longer.

3. Add zucchini, tomato, edamame, curry powder, and turmeric; cook and stir for another 3 minutes.

4. Add couscous and vegetable broth and bring to a simmer. Remove pan from heat, cover, and let stand for 8 minutes.

5. Remove lid, fluff couscous with a fork, top with parsley, and serve immediately.

PER SERVING: Calories: 236 | Total Fat: 9g | Saturated Fat: 1g | Cholesterol: 0mg | Protein: 10g | Sodium: 52mg | Potassium: 610mg | Fiber: 4g | Carbohydrates: 30g | Sugar: 3g

POTATO TORTA

Serve this delicious potato torta with a green salad tossed with sliced zucchini and grape tomatoes, and a glass of white wine.

SERVES 4

4 medium Yukon Gold potatoes, peeled

1 large sweet potato, peeled

2 tablespoons olive oil

2 medium onions, chopped

4 cloves garlic, minced

6 large eggs

¼ cup heavy cream

1 teaspoon minced fresh rosemary leaves

¼ teaspoon white pepper

1. Slice the potatoes and sweet potato ⅛" thick. Place in a large microwave-safe casserole dish and add water.

2. Cover and microwave for 6 minutes, then remove and rearrange potatoes with tongs. Cover and microwave for an additional 2 minutes until potatoes are almost tender. Drain well.

3. In medium saucepan, heat olive oil over medium heat. Add onions and garlic; cook, stirring frequently, for 8–10 minutes or until onions start to turn golden. Remove from heat.

4. Preheat oven to 375°F. Wrap the outside of a 9" springform pan completely with heavy-duty foil and spray the inside with nonstick cooking spray. Layer the potatoes, onions, and garlic in the pan.

5. In large bowl, beat eggs with cream, rosemary, and pepper. Slowly pour over the potatoes in the pan. Press down with a spatula.

6. Cover and bake for 20 minutes. Uncover pan and bake for another 25–30 minutes or until the top is browned and potato mixture is set.

7. Remove from oven and cool on rack for 10 minutes. Carefully remove the foil. Run a knife around the edges of the pan, unclamp the sides of the pan and remove sides. Slice into wedges to serve.

PER SERVING: Calories: 386 | Total Fat: 19g | Saturated Fat: 6g | Cholesterol: 337mg | Protein: 13g | Sodium: 129mg | Potassium: 730mg | Fiber: 3g | Carbohydrates: 40g | Sugar: 4g

VEGETABLE CALZONES

Calzones are stuffed pizzas; they are usually made with pie crust or pizza dough. This recipe uses your own homemade Flaky Crescent Rolls (Chapter 2) for a wonderful flaky crust and great flavor. You can use any of your favorite vegetables in this simple recipe. Have the kids help; they love to work with dough!

YIELDS 9 CALZONES

½ recipe Flaky Crescent Rolls (Chapter 2)

2 tablespoons unsalted butter

1 medium onion, chopped

4 cloves garlic, minced

1 (8-ounce) package mushrooms, sliced

1 carrot, sliced ⅛" thick

1 medium yellow bell pepper, chopped

1 medium red bell pepper, chopped

⅔ cup mascarpone cheese

2 tablespoons grated Parmesan cheese

1 tablespoon grated lemon zest

1 teaspoon dried thyme leaves

¼ teaspoon black pepper

1 large egg, beaten

1. Prepare the crescent roll dough; divide in thirds, cover, and refrigerate while preparing filling.

2. In large saucepan, melt butter over medium heat. Add onion, garlic, mushrooms, and carrot; cook and stir until tender, about 8–10 minutes.

3. Add yellow bell pepper and red bell pepper; cook for another 3 minutes, stirring occasionally. Remove from heat and place in large bowl. Let cool for 30 minutes.

4. Add mascarpone, Parmesan cheese, lemon zest, thyme, and pepper to vegetables and mix well. Preheat oven to 375°F.

5. Divide each dough third into thirds again so you have nine balls. Roll out each ball to a 7" round. Top each round with scant ½ cup of vegetable mixture; fold dough over and seal edges with a fork. Prick the top of the calzones with a fork.

6. Place calzones on a cookie sheet and brush with beaten egg. Bake for 25–35 minutes or until golden brown.

PER SERVING: Calories: 312 | Total Fat: 16g | Saturated Fat: 9g | Cholesterol: 100mg | Protein: 9g | Sodium: 79mg | Potassium: 292mg | Fiber: 1g | Carbohydrates: 32g | Sugar: 6g

VEGGIE LOAF

This vegetarian "meat" loaf is delicious and packed full of fiber and flavor. This is delicious served with Scalloped Potatoes (Chapter 13) and a fruit salad.

SERVES 6

1 ounce dried shiitake mushrooms

1 ounce dried portobello mushrooms

1 cup warm water

2 tablespoons olive oil

1 medium onion, chopped

1 (8-ounce) package cremini mushrooms, finely chopped

1 medium red bell pepper, minced

4 cloves garlic, minced

3 slices French Bread (Chapter 2), crumbled

1 cup cooked brown rice

¾ cup toasted chopped walnuts

2 tablespoons no-salt-added tomato paste

¼ cup Mustard (Chapter 4), divided

1 teaspoon dried marjoram leaves

2 large eggs, beaten

¼ cup mascarpone cheese

¼ cup grated Parmesan cheese

1. In medium bowl, combine both kinds of dried mushrooms and warm water; let stand for 30 minutes. Drain, reserving ⅓ cup soaking liquid. Remove stems from reconstituted mushrooms and discard; finely chop caps.

2. Preheat oven to 350°F. In large skillet, heat olive oil over medium heat. Add onion and cremini mushrooms; cook, stirring occasionally, until the mushrooms give up their liquid and the liquid evaporates.

3. Add reconstituted mushroom caps, red bell pepper, and garlic to skillet; cook and stir for another 3–4 minutes.

4. Transfer mixture from skillet to large bowl; let cool for 20 minutes.

5. Add bread crumbs, rice, walnuts, tomato paste, 2 tablespoons mustard, marjoram, eggs, mascarpone cheese, and Parmesan cheese to the vegetables and mix well.

6. Coat a 9" × 5" loaf pan with nonstick cooking spray. Add the vegetable mixture and press down gently; smooth the top with the back of a spoon. Spread top with remaining 2 tablespoons mustard.

7. Bake veggie loaf for 40–50 minutes or until a thermometer registers 165°F. Let stand for 10 minutes, then cut into slices to serve.

PER SERVING: Calories: 237 | Total Fat: 11g | Saturated Fat: 3g | Cholesterol: 79mg | Protein: 9g | Sodium: 118mg | Potassium: 470mg | Fiber: 2g | Carbohydrates: 25g | Sugar: 2g

SCRAMBLED EGG SPINACH SALAD

Spinach salad with egg is usually made with bacon. We'll use deeply browned mushrooms, called duxelles, instead. When mushrooms are cooked until very dark, they develop a meaty taste that is an excellent substitute for meat and salt. Serve this salad with a glass of white wine and some Garlic Bread (Chapter 6).

SERVES 4

¼ cup olive oil, divided

3 large eggs, beaten

2 tablespoons heavy cream

1 cup chopped cremini mushrooms

¼ cup sliced green onion

3 cloves garlic, sliced

10 cups baby spinach

2 tablespoons apple cider vinegar

2 tablespoons honey

1 tablespoon water

¼ teaspoon pepper

1. In large saucepan, heat 1 tablespoon olive oil. Beat eggs with cream in a small bowl; add to saucepan. Cook until eggs are done, stirring occasionally. Remove from pan and set aside in serving bowl; wipe out saucepan.

2. Add 3 tablespoons olive oil to the saucepan. Add mushrooms; cook and stir until the mushrooms give up their liquid and the liquid evaporates. Continue cooking for another 7–8 minutes. When mushrooms are deep golden brown, add green onion and garlic; cook for 1 minute longer. Using a slotted spoon, add to eggs in serving bowl. Top with spinach.

3. Carefully add vinegar, honey, water, and pepper to drippings remaining in pan; bring to a boil. Pour over the spinach mixture and toss to coat. Serve immediately.

PER SERVING: Calories: 260 | Total Fat: 20g | Saturated Fat: 4g | Cholesterol: 168mg | Protein: 7g | Sodium: 117mg | Potassium: 607mg | Fiber: 2g | Carbohydrates: 14g | Sugar: 9g

EGG AND POTATO SCRAMBLE

Small red potatoes cook very quickly, and they are delicious scrambled with fluffy eggs. This recipe usually has bacon, but we'll use mushrooms instead for a meaty flavor. Serve with freshly squeezed orange juice, hot coffee, and some Raisin Bread (Chapter 2), toasted and spread with unsalted butter.

SERVES 6

1 pound small red potatoes, cut in half

2 tablespoons water

2 tablespoons unsalted butter

1 cup sliced mushrooms

¼ cup sliced green onions

2 cloves garlic, minced

8 large eggs

½ cup whole milk

½ teaspoon dried thyme leaves

⅛ teaspoon pepper

3 tablespoons grated Parmesan cheese

1. In 2-quart microwave safe dish, place potatoes. Add water and partially cover. Microwave on high power for 6–9 minutes or until potatoes are almost tender; drain well.

2. In large skillet, melt butter over medium heat. Add mushrooms; cook and stir until mushrooms give up their liquid and the liquid evaporates, about 8 minutes. Cook until mushrooms start to brown.

3. Add potatoes, green onions, and garlic to skillet. Cook and stir for 4–5 minutes longer, until potatoes start to brown.

4. In large bowl, beat eggs with milk, thyme, and pepper. Add to skillet; cook, stirring occasionally, until eggs are set but still shiny.

5. Sprinkle with cheese and serve immediately.

PER SERVING: Calories: 223 | Total Fat: 12g | Saturated Fat: 5g | Cholesterol: 295mg | Protein: 12g | Sodium: 139mg | Potassium: 574mg | Fiber: 1g | Carbohydrates: 17g | Sugar: 2g

MUSHROOM FRITTATA

You can use any vegetables you'd like in this simple recipe. Look for more unusual mushrooms in the grocery store. You can often find cremini mushrooms, which are baby portobellos, along with dried wild mushrooms, chanterelles, and shiitake mushrooms.

SERVES 4

2 tablespoons olive oil

1 tablespoon unsalted butter

1 medium onion, chopped

2 cups mixed variety sliced mushrooms

2 cloves garlic, minced

9 large eggs

¼ cup whole milk

½ teaspoon dried marjoram leaves

⅛ teaspoon white pepper

2 tablespoons grated Parmesan cheese

1. In a 10" nonstick skillet with an ovenproof handle (or wrap foil around a wooden handle), heat olive oil with butter over medium heat.

2. Add onion; cook and stir for 3 minutes. Then add mushrooms; cook and stir until they give up their liquid and the liquid evaporates. Add garlic; cook for another minute.

3. In large bowl, beat eggs with milk, marjoram, and pepper. Add to the skillet with the vegetables.

4. Cook, lifting the edge of the frittata as it cooks to let uncooked egg flow underneath, until the bottom is golden brown and the edges start to puff.

5. While the frittata is cooking on the stovetop, preheat oven to broil.

6. Sprinkle frittata with cheese and broil 6" from heat for 8–12 minutes, watching carefully, until the frittata is puffed and light golden brown. Cut into wedges to serve.

PER SERVING: Calories: 187 | Total Fat: 14g | Saturated Fat: 5g | Cholesterol: 325mg | Protein: 11g | Sodium: 137mg | Potassium: 255mg | Fiber: 0g | Carbohydrates: 2g | Sugar: 0g

SPANISH OMELET

A Spanish omelet, also known as Tortilla Española, is made with potatoes, onions, and eggs. Many recipes add chorizo, a spicy sausage that is very high in sodium and obviously not vegetarian. We'll use our trusty mushrooms instead to add a meaty taste. Serve with a glass of red wine and a green salad.

SERVES 6

2 large russet potatoes

2 tablespoons olive oil

1 medium onion, chopped

1 cup chopped cremini mushrooms

3 cloves garlic, minced

8 large eggs

¼ cup light cream

⅛ teaspoon pepper

1. Peel the potatoes and thinly slice crosswise. Place in a bowl of ice water as you work. When both the potatoes are sliced, pat dry with kitchen towels.

2. In 10" nonstick skillet, heat the olive oil over medium heat. Add onion and mushrooms and cook, stirring occasionally, until the mushrooms give up their liquid and the liquid evaporates. Continue to cook until mushrooms are browned.

3. Add garlic; cook for 1 minute longer. Remove skillet from heat and remove vegetables from skillet.

4. Layer half of the sliced potatoes in the skillet. Top with the onion mixture, then the remaining potatoes. Press down with a spatula.

5. Beat eggs, cream, and pepper in a large bowl. Pour slowly over the potatoes in the pan, giving the egg time to seep down through the layers.

6. Return the pan to the heat. Cook over medium-low heat for 15–20 minutes, pulling up the edges with a spatula so uncooked egg can run underneath. When the mixture is almost set, preheat broiler.

7. Broil the omelet for 5–6 minutes or until the top starts to turn golden brown. Serve hot or at room temperature.

PER SERVING: Calories: 217 | Total Fat: 14g | Saturated Fat: 4g | Cholesterol: 293mg | Protein: 10g | Sodium: 100mg | Potassium: 347mg | Fiber: 1g | Carbohydrates: 12g | Sugar: 1g

SPANAKO-PITAS

Spanakopita is a Greek dish made by layering phyllo dough with butter, then sandwiching a filling of spinach, feta cheese, and onion in between. Let's omit the phyllo altogether, and use pita breads to hold a Greek-flavored spinach filling!

SERVES 4–6

4 Pita Breads (Chapter 2), cut in half

1 tablespoon extra-virgin olive oil

1 tablespoon unsalted butter

1 medium onion, chopped

3 cloves garlic, minced

3 tablespoons lemon juice, divided

4 cups baby spinach leaves

½ cup chopped flat-leaf parsley

2 tablespoons chopped fresh mint leaves

3 hard-cooked eggs, chopped

½ cup ricotta cheese

2 tablespoons crumbled feta cheese

½ teaspoon grated lemon zest

1. Prepare the pita breads, cool, and cut in half crosswise. Open the pocket in the center, then set aside.

2. In medium saucepan, heat olive oil and butter over medium heat. Add onion and garlic; cook and stir until the onion starts to turn golden around the edges, about 8–10 minutes. Remove from heat and stir in 2 tablespoons lemon juice.

3. Meanwhile, combine spinach, parsley, and mint in large bowl. Add the hot onion mixture and toss to coat; the spinach will wilt slightly. Add eggs and toss.

4. In small bowl, combine ricotta, feta, remaining 1 tablespoon lemon juice, and lemon zest and mix well. Spread this mixture inside the pita breads.

5. Add the spinach mixture to the pita breads and serve immediately.

PER SERVING: Calories: 252 | Total Fat: 13g | Saturated Fat: 5g | Cholesterol: 125mg | Protein: 10g | Sodium: 130mg | Potassium: 232mg | Fiber: 2g | Carbohydrates: 23g | Sugar: 1g

WHITE BEAN–STUFFED PEPPERS

This recipe uses white beans, brown rice, and kale to increase the nutritional value of the recipe and add lots of flavor. Lemon juice, dill, and onion add even more flavor. Serve this with a fruit salad and a nice glass of white wine or a cold beer.

SERVES 6

6 medium red or yellow bell peppers

½ cup brown rice

1 cup Vegetable Broth (Chapter 5)

2 tablespoons olive oil

1 medium onion, chopped

4 cloves garlic, minced

3 cups chopped kale

2 tablespoons water

1 (14-ounce) can no-salt-added cannellini beans, rinsed and drained

½ cup ricotta cheese

2 tablespoons lemon juice

½ teaspoon grated lemon zest

1 teaspoon dried dill weed

⅛ teaspoon white pepper

1. Cut the tops off the bell peppers and set aside. Chop the flesh around the stem. Remove and discard the seeds and membranes from inside the peppers.

2. Combine rice and vegetable broth in a small pan. Cover and bring to a simmer. Simmer on low for 20–30 minutes or until the rice is tender. Drain if necessary and set aside.

3. In large skillet, heat olive oil over medium heat. Add onion and garlic; cook and stir until tender, about 6–8 minutes. Add reserved chopped bell pepper tops; cook and stir for another 2 minutes.

4. Add kale and water; cover and steam until kale is wilted, stirring occasionally, about 3–4 minutes. Drain.

5. Remove pan from heat and stir in rice, beans, ricotta, lemon juice, zest, dill weed, and white pepper. Stuff peppers with this mixture.

6. Preheat oven to 375°F. Place peppers in a baking dish and add ½ cup water to the dish. Cover and bake for 30 minutes, then remove cover and bake until peppers are tender, about 10–15 minutes longer.

PER SERVING: Calories: 301 | Total Fat: 8g | Saturated Fat: 2g | Cholesterol: 10mg | Protein: 13g | Sodium: 53mg | Potassium: 1,035mg | Fiber: 7g | Carbohydrates: 45g | Sugar: 0g

MUSHROOM BROTH

This simple broth can add amazing flavor to so many of your dishes. Use it in Mushroom Risotto (see recipe in this chapter) to up the mushroom goodness or any of your recipes that call for a veggie broth for an extra punch of flavor.

SERVES 8

4 medium carrots, washed and cut into large pieces

2 large leeks, well-cleaned and cut into large pieces

2 large sweet onions, quartered

1 stalk celery, chopped

5 whole cloves

Pinch dried red pepper flakes

2 cups sliced fresh button or other fresh mushrooms

9 cups water

1. Put all the ingredients in a large pot and bring to a boil; reduce heat and simmer, covered, for 45 minutes.

2. Strain the broth for a clear stock. You can refrigerate the broth for up to 2 or 3 days, or freeze for up to 3 months.

PER SERVING: Calories: 5 | Total Fat: 0g | Saturated Fat: 0g | Cholesterol: 0mg | Protein: 0g | Sodium: 5mg | Potassium: 0mg | Fiber: 0g | Carbohydrates: 0g | Sugar: 0g

SWEET POTATO FRITTATA

Sweet potatoes are delicious when cooked until caramelized, then folded into an egg mixture and cooked on the stovetop. Fresh thyme and caramelized leek add lots of flavor and interest to this simple dish. This frittata is wonderful served with orange juice and coffee, and some sweet rolls for brunch.

SERVES 8

2 tablespoons olive oil

1 leek, chopped

1 large sweet potato, peeled and cubed

2 cloves garlic, minced

9 large eggs

¼ cup light cream

1 tablespoon minced fresh thyme leaves

⅛ teaspoon pepper

⅓ cup shredded mozzarella cheese

1. In 10" nonstick ovenproof skillet, heat olive oil over medium heat. Add leek and sweet potato. Cook, stirring frequently, until vegetables soften and start to turn brown, about 10–12 minutes. When they are tender, add the garlic and cook for 1 minute longer.

2. In large bowl, beat eggs with cream, thyme, and pepper. Add to skillet.

3. Cook the frittata over medium heat, lifting edges so uncooked egg flows underneath, until the bottom is golden and edges are puffy, about 8–10 minutes.

4. Preheat broiler. Top frittata with cheese and place 6" from heat source. Broil for 9–10 minutes, watching carefully, until the top is golden and the frittata is puffed. Serve immediately.

PER SERVING: Calories: 168 | Total Fat: 12g | Saturated Fat: 4g | Cholesterol: 249mg | Protein: 8g | Sodium: 117mg | Potassium: 154mg | Fiber: 0g | Carbohydrates: 6g | Sugar: 2g

BROCCOLI QUICHE

This crustless wonder is just as delicious as a traditional egg pie, but much easier to make. Lots of fresh broccoli, onion, and garlic add flavor to this classic recipe. Let the quiche stand for a few minutes after it comes out of the oven to firm up a bit and so the wedges cut perfectly. Serve with a green salad.

SERVES 8

2 tablespoons olive oil

1 medium onion, chopped

2 cloves garlic, minced

2 cups broccoli florets

2 tablespoons water

5 large eggs, beaten

1¼ cups almond milk or regular whole milk

1 tablespoon flour

1 teaspoon dried thyme leaves

⅛ teaspoon white pepper

1 cup shredded mozzarella cheese

1. Preheat oven to 375°F. In large skillet, heat olive oil over medium heat. Add onion and garlic; cook and stir until tender, about 6–7 minutes.

2. Add broccoli; cook and stir for 2 minutes. Add water to pan, cover, and steam until broccoli is tender, about 3–4 minutes. Drain well.

3. Spray a 9" pie pan with nonstick baking spray containing flour. Arrange vegetables in the pan.

4. In medium bowl, combine eggs, milk, flour, thyme, and pepper and mix well. Slowly pour over vegetables in pan. Top with cheese.

5. Bake for 30–40 minutes or until the quiche is set and the top is starting to brown. Let cool for 5 minutes, then cut into wedges to serve.

PER SERVING: Calories: 150 | Total Fat: 10g | Saturated Fat: 4g | Cholesterol: 147mg | Protein: 9g | Sodium: 138mg | Potassium: 174mg | Fiber: 0g | Carbohydrates: 4g | Sugar: 2g

SWEET POTATO RED PEPPER PIZZA

Roasted red peppers combined with sweet potatoes makes a wonderful pizza that is delicious served with a cold glass of beer. Pizzas don't need much cheese to taste good, which is good news for those on low-sodium diets. Make your own pizza crust to ensure that this recipe is healthy.

SERVES 4–6

1 Pizza Crust (Chapter 2), prebaked

1 large red bell pepper

2 tablespoons olive oil

1 medium onion, chopped

1 large sweet potato, peeled and cubed

⅓ cup ricotta cheese

1 tablespoon lemon juice

½ teaspoon grated lemon zest

1 tablespoon chopped fresh thyme leaves

½ cup shredded mozzarella cheese

2 tablespoons grated Parmesan cheese

1. Preheat oven to 400°F. Prebake the pizza crust for 5 minutes or until set. Remove from oven and set aside.

2. Preheat the broiler. Cut the bell pepper in half; remove seeds and membranes. Place on broiler pan, skin-side up. Broil the pepper until the skin starts to blacken. Place the pepper in a plastic bag; close bag and let steam for 4 minutes. Remove skin from pepper. Cut pepper into strips. Turn oven back to 400°F.

3. In large pan, heat olive oil over medium heat. Add onion and sweet potato; cook, stirring occasionally, until vegetables are tender, about 9–10 minutes.

4. In small bowl, mix ricotta with lemon juice, zest, and thyme; spread over crust. Top with sweet-potato mixture and bell pepper strips. Top with mozzarella and Parmesan cheese.

5. Bake pizza for 15–20 minutes or until the crust is deep golden brown and the cheese melts and starts to brown.

PER SERVING: Calories: 273 | Total Fat: 10g | Saturated Fat: 2g | Cholesterol: 8mg | Protein: 8g | Sodium: 125mg | Potassium: 208mg | Fiber: 2g | Carbohydrates: 37g | Sugar: 2g

SLOPPY TOFU SANDWICHES WITH ZIPPY COLESLAW

Tofu makes a remarkable substitute for ground beef in this easy recipe. Serve on your own homemade hamburger buns that have been split, spread with unsalted butter, and toasted. Some steamed carrots, a green salad, and some brownies will finish off this meal.

SERVES 4

1 (12-ounce) package firm tofu

2 tablespoons olive oil

1 medium onion, chopped

2 cloves garlic, sliced

1 cup chopped mushrooms

2 tablespoons no-salt-added tomato paste

½ cup Easy Homemade Ketchup (Chapter 4)

¼ cup Mustard (Chapter 4)

¼ cup water

2 tablespoons lemon juice

2 tablespoons brown sugar

⅛ teaspoon pepper

4 Hamburger Buns (Chapter 2), split and toasted

1½ cups Zippy Coleslaw (Chapter 3)

1. Remove tofu from package and drain. Place tofu between layers of paper towel and press down firmly to remove water. Crumble the tofu coarsely.

2. Heat olive oil in large nonstick pan over medium heat. Add onion, garlic, and mushrooms; cook until mushrooms give up their liquid and the liquid evaporates.

3. Add tofu; cook, stirring frequently, until tofu and vegetables start to brown, about 8–9 minutes.

4. Add tomato paste to pan; let brown in a few spots. Then stir in the ketchup, mustard, water, lemon juice, brown sugar, and pepper. Simmer for 5 minutes, stirring frequently.

5. Make sandwiches with the hamburger buns, tofu mixture, and slaw.

PER SERVING: Calories: 629 | Total Fat: 30g | Saturated Fat: 5g | Cholesterol: 40mg | Protein: 18g | Sodium: 20mg | Potassium: 626mg | Fiber: 6g | Carbohydrates: 73g | Sugar: 24g

VEGETABLE RISOTTO

You can make risotto with just about any veggie—but try this combo at least once. Leeks, mushrooms, spinach, and asparagus are a delicious combination. If you'd like, substitute ½ cup white wine for some of the broth.

SERVES 4

3½ cups Vegetable Broth (Chapter 5)

2 tablespoons unsalted butter

1 leek, chopped

1 cup sliced mushrooms

3 cloves garlic, minced

1¼ cups Arborio rice

½ teaspoon dried thyme leaves

⅛ teaspoon white pepper

½ pound asparagus, cut into 2" lengths

2 cups baby spinach leaves

2 tablespoons grated Parmesan cheese

1. Put the broth in a medium saucepan and warm over low heat.

2. In a large saucepan, melt butter over medium heat. Add leek and mushrooms to butter; cook, stirring occasionally, until vegetables are almost tender, about 6 minutes.

3. Add garlic, rice, thyme and white pepper to the vegetables; cook and stir for 2 minutes.

4. Add ½ cup of broth at a time, stirring frequently, until the broth is absorbed and liquid is tender. If you like a runnier risotto, add more liquid.

5. Add the asparagus and spinach to the risotto; cook for 2 minutes.

6. Stir in the cheese; cover and remove from heat. Let stand for 3 minutes, then stir again and serve immediately.

PER SERVING: Calories: 356 | Total Fat: 8g | Saturated Fat: 4g | Cholesterol: 17mg | Protein: 12g | Sodium: 121mg | Potassium: 522mg | Fiber: 2g | Carbohydrates: 58g | Sugar: 1g

CAULIFLOWER PATTIES WITH CORN COMPOTE

Not everyone loves cauliflower, although it's nutty with a wonderful texture: crunchy when raw, tender when cooked. Turn it into some golden patties with a corn compote, and everyone will love it! The compote can be served with other recipes too—try it on top of a stew or on a frittata just out of the oven.

SERVES 4

1 tablespoon olive oil

2 cups frozen corn kernels, thawed and drained

1 medium red bell pepper, chopped

2 cloves garlic, sliced

1 medium tomato, seeded and chopped

1 head cauliflower

2 large eggs

¼ cup ricotta cheese

⅓ cup shredded Swiss cheese

2 tablespoons grated Parmesan cheese

2 slices French Bread (Chapter 2), crumbled

½ teaspoon dried dill weed

⅛ teaspoon black pepper

2 tablespoons unsalted butter

1. In medium skillet, heat olive oil over medium heat. Add corn, bell pepper, and garlic; cook, stirring occasionally, until tender, about 5 minutes. Add tomato; cook for another 3 minutes. Remove from heat and set aside.

2. Cut the florets off the cauliflower and place in a microwave-safe dish. Peel the stems and chop into 1" pieces; add to florets in dish. Add water; cover and microwave for 8 minutes or until cauliflower is tender. Drain well.

3. Transfer cauliflower to bowl and coarsely mash. Stir in eggs, ricotta, Swiss cheese, Parmesan cheese, bread crumbs, dill weed, and pepper; mix well. Form into 8 patties.

4. Heat butter in large nonstick skillet over medium heat. Add the patties and cook in the butter, turning once, until golden brown, about 7–8 minutes total.

5. Place patties on a serving plate and top with the corn mixture.

PER SERVING: Calories: 336 | Total Fat: 118g | Saturated Fat: 8g | Cholesterol: 139mg | Protein: 14g | Sodium: 140mg | Potassium: 482mg | Fiber: 5g | Carbohydrates: 33g | Sugar: 7g

BLACK BEAN CAKES WITH CORN RELISH

Black beans can be made into delicious patties that are crisp on the outside and tender on the inside. Add corn relish for a wonderful dish that provides complete protein, something vegetarians need. Serve this dish with a green salad and some sparkling water.

SERVES 4

2 cups frozen corn, thawed and drained

1 large tomato, seeded and chopped

½ cup chopped red onion

¼ cup honey

¼ cup apple cider vinegar

½ teaspoon celery seed

¼ cup olive oil, divided

2 shallots, minced

3 cloves garlic, minced

2 (15-ounce) cans no-salt-added black beans, rinsed and drained

3 slices French Bread (Chapter 2), crumbled

2 large eggs

¼ cup flour

2 tablespoons chopped flat-leaf parsley

½ teaspoon dried marjoram leaves

⅛ teaspoon pepper

1. In medium saucepan over medium heat, combine corn, tomato, red onion, honey, vinegar, and celery seed. Bring to a simmer. Reduce heat to low and simmer for 15 minutes, stirring occasionally. Remove from heat and set aside.

2. In small saucepan, heat 1 tablespoon olive oil over medium heat. Add shallots and garlic; cook, stirring frequently, until tender, about 4 minutes. Remove to large bowl.

3. Add the black beans and mash with a potato masher, leaving some texture. Add bread crumbs, eggs, flour, parsley, marjoram, and pepper and mix well. Form into 8 patties.

4. In large nonstick skillet, heat remaining 3 tablespoons olive oil over medium heat. Add black bean patties; cook, turning once, until the patties are crisp, about 6–8 minutes total.

5. Remove patties to serving platter, top with corn relish, and serve.

PER SERVING: Calories: 559 | Total Fat: 4g | Saturated Fat: 1g | Cholesterol: 105mg | Protein: 27g | Sodium: 67mg | Potassium: 1,079mg | Fiber: 22g | Carbohydrates: 107g | Sugar: 22g

CHICKPEA LENTIL STEW

Chickpeas and lentils is another great combination that provides complete protein. Chickpeas are meaty and nutty tasting, with a slightly chewy texture, and lentils are nutty and sweet and tender. Combine them in a stew that is rich with vegetables for a hearty recipe that will warm you up on the coldest winter day.

SERVES 6

1 tablespoon olive oil

1 medium onion, chopped

2 cloves garlic, minced

1 tablespoon grated fresh ginger root

2 medium carrots, sliced

3 tablespoons no-salt-added tomato paste

2 teaspoons curry powder

3 cups Vegetable Broth (Chapter 5)

2 (15-ounce) cans no-salt-added chickpeas

⅔ cup Puy lentils, sorted and rinsed

1 (14-ounce) can no-salt-added diced tomatoes, undrained

⅓ cup chopped flat-leaf parsley

1 teaspoon grated lemon zest

1. In large pot, heat olive oil over medium heat. Add onion, garlic, and ginger root; cook and stir for 4 minutes. Add carrots; cook and stir for 2 minutes.

2. Add tomato paste; let it turn brown in a few spots, then stir. Add the curry powder; cook for 2 minutes.

3. Add broth and stir well to remove pan drippings. Add chickpeas and lentils and bring to a simmer. Reduce heat to low and simmer for 45 minutes or until lentils are almost tender.

4. Add tomatoes; simmer for another 15–20 minutes or until lentils are tender.

5. Meanwhile, combine parsley and lemon zest in a small bowl. Serve the stew with the parsley mixture as a garnish.

PER SERVING: Calories: 330 | Total Fat: 7g | Saturated Fat: 0g | Cholesterol: 0mg | Protein: 18g | Sodium: 80mg | Potassium: 918mg | Fiber: 14g | Carbohydrates: 52g | Sugar: 11g

MUSHROOM PAELLA

Saffron is the key to paella. It's very expensive; in fact, it's the world's most expensive legal crop. But you only need a tiny pinch to add indescribable flavor and beautiful color to this dish.

SERVES 6

Pinch saffron threads

¼ cup water

2 tablespoons olive oil

1 medium onion, chopped

1 leek, chopped

4 cloves garlic, minced

1 cup sliced cremini mushrooms

1 cup sliced button mushrooms

1 cup sliced shiitake mushrooms

1¼ cups brown rice

2½ cups Vegetable Broth (Chapter 5)

1 bay leaf

1 teaspoon dried thyme leaves

1 cup frozen peas, thawed

1. In small bowl, combine saffron threads and water; set aside.

2. In large skillet, heat olive oil over medium heat. Add onion, leek, and garlic; cook and stir until tender, about 6 minutes.

3. Add all of the mushrooms; cook and stir until mushrooms give up their liquid and the liquid evaporates, about 8–9 minutes.

4. Add rice to skillet; cook for 2 minutes, stirring frequently.

5. Add the broth, saffron in water, bay leaf, and thyme to the skillet. Bring to a simmer. Reduce heat to low, cover, and simmer for 30–40 minutes or until rice is tender and liquid is absorbed. Stir.

6. Stir in the peas; cover and let stand for 3 minutes. Remove and discard bay leaf, and serve.

PER SERVING: Calories: 255 | Total Fat: 6g | Saturated Fat: 1g | Cholesterol: 0mg | Protein: 7g | Sodium: 43mg | Potassium: 470mg | Fiber: 4g | Carbohydrates: 43g | Sugar: 6g

FRIED TOFU "FILLETS"

Regular tofu (also called Chinese-style tofu or bean curd) is more common than its softer cousin silken tofu. Firm tofu usually comes in a plastic container in the refrigerator or produce section of your grocery store and must be kept refrigerated.

SERVES 4

1 (19-ounce) block firm tofu

¼ cup nonfat, low-sodium chicken-flavored broth

¼ teaspoon low-sodium Worcestershire sauce

¼ teaspoon Bragg Liquid Aminos

Optional: A few dashes of hot pepper sauce

1 tablespoon water

1 tablespoon unbleached all-purpose flour

2 teaspoons masa harina or cornmeal

1 teaspoon white rice flour

¼ teaspoon dried basil

¼ teaspoon dried rosemary

Pinch dried sage

Pinch dried marjoram

Pinch dried thyme

Pinch dried oregano

1 large egg

2 teaspoons olive or canola oil

1. Slice the tofu into 4 equal pieces. Place the slices between layers of paper towels and fold the towels over in both directions to cover the tofu. Place a baking sheet on top of the tofu and weigh it down with a cast iron skillet or similar weight for 1 hour.

2. In a casserole dish wide enough to hold the tofu slices side by side, combine the broth, Worcestershire sauce, liquid aminos, hot pepper sauce, if using, and water. Place the tofu into the broth marinade; marinate for 15 minutes on each side.

3. Place the flour, masa harina or cornmeal, and rice flour into a shallow dish and mix until combined. Mix together the basil, rosemary, sage, marjoram, thyme, and oregano; grind using a spice grinder or a mortar and pestle, then add to the flour mixture and mix well. In a small bowl, beat the egg until frothy.

4. Heat the oil in a nonstick skillet over medium-high heat.

5. Remove the tofu from the broth marinade and drain on paper towels to remove any excess marinade.

6. Lightly dredge the tofu in the flour mixture, knocking off any excess flour. Dip the floured slices into the eggs until completely, but thinly, coated on both sides.

7. Gently place the tofu in the skillet and fry for 2 minutes per side, until golden brown.

PER SERVING: Calories: 170 | Total Fat: 9g | Saturated Fat: 1g | Cholesterol: 52mg | Protein: 14g | Sodium: 51mg | Potassium: 40mg | Fiber: 1g | Carbohydrates: 7g | Sugar: 0g

PASTA IN MUSHROOM ALFREDO-STYLE SAUCE

For a creamy tomato sauce, sauté 1 or 2 tablespoons of tomato paste along with the onions and garlic. If using the tomato paste, add a pinch each of sugar and baking soda and stir well before adding the milk; this helps cut the acidity of the tomato and prevents the milk from curdling.

SERVES 4

1 teaspoon extra-virgin olive oil

1 teaspoon unsalted butter

2 cups sliced button or cremini mushrooms

1 small onion, minced

4 cloves garlic, minced

2 teaspoons unbleached all-purpose flour

½ teaspoon basil or an herb seasoning blend

¼ teaspoon freshly ground black pepper

2 pinches dried red pepper flakes, divided

Pinch ground nutmeg

⅛ cup skim milk

2 cups nonfat cottage cheese

¼ cup grated Parmesan cheese

8 ounces dry oat bran or whole-wheat pasta

2 tablespoons fresh lemon juice

1 teaspoon dried parsley

Optional: 4 teaspoons chopped unsalted, dry-roasted peanuts

1. In deep nonstick skillet, heat the olive oil and butter over medium-high heat. Add the mushrooms and sauté for 2 minutes. Add the onion and garlic; sauté for 2 minutes or until the onion is transparent. Stir often to prevent the garlic from burning.

2. Sprinkle the flour over the mushroom mixture. Cook for 1 minute, stirring well so the flour absorbs any liquid and oil and makes a light roux. Add the basil, pepper, 1 pinch of the red pepper flakes, and the nutmeg; stir to combine.

3. Add the milk and stir to loosen the roux. Add the cottage cheese. (For a smoother sauce, purée the cottage cheese in a blender or food processor before adding it to the pan.) Cook and stir until the sauce is thickened and smooth. Add all but 4 teaspoons of the grated Parmesan cheese and stir well.

4. Lower the heat and keep the sauce warm while the pasta cooks. Consult the package directions for the amount of water and cooking time for the pasta. Add the lemon juice and the remaining dash of red pepper flakes to the boiling water, then add the pasta. Cook until al dente, then drain well. Toss the drained pasta with the sauce. Sprinkle with the parsley and the reserved Parmesan cheese. Top each serving with 1 teaspoon chopped peanuts, if desired.

PER SERVING: Calories: 286 | Total Fat: 5g | Saturated Fat: 2g | Cholesterol: 11mg | Protein: 22g | Sodium: 106mg | Potassium: 356mg | Fiber: 6g | Carbohydrates: 40g | Sugar: 5g

CASHEW CORN CHOWDER

This yummy low-sodium chowder is a little different from the standard variety but no less delicious and creamy. Pair this with some Cornbread (Chapter 2) for a warm and comforting meal.

SERVES 4

4 teaspoons canola oil

1 large sweet onion, chopped

4 stalks celery, chopped

1 medium-size sweet potato, peeled and diced

3 cloves garlic, minced

1 tablespoon unbleached all-purpose flour

6 cups water

1 (10-ounce) package frozen sweet corn, thawed

1 small red bell pepper, seeded and diced

1 small green bell pepper, seeded and diced

½ cup no-salt-added roasted cashew butter

1 tablespoon fresh lime juice

1 teaspoon dried cilantro, crushed

1/16 teaspoon cayenne

⅛ teaspoon freshly ground black pepper

1. Heat the oil in a large saucepan on medium-high. Add the onions and celery; sauté for 3–4 minutes, stirring frequently. Add the sweet potatoes; sauté for 1–2 minutes, mixing them in with the other vegetables. Add the garlic and sauté for 1 minute.

2. Lower the heat to medium and stir in the flour. Continue to stir for 5 minutes to completely cook the flour. Add the water and bring to a boil; reduce the heat, cover the pot, and simmer for 40 minutes or until the sweet potatoes are completely tender. Stir well, mashing the sweet potatoes somewhat with the back of a spoon, or use a hand blender to cream the soup.

3. Stir in the corn. Return the cover to the pan and simmer for 20 more minutes.

4. Add the bell peppers; cover and simmer for 5 minutes. Add the cashew butter, stirring to blend it completely. Stir in the lime juice, cilantro, cayenne, and pepper. Serve warm.

PER SERVING: Calories: 385 | Total Fat: 21g | Saturated Fat: 3g | Cholesterol: 0mg | Protein: 10g | Sodium: 85mg | Potassium: 781mg | Fiber: 6g | Carbohydrates: 45g | Sugar: 10g

BLACK BEAN CHILI

Using a combination of chili powders such as ancho, chipotle, or specialty salt-free chili powder blends in this recipe is an easy way to add layers of flavor. You can also substitute chunk pineapple canned in its own juice if fresh pineapple isn't available, or substitute 1 cup of fresh orange juice instead.

SERVES 8

1½ cups dried black beans

2 tablespoons canola oil

2 large sweet onions, chopped

5 medium-size cloves garlic, minced

1 tablespoon ground cumin

1 tablespoon dried oregano

3 tablespoons salt-free chili powder

1 teaspoon freshly ground black pepper

1 teaspoon dried red pepper flakes

1 teaspoon grated lemon zest

3 jalapeño peppers, seeded and minced

2 (14.5-ounce) cans no-salt-added diced tomatoes

1 cup chopped fresh pineapple

4 large carrots, peeled and sliced

1 cup uncooked long-grain brown rice

1 tablespoon apple cider vinegar or red wine vinegar

Optional: Tamari sauce or Bragg Liquid Aminos

Optional: No-salt-added peanut butter or other nut butter

Optional: Freshly ground black pepper

Fresh cilantro, for garnish

1. Rinse the beans and cover them with water in a large, heavy pot. Bring to a full boil over medium-high heat, drain, and rinse again. Return the beans to the pot over medium-high heat and add 7 cups of water, or a combination of water and mushroom broth. Once the water comes to a boil, reduce heat and simmer for 1 hour.

2. While the beans cook, heat a large nonstick sauté pan over medium heat. Add the oil and onions; sauté for 4 minutes, stirring frequently. Lower the heat to medium-low. Add the garlic and sauté for 1 minute. Stir in the cumin, oregano, chili powder, pepper, red pepper flakes, lemon zest, and jalapeños; sauté for an additional 4 minutes, then add the tomatoes. Simmer for 10 minutes, stirring frequently.

3. Stir the sautéed mixture into the pot of beans. Add the pineapple, carrots, and rice. Simmer partially covered for another hour, or until the beans are soft and the rice is done. Stir in the vinegar. Have tamari sauce or liquid aminos, peanut or other nut butter, and freshly ground black pepper available at the table to flavor individual servings of the chili, if desired. Garnish with cilantro.

PER SERVING: Calories: 235 | Total Fat: 4g | Saturated Fat: 0g | Cholesterol: 0mg | Protein: 6g | Sodium: 45mg | Potassium: 648mg | Fiber: 7g | Carbohydrates: 43g | Sugar: 10g

MUSHROOM RISOTTO

This risotto can be a side dish to your favorite dish, but it is so warm, thick, and creamy that it can also be a meal all on its own.

SERVES 8

2 tablespoons olive oil

4 cloves garlic, minced

1 tablespoon minced shallot

2 cups uncooked brown Arborio or basmati rice

½ cup dry white wine

2 cups Mushroom Broth (see recipe in this chapter)

1–2 cups boiling water

2 tablespoons unsalted butter

⅛ teaspoon ground mustard

Pinch cayenne pepper

2 tablespoons grated Parmesan cheese

1. Heat a large, deep nonstick sauté pan over medium heat. Add the olive oil, garlic, and shallot and sauté for 1 minute, being careful not to burn the garlic. Add the rice and stir to coat it with the olive oil. Add the wine and bring to a simmer, reducing the heat, if necessary, to maintain a simmer.

2. Pour the mushroom broth and 1 cup of the water into a saucepan over medium heat and bring to a simmer; adjust the heat to maintain a simmer.

3. Ladle about ½ cup of the warm mushroom broth into the rice. At this point, begin stirring the rice constantly, adding more broth ½ cup at a time once the broth is absorbed into the rice. Continue to cook until the rice is al dente, using the additional cup of water, if necessary. The entire cooking process should take about 20–25 minutes.

4. Lower the heat. Add the butter, ground mustard, cayenne, and Parmesan cheese; stir rapidly to combine and melt the butter and cheese into the risotto. The rice is ready when it retains a thick, creamy consistency.

PER SERVING: Calories: 247 | Total Fat: 8g | Saturated Fat: 2g | Cholesterol: 8mg | Protein: 5g | Sodium: 45mg | Potassium: 125mg | Fiber: 2g | Carbohydrates: 35g | Sugar: 0g

CHAPTER 13

VEGETABLES AND SIDE DISHES

REFRIED BEANS

Making your own refried beans will change your Mexican recipes. Freshly made refried beans taste nothing like the canned variety. You can make this recipe as spicy or as mild as you like.

YIELDS 4 CUPS; 8 SERVINGS

2 tablespoons olive oil

1 medium onion, finely chopped

3 cloves garlic, minced

1 or 2 jalapeño peppers, finely chopped

2 (16-ounce) cans no-salt-added kidney beans, rinsed and drained

1 cup Chicken Stock (Chapter 5) or Vegetable Broth (Chapter 5)

1 tablespoon chili powder

1 teaspoon ground cumin

2 tablespoons lemon juice

¼ teaspoon black pepper

1. In large skillet, heat olive oil over medium heat. Add onion, garlic, and jalapeño pepper; cook and stir for 4–5 minutes until crisp-tender.

2. Add the kidney beans. Mash with a potato masher until the beans are as smooth as you want. You can leave some of the beans whole for more texture. Add stock or broth, stirring so the beans absorb the liquid.

3. Simmer for 5 minutes, then add the chili powder, cumin, lemon juice, and pepper and mix well. Use immediately, or cool completely, then freeze in 1 cup measures. To thaw, let stand in refrigerator for several hours.

PER SERVING: Calories: 186 | Total Fat: 4g | Saturated Fat: 0g | Cholesterol: 0mg | Protein: 10g | Sodium: 21mg | Potassium: 526mg | Fiber: 8g | Carbohydrates: 27g | Sugar: 0g

GRILLED CORN WITH HONEY BUTTER

Grilling corn is a wonderful way to bring out the vegetable's sweetness and to add a delicious layer of smoky flavor. Serve these right as they come off the grill, with the honey butter to slather on them.

SERVES 6

6 ears corn

¼ cup honey

¼ cup unsalted butter

⅛ teaspoon cinnamon

1. Prepare and preheat grill. While the grill is preheating, pull back all the leaves on the corn cobs. Remove the silk. Smooth half of the leaves back over the corn kernels; tear off and discard the outer leaves.

2. In small bowl, combine honey, butter, and cinnamon. Mix well and set aside.

3. Grill the corn 6" from medium coals for 15–20 minutes, turning frequently, until the leaves look scorched. Use a kitchen towel to peel off the remaining leaves and serve immediately with honey butter.

PER SERVING: Calories: 169 | Total Fat: 8g | Saturated Fat: 4g | Cholesterol: 20mg | Protein: 2g | Sodium: 4mg | Potassium: 168mg | Fiber: 2g | Carbohydrates: 25g | Sugar: 13g

ROASTED CAULIFLOWER WITH SMOKED PAPRIKA

Cauliflower is an elegant vegetable that isn't used as often as it should be. It is a member of the brassica family, along with broccoli and Brussels sprouts, and is a great source of nutrition. It's very high in vitamin C and fiber. Break the florets from the stem and roast them with paprika and herbs for a delicious side dish.

SERVES 4–6

1 head cauliflower, broken into small florets

3 tablespoons extra-virgin olive oil

1 tablespoon smoked paprika

1 teaspoon dried marjoram leaves

½ teaspoon dried thyme leaves

¼ teaspoon pepper

2 tablespoons lemon juice

1. Preheat oven to 425°F.

2. On a baking sheet with sides, toss cauliflower florets and olive oil. Sprinkle with paprika, marjoram, thyme, pepper, and lemon juice and toss again.

3. Roast cauliflower for 8–12 minutes or until tender and light golden. Remove from oven, transfer to serving bowl, and serve immediately.

PER SERVING: Calories: 100 | Total Fat: 7g | Saturated Fat: 0g | Cholesterol: 0mg | Protein: 3g | Sodium: 42mg | Potassium: 459mg | Fiber: 4g | Carbohydrates: 8g | Sugar: 3g

GRILLED CORN SUCCOTASH

Succotash is a southern recipe that combines corn with lima beans. This is a great recipe to make with leftover grilled corn. If you're serving four people, grill eight to ten ears of corn and save the leftovers to make this dish in the next few days. It's a great side dish to grilled steak or chicken.

SERVES 4

4 ears Grilled Corn with Honey Butter (see recipe in this chapter)

1 (16-ounce) package frozen lima beans

2 tablespoons unsalted butter

1 medium onion, chopped

3 cloves garlic, minced

1 tablespoon grated fresh ginger root

¼ teaspoon white pepper

2 tablespoons honey

1. Cut the kernels off the cob and set aside. Thaw lima beans according to package directions and drain well.

2. In skillet, melt butter over medium heat. Add onion; cook and stir for 5 minutes or until crisp-tender.

3. Add garlic and ginger root; cook for another 1 minute or until fragrant. Add the corn, beans, pepper, and honey and bring to a simmer.

4. Simmer mixture for 5–6 minutes or until vegetables are tender, stirring frequently. Serve immediately.

PER SERVING: Calories: 266 | Total Fat: 6g | Saturated Fat: 3g | Cholesterol: 15mg | Protein: 9g | Sodium: 37mg | Potassium: 657mg | Fiber: 8g | Carbohydrates: 46g | Sugar: 12g

CITRUS-GLAZED CARROTS

You can make this recipe with sliced large carrots, or with whole baby carrots, which are simply a special variety of large carrot trimmed down to a petite size.

SERVES 6

1¾ pounds large peeled carrots, sliced ¼" thick, or 2 pounds baby carrots

1 cup water

½ cup orange juice

¼ cup lemon juice

¼ cup grapefruit juice

3 tablespoons honey

2 tablespoons unsalted butter

½ teaspoon grated orange zest

½ teaspoon grated lemon zest

1. In large pot, combine carrots with water, orange juice, lemon juice, grapefruit juice, and honey. Bring to a boil over high heat.

2. Reduce heat to low and cook, stirring occasionally, until carrots are almost tender, about 5–6 minutes.

3. With a slotted spoon, remove carrots from liquid and set aside.

4. Boil the remaining liquid in the pot until it is reduced and thickens to a thin syrup.

5. Return carrots to the liquid along with butter, orange zest, and lemon zest. Simmer for 1–3 minutes or until carrots are glazed and tender. Serve immediately.

PER SERVING: Calories: 102 | Total Fat: 0g | Saturated Fat: 0g | Cholesterol: 0mg | Protein: 1g | Sodium: 92mg | Potassium: 498mg | Fiber: 3g | Carbohydrates: 25g | Sugar: 17g

COUSCOUS PILAF

Couscous is actually pasta. Just soak the couscous in boiling water or stock for about 10 minutes and it's ready to use. It's delicious in a buttery pilaf with onions, leeks, and lots of herbs.

SERVES 4

1 cup unflavored couscous

2 cups Chicken Stock or Vegetable Broth (Chapter 5)

2 tablespoons unsalted butter

1 tablespoon olive oil

1 medium onion, minced

1 leek, chopped

½ cup toasted pine nuts

2 tablespoons chopped fresh basil leaves

2 tablespoons chopped flat-leaf parsley

2 teaspoons chopped fresh mint

1. In medium bowl, place couscous. Bring stock to a boil and pour over couscous; cover bowl with a plate and set aside.

2. In large saucepan, melt butter and olive oil over medium heat. Add onion and leek; cook and stir until vegetables are tender, about 7–9 minutes.

3. Uncover couscous and fluff with a fork. Add to the onion mixture along with pine nuts. Cook and stir for 2 minutes.

4. Stir in basil, parsley, and mint and stir to combine. Serve immediately.

PER SERVING: Calories: 317 | Total Fat: 21g | Saturated Fat: 5g | Cholesterol: 15mg | Protein: 8g | Sodium: 47mg | Potassium: 315mg | Fiber: 2g | Carbohydrates: 25g | Sugar: 1g

APPLE CRANBERRY COLESLAW

Coleslaw is a bright and delicious recipe to serve at any summer meal, especially one with grilled meats. The cool flavor, crunch, and texture are a great contrast to smoky grilled steak, pork, or chicken. You can also add leftover cooked cubed meat to this recipe to make a main dish salad.

SERVES 8

1 head green cabbage, shredded

2 Granny Smith apples, shredded

¼ cup sliced green onions

⅔ cup Mayonnaise (Chapter 4)

¼ cup lemon yogurt

¼ cup apple juice

2 tablespoons honey

1 tablespoon Mustard (Chapter 4)

1 tablespoon lemon juice

1 teaspoon dried thyme leaves

⅔ cup dried cranberries

1. In large bowl, combine cabbage, apples, and green onions.

2. In small bowl, combine mayonnaise, yogurt, apple juice, honey, mustard, lemon juice, and thyme and mix well.

3. Pour over vegetables in large bowl and toss to coat. Stir in cranberries, cover, and refrigerate for 1–2 hours before serving to blend flavors.

PER SERVING: Calories: 260 | Total Fat: 16g | Saturated Fat: 2g | Cholesterol: 22mg | Protein: 3g | Sodium: 34mg | Potassium: 343mg | Fiber: 5g | Carbohydrates: 29g | Sugar: 21g

SCALLOPED POTATOES

The recipe is easy to make, but unless you add salt, the potatoes can be bland. We'll fix that by adding your own homemade mustard and some caramelized onions to the mix. Serve this wonder with meatloaf, roasted turkey, or a grilled steak.

SERVES 8

6 russet potatoes

1½ cups Slow Cooker Caramelized Onions (Chapter 4)

5 cloves garlic, minced

1 cup heavy cream

1 cup whole milk

¼ cup Mustard (Chapter 4)

2 tablespoons unsalted butter

1. Preheat oven to 350°F. Peel the potatoes and slice them ⅛" thick. As you work, put the sliced potatoes in a bowl of cold water.

2. When all of the potatoes are sliced, dry with a kitchen towel and layer them in a 9" × 13" glass baking dish with the onions and garlic.

3. In medium bowl, combine cream, milk, and mustard and mix with a whisk until blended. Pour slowly over the potatoes. Dot the top with the butter.

4. Bake, covered, for 1 hour. Uncover the potatoes and bake for 25–35 minutes longer or until the potatoes are tender and the top is golden brown.

PER SERVING: Calories: 448 | Total Fat: 19g | Saturated Fat: 9g | Cholesterol: 51mg | Protein: 9g | Sodium: 56mg | Potassium: 1,462mg | Fiber: 6g | Carbohydrates: 60g | Sugar: 8g

BLACK RICE PILAF

Black rice, or forbidden rice, used to be served only to royalty in China. It is definitely black in color, and it's packed with healthy antioxidants, along with lots of fiber and minerals. Serve it with roasted chicken or meatloaf for a hearty meal.

SERVES 6

2 tablespoons unsalted butter

1 tablespoon olive oil

3 cloves garlic, sliced

½ cup sliced green onions

1 teaspoon grated lemon zest

1½ cups black rice

3 cups Chicken Stock (Chapter 5)

⅛ teaspoon pepper

2 teaspoons minced fresh thyme leaves

1. In heavy saucepan, melt butter with olive oil over medium-low heat. Add garlic and green onions; sauté for 2 minutes.

2. Add lemon zest and black rice; sauté for another 2–4 minutes, stirring constantly, until rice is slightly toasted.

3. Add stock and pepper and bring to a simmer. Reduce heat to low, cover the pan, and simmer for 30 minutes or until the rice is just tender.

4. Remove pan from heat, stir in thyme, and let stand, covered, for 5 minutes. Fluff rice with a fork and serve.

PER SERVING: Calories: 241 | Total Fat: 8g | Saturated Fat: 3g | Cholesterol: 10mg | Protein: 6g | Sodium: 38mg | Potassium: 248mg | Fiber: 3g | Carbohydrates: 36g | Sugar: 0g

MASHED SWEET POTATOES WITH CARAMELIZED ONIONS

Sweet potatoes make a nice change of pace from regular russet potatoes in this delicious recipe. You can make this ahead of time; just cover the mashed potatoes and refrigerate up to 24 hours. Bake for 40–50 minutes just before serving until hot.

SERVES 6

4 large sweet potatoes

3 tablespoons unsalted butter

⅓ cup whole milk

¼ cup heavy cream

2 tablespoons orange juice

2 tablespoons maple syrup

1 cup Slow Cooker Caramelized Onions (Chapter 4)

1 teaspoon dried thyme leaves

¼ teaspoon white pepper

1. Preheat oven to 375°F. Scrub the sweet potatoes and prick them with a fork. Place on a baking pan and bake for 55–65 minutes or until they are very tender.

2. Cool the potatoes for 20 minutes, then cut in half lengthwise and scoop out the flesh with a spoon into a large bowl. Add the butter and mash.

3. Stir in the milk, cream, orange juice, maple syrup, onions, thyme, and pepper. Pile into a 3-quart baking dish. Bake for 25–35 minutes or until hot and slightly brown on top.

PER SERVING: Calories: 203 | Total Fat: 12g | Saturated Fat: 6g | Cholesterol: 29mg | Protein: 2g | Sodium: 25mg | Potassium: 353mg | Fiber: 2g | Carbohydrates: 21g | Sugar: 10g

HASH BROWNS WITH PEAR AND APPLE

Hash brown potatoes are simple to make, especially if you start with premade frozen shredded potatoes. They do contain a little bit of sodium, but not enough to make much of a difference. These hash browns are cooked with pear and apple for a sweet taste. They're delicious for breakfast.

SERVES 6

2½ cups frozen hash brown potatoes, thawed and drained

⅓ cup shredded Granny Smith apple

⅓ cup shredded pear

1 tablespoon lemon juice

1 teaspoon dried thyme leaves

⅛ teaspoon white pepper

3 tablespoons unsalted butter, divided

2 tablespoons olive oil

1. In large bowl, combine the potatoes, apple, and pear. Sprinkle with lemon juice, thyme, and pepper and mix well. Preheat oven to 300°F.

2. In a large nonstick skillet, melt 2 tablespoons butter and olive oil over medium heat. Drop the potato mixture by ½-cup portions into the butter, making 3 patties at a time.

3. Cook, pressing down occasionally with a spatula, until the patties are brown on the bottom, about 4–6 minutes. Flip carefully with a spatula and cook on the second side until brown, about 3–5 minutes longer. Remove to a baking pan and place in the oven to keep warm. Cook the second batch as you did the first, adding another tablespoon of butter before cooking, and serve immediately.

PER SERVING: Calories: 172 | Total Fat: 10g | Saturated Fat: 4g | Cholesterol: 15mg | Protein: 2g | Sodium: 20mg | Potassium: 273mg | Fiber: 1g | Carbohydrates: 18g | Sugar: 1g

STEAMED GREEN BEANS AND ASPARAGUS

Steaming vegetables is the healthiest way to cook them. You don't need a fancy steamer to make this recipe; just put a metal colander on top of a pan of simmering water and cover the whole thing with heavy duty foil. The vegetables will become bright green and will have the most perfect tender-crisp texture.

SERVES 6

1 pound fresh green beans

1 pound fresh asparagus spears

3 tablespoons unsalted butter

⅓ cup toasted pine nuts

⅛ teaspoon white pepper

1. Cut both ends off the green beans and rinse well. Bend the asparagus until it snaps, then discard the ends. Rinse well.

2. Bring 1" of water to a simmer in a large saucepan. Put the green beans in a colander or steamer insert and place on top. Cover and steam for 2 minutes.

3. Carefully remove the cover and add the asparagus; mix with the green beans using tongs. Cover again and steam for 2–3 minutes or until the vegetables are bright green and crisp-tender.

4. Transfer vegetables to a serving dish and toss with the butter. Sprinkle with pine nuts and pepper and serve.

PER SERVING: Calories: 172 | Total Fat: 11g | Saturated Fat: 4g | Cholesterol: 15mg | Protein: 4g | Sodium: 3mg | Potassium: 309mg | Fiber: 4g | Carbohydrates: 9g | Sugar: 2g

SMASHED POTATOES WITH CARAMELIZED ONIONS AND GARLIC

Caramelized onions and garlic add wonderful flavor and texture to this homey dish. Serve with roasted chicken or meatloaf, along with a green salad tossed with sliced mushrooms and tomatoes, for a comforting meal.

SERVES 8

2 pounds small red potatoes, unpeeled

3 tablespoons unsalted butter

⅔ cup light cream

⅓ cup mascarpone cheese

1 cup Slow Cooker Caramelized Onions (Chapter 4)

1 head Roasted Garlic (Chapter 4), removed from skins

¼ teaspoon white pepper

1. Place potatoes in a large pot and cover with cold water. Bring to a simmer over high heat, then reduce heat to low and simmer for 20–30 minutes or until the potatoes are tender when pierced with a fork. Drain well.

2. Return the potatoes to the hot pot and mash coarsely with a potato masher. Beat in the butter, cream, and mascarpone.

3. Stir in the onions, garlic, and pepper and serve immediately, or cover and place in a 300°F oven to keep warm up to 30 minutes.

PER SERVING: Calories: 280 | Total Fat: 15g | Saturated Fat: 8g | Cholesterol: 43mg | Protein: 6g | Sodium: 33mg | Potassium: 768mg | Fiber: 3g | Carbohydrates: 31g | Sugar: 4g

SAUTÉED SPINACH AND GARLIC

When you buy fresh spinach to sauté it, buy much more than you need. Spinach cooks down to almost nothing; that's one reason why frozen chopped spinach is such a great buy. This delicious side dish pairs well with roasted chicken or a roast pork.

SERVES 6

2 (10-ounce) packages baby spinach leaves

2 tablespoons olive oil

1 tablespoon unsalted butter

8 cloves garlic, sliced

2 tablespoons lemon juice

1 tablespoon honey

⅛ teaspoon white pepper

Pinch nutmeg

2 tablespoons toasted sesame seeds

1. Rinse the spinach in cold water; it can be very sandy. Don't dry the spinach; just shake off excess water.

2. In a large saucepan with a lid, heat olive oil and butter over medium heat. Add garlic; cook and stir just until the garlic is fragrant, about 1 minute.

3. Add the spinach to pan and toss well with the garlic; cover. Cook for 2 minutes, shaking pan frequently.

4. Remove cover and add lemon juice, honey, pepper, and nutmeg. Cook, stirring frequently, until spinach is wilted, about 1 minute longer. Sprinkle with sesame seeds and serve immediately.

PER SERVING: Calories: 111 | Total Fat: 8g | Saturated Fat: 2g | Cholesterol: 5mg | Protein: 3g | Sodium: 76mg | Potassium: 563mg | Fiber: 2g | Carbohydrates: 8g | Sugar: 3g

OVEN-FRIED VEGGIES

Using your oven to "fry" vegetables is much healthier than deep-frying them. And the taste and texture are very similar to fried veggies. The trick is to roast them in a hot oven so the coating gets crisp by the time the vegetables are tender.

SERVES 4

3 slices French Bread (Chapter 2), crumbled

1 teaspoon dried thyme leaves

1 teaspoon paprika

⅛ teaspoon white pepper

1 cup cauliflower florets

1 cup zucchini slices

1 cup whole green beans

1 small red onion, cut into ¼" rings

1 large egg, beaten

1 tablespoon lemon juice

2 tablespoons olive oil

1. Preheat oven to 425°F. Combine bread crumbs, thyme, paprika, and pepper on a plate. Prepare the vegetables.

2. Combine egg and lemon juice in large bowl. Toss the vegetables in this mixture, then add the bread-crumb mixture and toss until coated.

3. Coat a baking sheet with sides with the olive oil. Add the coated vegetables in a single layer.

4. Bake for 14–18 minutes or until the vegetables are golden brown and crisp-tender.

PER SERVING: Calories: 165 | Total Fat: 8g | Saturated Fat: 1g | Cholesterol: 53mg | Protein: 5g | Sodium: 45mg | Potassium: 231mg | Fiber: 3g | Carbohydrates: 17g | Sugar: 1g

CONFETTI CORN

Corn is delicious on its own, of course, but it's even more wonderful when tossed with a colorful mélange of fresh veggies. This side dish is perfect with a roast chicken or grilled steak in the summer, or with meatloaf in the winter. Because it's made from frozen corn, it can be made year round.

SERVES 6

2 tablespoons unsalted butter

1 medium red bell pepper, chopped

1 medium green bell pepper, chopped

¼ cup sliced green onions

1 clove garlic, minced

1 (16-ounce) package frozen white and yellow corn, thawed

1 cup seeded and chopped tomato

½ cup heavy cream

½ teaspoon dried basil leaves

⅛ teaspoon black pepper

1. In large saucepan, melt butter over medium heat. Add red bell pepper, green bell pepper, green onions, and garlic; cook and stir until crisp-tender, about 4 minutes.

2. Add corn and tomato to saucepan; cook and stir until hot, about 2 minutes longer. Add cream, basil, and pepper and bring to a simmer. Simmer for 1–2 minutes or until slightly thickened. Serve immediately.

PER SERVING: Calories: 180 | Total Fat: 11g | Saturated Fat: 7g | Cholesterol: 37mg | Protein: 3g | Sodium: 15mg | Potassium: 291mg | Fiber: 3g | Carbohydrates: 19g | Sugar: 4g

CREAMY BROWN RICE PILAF

Rice pilaf is a more substantial and more interesting dish than just plain cooked rice. You can use your favorite vegetables in this easy recipe. Some sour cream and yogurt stirred into the cooked rice mixture add more flavor and texture. It's delicious served with steak or a roasted chicken.

SERVES 4

2 tablespoons unsalted butter

1 medium onion, finely chopped

3 cloves garlic, minced

2 medium carrots, diced

½ cup diced mushrooms

1⅓ cups brown rice

2 cups Vegetable Broth (Chapter 5)

⅔ cup water

1 tablespoon lemon juice

1 teaspoon dried marjoram leaves

½ cup plain yogurt

⅓ cup sour cream

⅛ teaspoon white pepper

1. In a large saucepan, melt butter over medium heat. Add onion, garlic, and carrots; cook, stirring occasionally, until tender. Add mushrooms; cook and stir for another 5 minutes.

2. Add rice; cook and stir for 2 minutes. Then add broth, water, lemon juice, and marjoram; bring to a simmer.

3. Reduce heat to low, cover pan, and simmer for 30–35 minutes or until rice is tender.

4. Remove from heat and stir in yogurt, sour cream, and pepper.

PER SERVING: Calories: 393 | Total Fat: 13g | Saturated Fat: 7g | Cholesterol: 29mg | Protein: 9g | Sodium: 95mg | Potassium: 521mg | Fiber: 5g | Carbohydrates: 60g | Sugar: 4g

CURRIED COUSCOUS

There's a big difference in taste between "raw" curry powder and that which has been toasted or sautéed. Sautéing curry powder boosts the flavors, releasing the natural aromatic oils in the spices. The Curry Powder from the recipe in Chapter 4 is one example: the spices are toasted before they're ground.

SERVES 8

1 tablespoon unsalted butter

1 teaspoon curry powder

1½ cups couscous

1½ cups boiling water

¼ cup plain nonfat yogurt

¼ cup extra-virgin olive oil

1 teaspoon white wine vinegar

¼ teaspoon ground turmeric

¼ teaspoon grated lemon zest

1 teaspoon freshly ground black pepper

½ cup diced carrots

½ cup minced fresh parsley

½ cup raisins

¼ cup blanched, sliced almonds

2 scallions, white and green parts thinly sliced

¼ cup diced red onion

1½ teaspoons Sesame Salt (Gomashio) (Chapter 4)

1. In a small nonstick skillet, melt the butter until sizzling, then add the curry powder. Stir for several minutes, being careful not to burn the butter. Place the couscous in a medium-size bowl. Pour enough of the boiling water into the pan with the sautéed curry powder to mix it with the water and rinse out the pan. Pour that and the remaining boiling water over the couscous. Cover tightly and allow the couscous to sit for 5 minutes. Fluff with a fork.

2. In a medium bowl, mix together the yogurt, olive oil, vinegar, turmeric, lemon zest, and pepper; pour over the fluffed couscous, and mix well.

3. Add the carrots, parsley, raisins, almonds, scallions, red onion, and sesame salt; mix well. Serve at room temperature.

PER SERVING: Calories: 208 | Total Fat: 11g | Saturated Fat: 2g | Cholesterol: 4mg | Protein: 4g | Sodium: 115mg | Potassium: 224mg | Fiber: 2g | Carbohydrates: 24g | Sugar: 6g

LEMON FINGERLING POTATOES

These tiny and tender potatoes are delicious when microwaved until almost tender, then quickly sautéed with some lemon and garlic. They are the perfect accompaniment to just about any main dish. You can use this cooking method with tiny new potatoes too, but the cooking time will be less.

SERVES 4

1 pound fingerling potatoes

1 cup water

2 tablespoons unsalted butter

1 tablespoon olive oil

3 cloves garlic, minced

2 tablespoons lemon juice

⅛ teaspoon white pepper

1. Wash the potatoes and slice in half lengthwise. Combine in microwave-safe dish with water.

2. Cover and microwave on high for 5–6 minutes or until potatoes are almost tender. Drain well.

3. In large saucepan, melt butter with olive oil over medium heat. Add garlic; cook for 1 minute until fragrant.

4. Carefully add the potatoes; they will splatter a bit, as they are not dry. Cook for 2–4 minutes, shaking pan frequently, until the potatoes are golden brown and tender. Drizzle with lemon juice, sprinkle with pepper, and serve.

PER SERVING: Calories: 186 | Total Fat: 9g | Saturated Fat: 4g | Cholesterol: 15mg | Protein: 2g | Sodium: 14mg | Potassium: 638mg | Fiber: 2g | Carbohydrates: 23g | Sugar: 1g

BAKED BEANS

Baked beans are a classic and thrifty winter recipe from the northwestern United States. This recipe is flavorful because it's made with homemade mustard and barbecue sauce. Serve this rich dish with meatloaf on a cold winter day for a comforting and hearty meal.

SERVES 6–8

2 cups dried navy beans

1 medium onion, chopped

3 cloves garlic, minced

5 cups water

½ cup BBQ Sauce (Chapter 4)

1 (8-ounce) can no-salt-added tomato sauce

¼ cup Mustard (Chapter 4)

¼ cup brown sugar

2 tablespoons molasses

2 tablespoons lemon juice

¼ teaspoon pepper

1. The night before, sort the beans, removing any sticks or stones. Rinse well, place in a large bowl, and cover with cold water.

2. In the morning, drain the beans and discard the soaking water. Combine in a 4-quart slow cooker with onion and garlic. Add 5 cups water. Cover and cook on low for 8 hours.

3. Add BBQ sauce, tomato sauce, mustard, brown sugar, molasses, lemon juice, and pepper to the slow cooker and stir.

4. Cover and cook on high for 2 hours or until the beans are tender.

PER SERVING: Calories: 272 | Total Fat: 2g | Saturated Fat: 0g | Cholesterol: 0mg | Protein: 12g | Sodium: 14mg | Potassium: 818mg | Fiber: 15g | Carbohydrates: 51g | Sugar: 12g

SAUTÉED SQUASH AND ZUCCHINI

This is a summer dish that is wonderful with grilled chicken or steak.

SERVES 4

1 tablespoon unsalted butter

1 tablespoon olive oil

1 shallot, minced

1 medium zucchini, sliced

1 medium yellow summer squash, sliced

2 tablespoons lemon juice

1 tablespoon minced fresh basil leaves

2 tablespoons minced flat-leaf parsley

1. Heat butter and olive oil in a large pan over medium heat. Add shallot; cook and stir for 2 minutes or until fragrant.

2. Add the zucchini and squash; cook, stirring frequently, for 5–7 minutes or until tender. Sprinkle with lemon, basil, and parsley, and serve immediately.

PER SERVING: Calories: 66 | Total Fat: 6g | Saturated Fat: 2g | Cholesterol: 7mg | Protein: 0g | Sodium: 2mg | Potassium: 154mg | Fiber: 0g | Carbohydrates: 2g | Sugar: 1g

OVEN-ROASTED CORN ON THE COB

Who says you have to grill corn! Here you get that sweet roasted flavor without ever having to step outside.

SERVES 4

4 ears fresh sweet corn

4 teaspoons fresh lime juice

Freshly ground black pepper

1. Preheat oven to 350°F.

2. Peel back the husks of the corn. Remove any silk. Brush the corn with the lime juice and generously grind black pepper over the corn. Pull the husks back up over the corn, twisting the husks at the top to keep them sealed over each ear.

3. Place the corn on the rack in a roasting pan large enough to hold the ears without overlapping. Roast for 30 minutes or until the corn is heated through and tender. Peel back the husks and use them as a handle, if desired, or discard the husks and insert corn holders into the ends of the cobs. Serve immediately.

PER SERVING: Calories: 60 | Total Fat: 0g | Saturated Fat: 0g | Cholesterol: 0mg | Protein: 2g | Sodium: 2mg | Potassium: 163mg | Fiber: 1g | Carbohydrates: 14g | Sugar: 0g

BAKED CAULIFLOWER CASSEROLE

To further crisp the bread crumbs that top this casserole, remove the cover once the casserole is baked and mist again with additional olive oil spray; then either return the casserole to the oven for an additional 5–10 minutes or place it under the broiler until the bread crumbs are lightly browned.

SERVES 6

1 (1¾-pound) head cauliflower

1 teaspoon lemon juice

⅛ teaspoon mustard powder

Olive oil spray

2 large eggs, beaten

1 teaspoon Sonoran Spice Blend (Appendix A)

¼ cup grated Parmesan cheese

½ cup bread crumbs

1. Preheat oven to 375°F.

2. Trim off the outer leaves of the cauliflower. Break the cauliflower apart. Bring a large pot of water to a boil over medium-high heat. Add the lemon juice and mustard powder; stir to mix. Add the cauliflower to the water and blanch for 5 minutes. Remove with a slotted spoon and drain.

3. Spray an ovenproof casserole dish with the olive oil spray. Spread the cauliflower evenly in the casserole dish.

4. In a small bowl, mix together the eggs, Sonoran Spice Blend, and cheese. Evenly pour the mixture over the top of the cauliflower. Sprinkle the bread crumbs over the top and lightly mist with the olive oil spray. Cover and bake for 15 minutes or until the eggs are set and the cheese is melted.

PER SERVING: Calories: 90 | Total Fat: 3g | Saturated Fat: 1g | Cholesterol: 74mg | Protein: 6g | Sodium: 139mg | Potassium: 225mg | Fiber: 3g | Carbohydrates: 9g | Sugar: 3g

GRILLED MUSHROOM AND VEGETABLE MEDLEY

This is a beautiful vegetable medley with bright color and taste. Cut the vegetables into equal-sized pieces to ensure even cooking.

SERVES 4

Olive oil spray

1 large red bell pepper, seeded

1 large green bell pepper, seeded

2 medium zucchini

2 medium yellow squashes

2 cups fresh button mushrooms

4 medium green onions, white and green parts minced

1 teaspoon dried thyme

1 teaspoon dried basil

½ teaspoon garlic powder

¼ teaspoon mustard powder

⅛ teaspoon freshly ground black pepper

Optional: Vinaigrette dressing of choice

1. Prepare a 20" × 14" sheet of heavy-duty foil by spraying the center with the olive oil spray.

2. Cut the bell peppers into ¼" strips; slice the zucchini and squashes crosswise into ¼" slices. Slice the mushrooms. Arrange the vegetables over the foil. Evenly sprinkle the green onions, thyme, basil, garlic powder, mustard powder, and black pepper over the vegetables. Lightly spray the mixture with the spray oil. Fold the ends of the foil up and over the vegetables, creating a packet and sealing it by crimping the edges well, leaving space for heat to circulate.

3. Grill on a covered grill over medium coals for 20–25 minutes, or until the vegetables are fork tender. Carefully open the foil packet and grill for an additional 5 minutes to let the juices from the vegetables evaporate, if desired.

PER SERVING: Calories: 50 | Total Fat: 0g | Saturated Fat: 0g | Cholesterol: 0mg | Protein: 3g | Sodium: 7mg | Potassium: 569mg | Fiber: 3g | Carbohydrates: 10g | Sugar: 5g

SWEET POTATO MASH

A dish for both casual meals and holiday affairs, this light and creamy concoction of sweet potatoes has hints of cinnamon and ginger.

SERVES 4

4 medium-size sweet potatoes, peeled and cubed

2 teaspoons lemon juice

4 teaspoons unsalted butter

¼ teaspoon ground cumin

¼ teaspoon ground cinnamon

¼ teaspoon dried ginger

Optional: ¼ teaspoon chipotle powder or other salt-free chili powder

½ cup skim milk

1. Put the sweet potatoes in a saucepan and cover with cold water. Add the lemon juice. Bring to a boil over medium heat. Cover and cook for 7–10 minutes, until the potatoes are fork tender. Once the sweet potatoes are fully cooked, drain the water from the pot and place them in a medium-size bowl.

2. Melt the butter in the saucepan over medium heat. Add the cumin, cinnamon, ginger, and chipotle powder, if using; sauté the spices for 30 seconds. Add the milk and bring to a boil. Pour over the cooked sweet potatoes. Mix together using a masher or wooden spoon. Serve immediately.

PER SERVING: Calories: 161 | Total Fat: 4g | Saturated Fat: 2g | Cholesterol: 10mg | Protein: 3g | Sodium: 57mg | Potassium: 409mg | Fiber: 3g | Carbohydrates: 28g | Sugar: 10g

OVEN-FRIED POTATO WEDGES

These potatoes come out soft and tender inside with a crisp outer coating. With all the flavor and none of the fat, you never have to go back to bagged fries again!

SERVES 4

Olive oil spray

4 large baking potatoes, washed and cut into 6 wedges each

¾ teaspoon freshly ground black pepper

1 teaspoon garlic powder

½ teaspoon dried rosemary, finely crushed

½ teaspoon grated lemon zest

1. Preheat the oven to 400°F.

2. Spray a baking sheet with the olive spray oil. Arrange the potato wedges on the sheet. Spray the potatoes with a thin layer of the olive oil spray. Sprinkle the potatoes with the pepper, garlic powder, rosemary, and lemon zest.

3. Bake for 30–35 minutes, turning the potatoes to the other cut side after 20 minutes, until the potatoes are lightly browned, crisp outside, and tender inside.

PER SERVING: Calories: 290 | Total Fat: 0g | Saturated Fat: 0g | Cholesterol: 0mg | Protein: 7g | Sodium: 41mg | Potassium: 1,644mg | Fiber: 6g | Carbohydrates: 64g | Sugar: 3g

GOLDEN DELICIOUS RISOTTO

When you prepare traditional rice, the ratio of liquid to rice is usually 2 parts to 1. One cup of broth and 3 cups of water for every cup of rice is the correct amount to use when preparing risotto.

SERVES 4

4–5 cups water

2 tablespoons extra-virgin olive oil

2 tablespoons minced onion or shallot

1 cup Arborio rice (short-grain white rice)

2 medium-size Golden Delicious apples, peeled, cored, and diced

¾ teaspoon low-sodium chicken base

¼ teaspoon sautéed vegetable base

⅓ cup dry white wine

2 tablespoons unsalted butter

2 tablespoons grated Parmesan cheese

Optional: Freshly grated nutmeg

1. In medium-size saucepan, heat the water to boiling; reduce heat to maintain a steady simmer.

2. In large nonstick sauté pan treated with nonstick spray, bring the olive oil to temperature over medium heat; add the onion (or shallot) and sauté for 3 minutes. Add the rice and half of the diced apples; sauté, stirring well, for 3 minutes. Add the bases and stir to dissolve. Add the wine and stir until the wine evaporates.

3. Stirring, ladle in enough of the water to just cover the rice (about ¾ cup). Lower the heat to maintain a steady simmer and cook the rice, stirring constantly, until almost all of the water has been absorbed, about 4 minutes.

4. Continue adding water ½ cup at a time, stirring and cooking until absorbed. After 15 minutes, stir in the remaining diced apples. The rice is done when it is creamy yet firm in the center (al dente). Total cooking time will be around 25–30 minutes.

5. Remove pan from heat and stir in the butter and Parmesan cheese. Grate nutmeg over the top of each serving, if desired, and serve immediately.

PER SERVING: Calories: 376 | Total Fat: 13g | Saturated Fat: 5g | Cholesterol: 17mg | Protein: 5g | Sodium: 39mg | Potassium: 125mg | Fiber: 1g | Carbohydrates: 55g | Sugar: 8g

ROASTED AND GLAZED ROOT VEGETABLES

Roasting brings out the natural sweetness of vegetables and turns them into a delectable side dish that complements any type of meal.

SERVES 4

Olive oil spray

4 small beets, peeled and diced

2 small white turnips, peeled and diced

4 large carrots, peeled and sliced

2 parsnips, peeled and diced

4 cloves garlic, minced

1 tablespoon candied ginger, minced

4 teaspoons honey

¼ teaspoon (or to taste) freshly ground pepper

Optional: Chopped watercress, for garnish

1. Preheat the oven to 350°F.

2. Spray a jellyroll pan with the olive oil spray. Arrange the vegetables in a single layer across the pan. Sprinkle the garlic and ginger over the vegetables. Spray lightly with the olive oil spray.

3. Bake for 30 minutes. Drizzle the honey over the top of the vegetables. Use a spatula to stir the vegetables and then spread them back out into a single layer across the pan. Sprinkle with the ground pepper. Bake for an additional 15 minutes or until the vegetables are fork tender.

4. Transfer the vegetables to a serving bowl, stirring well to mix; toss with chopped watercress, if desired.

PER SERVING: Calories: 156 | Total Fat: 0g | Saturated Fat: 0g | Cholesterol: 0mg | Protein: 3g | Sodium: 103mg | Potassium: 761mg | Fiber: 6g | Carbohydrates: 37g | Sugar: 21 g

EAST MEETS WEST CORN

To make ghee (clarified butter) melt unsalted butter in a saucepan over low heat. It will separate into foam, liquid, and milk solids. Skim off the foam and carefully pour off the golden liquid (ghee) into a bowl. Discard milk solids in the bottom of the pan.

SERVES 8

2 tablespoons ghee (clarified butter), divided

1 teaspoon yellow mustard seeds

⅛ teaspoon fenugreek seeds

¼ teaspoon dried red pepper flakes

¼ teaspoon ground ginger

½ teaspoon asafetida

1 large sweet onion, chopped

1 medium red bell pepper, seeded and chopped

1 medium green bell pepper, seeded and chopped

2 cloves garlic, minced

¼ teaspoon turmeric

2 jalapeño peppers, seeded and chopped

2 (10-ounce) packages frozen sweet corn, thawed

2 tablespoons freeze-dried shallot

1 teaspoon freeze-dried cilantro

2½ cups plain nonfat yogurt

1. Heat a large, deep nonstick sauté pan over medium heat. Melt 1 teaspoon of the ghee. Add the mustard and fenugreek seeds. Cover (because the mustard seeds will pop) and toast for 30 seconds, shaking the pan to move the spices and prevent them from scorching. Transfer to a mortar and pestle along with the red pepper flakes and ginger; pound into a paste. Set aside.

2. Add the remaining ghee to the sauté pan. Add the asafetida and sauté for 1 minute over medium heat. Add the onion and bell peppers; sauté until the onion is transparent. Add the garlic and cook for 1 minute, stirring the garlic into the onion-pepper mixture. Add the turmeric and mustard-seed paste; stir into the onion mixture. (Add 1 or 2 tablespoons of water at this point if the mixture is dry.)

3. Add the jalapeño peppers and corn; stir-fry with the onion-pepper mixture, cooking for 2 minutes. Stir in the shallot, cilantro, and yogurt. Lower the heat and simmer, covered, for 5 minutes. Serve immediately.

PER SERVING: Calories: 164 | Total Fat: 3g | Saturated Fat: 2g | Cholesterol: 9mg | Protein: 5g | Sodium: 67mg | Potassium: 516mg | Fiber: 9g | Carbohydrates: 28g | Sugar: 2g

BUTTERNUT SQUASH CHEESE MUFFINS

Here's a way to consume a bumper crop of butternut squash. These moist muffins are absolutely delicious and freeze beautifully, so you can bake several batches to enjoy in colder weather.

SERVES 12

1 tablespoon unsalted butter

1 tablespoon extra-light olive oil or canola oil

1 cup chopped sweet onion

1 cup sliced button mushrooms

¼ cup water

2 cups cubed Roasted Butternut Squash (see recipe in this chapter)

6 tablespoons unbleached all-purpose flour

3 tablespoons oat bran or wheat germ

2 large eggs

¼ teaspoon freshly ground black pepper

½ cup grated Jarlsberg cheese

1 tablespoon hulled sesame seeds

1. Preheat oven to 400°F.

2. Add the butter and oil to a nonstick sauté pan over high heat. When the butter begins to sizzle, reduce heat to medium and add the onion and mushrooms. Sauté until the onion is transparent, about 4–5 minutes. Set aside to cool.

3. In the bowl of a food processor or in a blender, combine the cooled sautéed mixture and all of the remaining ingredients except the cheese and sesame seeds; pulse until mixed.

4. Fold the cheese into the squash mixture. Spoon the resulting batter into muffin cups treated with nonstick spray (or lined with foil muffin liners), filling each muffin cup to the top. Evenly divide the sesame seeds over the top of the batter.

5. Bake for 35–40 minutes. (For savory appetizers, make 24 mini muffins; bake for 20–25 minutes.)

PER SERVING: Calories: 99 | Total Fat: 4g | Saturated Fat: 1g | Cholesterol: 42mg | Protein: 4g | Sodium: 30mg | Potassium: 142mg | Fiber: 0g | Carbohydrates: 10g | Sugar: 1g

ROASTED BUTTERNUT SQUASH

In the fall, try to get several scrumptious butternut squashes from a local organic farmer. Roast extra and freeze any leftovers in fork-mashed, ½-cup increments, so they're ready to add to your favorite recipes or to be seasoned and heated for a vegetable side dish.

SERVES 4

1 large butternut squash

1. Preheat oven to 350°F. Wash the outside skin of the squash.

2. Place the whole squash on a jellyroll pan or baking sheet. Pierce the skin a few times with a knife. Bake for 1 hour or until tender.

3. Once the squash is cool enough to handle, slice it open, scrape out the seeds, and scrape the squash pulp off of the skin.

PER SERVING: Calories: 93 | Total Fat: 0g | Saturated Fat: 0g | Cholesterol: 0mg | Protein: 2g | Sodium: 4mg | Potassium: 319mg | Fiber: 0g | Carbohydrates: 24g | Sugar: 0g

FRENCH GLAZED GREEN BEANS

Lively and flavorful, this green bean dish is a great partner to any meat dish. The walnuts add the perfect crunchy mouthfeel that rounds out this recipe.

SERVES 4

¼ cup chopped walnuts

4 teaspoons cold-pressed walnut or canola oil

2 (15-ounce) cans French-cut green beans

1 teaspoon lemon juice

1 teaspoon honey

1 teaspoon French Spice Blend (Appendix A)

⅛ teaspoon grated lemon zest

⅛ teaspoon mustard powder

⅛ teaspoon freshly ground black pepper

1. Heat a large, deep nonstick sauté pan over medium heat. Add the walnuts. Toast for 3 minutes, stirring frequently so the walnuts don't burn. Transfer to a bowl and set aside.

2. Add the walnut or canola oil to the pan. Drain the green beans and add to the pan; stir to toss in the oil. Once the green beans are hot, push them to the sides of the pan.

3. In a medium bowl, add the lemon juice, honey, French spice blend, lemon zest, mustard powder, and pepper; stir to combine. Toss the green beans in the lemon juice mixture. Pour into a serving bowl and top with the toasted walnuts.

PER SERVING: Calories: 88 | Total Fat: 5g | Saturated Fat: 0g | Cholesterol: 0mg | Protein: 1g | Sodium: 29mg | Potassium: 205mg | Fiber: 3g | Carbohydrates: 9g | Sugar: 1g

VEGETABLES IN WARM CITRUS VINAIGRETTE

You can substitute fresh orange juice for the frozen fruit juice concentrate and water called for in this recipe. Using a frozen fruit juice concentrate saves some time, however, because you can simply mix it for the strength you need.

SERVES 4

Pinch saffron

Pinch grated lemon or lime zest

2 teaspoons grapeseed oil

1 tablespoon water

Olive oil spray

1 (10-ounce) package frozen California-style vegetables, thawed

1 tablespoon frozen orange juice concentrate

⅛ teaspoon freshly ground black pepper

1. Preheat oven to 350°F.

2. Add the saffron, zest, grapeseed oil, and water to a microwave-safe bowl. Microwave on high for 20–30 seconds, until the water just boils; stir. Cover and set aside to infuse at room temperature while the vegetables bake.

3. Treat an ovenproof casserole dish with the olive oil spray. Add the thawed vegetables. Spray a light coating of olive oil spray over the top of the vegetables. Cover and bake for 15 minutes. Carefully remove the cover and stir the vegetables. Spray with an additional coating of the olive oil spray. Bake for an additional 15 minutes.

4. During the last few minutes of the baking time, add the frozen orange juice concentrate to the saffron-oil mixture. Whisk to combine.

5. Remove the vegetables from the oven. Pour the saffron-orange vinaigrette over the vegetables and add the pepper; toss to combine. Serve immediately.

PER SERVING: Calories: 72 | Total Fat: 2g | Saturated Fat: 0g | Cholesterol: 0mg | Protein: 2g | Sodium: 24mg | Potassium: 149mg | Fiber: 3g | Carbohydrates: 10g | Sugar: 3g

CARIBBEAN CORN ON THE COB

Here's corn with a sweet and tangy kick. Corn is high in vitamin C and a great source of both protein and fiber, and contains antioxidants associated with a reduced risk of cardiovascular disease.

SERVES 4

4 cups water

⅛ cup lime juice

1 teaspoon Caribbean Spice Blend (Appendix A)

4 medium-size ears yellow sweet corn

Optional: Freshly ground black pepper

In a large, deep nonstick sauté pan, bring the water to a boil. Stir in the lime juice and the Caribbean spice blend. Add the corn. Cover, reduce heat, and simmer for 4–6 minutes, until the corn is just tender. Remove corn from pan using tongs and drain briefly. Serve topped with freshly ground black pepper, if desired.

PER SERVING: Calories: 61 | Total Fat: 0g | Saturated Fat: 0g | Cholesterol: 0mg | Protein: 1g | Sodium: 2mg | Potassium: 166mg | Fiber: 1g | Carbohydrates: 14g | Sugar: 0g

BAKED POTATO LATKES

Latkes are potato pancakes that are best know as a Hanukkah food. While traditional latkes are made with potatoes, onions, and matzoh and then fried in oil, this recipe takes a healthier approach and bakes the pancakes.

SERVES 8

Olive oil spray

4 medium-size potatoes, peeled and grated

1 medium-size red onion, finely chopped

¼ teaspoon salt

⅛ teaspoon grated lemon zest

½ teaspoon freshly grated black pepper

1 teaspoon freeze-dried chives

1 large egg plus 1 large egg white, lightly beaten together

¼ cup unbleached all-purpose flour

1 teaspoon canola oil

1. Preheat oven to 350°F. Spray a baking sheet with the olive oil spray.

2. Mix together the remaining ingredients. Spoon the batter onto the baking sheet in 8 equal-sized portions, flattening them slightly. Spray the tops of the pancakes with a light coating of the olive oil spray.

3. Bake for 10 minutes or until brown on the bottom. Turn and bake for an additional 5–10 minutes, until evenly browned.

PER SERVING: Calories: 103 | Total Fat: 1g | Saturated Fat: 0g | Cholesterol: 26mg | Protein: 3g | Sodium: 92mg | Potassium: 329mg | Fiber: 1g | Carbohydrates: 20g | Sugar: 1g

BAKED STUFFED TOMATOES

Plum tomatoes are perfect for stuffing because they have thicker flesh and fewer seeds than a beefsteak tomato. To remove the seeds, just push them out with your thumb.

SERVES 4

1¼ cups chopped parsley

3 small cloves garlic, finely chopped

Pinch red pepper flakes

¾ cup bread crumbs

Olive oil spray

10 plum tomatoes, cut in half lengthwise and seeded

½ teaspoon freshly ground black pepper

¼ teaspoon grated lemon zest

½ cup water

1. Preheat oven to 400°F.

2. In the bowl of a food processor, combine the parsley, garlic, red pepper flakes, and bread crumbs; pulse to chop and mix. Set aside.

3. Prepare a casserole dish or baking pan large enough to hold the tomato halves side by side by spraying it with the olive oil spray. Fill the tomato halves with the bread crumb mixture and place them in the dish or pan. Spray a light layer of the olive oil spray over the tops of the filled tomatoes. Sprinkle the pepper and lemon zest over the top of the bread crumbs.

4. Add ½ cup water to the bottom of the pan. Cover tightly with an aluminum foil tent. Bake for 30–35 minutes or until the tomatoes are tender.

5. Remove the aluminum foil. Place the pan under the broiler and broil until crisp and slightly browned, about 2 minutes. (Watch closely so the bread crumbs don't burn!)

PER SERVING: Calories: 182 | Total Fat: 1g | Saturated Fat: 0g | Cholesterol: 0mg | Protein: 7g | Sodium: 22mg | Potassium: 326mg | Fiber: 4g | Carbohydrates: 38g | Sugar: 5g

CARROTS WITH AN ENGLISH ACCENT

Vibrant, crunchy, and sweetly delicious, carrots are a beloved vegetable among humans and animals alike. Carrots contain high levels of vitamin A and antioxidants and are believed to help prevent cancer.

SERVES 4

Olive oil spray

¼ cup water

1 teaspoon lemon juice

4 cups baby carrots, sliced

1 teaspoon English Spice Blend
(Appendix A)

1. Preheat oven to 350°F.

2. Spray an ovenproof casserole dish with the olive oil spray. Add the water and lemon juice, and stir to combine.

3. Spread the carrot slices over the water-lemon mixture. Mist the carrots with the olive oil spray. Sprinkle the English spice blend over the carrots. Cover and bake for 35 minutes.

4. Mist the carrots again with the olive oil spray, if desired. Uncover and bake for an additional 10 minutes or until the carrots are tender.

PER SERVING: Calories: 50 | Total Fat: 0g | Saturated Fat: 0g | Cholesterol: 0mg | Protein: 1g | Sodium: 84mg | Potassium: 391mg | Fiber: 3g | Carbohydrates: 11g | Sugar: 5g

CURRIED PARSNIP PURÉE

If the Curried Parsnip Purée ends up tasting hotter than you like it, you can counter the spices by adding a little unsweetened, no-salt-added applesauce.

SERVES 4

6 parsnips, peeled and cut into ½" cubes

1 teaspoon Hot Curry Spice Blend
(Appendix A)

4 teaspoons unsalted butter

½ cup warm skim milk

1. Cook the parsnip cubes in gently boiling water for 12 minutes or until tender. Drain well.

2. Add the parsnips to the bowl of a food processor along with the remaining ingredients; process until smooth.

PER SERVING: Calories: 215 | Total Fat: 4g | Saturated Fat: 2g | Cholesterol: 10mg | Protein: 4g | Sodium: 40mg | Potassium: 932mg | Fiber: 8g | Carbohydrates: 42g | Sugar: 13g

MIDDLE EASTERN GLAZED CARROTS

Remember: It's easier to add more seasonings than it is to subtract them if you add too much. Take a sample nibble before you serve a dish, and adjust the seasonings if necessary.

SERVES 4

4 cups sliced carrots

2 teaspoons canola oil

2 teaspoons unsalted butter

1 teaspoon Middle Eastern Spice Blend (Appendix A)

2 teaspoons granulated sugar

⅛ teaspoon freshly ground black pepper

1. Put the carrots in a microwave-safe casserole dish. Cover and microwave on high for 3 minutes; turn the dish. Microwave on high for 4 minutes or until the carrots are tender.

2. Bring a large, deep nonstick sauté pan to temperature over medium heat. Add the oil, butter, and spice blend; sauté the spices for 1 minute.

3. Add the carrots and stir to mix. Sprinkle the sugar and pepper over the carrots and stir-fry until the carrots are heated through and the sugar forms a glaze.

PER SERVING: Calories: 95 | Total Fat: 4g | Saturated Fat: 1g | Cholesterol: 0mg | Protein: 1g | Sodium: 84mg | Potassium: 391mg | Fiber: 3g | Carbohydrates: 13g | Sugar: 7g

OVEN-DRIED SEASONED TOMATOES

These tomatoes will add fabulous flavor to your salads, sauces, or pasta dishes.

SERVES 8

4 plum tomatoes, peeled, seeded, and cut into quarters

Olive oil spray

⅛ teaspoon freshly ground black pepper

½ teaspoon Pasta Blend (Appendix A)

1. Preheat oven to 250°F.

2. Put the tomatoes in a medium bowl. Lightly mist with the olives oil spray, toss, and then mist again. Add the pepper and Pasta Blend.

3. Arrange the tomatoes on a baking sheet and bake until somewhat dried, about 2½–3 hours. Store covered, in the refrigerator up to 4 days, or freeze for longer storage.

PER SERVING: Calories: 8 | Total Fat: 0g | Saturated Fat: 0g | Cholesterol: 0mg | Protein: 0g | Sodium: 2mg | Potassium: 106mg | Fiber: 0g | Carbohydrates: 1g | Sugar: 1g

BAKED CAJUN CAULIFLOWER

To create a savory-sweet vegetable entrée, mix the desired amount of Cajun Spice Blend seasoning mixture with ⅛ cup unsweetened, no-salt-added applesauce to make a paste. Spread the paste over the cauliflower and bake according to the Baked Cajun Cauliflower directions.

SERVES 6

1 (1¾-pound) head cauliflower

1 teaspoon lemon juice

⅛ teaspoon mustard powder

Olive oil spray

½–1 teaspoon Cajun Spice Blend (Appendix A)

1. Preheat oven to 375°F.

2. Trim off the outer leaves of the cauliflower. Cut the base so that the head will sit upright. Bring a large pot of water to a boil over medium-high heat. Add the lemon juice and mustard powder; stir to mix. Add the cauliflower, base down, and blanch for 5 minutes. Remove and drain.

3. Spray a deep ovenproof casserole dish with the olive oil spray. Place the cauliflower base down in the casserole dish. Lightly mist the cauliflower with the olive oil spray. Evenly sprinkle the Cajun Spice Blend over the top of the cauliflower. Cover and bake for 15 minutes.

PER SERVING: Calories: 30 | Total Fat: 0g | Saturated Fat: 0g | Cholesterol: 0mg | Protein: 2g | Sodium: 19mg | Potassium: 189mg | Fiber: 3g | Carbohydrates: 5g | Sugar: 2g

CHAPTER 14

DESSERTS

RASPBERRY ICE CREAM

Ice cream is a wonderful treat for hot summer days. If you've never made your own ice cream, it's easy, especially with this recipe. Frozen and fresh raspberries are used to add flavor and color to the simple combination of ingredients. You don't need an ice-cream freezer for this treat!

YIELDS 6 CUPS; 12 SERVINGS

1 (14-ounce) can sweetened condensed milk

1½ cups heavy whipping cream

2 tablespoons lemon juice

1 teaspoon vanilla

1½ cups frozen raspberries, thawed

1 cup fresh raspberries

1. In large bowl, combine sweetened condensed milk, cream, lemon juice, and vanilla. Beat with a mixer until soft peaks form.

2. Fold in the frozen raspberries to marble, then the fresh raspberries. Pour into a freezer container and freeze until firm, about 4–6 hours.

PER SERVING: Calories: 248 | Total Fat: 14g | Saturated Fat: 8g | Cholesterol: 52mg | Protein: 3g | Sodium: 53mg | Potassium: 200mg | Fiber: 2g | Carbohydrates: 28g | Sugar: 25g

COOKIE PIE CRUST

Pie crusts can be tricky to make, even for experienced bakers. This crust is simple and fun to make and is foolproof. It's just pressed into a pie pan, baked, and cooled. You can fill it with ice cream, with pudding, with mousse, or simply with fresh fruit glazed with some melted fruit jelly. It's versatile and delicious!

YIELDS 1 PIE CRUST; 8 SERVINGS

⅓ cup unsalted butter

¼ cup granulated sugar

2 tablespoons brown sugar

1 egg yolk

1 teaspoon vanilla

½ teaspoon grated lemon zest

1¼ cups flour

1. Preheat oven to 350°F. In medium bowl, combine butter with granulated sugar and brown sugar and mix well. Beat in egg yolk, vanilla, and lemon zest.

2. Add flour and mix until a dough forms.

3. Press into the bottom and up the sides of 9" pie pan. Flute edge if desired. Prick bottom of crust with fork.

4. Bake for 12–15 minutes or until the pie crust is light golden brown. Let cool completely and fill as desired.

PER SERVING: Calories: 180 | Total Fat: 8g | Saturated Fat: 5g | Cholesterol: 46mg | Protein: 2g | Sodium: 3mg | Potassium: 30mg | Fiber: 0g | Carbohydrates: 23g | Sugar: 8g

STRAWBERRY BASIL PIE

When fresh strawberries and fresh basil are in season in the summer, this is the dessert to make. Garnish with sweetened whipped cream and some fresh berries before serving, and top each piece with a fresh small basil leaf.

SERVES 8

1 recipe Cookie Pie Crust (see recipe in this chapter), baked and cooled

3 cups strawberry sorbet, slightly softened

1 tablespoon lemon juice

2 tablespoons chopped fresh basil leaves

2 cups sliced fresh strawberries

1. Prepare cookie pie crust and let cool.

2. In large bowl, combine strawberry sorbet, lemon juice, and basil and mix until combined. Stir in fresh strawberries.

3. Pile into the pie crust and freeze until firm, about 4–6 hours. Let stand at room temperature for 15–20 minutes before serving for easier slicing.

PER SERVING: Calories: 275 | Total Fat: 9g | Saturated Fat: 5g | Cholesterol: 46mg | Protein: 3g | Sodium: 29mg | Potassium: 155mg | Fiber: 2g | Carbohydrates: 44g | Sugar: 24g

TOFFEE SQUARES

Toffee is a difficult candy to make—you're using a candy thermometer, the timing is tricky, and you're working with boiling sugar syrup. But you can almost replicate the flavor and texture with these delicious and super easy bar cookies.

YIELDS 32 BAR COOKIES

¾ cup unsalted butter, softened

⅓ cup brown sugar

¼ cup granulated sugar

2 tablespoons powdered sugar

1½ teaspoons vanilla

¼ cup toffee bits, finely crushed

1½ cups flour

1 (11.5-ounce) package milk chocolate chips

½ cup toffee bits

½ cup chopped toasted pecans

1. Preheat oven to 350°F. Spray a 9" × 13" pan with nonstick baking spray containing flour and set aside.

2. In large bowl, combine butter, brown sugar, granulated sugar, powdered sugar, and vanilla and beat until smooth. Stir in finely crushed toffee bits.

3. Add flour and mix until a dough forms. Press into prepared pan.

4. Bake for 20–25 minutes or until bars are set and light golden brown. Immediately sprinkle with chocolate chips; cover pan with foil. Let stand 5 minutes, then spread the melted chips over the bars with a knife. Sprinkle with ½ cup toffee bits and toasted pecans; let cool completely.

PER SERVING: Calories: 164 | Total Fat: 10g | Saturated Fat: 3g | Cholesterol: 14mg | Protein: 1g | Sodium: 18mg | Potassium: 26mg | Fiber: 1g | Carbohydrates: 19g | Sugar: 12g

CHEWY APRICOT BARS

These chewy bars are rich with dried apricots and nuts. They travel well and are excellent for picnics and lunchboxes. After the bars are baked and cooled, they are cut into squares and rolled in powdered sugar so the sticky sides are coated in sweetness.

YIELDS 16 BARS

3 large eggs

¾ cup granulated sugar

¼ cup brown sugar

1 tablespoon lemon juice

1 teaspoon vanilla

¾ cup flour

1 teaspoon baking powder

1 cup chopped dried apricots

¾ cup chopped pecans

Optional: Powdered sugar

1. Preheat oven to 325°F. Spray a 9" square pan with nonstick baking spray containing flour and sprinkle with more flour; shake to distribute evenly. Set aside.

2. In large bowl, beat eggs until light and lemon colored. Gradually add granulated sugar, beating until light and fluffy. Beat in brown sugar, lemon juice, and vanilla.

3. By hand, stir in flour and baking powder until combined. Add apricots and pecans.

4. Spoon into prepared pan and spread evenly. Bake for 25–30 minutes or until light golden brown and set. Cool completely.

5. Cut bars into 16 squares and roll each square in powdered sugar to coat. Store in airtight container at room temperature.

PER SERVING: Calories: 140 | Total Fat: 4g | Saturated Fat: 0g | Cholesterol: 39mg | Protein: 2g | Sodium: 38mg | Potassium: 140mg | Fiber: 1g | Carbohydrates: 23g | Sugar: 17g

PEANUT BUTTER S'MORES BARS

S'mores are the classic Girl Scout treat, made by roasting marshmallows over a campfire, then building a sandwich with the smoky sweet marshmallow, a chocolate bar, and graham crackers. Serve these peanutty bars with a big glass of cold milk.

YIELDS 36 BAR COOKIES

½ cup unsalted butter, melted

1 cup unsalted peanut butter, divided

2 cups Graham Crackers (see recipe in this chapter) crumbs

½ cup chopped unsalted peanuts

4 cups mini marshmallows

1 (12-ounce) package semisweet chocolate chips

1. Preheat oven to 350°F. Spray a 13" × 9" pan with nonstick baking spray containing flour.

2. In large bowl, combine unsalted butter, ½ cup peanut butter, graham cracker crumbs, and unsalted peanuts and mix until combined. Press into bottom of baking pan.

3. Bake for 12–14 minutes or until crust is set. Remove from oven and sprinkle with marshmallows; turn oven to broil.

4. Put the pan under the broiler; watching carefully, broil until the marshmallows puff and start to turn brown, turning pan occasionally. Remove from oven and place on wire rack.

5. In small bowl, combine chocolate chips and remaining ½ cup peanut butter; microwave on high for 2 minutes. Remove from microwave and stir. Continue microwaving for 30-second intervals, stirring after each, until mixture is smooth. Pour over marshmallows. Let stand until set, then cut into bars.

PER SERVING: Calories: 190 | Total Fat: 11g | Saturated Fat: 3g | Cholesterol: 11mg | Protein: 4g | Sodium: 16mg | Potassium: 87mg | Fiber: 1g | Carbohydrates: 20g | Sugar: 12g

PEAR AND RASPBERRY FOSTER

Bananas Foster is usually made with bananas, but using different fruits is fun. This recipe is very colorful and delicious. Serve it over ice cream, pound cake, or freshly baked biscuits, topped with whipped cream.

SERVES 4

⅓ cup unsalted butter

⅓ cup brown sugar

1 tablespoon lemon juice

2 medium pears, peeled, cored, and sliced

1 teaspoon vanilla

1 cup fresh raspberries

1. In large saucepan, melt butter with brown sugar over medium heat. Add lemon juice and pears.

2. Sauté pears, stirring gently, until just tender, about 3–4 minutes. Add vanilla and raspberries; heat for another 1–2 minutes, then serve over ice cream or cake.

PER SERVING: Calories: 289 | Total Fat: 15g | Saturated Fat: 9g | Cholesterol: 40mg | Protein: 1g | Sodium: 8mg | Potassium: 218mg | Fiber: 5g | Carbohydrates: 39g | Sugar: 30g

ICE CREAM SHERBET BUNDT CAKE

Look at the label for the sodium content before you buy the ice cream and sherbet for this recipe. And you do need to know how much your bundt pan will hold before you buy the ice cream and sherbet for this recipe; just add cups of water to it, counting, until the pan is filled.

SERVES 16

2 quarts ice cream of various flavors

1 quart sherbet of various flavors

½ cup marshmallow crème

1. Layer the ice cream, sherbet, and marshmallow crème in the bundt pan, pressing down firmly so there are no air pockets.

2. Cover pan and freeze for at least 8 hours, preferably overnight.

3. An hour before you're ready to serve, remove pan from the freezer. Cover it with hot towels and shake until the ice cream mixture is loosened. Invert onto a serving tray, remove the pan, and immediately refreeze the "cake."

4. Remove from the freezer 10 minutes before serving to make the "cake" easier to slice.

PER SERVING: Calories: 215 | Total Fat: 8g | Saturated Fat: 5g | Cholesterol: 22mg | Protein: 3g | Sodium: 72mg | Potassium: 200mg | Fiber: 1g | Carbohydrates: 35g | Sugar: 28g

GRAHAM CRACKERS

This easy recipe is fun to make, but to make them simpler, the dough is rolled into balls and flattened right on the baking sheet, then baked until crisp. You can find whole-wheat pastry flour at most large grocery stores, or order it on the Internet.

YIELDS 36 GRAHAM CRACKERS

¾ cup unsalted butter, softened

½ cup dark brown sugar

¼ cup light brown sugar

⅓ cup honey

2 teaspoons vanilla

½ cup milk

¼ cup water

3 cups whole-wheat pastry flour

1½ cups all-purpose flour

1 teaspoon baking powder

¼ teaspoon baking soda

½ teaspoon cinnamon

⅛ teaspoon nutmeg

1. In large bowl, combine butter and brown sugars; beat until fluffy. Add honey, beating until fluffy. Beat in vanilla, milk, and water.

2. Sift together pastry flour, all-purpose flour, baking powder, baking soda, cinnamon, and nutmeg and add to creamed mixture.

3. Cover dough and refrigerate overnight.

4. When you're ready to bake, preheat oven to 350°F. Roll the dough into 1" balls, using floured hands, and place 4" apart on baking sheet. Press down with a glass or a spatula to make thin rounds. Prick each round with a fork.

5. Bake for 12–15 minutes or until the crackers are set and no imprint remains when lightly touched with your finger. Let cool for 5 minutes on baking sheets, then cool completely on wire racks.

PER SERVING: Calories: 116 | Total Fat: 4g | Saturated Fat: 2g | Cholesterol: 10mg | Protein: 2g | Sodium: 22mg | Potassium: 60mg | Fiber: 1g | Carbohydrates: 18g | Sugar: 7g

TRIPLE BERRY PAVLOVA

A Pavlova is a gorgeous and ethereal dessert that was invented to honor Anna Pavlova, the Russian ballerina. It has to be made ahead of time, so is perfect for entertaining. Take a picture of it before you dig in!

SERVES 6

5 egg whites

½ teaspoon lemon juice

1 cup sugar

2 teaspoons cornstarch

1 teaspoon apple cider vinegar

1½ teaspoons vanilla, divided

½ cup heavy whipping cream

3 tablespoons powdered sugar

½ cup Lemon Curd (Chapter 4)

1 cup raspberries

1 cup blueberries

1 cup blackberries

2 tablespoons orange juice

1. Preheat oven to 300°F.

2. In large bowl, place egg whites and lemon juice; beat until soft peaks form. Gradually add sugar, about a tablespoon at a time, beating until the meringue holds a stiff peak.

3. Stir in cornstarch, vinegar, and 1 teaspoon vanilla.

4. Place parchment paper on a baking sheet. Spoon the meringue onto the sheet, creating a 9" circle; smooth the top. Bake for 50–60 minutes or until the meringue is crisp on the outside. Cool on the paper on a wire rack.

5. When ready to eat, peel the paper off the meringue and turn it over onto a serving plate so the top is on the bottom.

6. In medium bowl, beat whipping cream with powdered sugar and remaining ½ teaspoon vanilla until soft peaks form. Fold in lemon curd. Pile this mixture on the meringue.

7. Top with berries and drizzle with orange juice. Refrigerate for an hour or two, or serve immediately.

PER SERVING: Calories: 317 | Total Fat: 10g | Saturated Fat: 6g | Cholesterol: 59mg | Protein: 5g | Sodium: 63mg | Potassium: 178mg | Fiber: 3g | Carbohydrates: 53g | Sugar: 47g

STRAWBERRY RHUBARB RASPBERRY CRISP

You can use any fruit you'd like in this easy home recipe, but in the spring, strawberries, rhubarb, and raspberries are an admirable combination. This dessert is good served warm or cold, topped with sweetened whipped cream, or served with ice cream.

SERVES 8

2 cups sliced fresh rhubarb

2 cups sliced strawberries

2 cups raspberries

¾ cup sugar

1 cup plus 2 tablespoons flour, divided

2 tablespoons lemon juice

½ teaspoon grated lemon zest

1½ cups rolled oats

1 cup brown sugar

½ cup chopped pecans

¾ cup unsalted butter, melted

½ teaspoon cinnamon

1. Preheat oven to 375°F. Spray a 9" × 13" glass baking dish with nonstick cooking spray containing flour and set aside.

2. Combine rhubarb, strawberries, and raspberries in the baking dish. Sprinkle with sugar, 2 tablespoons flour, lemon juice, and zest and toss gently to coat.

3. In medium bowl, combine remaining 1 cup flour, rolled oats, brown sugar, and pecans, and mix well. Add melted butter and cinnamon and mix until crumbly. Spoon on top of the fruit.

4. Bake for 40–50 minutes or until fruit mixture is bubbly and tender and the streusel topping is golden brown. Let cool 1 hour, then serve.

PER SERVING: Calories: 534 | Total Fat: 23g | Saturated Fat: 11g | Cholesterol: 45mg | Protein: 5g | Sodium: 12mg | Potassium: 349mg | Fiber: 6g | Carbohydrates: 79g | Sugar: 50g

LACE COOKIES

Lace cookies are fun to make and eat. They spread out into a very thin layer while they bake, and are flexible while warm. You can drape them over a rolling pin or form them around a stainless steel rod or cone to make fancy shapes. Then those shapes can be filled with whipped cream, pudding, or lemon curd.

YIELDS 48 COOKIES

½ cup unsalted butter

¾ cup brown sugar

¼ cup granulated sugar

1 cup rolled oats

¼ cup flour

1 tablespoon honey

1 tablespoon heavy cream

1 teaspoon vanilla

1. Preheat oven to 375°F. In large saucepan, melt butter over medium heat. Add brown sugar and granulated sugar and stir until smooth. Stir in rolled oats, flour, honey, heavy cream, and vanilla, beating well.

2. Line cookie sheets with silicone baking mats or parchment paper. Drop the batter onto the lined sheets with a teaspoon, leaving about 3" between each cookie, because they spread while they bake.

3. Bake for 6–7 minutes until golden brown. Remove from oven and set aside for about a minute, then carefully remove to a wire rack to cool. You can drape them over a rolling pin or around a form at this point.

PER SERVING: Calories: 45 | Total Fat: 2g | Saturated Fat: 1g | Cholesterol: 5mg | Protein: 0g | Sodium: 1mg | Potassium: 12mg | Fiber: 0g | Carbohydrates: 6g | Sugar: 4g

LEMON RASPBERRY ETON MESS

Eaton mess is a classic dessert from England, made by layering meringue cookies, whipped cream, and fruit in parfait glasses. This super simple version of this dessert is lovely and full of flavor. It's perfect for a summer party.

SERVES 4

¾ cup heavy whipping cream

2 tablespoons powdered sugar

⅓ cup Lemon Curd (Chapter 4)

16 Meringue Cookies (see recipe in this chapter), crumbled

1½ cups fresh raspberries

1. In medium bowl, combine whipping cream and powdered sugar; beat until soft peaks form. Beat in lemon curd.

2. Layer the cream mixture, crumbled cookies, and raspberries in parfait glasses or wine goblets. Serve immediately or cover and chill for 2–4 hours.

PER SERVING: Calories: 292 | Total Fat: 19g | Saturated Fat: 11g | Cholesterol: 97mg | Protein: 3g | Sodium: 36mg | Potassium: 135mg | Fiber: 3g | Carbohydrates: 28g | Sugar: 23g

PEANUT FUDGE POPS

Frozen treats are fun to eat in the summer. Kids love them, and they are easy to make. You can make them out of frozen juice, or frozen yogurt, or puréed fruit; let your imagination run wild! This recipe tastes like a Fudgsicle, but better. The peanut butter adds a rich and nutty taste and makes the pops very creamy.

YIELDS 8 POPS

3 tablespoons unsalted butter

⅓ cup flour

2 cups milk

⅔ cup brown sugar

3 tablespoons cocoa

½ cup semisweet chocolate chips

⅓ cup unsalted peanut butter

1 teaspoon vanilla

½ cup chopped unsalted peanuts

1. In medium saucepan, melt butter over medium heat. Add flour; cook and stir for 1 minute.

2. Add milk, brown sugar, and cocoa; cook, stirring constantly with a wire whisk, until thickened.

3. Add chocolate chips and peanut butter; cook and stir until melted.

4. Remove from heat and add vanilla. Let cool for 1 hour, stirring a few times with the whisk.

5. Pour ⅓ cup into each pop mold or 4-ounce paper cup. Add wooden sticks, then sprinkle with peanuts. Freeze until firm.

PER SERVING: Calories: 344 | Total Fat: 19g | Saturated Fat: 5g | Cholesterol: 16mg | Protein: 8g | Sodium: 33mg | Potassium: 283mg | Fiber: 3g | Carbohydrates: 39g | Sugar: 29g

MOCHA BROWNIES

Chocolate and coffee are natural partners. The depth of flavor in coffee brings out the nuttiness and richness of the chocolate. Using both cocoa and chocolate chips also makes the flavor richer, and the brownies creamier. You can frost these with any frosting, but for a real treat try the caramel coffee frosting as directed.

YIELDS 36 BROWNIES

1¼ cups unsalted butter, divided

¼ cup safflower or peanut oil

1¾ cups brown sugar, divided

1 cup granulated sugar

⅔ cup cocoa powder

½ cup milk chocolate chips

4 large eggs

¾ cup flour

1 tablespoon espresso powder

2 teaspoons vanilla, divided

½ cup crushed chocolate-covered coffee beans

3 tablespoons milk

2 cups sifted powdered sugar

1. Preheat oven to 325°F. Spray a 13" × 9" baking pan with nonstick baking spray containing flour and set aside.

2. In large saucepan, melt ¾ cup butter with oil over medium heat. Add 1 cup brown sugar and granulated sugar and cook, stirring, for 2 minutes.

3. Add cocoa powder and chocolate chips and stir for 2 minutes or until chips are melted. Remove from heat.

4. Beat in eggs, one at a time, beating well after each addition. Add flour and espresso powder and mix well, then stir in 1 teaspoon vanilla and coffee beans.

5. Pour into prepared pan. Bake for 22–27 minutes or until brownies are just set and have a shiny crust. Remove from oven and cool on wire rack.

6. For frosting, melt remaining ½ cup butter in small saucepan over medium heat. Add remaining ¾ cup brown sugar and stir until mixture just comes to a boil.

7. Remove from heat and add milk; stir with wire whisk until smooth. Beat in powdered sugar and remaining 1 teaspoon vanilla until smooth. Pour over brownies and let stand until set.

PER SERVING: Calories: 194 | Total Fat: 10g | Saturated Fat: 5g | Cholesterol: 41mg | Protein: 1g | Sodium: 13mg | Potassium: 60mg | Fiber: 0g | Carbohydrates: 25g | Sugar: 21g

CREAM PUFFS WITH RASPBERRY ICE CREAM

Cream puffs don't have a lot of flavor on their own, so add some with the filling; it should have a strong flavor. Strawberry or raspberry ice cream is delicious, and pretty too. Add some fresh berries to the plate for a nice finishing touch.

SERVES 6

⅔ cup water

⅓ cup unsalted butter

⅔ cup flour

2 large eggs

1 egg white

2 teaspoons vanilla

6 cups Raspberry Ice Cream (see recipe in this chapter)

1 cup fresh raspberries

1. Preheat oven to 400°F. Line baking sheets with parchment paper and set aside.

2. In medium saucepan, combine water and butter and bring to a rolling boil over high heat. Turn heat down to medium, add flour, and beat until a ball forms that cleans the sides of the pan. Remove from heat.

3. Add eggs and the egg white, one at a time, beating well after each addition until mixture is smooth and shiny. Beat in vanilla.

4. Drop batter by ¼-cup measures onto prepared baking sheets, about 4" apart. Bake for 25–35 minutes or until puffs are golden brown and firm to the touch.

5. Remove puffs from oven and cut a small slit in the top of each one; return to oven for 2 minutes. Let cool on wire racks.

6. When ready to eat, cut puffs in half crosswise. Remove any dough from the inside so you have hollow shells. Fill with ice cream; replace tops, and serve with raspberries.

PER SERVING: Calories: 675 | Total Fat: 39g | Saturated Fat: 24g | Cholesterol: 200mg | Protein: 11g | Sodium: 140mg | Potassium: 480mg | Fiber: 5g | Carbohydrates: 70g | Sugar: 51g

LEMON PEAR CRISP

This dessert is delicious served warm from the oven with a scoop of vanilla ice cream, or some soft whipped cream flavored with honey.

SERVES 8

6 large ripe pears, peeled, cored, and sliced

2 tablespoons honey

¼ cup sugar

1 cup plus 2 tablespoons flour, divided

2 tablespoons lemon juice

1 teaspoon grated lemon zest

2 teaspoons minced fresh thyme leaves

1½ cups rolled oats

1 cup brown sugar

¾ cup unsalted butter, melted

1 cup chopped walnuts

1. Preheat oven to 350°F. Spray a 13" × 9" baking dish with nonstick baking spray containing flour.

2. Place pears in the baking dish. Top with honey, sugar, 2 tablespoons flour, lemon juice, lemon zest, and thyme and toss gently to coat.

3. In medium bowl, combine remaining 1 cup flour, rolled oats, and brown sugar and mix well. Add melted butter and stir until crumbly. Add walnuts. Sprinkle over pears in baking pan.

4. Bake for 50–55 minutes or until pears are tender and bubbling around the edges and the topping is golden brown. Cool 30 minutes, then serve.

PER SERVING: Calories: 516 | Total Fat: 20g | Saturated Fat: 11g | Cholesterol: 45mg | Protein: 5g | Sodium: 12mg | Potassium: 296mg | Fiber: 6g | Carbohydrates: 82g | Sugar: 50g

BUTTERSCOTCH PUDDING

Make your own pudding from scratch for a delicious, homestyle dessert everyone will love. Top with a drizzle of caramel sauce or some whipped cream.

SERVES 4

2 tablespoons butter

2 tablespoons flour

1 tablespoon cornstarch

1 cup whole milk

⅓ cup light brown sugar

⅓ cup dark brown sugar

2 egg yolks

¾ cup light cream

1½ teaspoons vanilla

1. In heavy saucepan, melt butter over medium heat. Add flour and cornstarch and cook for 1 minute until mixture bubbles, stirring constantly with a wire whisk.

2. Add milk and stir until smooth, making sure the whisk gets into the corners of the pan. Then add sugars, egg yolks, and light cream and, stirring constantly with a wire whisk, cook until mixture comes to a boil. Cook for another 2 minutes until thickened.

3. Remove from heat and add vanilla; whisk until smooth.

4. Cool, stirring occasionally, for about 40 minutes, then pour into serving dishes. Cover and chill for 1–2 hours before serving.

PER SERVING: Calories: 410 | Total Fat: 23g | Saturated Fat: 14g | Cholesterol: 176mg | Protein: 4g | Sodium: 55mg | Potassium: 196mg | Fiber: 0g | Carbohydrates: 45g | Sugar: 38g

RED VELVET CUPCAKES

The classic red velvet recipe uses an entire bottle of red food coloring. That's really not something you want to feed your family. Make the cake with some puréed beets instead! You'll get that lovely red color and a slightly rich and roasted flavor in the cake. Frost with cream cheese frosting for a delicious and beautiful dessert.

YIELDS 12 CUPCAKES

1 large beet

1 tablespoon safflower or peanut oil

⅔ cup milk

2 tablespoons lemon juice

1¾ cups all-purpose flour

¼ cup cornstarch

2 tablespoons cocoa powder

⅛ teaspoon salt

½ teaspoon baking powder

¼ teaspoon baking soda

¾ cup granulated sugar

⅓ cup brown sugar

3 large eggs

½ cup unsalted butter, melted

2 teaspoons vanilla, divided

4 ounces cream cheese, softened

2 tablespoons unsalted butter, softened

2 cups powdered sugar

1. Preheat oven to 375°F. Line a 12-cup muffin tin with paper liners.

2. Place the beet on a cookie sheet and drizzle with oil. Roast for about 1 hour or until the beet is tender. Remove from oven and let cool completely; peel and chop (use gloves or your hands will be dyed red).

3. Purée beet in a food processor or blender. In small bowl, combine milk and lemon juice; mix and set aside.

4. In a medium bowl, combine flour, cornstarch, cocoa, salt, baking powder, and baking soda, and mix well with a wire whisk.

5. In a large bowl, beat granulated sugar, brown sugar, and eggs until light. Add milk mixture, ½ cup melted butter, puréed beets, and 1½ teaspoons vanilla and beat well. Beat in flour mixture just until smooth.

6. Spoon batter into prepared muffin cups. Bake for 25–30 minutes or until cupcakes spring back when lightly touched. Let cool completely on racks.

7. In medium bowl, combine cream cheese, 2 tablespoons softened butter, powdered sugar, and remaining ½ teaspoon vanilla and beat well. Frost cooled cupcakes.

PER SERVING: Calories: 384 | Total Fat: 15g | Saturated Fat: 8g | Cholesterol: 89mg | Protein: 4g | Sodium: 127mg | Potassium: 121mg | Fiber: 1g | Carbohydrates: 57g | Sugar: 39g

OLIVE OIL CAKE

Olive oil makes an interesting cake with a slightly spicy flavor. If you like a strong olive oil taste, use extra-virgin; otherwise, use ordinary olive oil for a milder taste. Serve after an Italian meal and enjoy every bite.

SERVES 9

3 large eggs

¾ cup granulated sugar

⅓ cup brown sugar

¾ cup olive oil

1½ cups cake flour

½ cup almond flour

½ teaspoon baking powder

¼ teaspoon baking soda

Pinch salt

1 cup milk

¼ cup heavy cream

1 teaspoon vanilla

2 tablespoons plus 2 teaspoons minced fresh basil leaves, divided

¼ cup hot water

1 tablespoon lemon juice

1⅓ cups powdered sugar

1 tablespoon honey

1. Preheat oven to 350°F. Spray a 9" round cake pan with nonstick baking spray containing flour and set aside.

2. In large bowl, beat eggs with granulated sugar until light and fluffy. Beat in brown sugar. Then beat in olive oil in a steady stream until blended.

3. In medium bowl, stir together cake flour, almond flour, baking powder, baking soda, and salt and whisk together. Add to the egg mixture in four batches, alternating with the milk and heavy cream.

4. Stir in vanilla and 2 teaspoons minced basil leaves. Pour into prepared pan.

5. Bake for 30–40 minutes or until cake springs back when lightly touched and just starts to pull away from sides of the pan. Cool 10 minutes, then cool completely on wire rack.

6. While cake is cooling, combine hot water, lemon juice, and remaining 2 tablespoons minced basil in a small bowl. Let stand for 30 minutes, then strain the liquid, discarding the basil leaves. Add powdered sugar and honey to the strained liquid and mix well. Pour over cooled cake.

Calories: 542 | Total Fat: 27g | Saturated Fat: 4g | Cholesterol: 75mg | Protein: 7g | Sodium: 137mg | Potassium: 106mg | Fiber: 2g | Carbohydrates: 68g | Sugar: 47g

LEMON CURD ICE CREAM

It's almost impossible to find lemon ice cream in grocery stores. But you don't need to look very hard; this super simple recipe is perfect and has the best flavor. Serve it in hollowed-out lemon halves for a special presentation.

YIELDS 1 QUART; SERVING SIZE ½ CUP

3 cups vanilla ice cream

1 cup Lemon Curd (Chapter 4)

½ teaspoon grated lemon zest

1. Let the ice cream stand at room temperature for 15 minutes or until slightly softened. Place in medium bowl.

2. Beat in lemon curd and lemon zest until smooth. Immediately pour into a freezer container and return to freezer. Freeze 4–6 hours until firm.

PER SERVING: Calories: 157 | Total Fat: 8g | Saturated Fat: 5g | Cholesterol: 66mg | Protein: 2g | Sodium: 47mg | Potassium: 107mg | Fiber: 0g | Carbohydrates: 18g | Sugar: 17g

BAKED PEARS WITH ROSEMARY

When fruit is baked, it takes on another dimension. The sugars in the fruit caramelize slightly, and the flesh becomes soft and tender. You can flavor these pears any way you'd like, but they are particularly good with some fresh rosemary.

SERVES 4

2 large pears, peeled, cored, and cut in half

2 tablespoons unsalted butter

2 tablespoons brown sugar

1 tablespoon granulated sugar

2 tablespoons honey

1 tablespoon lemon juice

1 teaspoon minced fresh rosemary leaves

1. Preheat oven to 400°F. Place the pears, cut side up, in a 2-quart baking dish and set aside.

2. In small saucepan, combine butter, brown sugar, granulated sugar, honey, lemon juice, and rosemary. Cook over low heat, stirring frequently, until sugar melts.

3. Drizzle this mixture over the pears. Bake for 20–30 minutes until pears are tender when pierced with a fork. Serve with rosemary leaves and whipped cream or ice cream, if desired.

PER SERVING: Calories: 181 | Total Fat: 5g | Saturated Fat: 3g | Cholesterol: 15mg | Protein: 0g | Sodium: 3mg | Potassium: 156mg | Fiber: 3g | Carbohydrates: 34g | Sugar: 27g

MERINGUE COOKIES

Most meringue recipes use salt to stabilize the foam, but cream of tartar and a drop of lemon have the same effect. For peppermint meringues, add some ground-up peppermint candies and peppermint extract. For lemon meringues, add some ground-up hard lemon candies and a bit of lemon zest.

YIELDS 48 COOKIES

⅔ cup sugar

2 egg whites

⅛ teaspoon cream of tartar

1/16 teaspoon lemon juice

½ teaspoon vanilla

1. Preheat oven to 300°F. Line a cookie sheet with parchment paper and set aside. Place the sugar in a blender or food processor and blend or process until it is finely ground.

2. In medium bowl, combine egg whites, cream of tartar, and lemon juice, and beat with a mixer until soft peaks form.

3. Gradually add the sugar, beating with mixer on high until the mixture is stiff and glossy. The sugar should be almost dissolved when you feel a bit of the meringue between your fingers. Beat in vanilla.

4. Drop by heaping teaspoons onto prepared cookie sheet. Bake for 25–35 minutes or until the meringues are firm to the touch. Turn off oven, open door, and cool for 30 minutes. Then transfer the paper with the cookies to a wire rack and cool completely. Store in an airtight container at room temperature.

PER SERVING: Calories: 11 | Total Fat: 0g | Saturated Fat: 0g | Cholesterol: 0mg | Protein: 0g | Sodium: 2mg | Potassium: 3mg | Fiber: 0g | Carbohydrates: 2g | Sugar: 2g

HERBED SUGAR COOKIES

These tender, slightly crisp cookies can be made simply, or rolled out and cut into shapes for the holidays. Let's make them, but with a twist; use Herbed Sugar instead of ordinary granulated sugar for a wonderful taste. Store them in a cookie jar, tuck them into lunchboxes, and enjoy with tea for a snack on the porch.

YIELDS 48 COOKIES

1 cup unsalted butter, softened

¾ cup Herbed Sugar (Chapter 4)

⅓ cup powdered sugar

1 large egg

2 egg whites

¼ cup light cream

¼ teaspoon vanilla

2⅔ cups flour

½ teaspoon baking powder

¼ teaspoon baking soda

1. Preheat oven to 350°F.

2. In large bowl, combine butter with herbed sugar and powdered sugar; beat well until fluffy.

3. Add egg and beat well, then beat in egg whites. Beat in light cream and vanilla.

4. Add flour, baking powder, and baking soda and mix just until a dough forms. Cover dough and chill for at least 4 hours.

5. Roll out the dough onto floured work surface to ¼" thick and cut with cookie cutters. You can also roll the dough into 1" balls; place on ungreased cookie sheets and flatten with a glass or a spatula.

6. Bake for 8–10 minutes or until the cookies are set and very light gold on the bottom. Let cool on cookie sheets for 2 minutes, then remove to wire rack to cool completely. Frost when cool, if desired.

PER SERVING: Calories: 82 | Total Fat: 4g | Saturated Fat: 2g | Cholesterol: 16mg | Protein: 1g | Sodium: 15mg | Potassium: 14mg | Fiber: 0g | Carbohydrates: 9g | Sugar: 4g

ANGEL FOOD CAKE

This recipe is easy to make; it just takes a bit of patience and some time. Angel food cake is also very easy to dress up. Frost with a simple powdered sugar glaze, or melt chocolate with some cream and drizzle that over the beautiful finished cake.

SERVES 12

11 egg whites, at room temperature

1 teaspoon cream of tartar

½ teaspoon lemon juice

1¼ cups granulated sugar

½ cup powdered sugar

1 cup cake flour

1½ teaspoons vanilla

1. Preheat oven to 325°F. Place the oven rack in the lowest position in the oven.

2. In large bowl, combine egg whites, cream of tartar, and lemon juice. Beat until soft peaks form.

3. Gradually beat in granulated sugar, about a tablespoon at a time, until the meringue is stiff and glossy. Beat in powdered sugar until combined.

4. Fold in half of the cake flour until combined, then fold in remaining flour. Stir in vanilla.

5. Spoon batter into an ungreased 10" angel food tube pan. Rap the pan on the counter gently once to remove any large air bubbles.

6. Bake for 40–50 minutes or until the cake is light golden brown and set. Immediately invert pan onto a bottle. It must cool upside down so the delicate structure doesn't collapse while cooling.

7. To remove from pan, run a sharp knife around the outside and around the center tube. Gently push cake out of pan. Turn onto serving plate.

PER SERVING: Calories: 145 | Total Fat: 0g | Saturated Fat: 0g | Cholesterol: 0mg | Protein: 1g | Sodium: 5mg | Potassium: 59mg | Fiber: 0g | Carbohydrates: 35g | Sugar: 25g

LEMON MERINGUE ANGEL FOOD DESSERT

This dessert serves a crowd and is perfect for entertaining. It looks like a lemon meringue pie, but you don't have to bother with a crust. The meringue is cooked before it's put on top of the dessert so it won't weep or turn liquid at the bottom. This is called a Swiss meringue. This process just takes a little bit of patience, and results in the perfect dessert.

SERVES 12

1 Angel Food Cake (see recipe in this chapter), cut into cubes

1¼ cups heavy whipping cream

⅓ cup powdered sugar

1 teaspoon vanilla

2 cups Lemon Curd (Chapter 4)

¼ cup finely ground hard lemon candies

4 egg whites

1 tablespoon lemon juice

⅔ cup granulated sugar

1. Place cake cubes in a bowl, cover, and set aside.

2. In large bowl, beat whipping cream with powdered sugar and vanilla until stiff peaks form. Fold in lemon curd.

3. Layer the cake cubes and lemon mixture in a 13" × 9" glass baking pan, pressing the cake down slightly so it is all covered with the lemon mixture. Sprinkle with crushed candies. Cover and refrigerate while you prepare the meringue.

4. For meringue, combine egg whites, lemon juice, and granulated sugar in the top of a double boiler. Place on a pan of simmering water, making sure the bottom of the double boiler doesn't touch the water below. Stir with a wire whisk until the sugar dissolves.

5. Beat with a hand mixer until the mixture is stiff and glossy and a thermometer registers 160°F. This should take about 10–15 minutes.

6. Remove the dessert from the refrigerator and top with the meringue, spreading to cover and sealing the edges.

7. Preheat oven to broil. Place the dessert 6" from heat source and broil for about 2 minutes, watching carefully, until the meringue is browned on the peaks. Refrigerate for at least 4 hours before serving.

PER SERVING: Calories: 389 | Total Fat: 14g | Saturated Fat: 8g | Cholesterol: 97mg | Protein: 4g | Sodium: 51mg | Potassium: 129mg | Fiber: 0g | Carbohydrates: 62g | Sugar: 51g

GRILLED STRAWBERRY SHORTCAKE

Strawberry shortcake can be made with pound cake or with actual shortcake, which is more like a biscuit. But try it with grilled Angel Food Cake! Grill the strawberries a bit too, to soften them and add a smoky flavor. This dessert is perfect for the Fourth of July or after a cookout.

SERVES 6

¾ cup heavy whipping cream

¼ cup powdered sugar

¼ cup Lemon Curd (Chapter 4)

2 cups strawberries

6 slices Angel Food Cake (see recipe in this chapter)

1. In medium bowl, combine whipping cream with powdered sugar; beat until soft peaks form. Fold in the lemon curd, cover, and refrigerate.

2. Prepare and preheat grill. Remove the stems and leaves from the strawberries and wash gently; pat dry. Place strawberries in a grill basket.

3. Grill the berries for a minute or two until they are warm. Remove from grill basket and let cool. Crush ½ cup of the strawberries in a small bowl. Slice remaining strawberries in about ¼" slices.

4. Grill the angel food cake for a minute or two on each side until grill marks form. Place cake slices on serving plates.

5. Drizzle with the crushed strawberries and top with sliced strawberries. Top with the whipped-cream mixture and serve immediately.

PER SERVING: Calories: 309 | Total Fat: 12g | Saturated Fat: 7g | Cholesterol: 56mg | Protein: 2g | Sodium: 21mg | Potassium: 180mg | Fiber: 1g | Carbohydrates: 48g | Sugar: 36g

APPLE PEACH CRISP

Apple crisp is a classic dessert that is perfect for fall. This simple and homespun recipe is dressed up with another fruit that comes into season in the fall: peaches. The combination of apples and peaches is really delicious. Serve this warm from the oven, topped with vanilla ice cream, for a wonderful treat.

SERVES 8

3 cups Granny Smith apple slices, peeled, cored, and sliced ¼" thick

2 cups peach slices, peeled, sliced ½" thick

2 tablespoons lemon juice

1 cup granulated sugar, divided

2 tablespoons cornstarch

½ teaspoon cinnamon

⅛ teaspoon nutmeg

2 cups flour

2 cups quick-cooking oats

1 cup brown sugar

1 cup unsalted butter, melted

1. Preheat oven to 350°F. Combine apples and peaches in a 13" × 9" glass baking dish. Sprinkle with lemon juice. In a small bowl, combine ½ cup granulated sugar, cornstarch, cinnamon, and nutmeg and sprinkle over fruit; toss to coat.

2. In large bowl, combine flour, oats, brown sugar, and remaining ½ cup granulated sugar and mix well. Add melted butter and mix until crumbly. Sprinkle over fruit in the baking dish.

3. Bake for 45–55 minutes or until fruit is tender. Remove from oven and let cool for 45 minutes before serving.

PER SERVING: Calories: 634 | Total Fat: 24g | Saturated Fat: 14g | Cholesterol: 60mg | Protein: 6g | Sodium: 12mg | Potassium: 263mg | Fiber: 3g | Carbohydrates: 100g | Sugar: 59g

PEANUT BUTTER BROWNIES

This simple recipe is great for packing into lunchboxes or as a picnic treat. Be sure to buy unsalted peanut butter, since the salted type is high in sodium. By the way, using a glass baking dish instead of a metal one helps the brownies stay softer and chewier, because it doesn't hold heat as well and the brownies cool faster.

YIELDS 36 BARS

1¾ cups unsalted peanut butter, divided

½ cup unsalted butter, softened

1 cup brown sugar

1 cup granulated sugar

3 large eggs, beaten

2 teaspoons vanilla

1¾ cups flour

½ teaspoon baking powder

1 cup chopped unsalted peanuts

1 (12-ounce) package semisweet chocolate chips

1. Preheat oven to 325°F. Spray a 13" × 9" glass baking dish with nonstick baking spray containing flour and set aside.

2. In large bowl, combine 1¼ cups peanut butter and butter; mix until combined. Add brown sugar and granulated sugar and mix until combined.

3. Add eggs and beat until combined; do not overbeat. Mix in vanilla.

4. Stir in flour and baking powder and mix. Add the unsalted peanuts. Spoon into prepared pan and smooth top.

5. Bake for 30–35 minutes or until the bars are just set. Cool on wire rack for 30 minutes.

6. In small microwave-safe bowl, combine chocolate chips and remaining ½ cup peanut butter. Microwave on high power for 2 minutes, then remove and stir until chips are melted and mixture is smooth. Pour over brownies and spread to coat. Let stand until the glaze is set, then cut into bars.

PER SERVING: Calories: 237 | Total Fat: 13g | Saturated Fat: 3g | Cholesterol: 24mg | Protein: 5g | Sodium: 15mg | Potassium: 129mg | Fiber: 1g | Carbohydrates: 25g | Sugar: 17g

WALNUT CARAMEL APPLE PIZZA

The best apples for baking include Granny Smith, Braeburn, Gala, Fuji, Honeycrisp, Northern Spy, and Winesap. They hold their shape well when baked and have a wonderful sweet and tart flavor. Serve this pizza warm from the oven.

SERVES 8

2 recipes unbaked Cookie Pie Crust (see recipe in this chapter)

4 large apples, peeled and sliced

2 tablespoons lemon juice

¼ cup granulated sugar

1 teaspoon cinnamon

⅛ teaspoon nutmeg or cardamom

¾ cup brown sugar

½ cup corn syrup

3 tablespoons unsalted butter

¼ cup heavy cream

1 teaspoon vanilla

20 caramels, unwrapped, and quartered

1. Preheat oven to 375°F. Make the cookie pie crust and press into a metal 13" × 9" baking pan. Bake for 5 minutes or until just set.

2. In large bowl, toss apples with lemon juice, granulated sugar, cinnamon, and nutmeg; set aside.

3. In heavy saucepan, combine brown sugar, corn syrup, and butter and bring to a boil over medium heat. Cook, stirring constantly with a wire whisk, for about 5 minutes until thickened. Remove from heat and stir in cream; stir until mixture stops bubbling. Stir in vanilla.

4. Arrange apple mixture over the crust. Top with the quartered caramels and drizzle with the caramel syrup. Bake for 25–30 minutes or until the apples are tender and the crust is light golden brown. Serve warm.

PER SERVING: Calories: 692 | Total Fat: 24g | Saturated Fat: 14g | Cholesterol: 115mg | Protein: 5g | Sodium: 100mg | Potassium: 214mg | Fiber: 2g | Carbohydrates: 118g | Sugar: 60g

HIDDEN SURPRISE CAKES

Cupcakes are always fun, but these are extra special: There's a piece of candy hidden inside each one! You could substitute any candy for the peppermint cups in this recipe; just cut into pieces about 1" wide.

SERVES 12

1 cup unbleached all-purpose flour

⅛ teaspoon salt

1 teaspoon baking powder

3 large eggs

¾ cup vanilla sugar (see Fruit Sauce recipe in this chapter)

1 tablespoon lemon juice

Optional: ½ teaspoon grated lemon zest

6 tablespoons hot skim milk

1 (1.2-ounce) package dark chocolate peppermint cups

1 tablespoon cocoa powder

1. Preheat oven to 350°F. Treat a 12-cup muffin pan with nonstick spray or line with foil liners.

2. In a small bowl, mix together the flour, salt, and baking powder. Add the eggs to the bowl of a food processor or a mixing bowl; pulse or beat until fluffy and lemon colored. Add the vanilla sugar, lemon juice, and the optional lemon zest, if using; pulse or beat to mix. Add the flour mixture; process or mix just enough to blend. Add the hot milk and process or mix until blended.

3. Spoon the batter halfway up the muffin cups in the prepared muffin pan. Cut each peppermint cup into 4 equal pieces. Add 1 piece to each muffin section. Spoon the remaining batter over the top of the candy.

4. Bake for 15 minutes or until the cakes are light golden brown and firm to touch. Dust the tops of the cakes with cocoa powder. Move to a rack to cool.

PER SERVING: Calories: 120 | Total Fat: 1g | Saturated Fat: 0g | Cholesterol: 53mg | Protein: 3g | Sodium: 75mg | Potassium: 50mg | Fiber: 0g | Carbohydrates: 23g | Sugar: 14g

FRUIT SAUCE

To make the vanilla sugar in this recipe, put 2 cups of sugar and 1 snipped vanilla bean in a blender or food processor; process until the sugar is fine-ground and the vanilla bean is pulverized. Store in an airtight container in the refrigerator or freezer.

SERVES 4

1 teaspoon ground cinnamon

4 teaspoons vanilla sugar

1½ teaspoons rosewater

1½ teaspoons orange flower water

4 teaspoons unsalted butter

1. In a small microwave-safe bowl, combine the cinnamon, sugar, and flower waters; microwave on high for 30 seconds.

2. Stir until the sugar is dissolved, then whisk in the butter. Serve immediately.

PER SERVING: Calories: 51 | Total Fat: 3g | Saturated Fat: 2g | Cholesterol: 10mg | Protein: 0g | Sodium: 0mg | Potassium: 4mg | Fiber: 0g | Carbohydrates: 4g | Sugar: 4g

APPLE APRICOT FROZEN YOGURT

If you don't have an ice-cream freezer you can still make this delicious dessert. Just pour the mixture into ice cube trays treated with nonstick spray; freeze until firm. If your blender can make shaved ice, transfer the cubes to the blender and process.

SERVES 4

1 large Golden Delicious apple, peeled, cored, and diced

¼ cup frozen apple juice concentrate

¾ cup cold water

4 apricots, peeled and pitted

1 large banana, peeled and sliced

¾ cup plain nonfat yogurt

1 tablespoon honey

1. Add the apple, apple juice concentrate, water, apricots, and banana to a blender or food processor; process until smooth.

2. Stir in the remaining ingredients. Add to ice-cream freezer and freeze according to manufacturer's directions.

PER SERVING: Calories: 120 | Total Fat: 0g | Saturated Fat: 0g | Cholesterol: 0mg | Protein: 2g | Sodium: 39mg | Potassium: 349mg | Fiber: 1g | Carbohydrates: 27g | Sugar: 22g

STEAMED RASPBERRY LEMON CUSTARD

To steam custards at the same time as other dishes that might affect taste, wrap the ramekins in plastic wrap (so they won't pick up the other aromas) and put them in the top tier of the steamer.

SERVES 4

2 large eggs

¼ teaspoon cream of tartar

1 lemon, zested and juiced

¼ teaspoon pure lemon extract

3 tablespoons unbleached all-purpose flour

¼ cup granulated sugar

40 fresh raspberries

Optional: 12 additional fresh raspberries

Optional: Fresh mint leaves

Optional: 2–4 teaspoons powdered sugar

1. Separate the egg yolks and whites. Add the egg whites to a large bowl and set aside the yolks. Use an electric mixer or wire whisk to beat the egg whites until frothy. Add the cream of tartar; continue to whip or whisk until soft peaks form.

2. In a small bowl, mix together the lemon zest, lemon juice, lemon extract, flour, sugar, and egg yolks; gently fold into the whites with a spatula.

3. Treat 4 (6-ounce) ramekins with nonstick spray. Place 10 raspberries in the bottom of each. Spoon the batter into the ramekins and set them in a steamer with a lid; cover and steam for 15–20 minutes.

4. To remove the custards from the ramekins, run a thin knife around edges; turn upside down onto plates. Garnish with raspberries, mint, and a dusting of powdered sugar, if desired.

PER SERVING: Calories: 137 | Total Fat: 3g | Saturated Fat: 0g | Cholesterol: 105mg | Protein: 4g | Sodium: 35mg | Potassium: 163mg | Fiber: 4g | Carbohydrates: 25g | Sugar: 15g

WATERMELON SORBET

Delightfully cool and tingly, this refreshing dessert is the perfect end to a summer meal. Garnish with fresh mint leaves and extra cubed watermelon if you like.

SERVES 4

4 cups seeded cubed watermelon

2 tablespoons water

1 teaspoon unflavored gelatin

2 tablespoons lime juice

2 tablespoons honey

1. If you're using an ice-cream freezer, place the watermelon cubes in the freezer while you prepare the gelatin. Add the water to a microwave-safe bowl and sprinkle the gelatin over it; let stand for 2 minutes or until the gelatin softens. Microwave on high for 40 seconds; stir until the gelatin is dissolved. Pour into a blender or food processor and add half of the watermelon, the lime juice, and honey. Cover and process until smooth. Add the remaining melon and process until smooth. Pour into prepared ice-cream freezer (see manufacturer's instructions); put the cover in place and plug in the machine. The mixture will take about 15–20 minutes to freeze.

2. If you're not using an ice-cream freezer, pour the melon mixture into ice cube trays treated with nonstick spray; freeze until firm. If your blender can make shaved ice, transfer the cubes to the blender and process. Otherwise, transfer to a chilled bowl and beat with an electric mixer until the mixture is bright pink.

3. You can put the sorbet in serving dishes and place them in the freezer until needed. If you do so, remove from the freezer about 20 minutes before you plan to serve, or at the beginning of the meal.

PER SERVING: Calories: 85 | Total Fat: 0g | Saturated Fat: 0g | Cholesterol: 0mg | Protein: 2g | Sodium: 5mg | Potassium: 187mg | Fiber: 0g | Carbohydrates: 20g | Sugar: 18g

VIRGIN BELLINI

A traditional Bellini is a mixture of Prosecco sparkling wine and white peach purée or nectar. It is usually served straight up (without ice) in a champagne flute. The Bellini is said to have been invented sometime between 1934 and 1948 in Venice, Italy.

SERVES 4

2 large peaches, peeled, pitted, and cubed

1 tablespoon honey

Optional: Drop of natural almond extract or flavoring or food-grade peppermint oil

Ice cubes

Seltzer water

Optional: Mint sprigs

1. In a blender or food processor, combine the peaches, honey, and almond extract or flavoring, if using; process until puréed.

2. Divide among 4 champagne flutes or tall glasses filled with ice cubes. Add enough seltzer water to fill the glasses, and stir. Garnish the glasses with fresh mint, if desired. Serve immediately.

PER SERVING: Calories: 50 | Total Fat: 0g | Saturated Fat: 0g | Cholesterol: 0mg | Protein: 0g | Sodium: 0mg | Potassium: 168mg | Fiber: 1g | Carbohydrates: 12g | Sugar: 11g

FRUIT MOLD

In 1889 Charles B. Knox discovered a way to granulate gelatin, turning the product from a cumbersome time-consuming one into an easy-to-use mainstay of the modern kitchen.

SERVES 8

1 envelope unflavored gelatin

¼ cup cold water

1½ cups hot water

¼ cup fresh lemon or lime juice

3 tablespoons peach or apricot preserves

1 tablespoon granulated sugar

1 large banana, peeled and sliced

1 cup unsweetened canned peach slices, drained

1. In a blender container, soak the gelatin in the cold water for 2 minutes.

2. Add the hot water and blend for about 2 minutes, until the gelatin is dissolved.

3. Add the juice, preserves, and sugar; blend until the sugar is dissolved.

4. Stir in the banana and peach slices. Pour into a dish or mold and refrigerate until set, about 4 hours.

PER SERVING: Calories: 63 | Total Fat: 0g | Saturated Fat: 0g | Cholesterol: 0mg | Protein: 3g | Sodium: 10mg | Potassium: 106mg | Fiber: 0g | Carbohydrates: 13g | Sugar: 8g

TRIPLE FRUIT MOLD

When making this dish be careful not to chill it too long after you add the sparkling water or it will solidify and you won't be able to add the fruit. Fifteen minutes should be the maximum chill time at this step.

SERVES 6

2 envelopes unflavored gelatin

½ cup frozen, unsweetened apple juice concentrate

3 cups unsweetened sparkling water

1 cup sliced strawberries

1 cup blueberries

2 large bananas, peeled and sliced

1. Mix together the gelatin and apple juice in a small saucepan; let stand for 1 minute. Stir the gelatin over low heat until completely dissolved, about 3 minutes. Let cool slightly.

2. Stir in the sparkling water. Refrigerate until the mixture begins to gel or is the consistency of unbeaten egg whites when stirred, about 15 minutes.

3. Fold the fruit into the partially thickened gelatin mixture. Pour into a 6-cup mold. Refrigerate for 4 hours or until set.

PER SERVING: Calories: 126 | Total Fat: 0g | Saturated Fat: 0g | Cholesterol: 0mg | Protein: 8g | Sodium: 24mg | Potassium: 313mg | Fiber: 2g | Carbohydrates: 24g | Sugar: 16g

BAKED APPLES

This dish is a fabulous use for fall fruit. Vary the types of apples you use to subtly change the flavor, or use pears or peaches.

SERVES 4

2 large apples, cored and cut in half

2 teaspoons lemon juice

4 teaspoons brown sugar

4 teaspoons rolled oats

Nonstick cooking spray

⅛ cup water

1. Preheat oven to 375°F. Treat an ovenproof dish with nonstick cooking spray.

2. Place the apples cut-side up in the prepared dish. Brush 1 teaspoon of the lemon juice over each apple half.

3. In a small bowl, mix together the brown sugar and rolled oats; evenly divide over the apples. Mist the top of the apples with the cooking spray.

4. Add the water to the bottom of the baking dish. Bake for 35 minutes or until the apples are fork tender. Serve hot or cold.

PER SERVING: Calories: 70 | Total Fat: 0g | Saturated Fat: 0g | Cholesterol: 0mg | Protein: 0g | Sodium: 0mg | Potassium: 110mg | Fiber: 1g | Carbohydrates: 18g | Sugar: 14g

FRUIT CUP WITH CREAMY DRESSING

Here's a healthy dessert that also makes a great side dish or breakfast. The combination of carrots, raisins, and grapes is unusual and delicious.

SERVES 1

⅛ cup peeled and grated carrots

1 tablespoon raisins

¼ cup cubed or sliced apple

6 seedless red or green grapes

4 ounces plain nonfat yogurt

1 tablespoon unsweetened, no-salt-added applesauce

1 teaspoon lemon juice

¼ teaspoon honey

⅛ teaspoon Pumpkin Pie Spice (Appendix A)

⅛ teaspoon finely grated fresh lemon zest

1. Arrange the carrots and fruit in a dessert cup.

2. In a medium bowl, mix the yogurt, applesauce, lemon juice, honey, and pumpkin pie spice together and drizzle over the fruit.

3. Sprinkle lemon zest over the top.

PER SERVING: Calories: 158 | Total Fat: 0g | Saturated Fat: 0g | Cholesterol: 2mg | Protein: 4g | Sodium: 99mg | Potassium: 541mg | Fiber: 1g | Carbohydrates: 33g | Sugar: 28g

APPENDIX A

SPICE BLENDS

Using herbs is a delicious way to season dishes and to cut down on the amount of salt needed for flavor, too. Dried herb mixtures can be prepared in advance and stored in an airtight container. Dried spices and herbs tend to lose flavor the longer they're stored, so the age of your seasoning mixes can directly affect the amount you should add to a recipe. Grinding them can help revive the potency because it releases their essential oils; for that reason, wait to grind spices until just before you need them.

To grind the spices and dried herbs in seasoning blends, a spice grinder or mortar and pestle works best. Alternatively, you can use a small food processor or a blender. Unless advised otherwise by a recipe, process a seasoning blend until it is crushed and coarsely ground.

CAJUN SPICE BLEND

2 tablespoons paprika

1½ tablespoons garlic powder

1 tablespoon onion powder

½ tablespoon black pepper

2 teaspoons cayenne pepper

2 teaspoons dried oregano

2 teaspoons dried thyme

MIDDLE EASTERN SPICE BLEND

1 tablespoon ground coriander

1 tablespoon ground cumin

1 tablespoon turmeric

1 teaspoon ground cinnamon

1 teaspoon crushed dried mint

OLD BAY SEASONING

1 tablespoon celery seeds

1 tablespoon whole black peppercorns

6 bay leaves, ground

½ teaspoon whole cardamom

½ teaspoon mustard seeds

4 whole cloves

1 teaspoon sweet Hungarian paprika

¼ teaspoon mace

PACIFIC RIM

1 tablespoon Chinese five-spice powder

1 tablespoon paprika

1 tablespoon ground dried ginger

1 teaspoon black pepper

PASTA BLEND

5 tablespoons dried basil

3 tablespoons dried oregano

2 tablespoons dried thyme

1 teaspoon garlic powder

POULTRY SEASONING

2 tablespoons dried basil

2 teaspoons dried rosemary

2 teaspoons dried marjoram

1 teaspoon dried thyme

1 teaspoon dried oregano

½ teaspoon dried sage

¼ teaspoon mustard powder

¼ teaspoon dried lemon granules, crushed

PUMPKIN PIE SPICE

4 teaspoons cinnamon

2 teaspoons ground dried ginger

½ teaspoon ground allspice

½ teaspoon ground cloves

1 teaspoon ground nutmeg

SONORAN SPICE BLEND

1 tablespoon ground chili powder

1 tablespoon black pepper

1 tablespoon crushed dried oregano

1 tablespoon crushed dried thyme

1 tablespoon crushed dried coriander

1 tablespoon garlic powder

STUFFING BLEND

2 tablespoons dried rubbed sage

1 tablespoon dried sweet marjoram

2 teaspoons dried parsley

1¼ teaspoons dried celery flakes

TEXAS SEASONING

3 tablespoons dried cilantro

2 tablespoons dried oregano

4 teaspoons dried thyme

2 tablespoons salt-free chili powder

2 tablespoons freshly ground black pepper

2 tablespoons ground cumin

2 small crushed dried chili peppers

1 teaspoon garlic powder

CARIBBEAN SPICE BLEND

1 tablespoon curry powder

1 tablespoon ground cumin

1 tablespoon ground allspice

1 tablespoon ground dried ginger

1 teaspoon ground cayenne pepper

COUNTRY TABLE SPICE BLEND

5 teaspoons dried thyme

4 teaspoons dried basil

4 teaspoons dried chervil

4 teaspoons dried tarragon

ENGLISH SPICE BLEND

1 tablespoon juniper berries, crushed

1 tablespoon dried thyme

1 teaspoon black pepper

1 teaspoon ground cloves

1 tablespoon onion powder

FINES HERBES

3 tablespoons dried parsley

2 teaspoons dried chervil

2 teaspoons dried chives

1½ teaspoons dried tarragon

FISH AND SEAFOOD HERBS

5 teaspoons dried basil

5 teaspoons fennel seeds, crushed

4 teaspoons dried parsley

1 teaspoon dried lemon granules, crushed

FRENCH SPICE BLEND

1 tablespoon crushed dried tarragon

1 tablespoon crushed dried chervil

1 tablespoon onion powder

HERBES DE PROVENCE

4 teaspoons dried oregano

2 teaspoons dried basil

2 teaspoons dried sweet marjoram

2 teaspoons dried thyme

1 teaspoon dried mint

1 teaspoon dried rosemary

1 teaspoon dried sage leaves

1 teaspoon fennel seeds, crushed

1 teaspoon dried lavender

ITALIAN SPICE BLEND

1 tablespoon dried basil

1 tablespoon dried thyme

1 tablespoon dried oregano

2 tablespoons garlic powder

BLACKENED CATFISH SPICE BLEND

1 tablespoon sweet paprika

1 tablespoon garlic powder

1 tablespoon onion powder

2 teaspoons cayenne

2 teaspoons cracked black pepper

2 bay leaves, ground

1 teaspoon ground white pepper

1 teaspoon brown sugar

1 teaspoon mustard powder

1 teaspoon dried lemon granules, crushed

½ teaspoon dried thyme

¼ teaspoon dried oregano

¼ teaspoon ground cloves

Optional: 1 tablespoon hot paprika

CHIPOTLE CHILI POWDER SPICE BLEND

2 tablespoons ground chipotle

1 tablespoon onion powder

1 tablespoon garlic powder

1 teaspoon unsweetened cocoa powder

½ teaspoon dried Mexican oregano

¼ teaspoon cayenne

¼ teaspoon cumin

¼ teaspoon cinnamon

⅛ teaspoon ground cloves

⅛ teaspoon dried mustard powder

Pinch dried lemon granules, crushed

HOT CURRY SPICE BLEND

½ tablespoon ground coriander

½ tablespoon ground cumin

½ tablespoon turmeric

1 teaspoon salt-free chili powder

1 teaspoon ground dried ginger

1 teaspoon ground black pepper

½ teaspoon ground cardamom

½ teaspoon mustard powder

¼ teaspoon cayenne

¼ teaspoon ground cloves

⅛ teaspoon nutmeg

⅛ teaspoon cinnamon

Pinch saffron

GARAM MASALA SPICE BLEND

1 tablespoon ground coriander

2 teaspoons ground cardamom

1 teaspoon cracked black pepper

1 teaspoon ground cinnamon

1 teaspoon charnushka

1 teaspoon caraway seeds

½ teaspoon ground cloves

½ teaspoon freshly ground ginger

¼ teaspoon ground nutmeg

GREEK SPICE BLEND

1 tablespoon garlic powder

1 tablespoon dried mint

1 teaspoon dried dill (dill weed)

1 teaspoon freeze-dried chives

½ teaspoon ground cinnamon

½ teaspoon dried oregano

¼ teaspoon ground nutmeg

⅛ teaspoon cayenne

JERK SPICE BLEND

1 tablespoon brown mustard seeds

1 tablespoon onion powder

2 teaspoons ground dried ginger

2 teaspoons garlic powder

1 teaspoon ground allspice

1 teaspoon hot paprika

½ teaspoon dried thyme

½ teaspoon fennel seeds

½ teaspoon ground black pepper

¼ teaspoon cayenne

¼ teaspoon ground cloves

CITRUS PEPPER

1 tablespoon cracked or freshly ground black pepper

1 teaspoon dried orange zest

½ teaspoon dried lemon zest

½ teaspoon dried mint

½ teaspoon ground dried ginger

¼ teaspoon dried lime zest

¼ teaspoon ground cardamom

¼ teaspoon garlic powder

¼ teaspoon ground coriander

2 drops orange oil

Pinch cayenne

BOUQUETS GARNIS

Leafy part of 1–2 celery stalks

2–3 sprigs fresh thyme

1 bay leaf

1 small bunch fresh parsley

1–2 sprigs fresh marjoram or oregano

STANDARD U.S./METRIC MEASUREMENT CONVERSIONS

VOLUME CONVERSIONS

U.S. Volume Measure	Metric Equivalent
⅛ teaspoon	0.5 milliliter
¼ teaspoon	1 milliliter
½ teaspoon	2 milliliters
1 teaspoon	5 milliliters
½ tablespoon	7 milliliters
1 tablespoon (3 teaspoons)	15 milliliters
2 tablespoons (1 fluid ounce)	30 milliliters
¼ cup (4 tablespoons)	60 milliliters
⅓ cup	90 milliliters
½ cup (4 fluid ounces)	125 milliliters
⅔ cup	160 milliliters
¾ cup (6 fluid ounces)	180 milliliters
1 cup (16 tablespoons)	250 milliliters
1 pint (2 cups)	500 milliliters
1 quart (4 cups)	1 liter (about)

WEIGHT CONVERSIONS

U.S. Weight Measure	Metric Equivalent
½ ounce	15 grams
1 ounce	30 grams
2 ounces	60 grams
3 ounces	85 grams
¼ pound (4 ounces)	115 grams
½ pound (8 ounces)	225 grams
¾ pound (12 ounces)	340 grams
1 pound (16 ounces)	454 grams

OVEN TEMPERATURE CONVERSIONS

Degrees Fahrenheit	Degrees Celsius
200 degrees F	95 degrees C
250 degrees F	120 degrees C
275 degrees F	135 degrees C
300 degrees F	150 degrees C
325 degrees F	160 degrees C
350 degrees F	180 degrees C
375 degrees F	190 degrees C
400 degrees F	205 degrees C
425 degrees F	220 degrees C
450 degrees F	230 degrees C

BAKING PAN SIZES

U.S.	Metric
8 × 1½ inch round baking pan	20 × 4 cm cake tin
9 × 1½ inch round baking pan	23 × 3.5 cm cake tin
11 × 7 × 1½ inch baking pan	28 × 18 × 4 cm baking tin
13 × 9 × 2 inch baking pan	30 × 20 × 5 cm baking tin
2 quart rectangular baking dish	30 × 20 × 3 cm baking tin
15 × 10 × 2 inch baking pan	30 × 25 × 2 cm baking tin (Swiss roll tin)
9 inch pie plate	22 × 4 or 23 × 4 cm pie plate
7 or 8 inch springform pan	18 or 20 cm springform or loose bottom cake tin
9 × 5 × 3 inch loaf pan	23 × 13 × 7 cm or 2 lb narrow loaf or pâté tin
1½ quart casserole	1.5 liter casserole
2 quart casserole	2 liter casserole

INDEX

Note: Page numbers in **bold** indicate recipe category lists.